Edexcel

AS
Psychology

AS
Psychology

Christine Brain

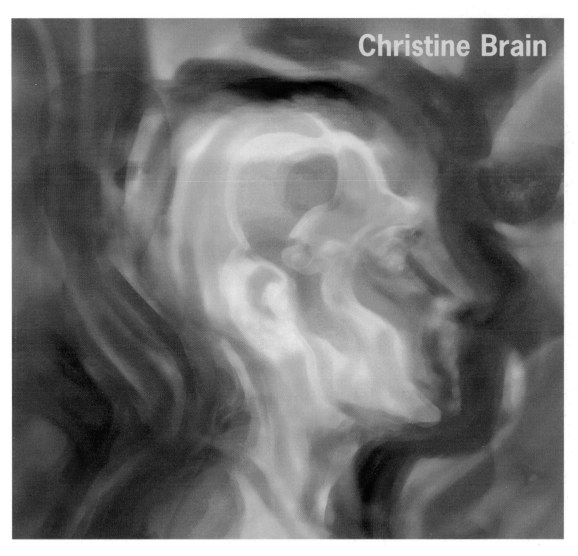

Warm thanks are due to David, Ash, Patrick and everyone at Philip Allan Updates for their kindness, help and professionalism. Thanks to my friends for their encouragement and for continuing to support me. Thanks, above all, to Alex, Jenny, Doug and Sarah — and wonderful new addition Jonathan, born 9 October 2007. I would be lost without them. And remembering Paul and Kevin too, of course.

This book is dedicated to the memory of Lee Alexander Brown, 11 December 1948 to 12 July 2007.

Philip Allan Updates, an imprint of Hodder Education, an Hachette UK company, Market Place, Deddington, Oxfordshire OX15 0SE

Orders
Bookpoint Ltd, 130 Milton Park, Abingdon, Oxfordshire OX14 4SB
tel: 01235 827720
fax: 01235 400454
e-mail: uk.orders@bookpoint.co.uk

Lines are open 9.00 a.m.–5.00 p.m., Monday to Saturday, with a 24-hour message answering service. You can also order through the Philip Allan Updates website: www.philipallan.co.uk

© Philip Allan Updates 2008

ISBN 978-0-340-96683-9

Impression number   5 4 3 2
Year   2012   2011   2010   2009

This material has been endorsed by Edexcel and offers high quality support for the delivery of Edexcel qualifications.

Edexcel endorsement does not mean that this material is essential to achieve any Edexcel qualification, nor does it mean that this is the only suitable material available to support any Edexcel qualification. No endorsed material will be used verbatim in setting any Edexcel examination and any resource lists produced by Edexcel shall include this and other appropriate texts. While this material has been through an Edexcel quality assurance process, all responsibility for the content remains with the publisher.

Copies of official specifications for all Edexcel qualifications may be found on the Edexcel website — www.edexcel.org.uk.

Printed in Italy

Hachette UK's policy is to use papers that are natural, renewable and recyclable products and made from wood grown in sustainable forests. The logging and manufacturing processes are expected to conform to the environmental regulations of the country of origin.

P01512

Contents

Introduction

This textbook is written specifically for students following the Edexcel AS Psychology course.

The AS course

Some features of the AS course are:

- that there are five approaches to psychology
- that there is a strong emphasis on how science works, in particular, how psychology works
- in each approach, there is the study of methodology of that approach, a key issue to help you to link the theory to an everyday issue and a practical

Unit 1 covers the social and cognitive approaches:

- The social approach examines how people are affected by others and by groups and social rules; the focus is on obedience to authority, and prejudice.
- The cognitive approach examines how information is processed in the brain; the focus is on memory and forgetting.

Unit 2 covers the psychodynamic, biological and learning approaches:

- The psychodynamic approach examines the role of unconscious wishes and desires and how they affect personality; the focus is on Freud's work including the power of the id, the oral, anal and phallic stages, and on how gender behaviour develops.
- The biological approach examines how genes, hormones and brain structures work together to affect each individual; the focus is on sex differentiation and gender development.
- The learning approach examines behaviour and how experiences affect the individual; the focus is on conditioning, the role of reinforcement and punishment, learning by observation and the application of learning principles to treating mental health problems.

Structure of each approach

Each approach follows the same structure, to help your learning:

- a definition of the approach and some key terms to learn
- methodology, to see how psychology works
- content, which involves some theories and studies from within the approach
- two studies in detail
- one key issue of your choice
- one practical of your choice

The unit tests

- The Unit 1 test is a written paper of 1 hour 20 minutes' duration. It is worth 60 marks, and is 40% of the total AS marks.
- The Unit 2 test is a written paper of 1 hour 40 minutes' duration. It is worth 80 marks, and is 60% of the total AS marks.
- Both exams start with multiple-choice questions, which are followed by a short-answer section and an extended-writing section. Questions about any area of each approach can be within any of these three sections. You should expect a 12-mark extended-writing question in each AS paper.

Assessment objectives

You are being tested on three assessment objectives (AOs):
- AO1 — knowledge with understanding, good use of terminology and answers communicated clearly
- AO2 — application and evaluation of what you have learnt
- AO3 — knowing of psychology in practice, of the methodology you have studied and the methodology of studies carried out by others

About this book

Each chapter in this textbook covers one of the approaches and is divided into the relevant areas, following the specification.

Throughout the book there is advice to guide you through your course:
- Key terms — these are emboldened in the text and, where further explanation is needed, accompanied with a definition in the margin.
- 'Explore' boxes — suggestions for you to extend your study of particular areas.
- 'Practical' boxes — to help with the required practical for each approach.
- 'Study hint' boxes — to help with the exams.
- 'Practice' boxes — to help you to learn the methodology and relevant terminology; there are answers to the 'practice' boxes at the end of each chapter.
- Examination-style questions — to help you revise.
- Extension questions — to help you learn the material by answering broader questions that will extend your learning; this will help you in the exams.

How to use this book

This book is planned for you to read through from this introduction to the final chapter. In each approach, the sections follow the sections of the specification. You will probably find that your course is structured to follow the course structure. However, if this is not the case, the chapters can be studied in a different order.

Active learning is best

You are advised to read through each chapter without taking notes. Then, go back through each section and make your own notes. Focus on terminology; making your own definitions for each term can be particularly useful. Use lots of headings in your notes and make your notes as clear as possible. For example, each study, theory or concept could have its own heading and summary. When carrying out your practical, keep a separate folder for your notes. Your teacher should be able to give you a pro forma for keeping notes about practicals

How psychology works

Throughout the Edexcel AS Psychology course, there is a strong emphasis on how science works. Each chapter has a section on methodology — how psychology works. Reading through the methodology sections of the chapters, starting with Chapter 1, will give you a clear picture of how psychology works and how scientific it is.

About practicals

For each approach, you will carry out a practical to practise the skills you have learnt in the methodology and content sections. The research method is specified for this practical, but the investigation you carry out will depend on the way your particular course is structured.

Psychology is a science and science involves:
- putting forward a theory
- developing a hypothesis of what might be expected from the theory
- testing the hypothesis

Each practical that you carry out should come from a theory and be planned to test that theory. Check that you understand the theory that your practical is testing. This will make for a more interesting and better investigation and will also mean that you will have a better understanding of the issues.

The Edexcel website

- Edexcel has its own website (**www.edexcel.org.uk**), with a section for psychology. Use it to find out more about your course, including the specification. The specification outlines everything you need to know for your course, and this textbook follows every aspect of Units 1 and 2 of the specification.
- Use the specimen assessment materials, which include specimen exam papers and mark schemes. The mark schemes will help you to see how to answer the questions and score the marks.
- You can ask questions using the website, using the 'Ask the Expert' service.

Take charge of your own learning and you will do very well.

Maintaining your interest in psychology

You will have had clear reasons for choosing to study AS psychology. Remember those reasons and make sure that you get what you want out of studying. Use websites and other sources, such as books and magazines, to maintain your interest. Treat your studies separately from your interest and towards the end of the year, try to bring the two together. This takes time and practice — you won't become a psychologist in 1 year — but it is worth being patient. If you joined the course because you want to know what makes people do certain things or what makes us like we are, then you *will* find the answers by studying psychology, even though some of what you learn at first may not seem relevant — it is relevant and its relevance will become more obvious as you move through the course.

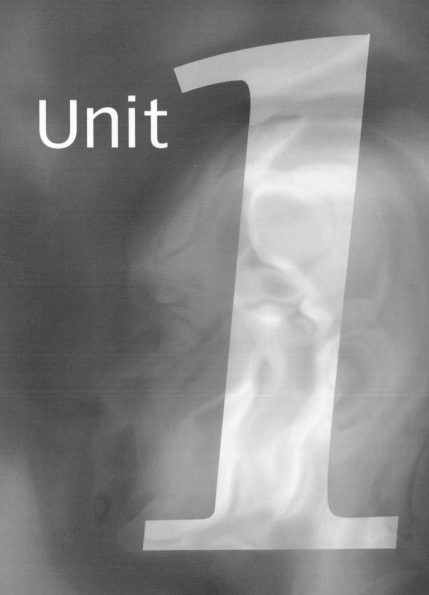

Unit 1

Social and Cognitive Psychology

Chapter 1

The social approach

This chapter is about the social approach to explaining human behaviour. It is about the effects of people, society and culture and how behaviour is guided by such effects. For example, people belong to groups ('in-groups'); rival groups become 'out-groups'. You could belong to several in-groups — for example, a gender group, an interest group, a psychology group, a family group, a race group or a work group. There are many others. Social psychology suggests that you will be prejudiced towards your in-groups and against your out-groups.

Another example of social psychology is how people obey other people, and in what circumstances. You might think that you would never give strong electric shocks to another person, but social psychology holds that it is quite likely that you would, if ordered to by someone in authority.

Study of interest Salvatore and Shelton (2007) carried out a study to examine the effect of racism on the individual. They asked 250 Princeton University undergraduates to read some fictitious CVs and fictitious employer comments. In some cases, there was blatant racism — for example, a white employer 'rejected' a well-qualified black applicant in favour of a white applicant saying that they had too many employees from ethnic minorities. In some cases there was ambiguous racism — for example, a white employer accepted a white applicant in favour of a better-qualified black applicant, without giving a reason. The undergraduates then carried out a task to test their cognitive (mental) abilities. It was found that the black undergraduates were more affected by ambiguous racism than blatant racism; the white undergraduates were more affected by blatant racism. It was thought that black people were used to blatant racism and had strategies to cope with it; those who were white were not used to it and had no such strategies. The study highlighted the effect of racism on cognitive abilities and the seriousness of such issues for the individual.

Summary of learning objectives

Definitions
You have to be able to define the terms:

- agentic state
- autonomous state
- moral strain
- in-group/out-group
- social categorisation
- social identification
- social comparison

Methodology comprises:

- the survey method, including questionnaires and interviews
- structured, unstructured and semi-structured interviews, open-ended and closed-ended questions, alternative hypotheses and issues around designing surveys
- an evaluation of the survey method, including reliability, validity and subjectivity
- qualitative and quantitative data, including their strengths and weaknesses
- ethical guidelines, such as British Psychological Society guidelines, in particular consent, deception, right to withdraw, debriefing and competence
- sampling techniques, including random, stratified, volunteer/self-selected and opportunity; the disadvantages and advantages of each technique

Content
You have to be able to:

- define obedience, as it is studied in the approach
- describe and evaluate:
  - Milgram's (1963) study and one of his variations
  - Milgram's agency theory
- describe and assess ethical issues arising from Milgram's research
- describe and evaluate a study based on Milgram's study but in a different culture; a Dutch study is suggested, but there are others and you have a free choice
- compare Milgram's study with the findings about obedience in another culture to show mainly that the issue of culture needs to be considered in psychology when drawing conclusions
- describe what prejudice and discrimination mean and describe and evaluate the social identity theory as an explanation of prejudice

Studies in detail:
You have to be able to describe and evaluate in detail:

- the study by Hofling et al. (1966)
- one other from Sherif (1954, 1961, 1988), Tajfel et al. (1970, 1971), and Reicher and Haslam (2003, 2006)

All four studies are described and evaluated in this chapter.

Unit 1

Chapter 1 The social approach

Key issues

You have to able to describe one key issue of your choice that can be explained using concepts and research from the social approach. There are five key issues suggested in the specification. They all look at explanations of certain types of behaviour of interest to society. All five issues are covered in this chapter to help you choose. However, you could choose a completely different issue.

Practical

- You have to carry out one practical of your (or your teacher's) choice, which must be a survey, using either a questionnaire or an interview.
- The survey must gather both qualitative and quantitative data and must be designed and carried out ethically.
- You must focus on design and sampling decisions, as well as collecting data and presenting an analysis of the data. Brief conclusions must be drawn.

One suggested practical is given in this chapter.

> **Study hint** Make the summary of learning objectives into a checklist. Table 1.1 gives a suggested list. However, you could add detail, which would help your learning.

Table 1.1 A checklist of what you need to know for the social approach and for your progress

I need to know about	Done	More work	I need to know about	Done	More work
Agentic state, autonomous state and moral strain			Opportunity sampling		
Social categorisation, social identification, social comparison			Strengths and weaknesses of different sampling methods		
In-group, out-group			BPS ethical guidelines of consent, debriefing, right to withdraw, competence, deceit		
Questionnaires			Definitions of obedience, prejudice and discrimination		
Interviews (structured, unstructured, semi-structured)			Milgram's main study and one variation (and evaluate)		
Open/closed-ended questions			A 'Milgram'-type study from another culture (and evaluate)		
Qualitative and quantitative data			Compare Milgram's findings with those from another culture		
Strengths and weaknesses of qualitative and quantitative data			Ethical issues arising from Milgram's work		
Analysis of qualitative data			Agency theory		
Evaluation of surveys including reliability, validity, subjectivity			Social identity theory		
Alternative hypotheses			Hofling et al. (1966) study		
Random sampling			One other study from Sherif; Tajfel et al.; Reicher and Haslam		
Stratified sampling			One key issue		
Volunteer/self-selected sampling			One practical — a survey		

Definitions

The following terms are connected with Milgram:
- agentic state
- autonomous state
- moral strain

The following terms are connected with Tajfel's social identity theory:
- in-group/out-group
- social categorisation
- social identification
- social comparison

All the above terms are defined in this chapter.

An introduction to the social approach

Social psychology examines human behaviour — the role of the individual's relationships with other people and groups, and how culture and society affect behaviour. This is a large field and the AS course covers only obedience and prejudice.

Key assumptions

The social approach examines how individuals interact with one another and how people behave in groups. When people are studied as social beings, the social approach is involved.

> **Study hint** It is useful to study the approach as a whole rather than the methodology, content, studies in detail, key issues and practical as separate sections. Read each chapter as a whole, taking in some of the information but without taking notes or learning the terms. After reading the whole chapter, you can then start learning in earnest.

The effect of interaction between individuals

Individuals interact with other individuals and they affect one another's behaviour. Agency theory suggests that people are agents for society and behave in such a way as to benefit their society. People help other people, they send signals to other people by the way they look and behave, and they obey certain people and not others. Helping behaviour, body language and obedience are studied within the social approach.

The effect of being in groups within society

The social approach assumes that people live within a culture and society and that their behaviour is affected by their experiences within a society, where they are members of certain groups. For example, a child is a girl or boy, a sister or brother perhaps, a daughter or son, a friend, a pupil at school, maybe a member of a club. Individuals describe themselves in these ways. Social identity theory suggests that by identifying oneself as being a member of a group, a person can become prejudiced against members of another rival group. Groups are prejudiced against each other,

1

members of a peer group copy one another and crowds can become unruly. Prejudice, peer group pressure and crowd behaviour are studied within the social approach.

Explore Try asking a few people to describe themselves briefly, in writing. They may describe themselves in terms of personality, such as generous, happy or quiet; they will probably also give their social roles. People describe themselves according to how others see them and how they fit into their social world.

The effect of the social situation

It is not just people and groups that affect behaviour, but the social situation itself. For example, when out for the evening with friends, you might not worry about expressing a view about religion; in a business meeting in another country, you would probably not comment.

Explore Use the internet or some other source to research social representation theory or social constructionism. The idea is that what we do and say is set within a particular society or culture. We represent the world to ourselves through our experiences and it is not that there are truths in the world to discover, such as what is right and wrong. All understanding is within a setting and can only be judged by knowing that setting. So for us to have any understanding of ourselves or others, society and culture must be studied. The theory holds that there are no general laws to discover and that knowledge is relative. This goes against the idea of a scientific approach to studying human behaviour.

Methodology

Methodology is the study of how research is carried out and is about how science works. In the AS psychology course, methodology is covered in each approach.

Study hint One of the main areas within your course is 'how science works'. You may not feel that methodology is why you chose to study psychology, but if you want to know why people act in certain ways, or how you make decisions when with others, you need to learn about the research of others. To know whether their findings are worth considering, you need to know about their methodology — for example, whether they asked enough people, or whether something else could have caused their findings. Psychology is a science and you have to be scientific when studying it. In each examination, some questions will focus on how science works.

Why study research methods?

Methodology involves looking at how psychology is studied. If you do not know how information has been obtained, how can you know how useful or accurate it is? For example, if you are told that males are better map-readers than females, you might ask how people know that (the biological approach will give you some evidence for the claim that male and female brains are different). If you are told that people tend to form relationships with people who are like their fathers/mothers, you might wonder what the evidence is for that claim (the psychodynamic and learning approaches help to explain why this might be the case). As you have chosen to study psychology, you will be interested in how evidence is gathered — both 'how do they do that?' and 'how do they know that?'

Why evaluate research methods?

When studying psychology you need to evaluate how secure the information is that you are reading or finding out.

In this textbook, **evaluation** is usually presented in the form of strengths and weaknesses; occasionally advantages and disadvantages are given. If what you discover goes against common sense, then it is unlikely to be true. However, you need evidence in order to argue whether it is true or untrue. For example, you might want to claim that no one would obey someone in authority and give electric shocks to a person they have just met. However, psychologists claim that we obey authority figures even when they tell us to do something that we think is unacceptable. Milgram did an experiment that used good methodology and showed just that. Psychological investigations into obedience have suggested that in 1968, when US soldiers in My Lai, Vietnam, shot and killed civilian women and children because they were told to, they just did what many of us are likely to do — obeyed orders. Such claims need to be substantiated by strong evidence, which is why all studies and theories are evaluated.

> Evaluation means weighing up different points of view.

The My Lai massacre, where soldiers killed civilian women and children in Vietnam because they were ordered to do so, was a shocking event

> **Study hint** This first methodology section introduces and defines new terms. When they occur again, they are defined simply. Therefore, you should read this section carefully and make notes so that you can build on your learning about methodology.

For the social approach you study **surveys**, **sampling** and **ethics** in depth.

Surveys in general

In the AS course, the term 'survey' covers both **question-naires** and **interviews**. Surveys are used for a number of reasons and you are likely to have been involved in surveys as a **participant**. For example, market research is carried out to find out what people want so that businesses can provide it, and glossy magazines provide brief questionnaires for their readers to find their likes and dislikes. The internet is a good source of surveys of various kinds.

> **Explore** Use the internet to find three question-naires about different issues. Note three similari-ties and three differences between them. Consider the construction of each questionnaire, what the aim is and how well it succeeds.

Aims and hypotheses

Surveys are planned with an **aim** or aims in mind — for example, 'to find out attitudes to prejudice' or 'to look at why we obey those in authority'. The aim of a study should be summed up in a general statement without detail of what is to be measured or examined in order to find the answers.

From such aims a researcher needs to generate one or more **hypotheses**. A hypothesis is a statement about what is being tested and involves things that are measurable. For example, you could ask people about their attitudes to prejudice (the aim) but you would find out more if you decided what you were looking for in more detail (the hypothesis) — for example, to try to find out if older people are more prejudiced than younger people.

For another study, you could decide what aspect of prejudice to measure. For example, you could measure discrimination in employment (you could investigate the race of employees or applicants) or prejudice at a personal level (you could ask who people like to have living next door to them). Possible hypotheses are: 'there are more white people than black people in well-paid jobs' (over a particular salary) and 'there are more people who prefer those of the same race to live nearby than don't mind who lives nearby'.

A hypothesis about obedience might be: 'When told to queue in a bank, more older people than younger people obey'.

The hypothesis in a study is the statement of the predicted result and should involve testable elements. Questionnaires and interviews require **alternative hypotheses**; they are alterna-tives to the **null hypothesis**, which is tested using statistics.

> Experiments also have hypotheses that are alternatives to the **null hypothesis**. In an experiment, the **alternative hypothesis** is called the experi-mental hypothesis.

> **Study hint** This section looks at how surveys (both questionnaires and interviews) are used in psychology, perhaps covering areas you studied at GCSE. So, when you can, use your previous learning.

Surveys using questionnaires

There is some terminology associated with questionnaires that you need to understand and learn.

Planning questionnaires

Questionnaires involve asking people questions about a topic of interest, which seems quite a simple thing to do. However, questionnaires have to be designed carefully. They ask for **personal data** such as age, gender and background, and have other questions relevant to the topic. Ethically, surveys must only ever ask what the researcher really needs to know. Questionnaires also gather **data** needed to answer the questions posed in the aim and hypothesis. Questions in a questionnaire can take different formats and there is no right or wrong way of writing a questionnaire. Four formats for the topic of 'finding out about yourself and your friends' are given below.

A Likert-type scale

Tick the appropriate box in the statements below.

Key: SA = strongly agree, A = agree, DK = don't know (unsure), D = disagree, SD = strongly disagree

Statement	SA	A	DK	D	SD
I like meeting new people	☐	☐	☐	☐	☐
I enjoy finding out about others	☐	☐	☐	☐	☐
I prefer the company of people like myself	☐	☐	☐	☐	☐
I prefer to go out with my friends	☐	☐	☐	☐	☐

A rating scale

Rate yourself on the following scales by putting a mark in the appropriate place on the line:

Happy	0	_____	10	Sad
Generous	0	_____	10	Mean
Friendly	0	_____	10	Unfriendly

Identifying characteristics

Circle those characteristics that you think apply to your best friend.

Mean   Caring   Unkind

Kind   Spiteful   Only child   Slow

Thoughtful   Intelligent   Sporty   Fussy

Sweet   Untidy   Gentle   Pretty

Handsome   Neat

An open question

How do you think that you are perceived by others?

Some general points about questionnaires include the following:

- You can use any question format that you like, depending on your aim.
- More straightforward questions usually come first, followed by more in-depth questions.
- Questions gathering personal data are best placed at the end, so that they do not take up the time of the **respondent** (the person giving the answers), who might get bored too quickly.
- For ethical and practical reasons, questionnaires should not be very long — you do not want the respondent to give up halfway through. Two sides of A4 are often enough; longer than four sides is probably too long, although there are exceptions.
- A **pilot survey** is usually carried out perhaps using friends and family as the respondents. This tests questions for clarity and allows the person conducting the survey to make sure that the required information will be gathered.

Questions should be put so that the respondent will read them carefully and respond accurately. If, for a particular respondent, the answer to the first four questions is likely to be 'no', the respondent might continue to answer 'no'. For example, when asking about gender and driving, if the first four questions were whether females drive bigger cars better, whether females pass their tests sooner, whether females are better drivers and whether females are good at parking, a respondent might want to answer 'no' to each one and a pattern might be formed. It would be better to change at least one of the questions — for example, ask whether males are better at parking. A **response set** or **response bias** is the tendency to stick to one response throughout and the way questions are asked can lead to a response bias. Questions should be set up in order to obtain a range of responses.

In general, negatives in questions should be avoided — for example, asking whether a person is *not* a racist or whether females do *not* drive bigger cars better than males. In a face-to-face situation when carrying out a questionnaire, care should be taken to ask questions impartially. This is to avoid any bias, either from the tone in which the questions are asked or from other bias from the researcher, such as facial expression.

Closed-ended and open-ended questions

Questionnaires involve **closed-ended questions** (or **closed questions**) in which the response choices are limited — for example, **dichotomies** (e.g. yes/no answers).

> **Dichotomy** means division into two parts.

In the examples of questionnaires given on page 9–10, the Likert-type scale, the rating scale and 'identifying characteristics' show closed-ended questions. There are also **open-ended** questions (or **open questions**) such as 'How do you think others see you?' Open-ended questions allow the respondent to state their attitudes and opinions. Both types of question have strengths and weaknesses, so questionnaires usually include both.

Strengths and weaknesses of closed-ended questions

- All respondents give standard answers (e.g. 'yes', 'no' or 'unsure', or a rating out of 5). Therefore, numbers can be generated (e.g. how many say 'yes' or 'no', or a score from adding up the ratings). Analysis is straightforward because one set of responses can be compared fairly with another set. Percentages and averages can be calculated.
- They are the same for all respondents and the set of answers. The question wording can be used to make the sense of the question clear. If the meaning is the same for all respondents then the questionnaire is more reliable. **Reliability** is when the test is repeated and the same results are found. Questionnaires using closed-ended questions are reasonably reliable.
- One weakness of closed-ended questions is that they force a respondent to choose from a set of answers, when the respondent might not agree with any of the choices. For example, if asked whether someone is being obedient or not, even if there is an 'unsure' category, respondents have to consider obedience, and they may not see the situation in that way. If respondents cannot say what they want to say, then the answers are not accurate and are therefore not valid. **Validity** is when results represent real life and researchers are testing what they think they are testing. Questionnaires using closed-ended questions may not be valid.
- A second weakness is that the choice answers could mean different things to different respondents. For example, 'unsure' could mean 'don't know' or 'sometimes yes and sometimes no', but would be scored the same. This would mean that the questionnaire is not producing valid data.

Strengths and weaknesses of open-ended questions

- One strength of open-ended questions is that respondents are not forced into specific answers but can say what they want to say. Questionnaires using open-ended questions tend to obtain richer, more detailed data.
- Not only are the answers more detailed, but the questions can be interpreted by the respondents. If the question asks what respondents think about prejudice, the reply can interpret what 'prejudice' means to them. For example, some might write about the rights of immigrants; others might write about the rights of the indigenous population (those 'naturally' from that country). Questionnaires using open-ended questions are, therefore, more valid because they enable respondents to talk more about what they 'really' think.
- One weakness of open-ended questions is that they are difficult to analyse because the answers are likely to be detailed and also different from one another.
- A second weakness is that, because the data are qualitative, averages cannot be calculated and the data cannot be displayed in tables or graphs.

- A third weakness is that respondents often fail to complete their answers to open-ended questions, probably because such responses take longer and also because it is more difficult to think of the answer than it is to tick a forced-choice set of boxes.

Table 1.2 *Strengths and weaknesses of closed-ended questions*

Strengths	Weaknesses
• Generate standard replies that can be counted for ease of comparability and analysis • Same clearly expressed detailed questions, so if repeated tend to get the same responses; reliable	• Force a choice of answer (even 'unsure') so may not have the answer respondents would prefer, so they are not valid • 'Unsure' can mean 'don't know' or 'sometimes yes and sometimes no'; answers may mean different things to different respondents, so they are not comparable

Table 1.3 *Strengths and weaknesses of open-ended questions*

Strengths	Weaknesses
• Respondent is not constrained but free to answer as they wish, so will give more detailed, in-depth and rich data • Allows respondent to interpret the questions as they wish, so produces more valid 'real' data than when constrained by the questions	• Difficult to analyse because tend to be interpreted by the respondent; too difficult to compare data with those of other respondents • Often are not answered in full as they take more time and it is more difficult to think of the answer than when ticking a forced-choice box

Quantitative and qualitative data

Questionnaires tend to gather both qualitative and quantitative data:

- **Qualitative data** involve ideas and opinions. People relate a story in answer to a question, such as why they would not obey orders and give electric shocks.
- **Quantitative data** involve numbers (e.g. numbers of 'yes' and 'no' answers) or percentages (e.g. percentage of people saying that they would give electric shocks to a stranger if told to).
- Open-ended questions produce qualitative data; closed-ended questions produce quantitative data.

Practice 1.1

Decide whether the following questions would produce qualitative or quantitative data:

1 Do you agree that we should obey everyone in authority? Yes or no?

2 Rate on a scale of 0–5 (0 = not at all; 5 = totally) how much you think soldiers are responsible for their own actions.

3 What do you think about people who, when obeying orders, do wrong?

Answers are at the end of Chapter 1.

Strengths and weaknesses of qualitative data

- They give detailed information on a subject and allow in-depth analysis. For example, a respondent might say 'I think it is right to obey orders to control society *and* I want to know more' and another respondent might say 'I think it is right to obey orders to control society *but* I want to know more'. The first respondent wants to obey; the second respondent thinks it is right to obey, but perhaps only to an extent. The use of 'and' or 'but' has changed the meaning. Such in-depth analysis adds useful understanding.
- Another strength of qualitative data, which in a questionnaire comes from open-ended questions, is that there is more validity. Respondents can say what they really think about an issue.
- One weakness of qualitative data is that they are hard to analyse in order to compare responses. Answers might be so different that they are difficult to categorise, and the results can be long and hard to summarise.
- A second weakness is that they are not easy to gather because respondents might be reluctant to give an in-depth response or because the data might take a long time to gather. On questionnaires, respondents often miss out the open-ended questions — perhaps because it takes longer to write out answers than to tick boxes or because it is more trouble. Qualitative data are also gathered from other research methods. Whatever the method used, it takes a long time to gather such data compared with gathering quantitative data.

Strengths and weaknesses of quantitative data

- They can be fairly quickly and easily analysed, and averages, percentages and other statistics can be calculated. The data can be represented in graphs and tables, which means that research results can be more easily and efficiently communicated to others.

Study hint   When learning strengths and weaknesses make sure that you don't make your notes too short. The text here says that quantitative data can be fairly easily analysed, but if you write in an exam that 'they are easy to analyse' you will not get the mark. You need to say what you mean by 'easy', e.g. averages can be calculated and put into tables, which is easier than generating themes as is done for qualitative data.

- They are reliable, because the way that they are gathered is controlled sufficiently well for the test to be repeated to see if similar results are found. Quantitative data in questionnaires come from closed-ended questions, so the strengths of closed-ended questions apply. However, quantitative data can also be gathered by other research methods, such as experiments.
- A researcher puts **controls** into place to make sure that any test can be repeated and give the same results. Control of the setting and the tools used are all important.
- One weakness of quantitative data is that they may not be valid because the respondents have a forced choice of answer. They may have to reply 'untruthfully'.

> The same strengths of gathering quantitative data apply in all research methods — good **controls**, giving reliable data.

- A second weakness of quantitative data is that respondents may be answering so quickly that they do not check their answers or simply do not bother about their answers.
- A third weakness is that respondents may be so guided by how the questions are set that they do not answer 'truthfully'. When writing their opinions in answer to open-ended questions (or talking about themselves for a case study) they are unlikely to lie — they would probably miss out the question instead. However, with quantitative data from closed-ended questions respondents could lie or be misled:
  - One aspect of 'lying' in answer to a questionnaire is **social desirability**. Respondents might say what they think they ought to say. For example, in British culture, if asked if they are racist, with options of 'yes', 'no' and 'unsure', respondents are unlikely to say 'yes' or 'unsure', because it is not acceptable in Britain to be racist. Social desirability may also affect answers to open-ended questions and qualitative data. However, the opportunity to analyse the wording used and the detail of the answer may mean that such a tendency comes to light, whereas with quantitative data, social desirability is less likely to be detected.
  - A second aspect of 'lying' in answer to a questionnaire is **demand characteristics** (guessing the purpose). Questions that produce quantitative data and give forced-choice answers might hint at the aim of the questionnaire. Respondents might want to help the researcher, so they give the answers that they think are wanted — or they might not want to help and give different answers. In either case, the responses lack validity because they are not 'true' answers. Quantitative data tend to come from controlled studies and are more likely to suffer from demand characteristics than do qualitative data. This is because, with a clear aim and hypothesis, there are more likely to be clues about what the researcher is investigating.
  - A third aspect of 'lying' in a questionnaire is when there is a **response set** or **response bias**. If questions are listed so that respondents are likely to be answering 'no' to a number of questions in a pattern, they might continue to answer 'no' out of habit. It is also possible that a respondent may have a personality trait to agree, or to disagree, all the time.

Table 1.4 *Strengths and weaknesses of qualitative data*

Strengths	Weaknesses
• Allow more in-depth analysis because of greater detail • More valid because respondents can say what they really think	• Difficult to analyse because the data can be so different that they are hard to summarise • There is more detail and depth and it can take longer both for the researcher and participant

Table 1.5 *Strengths and weaknesses of quantitative data*

Strengths	Weaknesses
• Data can be summarised in graphs and tables, so are easier to analyse and easier to communicate to others • Usually involve good controls such as well-structured questions or a clearly specified set of answers, so can be replicated and tested for reliability	• Have specified responses that are required, so tend not to be valid • Responses may not be truthful; people may respond in a socially desirable way

Ethical and sampling issues

Ethical and sampling issues are discussed in-depth on pages 23–35. They are both important issues when carrying out questionnaires.

Analysing questionnaires

Analysis of a questionnaire depends on whether the questions are open-ended or closed-ended. Closed-ended questions need the answers adding up (for example, the total number of 'yes' answers compared with the total number of 'no' answers). From totals, percentages can be calculated.

Analysing quantitative data from closed-ended questions

Example 1   Using a Likert-type scale

Key: SA = strongly agree, A = agree, DK = don't know (unsure), D = disagree, SD = strongly disagree

Statement	SA	A	DK	D	SD
1 I like meeting new people	☐	☐	☐	☐	☐
2 I enjoy finding out about others	☐	☐	☐	☐	☐
3 I prefer the company of people like myself	☐	☐	☐	☐	☐
4 I prefer to go out with my friends	☐	☐	☐	☐	☐

This scale is scored with a high score for 'liking new people'. The range of scores for statements 1 and 2 is from 5 for 'strongly agree' to 1 for 'strongly disagree'; the range for statements 3 and 4 is from 1 for 'strongly agree' to 5 for 'strongly disagree'.

Participant 1:

Statement	SA	A	DK	D	SD
1 I like meeting new people	☑ (5)	☐	☐	☐	☐
2 I enjoy finding out about others	☐	☑ (4)	☐	☐	☐
3 I prefer the company of people like myself	☐	☐	☑ (3)	☐	☐
4 I prefer to go out with my friends	☐	☐	☐	☑ (4)	☐

Participant 1 scores 16. The highest possible score is 20, so this is a high score and suggests that the participant likes other people.

Participant 2:

Statement	SA	A	DK	D	SD
1 I like meeting new people	☐	☐	☐	☑ (2)	☐
2 I enjoy finding out about others	☐	☐	☐	☐	☑ (1)
3 I prefer the company of people like myself	☐	☑ (2)	☐	☐	☐
4 I prefer to go out with my friends	☐	☑ (2)	☐	☐	☐

Participant 2 scores 7. This is a low score and suggests that this participant does not like other people.

Example 2 Yes/no/unsure answers

Fifty people answered a question on liking new people. The results are shown in the table below.

Sixty per cent of those asked said they liked meeting new people compared with 20% who said they did not; 20% were unsure.

Answer	Number of answers	Percentage
Yes	30	60
Unsure	10	20
No	10	20
Total	**50**	**100**

Analysis of qualitative data from open-ended questions

Since respondents present their answers to open-ended questions in different ways, analysis of such qualitative data is in the form of generating themes. For example, participants were asked the question, '*How do you think you are perceived by others?*' Their responses were:

> **Participant 1:** I think in general everyone likes me, but I'm not attractive.
>
> **Participant 2:** I don't think I'm liked much, but they think I'm clever.
>
> **Participant 3:** I'm seen as fat and jolly, so they think I'm fun.

From these responses, the following four themes could be generated:

- being liked
- being clever
- physical appearance
- being fun

The participants' responses are then analysed by theme:

- being liked — yes, 1; no, 1
- being clever — yes, 1; no, 0
- physical appearance — 2 (fat, unattractive)
- being fun — yes, 1

Conclusions

More data would be analysed and assuming similar themes were involved, a conclusion could be that people judge how others see them in terms of physical appearance, whether they are liked or not, and using other traits like 'fun to be with' or 'clever'. With regard to physical appearance, perhaps people are insecure and think they are seen in a negative way (fat, unattractive). There is also one theme here of fat = jolly = fun, which may be found in other data too.

TopFoto

In general, young people like having friends around them — perhaps those with more friends are happier meeting new people

Checklist for planning a questionnaire

- Do the questions address the aim/hypothesis?
- Are the questions clear and unambiguous?
- Is the sample size of respondents large enough and representative?
- Are ethical issues, such as confidentiality, addressed?
- Is the survey a reasonable length?
- When will the survey be carried out and over what length of time?
- Has a pilot study been carried out?
- How will the survey be administered (e.g. post, face-to-face)?
- Will the data be both qualitative and quantitative, and how will the data be analysed?
- Will the respondents answer on the questionnaire or on a separate grid?

Study hint **Keeping a practical notebook**

During the AS course you will carry out five main practicals and you will be asked questions about them in the unit tests. From the start, keep a practical notebook folder for your own practical work and keep your class practical notes, data and comments in the folder. This will make it easier to revise for the exams.

Evaluation of questionnaires

Strengths

- The same questions are asked of all participants, using a set procedure. There is little variation in how people are asked for the information, so the answers should not be affected by anything other than the opinions of the respondent.

  A questionnaire can be carried out by post, which removes any potential bias from the presence of the researcher. If the researcher does not affect the situation, then in that sense there is also **validity** — responses are real as they are not affected by someone else. If you use methods that do not gather valid (real-life) data, then you are not really studying people at all. Validity exists when a study is measuring what it claims to measure. Of course, if questions restrict possible answers, then in that sense they do not give valid (real-life) data.

- Another strength of questionnaires is again that they can be repeated accurately because:
  - they use set procedures
  - the same questions are asked of all the participants

Study hint Note that research methods can be valid in one sense and not valid in another. A questionnaire is valid if the person asking the questions and the situation itself do not affect the responses; it is not valid if forced-choice questions can miss 'real' answers. These distinctions need to be made. In an exam, saying 'questionnaires are valid' or 'questionnaires are not valid' will not gain a mark; expanding the answer with a reason will score the mark.

This means that they are fairly easily and cheaply **replicable** — simply by administering the questionnaire again. When a replicable study is repeated and similar data are gathered, the study is said to be reliable. **Reliability** is another important issue in psychology. If you gather one set of results and on repeating the study get different results, then the study is not reliable. Before they can be relied upon, studies have to be repeated and the same results found. However, to a large extent, questionnaires are reliable.

Weaknesses

- Although questionnaires have set procedures and are replicable, they have to be administered, and the way that this is done might vary, which challenges reliability. For example, on one occasion, a female student might find respondents in a local shopping centre on Saturday and ask them the questions personally. On another occasion, a male adult might find respondents at a golf club on a Tuesday lunchtime and might leave the questionnaires at the bar for completion. In these two instances, there are several differences that could affect the results. Usually a researcher will control the way the questionnaire is administered, but differences may still arise.

- A second weakness of questionnaires is that they usually have fixed questions that do not allow respondents to expand on their answers. Therefore, the responses might not be valid. (This point is discussed in more detail under weaknesses of closed-ended questions.) Open-ended questions are often restricted in the length of the answers allowed, so qualitative data can also be limited in a questionnaire, again raising the question of validity. If respondents are not free to say exactly what they want to say, then their answers may not be 'true' and are, therefore, not valid.

Study hint Validity and reliability are issues that occur throughout your course. Make sure that you understand what they mean. Learn one or two examples, so that you can always refer to validity and reliability when discussing a study.

Practice 1.2

Two scenarios are described above to show how the same questionnaire could be administered differently. List the differences between them and suggest how these differences might affect the results.

Answers are at end of Chapter 1.

Table 1.6 *Strengths and weaknesses of questionnaires*

Strengths	Weaknesses
• They are often reliable because bias from the researcher can be avoided by having set questions and a set procedure • If questions and procedure are set so that bias is avoided, data should be valid	• They could be administered differently by different people, so data may be biased by the situation, which would make them unreliable • If fixed questions are mainly asked then useful relevant data can be missed, making data not valid. Respondents are not free to say what they want to say, even if open questions are chosen

Studies involving the methodology Adorno et al. (1950) used a questionnaire to see if authoritarian personality linked to prejudice. They developed a 'fascism' scale. Their findings suggested that people who were more fascist (authoritarian) were more prejudiced in their views. This suggests that prejudice relates to personality.

Explore A web version of the F-scale (www.anesi.com) is available for you to try. It has some comments at the end about the questionnaire and the findings.

Surveys using interviews

Planning interviews

Interviews involve a face-to-face situation and a series of questions. They can involve a complete set of questions (such as a questionnaire), the difference being that the face-to-face situation allows the opportunity to expand, or clarify, the questions.

An interview is chosen instead of a questionnaire:
- if some questions are to be explored in more depth
- when the respondent may need reassurance
- when access is difficult

Access refers to reaching the participants — physically reaching them and also finding them in the first place. Access can be a difficult issue, e.g. if data are to be gathered from a child, from someone with mental health problems or from a business or venture. The appropriate people have to be contacted and have to agree to co-operate. Issues around access can involve ethical and practical considerations, which can restrict the data that can be gathered.

Practical When you decide to carry out a practical, you must consider ethical issues and issues of access. Will you be able to find easily the participants/ respondents that you need? Choose to focus on areas where you can access participants/respondents ethically and easily.

Explore Use your textbooks or the internet to find some interviews or case studies. They do not have to be psychological studies — for example, they could be interviews with media personalities. In each case, consider the issue of access. How was the person reached? What were the ethical issues involved? Was it possible to ask all the required questions? What restrictions did problems with access impose on the interview findings?

Types of interview

- A **structured interview** follows a set format. It is a questionnaire administered by an individual. There might be extra instructions for using the questionnaire, such as where and how to expand on answers.
- An **unstructured interview** involves questions that are not in a set format and which allow the interviewer to explore the area with further questions arising from the respondent's answers.
- A **semi-structured interview** has set questions, some of which can be explored further by the interviewer.

Interviews gather mainly qualitative data

Interviews are usually used when in-depth and detailed information is required, so the data are qualitative and can be in the form of a story, or attitudes. There are likely to be some quantitative data, such as age, length of time in a job, or other personal data. There might also be some 'yes'/'no' questions or interviewees might be asked to rate some information, but the data are mainly qualitative. The more structured

an interview is, the more likely it is to include quantitative data; the less structured the interview, the more qualitative is the information likely to be gathered.

Issues to consider when conducting interviews

Interview schedules must be prepared in advance so that the aims and research hypotheses are addressed. During an interview, notes can be taken or the interview can be recorded. Whichever format is used to record the interview, all notes must be **transcribed** (copied out) in full after the interview. This is time-consuming but necessary, so that all data are available for analysis.

In order to carry out these steps, the participants must be involved at each stage:

- They must see the **schedule** (which is the set of questions and time required and so on) before the interview, so that they can be ready.
- They must agree to the chosen format for recording the interview.
- They must see the full transcript (copy) of the interview afterwards and agree that it is what was said or occurred.

There are both ethical and practical issues here. Ethical issues in carrying out research in psychology are outlined on pages 23–30). Practical issues are mainly to do with reliability, validity and objectivity.

Subjectivity and objectivity

In all research, the researcher can cause bias. The issues that can affect question-naires, such as social desirability, demand characteristics and response bias, can also affect interviews. Researchers can also cause bias by interpreting the results using their own views and judgements: **Subjectivity** is when the analysis of the results includes input from the person doing the analysis. **Objectivity** is when there is no bias affecting the results, including no bias from the researcher's opinions. Scientific studies must be objective.

Psychology as a science Science is defined by how knowledge is gained and how findings are built upon, as much as by the subject matter. For example, we can be scientific in our choice of friends or scientific in our study of archaeology. Psychology is a science because of its methodology. When psychology involves studying, for example, the genes or the structure of the brain, then it is easy to show that it is a science because techniques for microbiology and brain scanning are involved. However, psychology involves areas such as prejudice and obedience. Here, science refers to the research methods used, not the subject matter. Science involves:

- objectivity — it is important not to let subjective (personal) opinions affect results
- generating hypotheses — such as in psychology about differences between male and female driving behaviour
- careful controls — to avoid bias
- measurable concepts

Psychology involves all these factors.

Objectivity when interviewing

Interviewing involves a face-to-face situation. Researchers must not be affected by whether or not they like, or agree with, the **interviewee**. Ways of remaining objective include:

- producing a complete transcript of the interview. This makes sure that researchers cannot select what they include
- ensuring that the interviewee sees the results and agrees that they are accurately recorded
- having another researcher analyse the results

If results are not objective, then the findings will not be useful.

> It is important to maintain objectivity both when asking questions and when analysing results.

Justin Kasezthreez/Alamy

Interviewing must be objective and ethical

Practical **Checklist for carrying out an interview**

- Have you decided whether to use a structured, unstructured or semi-structured interview?
- Have you decided how to record the interview (written, tape-recorded)?
- Have you drawn up the interview schedule?
- Have you included a question for each area in which you are interested?
- Have you included questions requesting necessary personal data?
- Have you included an explanation, so that the interviewee knows what is expected?
- Have you prepared the interviewee appropriately beforehand, including obtaining permission?
- Have you prepared all the materials, such as, if appropriate, a record sheet for the answers?
- Have you made sure you will gather both qualitative and quantitative data?

After the interview, for the results:

- Have you completely transcribed the interview, with all the detail?
- Have you generated the themes and categories from the data, not from your own ideas?

Social and Cognitive Psychology

Evaluation of interviews

Strengths

- The interviewer can explain questions and can explore issues by asking further questions. A questionnaire is limited to the questions written down and even when gathering qualitative data, usually there will be limited space available. When a researcher needs to be able to explain issues to a participant or to investigate further, an interview is the ideal method.
- Interviews obtain in-depth and detailed data that are likely to be valid. Interviewees talk in their own words and are not restricted. The data are 'real life' and 'true', and so are valid. For these reasons, an interview is often an important part of a case study.

Weaknesses

- When asking questions, interviewers might find it hard not to influence the answers. They might ask in a particular way or with a certain emphasis, such as 'You are not prejudiced, are you?' How they look or act may also affect responses — for example, interviewees might give different responses to male and female interviewers. These would be forms of **researcher bias**.
- The researcher might find it hard not to interpret the responses when analysing the data and forming themes. It might be difficult to maintain objectivity; subjectivity can be a problem with analysing interviews. Generating themes involves selection and the appropriate grouping of data — that choice can be subjective.

Table 1.7 Strengths and weaknesses of interviews	
Strengths	**Weaknesses**
• Questions can be explained and enlarged upon, so this is a good method when in-depth and detailed data are required	• The interviewer may influence the data (e.g. by tone, dress, gender), which would result in researcher bias
• Data tend to be valid because interviewees use their own words and are not as constrained by the questions as they are in a questionnaire	• Analysis may be subjective (e.g. generating themes) and the researcher's views may influence the analysis

Studies involving the methodology Broadhead and Abas (1997) carried out interviews in Harare, Zimbabwe, about causes of depression. They had already carried out interviews in London and found that depression was associated with life events and difficulties, as previously shown by Brown and Harris (1978). In the later study, the participants were 172 randomly selected residents of Harare. The researchers used the same interview schedule as they had in London and again found that life events and difficulties were associated with depression; there were more severe events in Harare than in London. In both London and Harare, certain types of event — for example, bereavement, entrapment in a situation or a woman's humiliation — were found to be particularly likely to lead to depression. It was concluded that such causes are universal and that there is a common mechanism. The same events were more severe in Harare, which accounted for the higher level of depression. The study suggested that despite cultural differences, universal similarities can be found.

Comparing questionnaires and interviews

In all research methods, there can be a trade-off between reliability and validity; subjectivity has to be avoided, so that knowledge is secure and can be relied upon. In general:

- Interviews tend to give data with more validity. However, they can involve subjectivity and are hard to repeat. Therefore, it is hard to test for reliability.
- Questionnaires are reliable and are less likely to involve subjectivity. However, they tend to be less valid, as any open questions may be missed out or answered only briefly.

Data can be collected from questionnaires more quickly than from interviews because questionnaires can be given to a number of people in the time it takes to interview one person in depth. However, it is not true that questionnaires are quick because:

- they take a long time to draw up
- it is more important to run a pilot study because the questions are more fixed
- they can take as long to analyse as interviews, since a lot of data are gathered

The usefulness of interviews and questionnaires, in terms of reliability, validity and subjectivity is shown in Table 1.8

Table 1.8 *Comparing questionnaires and interviews in terms of reliability, validity and subjectivity*

	Questionnaires	Interviews
Reliability	Structured questions; the same for all respondents; so replicable and likely to be reliable	Each person interviewed separately in different settings and on different occasions and perhaps by a different person; difficult to replicate and test for reliability
Validity	Set questions with forced-choice answers are likely to be less valid as may not yield 'true' data	Questions can be explained and explored, so likely to be valid and give 'real-life' and 'true' data
Subjectivity	Structured format; less open to researcher bias in the analysis; closed questions do not require interpretation; open questions are likely to give short answers, so themes are clearer	Open to bias in analysis as generating themes requires interpretation; open to subjectivity, but analysis can be objective if the steps are made clear

Ethical issues in research in psychology

Ethics are issues around what is seen as right and wrong with regard to the actions of others or of societies. Psychology uses both humans and animals in studies and there are associated ethical issues. In our society, it is felt that animals have rights. However, not all animals appear to be considered equal. Some people may think, for example, that spiders cannot be treated unethically. Others would not agree, thinking that it is unethical to use any animals in research. The issue of using animals in research is explored in detail in Chapters 4 and 5. Here, the focus is on ethical issues surrounding the use of humans as participants in psychological studies.

1

Study involving the methodology

Adams et al. (1996) carried out a study to investigate homophobia. There were two groups of male heterosexual participants, but one group was more homophobic than the other. They measured changes in penile circumference when the men were shown erotic stimuli of three sorts — heterosexual, male homosexual and lesbian. All men showed greater penile erection for the heterosexual images. Only the homophobic men showed penile erection for the male homosexual images. It was concluded that homophobia masks homosexual feelings of which men are either unaware or which they deny.

Ethical guidelines for psychologists

Ethics is not a new focus for psychologists. Ethical issues were discussed from the time that the American Psychological Association (APA) was set up in 1900. In 1959, the APA published an abbreviated code of ethics and a Canadian psychology association adopted the code in 1963.

■ The APA has a set of ethical principles that covers issues such as the competence of the psychologist and issues of assessment and therapy. The most recent code was published in 2002. The APA advocates responsible conduct research (RCR), which covers professional activities under nine headings, including research misconduct, human participants, research involving animals and data acquisition.

> Remember that studies should be assessed for their ethics according to the code of their time.

■ UNESCO (United Nations Educational, Scientific and Cultural Organisation) has a set of ethical principles for social scientists, which focus on issues such as confidentiality, responsibility and care.

■ Health workers have their own ethical guidelines and psychologists working with health workers also have to obey rules.

■ The British Psychological Society (BPS) was formed in 1901. It put forward a code of conduct in 1985 and adopted it in 1993. That code of conduct still applies. It includes guidelines about research practice, the use of animals in research, and advertising. Some of the BPS ethical guidelines that affect you as students of psychology are outlined below.

The British Psychological Society guidelines

The BPS is the association that supports psychologists and regulates the profession. It is based in Leicester and has a website (**www.bps.org.uk**) containing a great deal of information. One purpose of the BPS is to make sure that people involved in psychology, including clients and research participants, are treated ethically. Students of psychology must work within BPS ethical guidelines. Some of the guidelines are for practitioners — for example obtaining a practising certificate and completing an annual continuing professional development log. Others apply to research, and all researchers must follow these guidelines.

> **Practical** All practical work must follow ethical guidelines. You will be guided about this throughout your course, but you are responsible for your research. Always note in your practical folder the ethical issues that arose from the study and how they were addressed. You are likely to be asked exam questions about such issues.

Although there are others that are equally important, for your course you have to consider five ethical guidelines:

- informed consent
- debriefing
- deceit
- competence
- right to withdraw

Some other ethical issues are covered in Chapter 3.

Getting informed consent

All participants should consent to the study, whatever the research method and whatever the study is about. It is usually easy to ask people if they will take part, but there is more to it than that. What is the value of their consent if they do not know what is going to happen? There should be **informed consent**. This means that those who agree to take part must know (be informed about) what the study is about. Observations may be carried out without consent (because you don't know who you will observe — it will depend on who is there). They should be carried out in a public setting where people know that they are likely to be seen.

Assessing the guideline 'getting informed consent'

It is often difficult to get informed consent without affecting the data. For example, Milgram (1963) carried out a study in the USA in which participants were asked to give what they thought were strong electric shocks to another participant, when that person gave incorrect answers to questions. In this obedience study, if the participants had known that the electric 'shocks' were not real, then the results would not have been about obedience in the same way because the participants would have known that the consequences were not 'real'. Milgram could not get informed consent, but he did try to make his study ethical:

- He asked for volunteers, so participants knew that they were taking part in a study.
- He asked other people before the study if they would agree to take part in such a study and they said that they would. This is **presumptive consent**.
- He asked others, including psychologists, whether they thought that the consequences for the participants would be severe, to which they said no.

Another way is to obtain consent sometime before the study starts. This is **prior consent** and involves asking people beforehand to volunteer and explaining that

sometimes deception will be necessary. So even if informed consent is not possible, there are other ways of making a study reasonably ethical, although Milgram's study is criticised widely as being unethical.

Milgram said the following about one of his participants:

> I observed a mature and initially poised businessman enter the laboratory smiling and confident. Within 20 minutes he was reduced to a twitching, stuttering wreck, who was rapidly approaching nervous collapse. He constantly pulled on his ear lobe, and twisted his hands. At one point he pushed his fist into his forehead and muttered 'Oh God, let's stop it'. And yet he continued to respond to every word of the experimenter and obeyed to the end.

Informed consent is not as difficult to obtain for questionnaires and interviews as it is for experiments because the questions in the survey will suggest what the survey is about (e.g. prejudice). Therefore, the participant is likely to guess the purpose and so it is sensible for the participant to be fully informed for ethical reasons.

However, if it is not possible to obtain informed consent because the data could not then be gathered, a thorough debriefing can make the study more ethical. An offer could also be made to withdraw data from the study if the participant is not happy with having taken part. If this is the case, then follow-up contact should be made to ensure that there is no lasting damage. No study should be carried out if the participant leaves the study in a different state from that when the study began.

Avoiding deception

Deception in a study can take many forms. One way of deceiving participants is when informed consent is not obtained. Participants can be deceived when they are not told what they have to do or if they are not told the truth about what they have to do. They can be deceived by not telling them what results are expected, by not telling them how the results will be used or not telling them the roles of other participants within the study.

Assessing the guideline 'avoiding deception'

In experiments in particular it is sometimes necessary to deceive participants because otherwise their knowledge would affect the results. Milgram (1963) deceived his participants in a number of ways. He told them that the shocks that they would give were real and even gave them a small shock (45 volts) to back this up. He told them that the person they were to give shocks to was another participant, when in fact it was one of his colleagues. He did not tell them that the colleague knew about the study and had been asked to scream and shout to pretend that he was receiving shocks. The participants were deceived from the start because they had volunteered for a memory experiment whereas the study was about obedience. You can see why Milgram's study has been criticised so strongly as not being ethical.

In questionnaires and interviews there is often no need for deception, and questions need to be clear. However, even in surveys there is sometimes deception — for example, asking more questions than necessary in order to hide the 'real' question within the set. This is done to avoid demand characteristics (the respondent guessing the aim of the study). However, there should not be too many 'other questions' so that the respondent is not inconvenienced.

If there is deception, then thorough debriefing can help to make the study more ethical. As with lack of informed consent, if participants are unhappy about having taken part, their data should be withdrawn and follow-up contact made to make sure that there are no long-term effects. Milgram contacted his participants after the 1963 study and found that most were happy to have taken part, which went some way towards making his study more ethical.

Giving the right to withdraw

Throughout any study, participants should be given the right to withdraw. At the start, when they have been told all that they can be told about the study without affecting the results, participants should be asked if they want to continue. They should be asked periodically whether they are still happy to continue. At the end, they should be given the right to withdraw their data.

Assessing the guideline 'giving the right to withdraw'

Usually it is quite easy to ask participants if they are happy to continue. However, in some studies this would affect the results. One example is in the study of obedience. To be obedient, participants have to do as they are told by someone in authority — usually the researcher. That won't work if participants can say they want to leave. Milgram did not give the right to withdraw and when participants seemed to want to leave he used planned verbal comments to make them continue. Of course, they could still leave the study, as some did, so Milgram was able to say that they always had the right to withdraw. However, this right should have been more explicit.

In interviews, it is easy to give the right to withdraw both at the start and through-out, because the interviewer is interacting with one participant and talking with him or her. However, in questionnaires it is likely that the right to withdraw will be outlined only at the start. Without anyone there to press the respondent to continue, questions can be missed out or the questionnaire not completed at all, which is equivalent to withdrawing from the study.

There should never be an occasion when a participant in any psychology study is not given the right to leave the study. Children or vulnerable people might not feel that they can leave and should be reminded that they can leave at any time.

Debriefing the participants

Participants are briefed at the start of a study to tell them about it — as far as is possible without affecting the data. Then they are asked to give informed consent. It is likely that fully informed consent from a full briefing will not be achieved, because something has to be held back for the sake of the study. This means that a complete **debrief** should take place immediately after the study. Participants should also be told at this point that, if they wish, they can withdraw their data. Participants should not be left upset or confused. The debrief should:

- explain the study
- explain what results were expected
- explain the participant's results
- ask the participant about possible withdrawal of results
- check that the participant has no further questions and is not distressed by the study

Assessing the guideline 'debriefing the participants'

Debrief is usually straightforward because the study is over and the participants can be told all about it. However, there are occasions when it is difficult — perhaps because the study involved observing crowds, and individuals in the crowd cannot be found later. The people in the crowd would be unaware of the study. If they are not being studied as individuals but as members of a crowd, and if they are not individually identifiable, then this might be considered ethical. If, however, the participants are picked out and are identifiable, they ought to be found and debriefed.

Debriefing can also be difficult in observations of people in public places, because by the time the observation is over, they will have moved on. It might be thought that as long as they are not looked at as individuals in the observation (for example, they may be studied for their gender alone), then no real personal data are recorded and a debrief is unnecessary. Observations are usually considered to be ethical if they take place in a public setting where those being observed would expect to be seen.

Being competent to run the study

No researcher should try to carry out a study for which they are not competent, including students and all psychologists. If in doubt, the researcher should ask the opinion of a qualified person. Competence includes:

- understanding the implications of the study
- knowing the ethical guidelines
- getting advice in any area about which the researcher does not feel confident
- being suitably qualified
- adhering to safe practice
- adhering to the Data Protection Act
- knowing where and how to store data

Assessing the guideline 'being competent to run the study'

There is the problem of not knowing what the results of a study will be and it is hard to assess competence without knowing this. Milgram asked colleagues what they thought and he was careful to obtain advice from other qualified people. With hindsight, it is clear that Milgram's study upset his participants a great deal, but at the time nobody thought that this would be the case. It is interesting to ask whether this makes it more ethical, since it is hard to know if the researcher is competent to run the study or not.

Explore Do some research into Milgram's views on his study. He was criticised widely for the ethics of his work but he defended himself and made some excellent points — for example, that it is our duty to study tricky areas such as obedience.

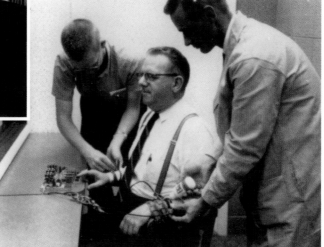

Milgram asked participants to give what they thought were very strong electric shocks to another person, and 65% obeyed

Figure 1.1 *Five ethical guidelines*

1 Getting informed consent
Researchers should get consent from participants; where possible this should be informed consent. This means that, at the start, they should be as fully informed as is possible, without spoiling the study.

2 Not deceiving participants
Ideally, participants should not be deceived. They should be told everything about the study. If some deceit is necessary, so that the study will not be affected, then prior consent should be obtained, confirming that the participant is willing to take part without knowing everything about the study.

5 Competence of the researcher
Researchers must have the necessary qualifications and be competent to carry out the study. If in doubt, they must refer to, and seek advice from, a competent person.

Ethical guidelines

4 Debriefing participants afterwards
Participants should be debriefed, which means explaining fully what the study was about and what their results mean. They should be unaffected by the study and be in the same emotional state at the end as they were at the beginning.

3 Allowing the right to withdraw
Participants can withdraw from the study at any time, should be reminded of this throughout and can withdraw their data.

Other ethical guidelines when using human participants

Other ethical guidelines include the following:

- Participants should not be harmed or distressed by the study.
- Children and other vulnerable groups should be treated with particular care to make sure that everything is understood, permission given, and that advantage is not taken of any participant.
- Confidentiality should be maintained throughout, with no names being used. Data must not be shared with anyone not connected with the study.

Ethical rules when using animal participants

The ethical rules for using animal paticipants are explained in detail in Chapter 4. They include requirements regarding caging and rules about the number of animals used, the use of endangered species and the use of anaesthetics. A Home Office licence is needed. When discussing ethical issues regarding the use of animals in psychological research, do not refer to the guidelines for using humans. Special rules to protect them are needed and it is these that you should discuss when considering non-human animals.

Animals are used in psychological research and guidelines must be followed to protect them

Sampling

When any study is carried out, it is rarely possible to include everyone who should be involved as participants. For example, the findings of a study about prejudice will potentially be applied to everyone, but it would be impossible to include everyone in the study. Even if a study is to look at a smaller group, for example, differences in obedience between male and female soldiers, there are too many to test them all. Almost always in psychology a study involves a sample of the population of interest. The **target population** is all the people the study is about — those to whom the findings will be applied. The chosen sample must be representative of the population and, if possible, not biased. **Representative** here means including members of each type of person in that population, usually in the correct proportion. An example of bias would be having only young males and older females in the sample of a study where gender is important.

It is difficult to get a representative sample because there are problems in obtaining participants. Even if you can get access to the relevant people, you still have to choose who will be involved. There are a number of sampling techniques in use, none of which is ideal for getting a representative sample, although some techniques are better than others.

Practical **How sampling takes place**

- Define the population of interest.
- Specify the sampling frame (items or events that can be measured).
- Choose a sampling method to measure items or events from the frame.
- Decide the sample size.
- Find the sample.
- Collect the data.
- Review the sampling process to evaluate the findings.

Sample size

The sample size depends on the confidence interval and the confidence level:

- The **confidence interval** is how far it is thought that answers, for example, might not be reliable/valid. For example, a researcher might say that the results are true within plus or minus (±) 3 in the scoring. So a score of 10 on a questionnaire rating prejudice may have a confidence interval of ±3 — the true score being between 7 and 13.
- The **confidence level** is the percentage of the sample that is likely to represent the population.

It is common for researchers to choose a confidence level of 95%; and a confidence interval of ±3 is also a sensible choice. To decide on sample size, you need to know:

- the size of the sampling frame (those you are choosing from)
- the confidence interval (e.g. ±3)
- the confidence level (e.g. 95%)

The internet has calculators for the sampling process, but there are variations in the advice — for example, about the size of the sampling frame. One example is that, with a confidence interval of ±3, a confidence level of 95% and a sampling frame of 2,000 people, the sample size should be 704. You could assume, therefore, that if you have a sampling frame of 200, the sample should be around 70. In practice, when studying psychology as you are, a sample size of 20 will give you some idea of the results you would find if you asked more people.

Simple random sampling

This method gives everyone an equal chance of being chosen. The main rule is that everyone in the target population is available for selection each time a participant is picked out. However, the larger target population is usually reduced to a manageable **sampling frame**. For example, to examine obedience in male and female soldiers, researchers could choose one regiment. Then, to get a random sample, the names of all the soldiers in the regiment could be put into a box and one picked out each time until the required number of participants was reached.

Another way of taking a random sample is to use random number tables or a random number generator. People are allocated numbers and whatever number occurs, that participant is chosen.

Explore Do some research using the internet or some other source to see how many participants are used in studies. Four studies are explained in detail in this chapter. Look at them now and note down the numbers used. For example, Tajfel et al. (1970, 1971) used groups of boys, but there were not many boys in each group; Hofling et al. (1966) used data from 22 nurses from which to draw their conclusions. So if you carry out a study and don't have many participants, it is worth noting that neither did many researchers.

Explore Make up some figures for confidence levels and confidence intervals and find out what sample sizes you would need for different population sizes. Check the different advice given by various internet sites. Note that in the studies covered in this section the sample sizes have been relatively small. For example, Adams et al. (1996) used around 30 men in each group,

Unit 1

Advantages of simple random sampling

- There is no bias in the way the participants are chosen; everyone has the opportunity to be chosen and no one is systematically excluded from the sample. Therefore, the sample is likely to be representative of the target population.
- It is clear to everyone how the sample was chosen. Each step of the process can be explained and understood. When studies are carried out scientifically, their results and conclusions are more widely recognised and can be added more easily to the body of psychological knowledge. With random sampling, any possible bias (as explained below) can be worked out mathematically and taken into account.

Disadvantages of simple random sampling

- It is difficult to ensure that everyone in the target population is available to be included in the sample, which may cause bias. There is a problem, for example, in getting the names of people because of the Data Protection Act (1998). Even if everyone's name were included, it would not be known if they were available to take part. For example, someone might not be available on the required day; someone might not want to take part. So even if random sampling took place, it would not mean that all those chosen would be part of the study, so there could be bias.
- Even with simple random sampling, when everyone has an equal chance of being chosen, there can be a bias in the sample. For example, if the hypothesis was to examine obedience in male and female soldiers, it is possible that a random sample would not include any female soldiers, which would not be useful.

Table 1.9 Strengths and weaknesses of simple random sampling

Strengths	Weaknesses
• Low bias because everyone has an equal chance of being chosen • Sample can be checked math-ematically for bias	• Cannot be certain that the sample is representative of all groups/types etc. • Difficult to access all the population so that random sampling can take place

Study hint In your practical work you are unlikely to use random sampling, so avoid saying that your sample was 'random'. If you find yourself writing about something being random, check your use of the term.

Stratified sampling

To make sure that certain groups are represented in the sample, stratified sampling is used. Groups arise from the study and it is decided how many participants are needed within each group. The number of participants from each group should represent the numbers of that group in the target population. For example, if the study was about obedience in male and female soldiers, there are two main groups; within those, age could be a factor, so there might be four groups:

- young male soldiers
- young female soldiers
- older male soldiers
- older female soldiers

These are the four strata for the stratified sampling. If there are five times as many male soldiers as female soldiers, then there should be five times as many male soldiers in the sample.

Advantages of stratified sampling

- Each group is bound to be represented, so conclusions about differences between those groups can be drawn.
- Stratified sampling is an efficient way of ensuring that there is representation from each group. Random sampling would probably still provide some participants from each group, but the researcher cannot be sure of this and may, therefore, need a larger sample. Stratified sampling limits the numbers needed to obtain representation from each group.

Disadvantages of stratified sampling

- It is difficult to know how many of each group to choose in order to make sure that the findings are **generalisable**. It is always difficult to know how many individuals make up an appropriate sample; with stratified sampling, where the numbers in each group may be small, it is harder.
- The groups set by the study may not be the important groups. Having the groups already decided means that some people will be ruled out as participants. This could mean that the sample is not representative of the population. For example, obedience in soldiers may depend on whether or not they have a family. That grouping was not considered in the sampling, so may not be represented.

> A study is **generalisable** if the findings can be said to be true of the target population.

Table 1.10	Strengths and weaknesses of stratified sampling

Strengths	Weaknesses
• All relevant groups/strata will have at least some representation • Limits the numbers of participants needed	• It is difficult to know how many of each group is needed in order to represent the target population accurately • Relies on researchers knowing all the required groups/strat; forces choice of participants and proportions of all groups so can give bias by excluding people

Volunteer/self-selected sampling

Sometimes it is best to ask for volunteers for a study — volunteers select themselves by volunteering. They might answer an advertisement or respond to a letter. When the sample is a **volunteer sample** it is **self-selected**. Milgram (1963) used a volunteer sample. His participants answered an advertisement.

Advantages of volunteer/self-selected sampling

- It is more ethical than other methods (e.g. simple random sampling) because the participants come to the researcher rather the researcher seeking them out.
- Volunteers are interested and are, therefore, perhaps less likely to give biased information or to go against the researcher's instructions. There is less likely to be social desirability or demand characteristics — unless they are so keen that they do what they think the researcher wants, having guessed what that is (demand characteristics). In general, it is an advantage to have volunteers, in that they are willing to be involved in the study.

Disadvantages of volunteer/self-selected sampling

- It can take a long time to get sufficient numbers of participants because the researcher has to wait for volunteers to apply. For example, one advertisement or request may not raise enough people.
- Because the participants select themselves, they might be similar in some way. For example, Milgram's participants all read the advertisement, so they read the same publication. They also had to have time to take part, which could rule out those in certain occupations. Therefore, a volunteer sample, being self-selected, is biased and is not likely to be representative of the target population.

Table 1.11 *Strengths and weaknesses of volunteer/self-selected sampling*

Strengths	Weaknesses
• Ethically good because people volunteer, so are willing to be involved	• Only certain types of people may volunteer, so there is bias
• More likely to cooperate, which means there may be less social desirability and such biases	• May take a long time to get enough volunteers

Opportunity sampling

Opportunity sampling is not really a true method of sampling, because it means taking whoever is available. Researchers use whoever they can find to take part — they take the opportunity to involve participants. The way participants are chosen is not structured. Psychology students tend to use opportunity sampling, as the people to whom they have access are limited.

> **Opportunity sampling** is sometimes called grab sampling or convenience sampling.

Advantages of opportunity sampling

- It tends to be more ethical because the researcher can judge if the participant is likely to be upset by the study or is too busy to take part. Other forms of sampling often do not give this information readily.
- The researcher has more control over who is asked, so finding participants should be quick and efficient, because access is not a problem.

Disadvantages of opportunity sampling

- There is more chance of bias than with other methods. One source of bias is that researchers have more control over who is chosen and may be biased towards people who are easy to access, such as people they know. They may be biased towards choosing people like themselves, people of their own age or people who look friendly. These issues connected with researchers are likely to lead to a biased sample.
- Those who are picked are available and willing to take part in the study, so they are self-selected. This would rule out anyone not available or not willing, which again will cause bias. These issues connected with participants are likely to lead to a biased sample.

> **Study hint** For your practicals, you will almost certainly use opportunity sampling so be prepared to answer a question about sampling methods by explaining the advantages and disadvantages of opportunity sampling. If you used a different sampling method, then you must be ready to answer questions about that method.

Table 1.12	Strengths and weaknesses of opportunity sampling

Strengths	Weaknesses
• More ethical because the researcher can judge if the participant is likely to be upset by the study or is too busy to take part • The researcher has more control over who is chosen and should, therefore, be able to get the sample quickly and efficiently	• Only people available are used and they may be a self-selected group (e.g. not working, so available during the day) • May not get representatives from all groups so there may be bias

Figure 1.2 Four sampling procedures

Simple random sampling
Everyone in the sampling frame or population has an equal chance of being chosen for the sample

Opportunity sampling
The researcher takes whomsoever they can to take part in the study

Sampling methods

Stratified sampling
The population is divided into the required groups and the correct proportions of people are picked out for the sample

Volunteer/self-selected sampling
People are asked to volunteer for the study, either personally or via an advertisement or some such means. By volunteering, they self-select

Examination-style questions

1 Describe and evaluate the interview as a research method in psychology. *(12 marks)*

2 Outline *three* ethical guidelines and assess *two* of the guidelines you have chosen. *(12 marks)*

3 Outline *one* advantage and *one* disadvantage of *two* sampling methods used in psychology. *(8 marks)*

Extension questions

1 Compare the use of questionnaires and interviews as research methods in psychology. *(10 marks)*

2 Discuss why ethical guidelines for research are necessary. *(12 marks)*

3 Compare *three* different methods of sampling used in psychology. *(9 marks)*

Content

The Milgram study is compulsory, together with a non-US study of obedience. The study described here is from the Netherlands, but you have a free choice. Obedience is studied in some depth; prejudice is touched upon by looking at one theory.

What is meant by obedience?

Obedience means obeying direct orders from someone in authority. This is not the same as conforming to the behaviour of others. **Conforming** is doing something

1

which is against the individual's own inclinations, but not doing it because of an order. **Compliance** means going along with what someone says, while not necessarily agreeing with it. **Internalising** is obeying with agreement.

Compliance is, therefore, part of obedience and is referred to as such by Milgram. His research into obedience focused on issues such as why Nazi soldiers obeyed orders to perpetrate genocide on the Jewish race. He wanted to know if all people would obey in similar circumstances or whether there was something different about those soldiers. At the time when Milgram was focusing on obedience, Adolf Eichmann was being tried in Jerusalem for crimes committed against the Jews in the **holocaust**.

> The **holocaust** was the slaughter of millions of Jews, gypsies, homosexuals and others by the Nazis during the second World War.

Eichmann was the officer most responsible for the holocaust. He did not appear to be evil, he was mild and ordinary-looking. He kept repeating that he did it because he was ordered to. This was frightening because people wondered if they would have done the same.

> **Explore** Investigate the holocaust and subsequent trials of those involved in it.
> Do you think they were evil people? Or do you think they were 'just obeying orders'?

The study of obedience by Milgram (1963) and variations

In 1963, Milgram carried out what is now a well-known experiment. Subsequently, he carried out variations of that study. You have to know the main study and one of the variations.

Milgram's (1963) basic study

Milgram wanted to see if people would obey orders when the consequences were severe. He decided to let people think that they were giving another person an electric shock and to see how far they would go.

Aim

The aim of Milgram's (1963) basic study was to test the idea that the Germans were somehow different from other people, in that they were able to carry out barbaric acts against the Jews and other minority groups. Milgram wanted to see if volunteer participants would obey orders to give electric shocks to someone they thought was just another participant. He wanted to answer the question 'How far would they go?'

Procedure

Milgram advertised for participants and told them that they were taking part in an experiment on human learning. He had a helper — called a **confederate** or **accomplice** — who was the learner who would 'receive' the (fake) shocks. There was one real shock of 45 volts, which the participants received to convince them that the shock generator was real. The confederate-learner, who was middle-aged and pleasant looking, was primed. The study took place at Yale University and the participants took part one at a time.

Yale is a prestigious university in the USA.

In the account of the study, Milgram is treated as being the experimenter but in fact someone else took that role.

Each participant arrived at the laboratory and waited in a room with the confederate. The participant was led to believe that the confederate was also a participant. They drew lots to decide who would be the learner. However, this was rigged so that the confederate was always the learner and the participant was always the teacher. Milgram reassured participants that the shocks would be painful but that there would be no permanent tissue damage. The participant-teacher watched the confederate-learner being strapped into a chair and wired up so that the 'shocks' could be felt. Milgram then took the participant-teacher into another room where there was a long counter in front of an array of switches and an impressive-looking machine — the generator. The switches were in a row and were labelled as running from 15 volts to 450 volts. Above the switches there were comments such as 'slight shock' and 'danger'. This left the participant in no doubt that the shocks would be increasingly painful and dangerous as the voltage increased. The participant sat in front of the 15-volt switch and began the experiment, having been given instructions by Milgram. The participant was to move up one switch at a time each time the learner gave a wrong answer.

The task required the participant to read out word pairs such as blue-box, nice-day, wild-duck, then read out the key word and four possible pairs. For example, he might read out blue-sky, ink, box, and lamp. The confederate-learner had four buttons and had to press the correct one. In this example, the correct response is 'box'. An incorrect response was given a 15-volt 'shock'; each successive wrong answer was given a shock 15 volts higher — 30 volts, 45 volts and so on.

At first the learner gave correct responses, then a few wrong responses. Up to 75 volts there was no indication that the shocks were causing distress. However, the learner then gave some grunts, and at 120 volts shouted that the shocks were becoming painful. The question was, 'When would the participant stop carrying out the task?'

Milgram and the confederate were working to a script, so that each participant had the same experiences. At 150 volts, the learner shouted that the shocks were becoming painful and that he did not want to go on with the study. At 270 volts, these shouts became agonised screams. At 300 volts, the learner refused to give answers. The experimenter told the participant to treat the absence of a response as no response and ordered him to go on with the shocks. If 450 volts was reached, participants were to continue with that switch. The experimenter was in the room with the participant, so the participant would think that no one was with the learner — who was now silent and could be in a bad way. It was pointless to continue with the study because the learner was not responding — no learning would take place. Would participants continue just because they were ordered to? They were, after all, free to leave.

It is worth noting that the experimenter had a script. On occasion, he prompted the participant to continue, by saying such things as 'You must continue', or 'It is absolutely essential that you continue'. These prompts are called verbal prods, and may have affected the outcome. They are shown in Table 1.13.

Table 1.13	Milgram's planned prompts to give to participants if they refused to continue

Order of prompt	Verbal prod
1	Please continue/please go on
2	The experiment requires that you continue
3	It is absolutely essential that you continue
4	You have no other choice — you must go on
5	If the participant was still refusing, then the study was stopped

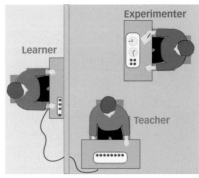

Figure 1.3 A plan of the experiment showing the teacher and experimenter in one room and the victim wired up in another room

Milgram thought the participants would refuse to go up to 450 volts. He expected to have to modify the pattern of screams and responses because participants would not agree to continue. Before carrying out the study, he asked students and colleagues what they thought; the opinion was that 2% or 3% would continue to the end. When people were asked what they would do, none said they would continue to the end.

Results

The results showed that 26 of the 40 men who took part in the study and 26 of the 40 women, who were tested in a separate study, continued to the end. In the main study, which used male participants, 14 participants therefore stopped before 450 volts (see Table 1.14). Sixty-five per cent obeyed to 450 volts; 100% obeyed to 300 volts.

Table 1.14	The number of participants who stopped before 450 volts was reached

Voltage	Number that stopped
Up to 300	0
300	5
315	4
330	2
345	1
360	1
375	1

Total stopped = 14 (out of 40)

Most participants thought that the experiment was real. After the study, they were asked to rate the shocks; most rated them as 14 on a scale in which 14 meant extremely painful. The average rating was 13.42. Many participants showed signs of nervousness, especially when 'giving' the most painful shocks. Participants were seen to sweat, tremble, stutter, groan and dig their fingernails into their flesh. Fourteen of the 40 showed nervous laughter and smiling (though after the study they made it clear that they did not think it was funny). Participants often heaved a sigh of relief when the study was ended.

Conclusions

Social influence is strong and people obey orders even when this causes them distress. It was not thought that people would obey and such obedience is surprising. Milgram summarised the features that led to obedience:

- Yale University is a prestigious institution and unlikely to allow anything unethical to occur.
- The study seemed to have a worthy cause — to learn about memory.
- The victim was not unwilling and had agreed to take part.
- The participant had volunteered and had made a commitment.
- The participant was paid and so felt an obligation.
- The learners was there by chance — he or she could have been the participant.
- This was a new situation for the participant, who had no idea of what was suitable behaviour.
- It was thought that the shocks were painful, but not dangerous.
- Up to 300 volts, the learner plays the game and seems willing.

Evaluation of the basic study by Milgram (1963)

Milgram's basic study has both strengths and weaknesses.

Strengths

- Milgram carried out a very well-controlled procedure. He had set prompts, in a set order, and had prepared the victim's responses carefully. He made every effort to make the experience of each participant the same, to avoid any bias. This lack of bias means that the conclusion — that obedience was due to a response to an authority figure — was firm. It is unlikely that other factors led to the results. This means that cause-and-effect conclusions can be drawn.
- The controlled procedures mean that the study is replicable and so can be tested for reliability. The precise procedure cannot be repeated for ethical reasons. However, there have been replications using the same idea, but with a different 'punishment'. These studies have also shown that people obey those in authority, even when it goes against their own moral code.

Weaknesses

- There are ethical problems with regard to repeating it. Milgram was aware of the ethical implications. He asked colleagues and others if they thought that the participants would obey, and it was generally thought they would not — certainly not to the level that they did. So he did not expect the level of anxiety and stress that he found. He debriefed the participants carefully and introduced them to his accomplice, as well as checking on their well-being. However, he described shaking, trembling, sweating and seizures, so it cannot be denied that the study was unethical. Milgram showed himself to be competent, and asked others to confirm this. He debriefed the participants thoroughly. In theory, he gave the right to withdraw because participants could leave

> The BPS guidelines listed for your course are lack of deceit, informed consent, right to withdraw, debriefing and competence.

at any time (some did). However, he pressurised participants to stay by using prompts, which means that, to an extent, he did not give the right to withdraw. He deceived participants by saying that the study was about memory and by pretending that the shocks were real. He gained consent and asked for volunteers. He pointed out that they could keep their payments even if they did not continue with the study. However, the consent he obtained was not fully informed consent because of the deceit.

■ The basic study lacked validity. For example, the participants trusted that what happened at Yale University would be acceptable (they were right — the shocks were not real). It could be argued that in a more realistic situation they would not have continued, although that is conjecture.

Table 1.15	Strengths and weaknesses of the basic study by Milgram (1963)	
Strengths		**Weaknesses**
• Good controls avoid bias and mean that the situation was the same for all, so cause-and-effect conclusions could be drawn • The well-controlled procedures mean that the study is replicable and can be tested for reliability		• The study is unethical because the participants were deceived, did not give informed consent, were distressed and did not have the full right to withdraw • The study lacks validity because of the artificial procedures

Variations of Milgram's 1963 procedure

Milgram carried out variations on his original study.

Aims

Milgram considered what might have affected the participants in his first study and then altered the situation to see the effect. For example, he thought that obedience might have been because the study was at Yale University, so he repeated it in an office. He wondered if having the experimenter in the room affected the level of obedience, so he carried out the study with the experimenter in touch by telephone. In another variation he used two other 'teachers' (both confederates) who stopped before the 300-volt level — to which all his initial participants had gone. As he made a change, he kept everything else constant so that he could make comparisons. The procedures and results are shown in Table 1.16.

Table 1.16 shows that in all the variations from the basic study, the level of obedience was reduced:

■ The original study produced the highest level of obedience (100% went to 300 volts and 65% went to 450 volts).

■ The study with the next highest level of obedience was the one held in a rundown office block, where 47.5% continued to 450 volts.

■ When the teacher had to hold the victim's hand down to receive the shock, 30% obeyed.

■ With the experimenter not in the room, 22.5% obeyed.

■ With two 'colleagues', who both refused to proceed before the 300 volt level, there was a 10% level of obedience.

■ When there were two experimenters, one of whom told the participant to stop, no one continued to the end.

Table 1.16 *Milgram's variations on his basic study*

Situation/procedures	Result
Original study	26 out of 40 (65%) continued to the end
Two experimenters; at 110 volts, one tells the participant to stop and the other tells the participant to continue	All participants stopped
Three teachers (two were confederates); one confederate-teacher stops at 150 volts and the other at 210 volts	Only 10% of participants continued to the end
Experimenter's instructions are given by tape and the participant can speak to the experimenter (who is not in the room) by phone	Nine of the 40 (22.5%) participants continued to the end
Moving the victim closer until the participant held the victim's hand down to receive the shock	12 of the 40 participants obeyed (30%)
Held in Research Associates of Bridgeport offices, in a fairly rundown office building	19 of the 40 participants obeyed (47.5%)

Conclusions

The level of obedience was highest in the basic experiment; all the variations led to a lower level. The setting had the least effect; the orders of the experimenter had the most effect. This suggests that the conclusion that obedience results from orders given by an authority figure is correct.

Evaluation of variations of Milgram's (1963) procedure

The strengths and weaknesses of Milgram's variations are similar to those of his basic procedure:

■ The strong controls avoid bias and make the experience the same for all participants, so cause-and-effect conclusions can be drawn.
■ Because of the clear procedures and controls, the studies are replicable and so can be tested for reliability. The findings from the studies with variations are different from each other and from the basic study, but they show obedience in similar situations and back up Milgram's conclusions.
■ The studies are not ethical because they put pressure on the participants, they deceive the participants and they do not give the full right to withdraw.
■ The studies lack validity because the situations are artificial.

The agency theory of obedience (Milgram 1973, 1974)

In Milgram's studies of obedience, participants who obeyed to the end tended to say that they were just doing what they were told to do and would not have done it otherwise. They knew that what they were doing was wrong. The participants showed **moral strain**, in that they knew that obeying the order was wrong, but they felt unable to disobey. Moral strain — when people become uncomfortable with their behaviour because they feel that it is wrong and goes against their values — comes from various sources. In this study:

- The participants heard the cries of the victim.
- They might have feared retaliation from the victim.
- They had to go against their own moral values.
- There was a conflict between the needs of the victim and the needs of the authority figure.
- The participants would not want to harm someone, because this would go against their opinions of themselves.

Having agreed to take part, all participants in the basic study obeyed until the 'shock level' reached 300 volts. It was as if, having agreed to take part, they were in an **agentic state**. This means that they were agents of the experimenter and so obeyed his orders. The agentic state is the opposite of autonomy. **Autonomy** is being under one's own control and having the power to make one's own decisions. The participants were not simply agents of the experimenter — the grey technician's coat that the experimenter wore and the Yale University setting, added to the power of the experimenter and to the role of the participants as agents.

Milgram (1973, 1974) used the idea of being in an agentic state to put forward his **agency theory**.

This is the idea that our social system leads to obedience. If people see themselves as individuals, they will respond as individuals and will be autonomous in a situation. For example, in a threatening situation, many people avoid aggression and turn away. This is likely to happen because avoiding aggression avoids being hurt and will aid survival. **Evolution theory** suggests that avoiding aggression is a good survival strategy.

> **Evolution theory** is the idea of natural selection — any tendency that aids survival would lead to the gene or gene combination for that tendency being passed on.

Early humans had a better chance of survival if they lived in social groups, with leaders and followers. A tendency to have leaders and followers may also have been passed on genetically. A hierarchical social system, such as the one that Milgram's participants were used to, requires a system in which some people act as agents for those 'above' them. According to the agency theory, the agentic state is what led the participants in Milgram's basic study to obey.

In an autonomous state:
- individuals see themselves as having power
- they see their actions as being voluntary

In an agentic state:
- individuals act as agents for others
- their own consciences are not in control

Milgram thought that, as well as the agentic state being a survival strategy, people learn it from their parents. In schools there are also hierarchies — it is clear who has the power, so children learn the same lesson there. In the agentic state, people do not feel responsible for their actions. They feel that they have no power, so they might well act against their own moral code, as happened in Milgram's basic study.

In the variation in Milgram's study in which the victim was nearer to the teacher, and the teacher had to hold the victim's hand on to the plate to receive the 'shock', there was less obedience. This suggests that the learners felt that they had to take greater responsibility for what they were doing. In a variation in which another experimenter ordered the participants to stop, they all stopped. This reinforces the idea that they were agents of the experimenter because they obeyed and stopped when they could.

Examination-style questions

1 What is meant by the terms 'agentic state' and 'autonomous state'? *(4 marks)*

2 Give a definition of the social approach, drawing on two of its main assumptions *(6 marks)*

Evaluation of the agency theory of obedience

Strengths

- The agency theory explains the different levels of obedience found in the variations to the basic study. In the basic study, the participants did not take responsibility and said that they were just doing what they were told. However, as they were made to take more responsibility because they had, for example, to hold the victim's hand down, the obedience level decreased. As they moved away from being in an agentic state, such as when in a less prestigious setting, fewer participants obeyed up to the 'shock level' of 450 volts. Evidence from the different studies reinforces the agency theory explanation of obedience.

- The theory helps to explain the issue that triggered Milgram's research into obedience — the holocaust, where so many Jews and members of other minority groups were slaughtered. Eichmann said that he was just obeying orders; agency theory helps to explain why he (and others) would obey to such a degree. Agency theory, which is rooted in the theory of natural selection, helps to explain seemingly inexplicable actions like the holocaust and other atrocities, such as the My Lai massacre (see page 7).

Weaknesses

- There are other possible explanations for obedience, such as social power. French and Raven (1959) proposed five different kinds of power:
  - Legitimate power is held by those in certain roles; Milgram's role would have had legitimate power.
  - Reward power is held by those with certain resources; Milgram may have held reward power because he paid the participants.
  - Coercive power is held by those who can punish another; Milgram gave the participants a small shock, so they may have felt that he could punish them. However, he did say that they could keep the money whatever the outcome, so they would not have thought he could punish them by taking the money away.

Unit 1

- Expert power is held by those with knowledge; the participants would see Milgram as an expert.
- Referent power is held by those who can win people over; the participants would probably not have seen Milgram in this light.

The obedience shown by the participants could be explained by social power theory. When another explanation is equally possible, this makes a theory less powerful as an explanation.

- Agency theory is more a description of how society works than an explanation. It suggests that the participants obeyed because they were agents of authority. However, obedience is defined as obeying authority figures, so agency theory does not really explain in much more detail why obedience occurs. The theory says that people are agents of others in society because that is the way society works, and natural selection means that people have evolved to obey those in 'higher' positions. There is no evidence for this, other than that it is a claim that makes sense.

A study of obedience from a country other than the USA

There have been studies in other countries that have partly replicated Milgram's procedures. To an extent, they have obtained different results, although still finding a level of obedience to authority that reinforces Milgram's findings. One such study was carried out by Meeus and Raaijmakers (1986).

A study into administrative obedience by Meeus and Raaijmakers (1986)

Meeus and Raaijmakers wanted to replicate Milgram's baseline condition (his basic study) focusing on what they saw as ambiguities in the study. One such ambiguity was that some levels of shock appeared to be dangerous because the victim went silent and the levers were labelled 'severe shock' and so on, but the participants were told that there would be no permanent tissue damage. Meeus and Raaijmakers (1986) saw this as an ambiguity. Another problem they saw with Milgram's study is that the punishment is old-fashioned, in that people today are unlikely to receive shocks — psychological punishment is more likely.

The aim of Meeus and Raaijmakers (1986) was to make the situation more real by using psychological violence. They wanted their participants to believe that they were doing definite harm to the victim. Their study used the kind of violence that might be found in Western societies. They also carried out a second study with the aim of seeing if two variations would reduce obedience, as Milgram's variations did. The two variations were:

- a study with the experimenter absent
- a study with two peer-confederates present, i.e. three people administering the punishment

General procedure

Meeus and Raaijmakers (1986) used a university researcher, the participant and someone applying for a job, so there were three people, as in Milgram's study. The applicant was a trained accomplice who had come to the laboratory to take a test — if he 'passes' the test, he gets the job. The participant had to interrupt the applicant by making 'stress remarks' — negative remarks about the applicant's performance and personality. Participants were told that being able to work under pressure was a requirement of the job for which the applicant was applying. They were also told that the procedure was to help the experimenter's research into the relationship between psychological stress and test achievement. The applicant objected to the interruptions. The participants were told to ignore these objections, which increased as the procedure continued. Due to the stress remarks, the applicant 'failed' the test and 'did not get the job'. The dilemma here for the participant is whether scientific research should affect someone's job and career. The question is whether the participants will cooperate. There were two studies, one is the main study; the other uses the two variations.

Procedure for experiment 1

There were 39 participants, both male and female, aged between 18 and 55 years, with at least Dutch high school education. They were recruited through newspaper advertisements and were paid the equivalent of $13. Fifteen people were in the control group and 24 in the experimental group. The experiment took place in a modern building on a university campus. The experimenter was a man, approximately 30 years old, well dressed and friendly, though stern. Instructions were given, the experiment lasted about 30 minutes and then there was a debriefing. The test that the applicant-confederate took consisted of 32 multiple-choice questions. It was administered orally, with the applicant in a different room listening via a speaker.

The study was said to be about whether stress resulted in the applicant's test score being better or worse. The participants were told that the applicant did not know about the study and that the job application was real. They were told to make negative comments 15 times during the test; the remarks were meant to make the applicant think that he was not doing well. Electrodes on the applicant's skull measured tension. A television monitor and sequence panel told participants when to make the stress remarks. The (apparent) stress level of the applicant was indicated by a number from 15 to 65 and also by being told verbally (e.g. 'normal' or 'intense'). The participants thought that poor performance on the test would mean the applicant would not be

Job applications can be very stressful

Trish Gant/Alamy

1

offered the job. They also heard the applicant ask if cooperating with the study would affect test performance, to which the answer was 'no'. So the participant thinks that there has been deceit.

The test questions were given in four sets. The first set was undertaken by the applicant without any stress comments from the participant. This gave a **baseline measure** against which to compare the other sets. For the next three sets, there were five stress comments for each set.

> **Study hint** When learning about studies, look for examples of aspects of methodology to use in answering questions about methodology. The study by Meeus and Raaijmakers (1986) can be used as an example of the use of a baseline measure — 'normal' achievement is measured. Achievement within the experimental conditions is compared with this, to see how it differs. There are also ethical issues here, such as deceit.

The applicant made errors in the last three sets, and the applicant 'failed' the test. (Remember, the applicant was a trained accomplice.) Ten errors were made; eight errors meant a fail. The applicant protested at the negative remarks, for example, by saying 'But surely…' and 'My answer wasn't wrong was it?' By the eighth and ninth stress remarks, the applicant asked the participant to stop making the negative comments. The applicant also said that the participant lied to him about the study and that he was withdrawing consent. If the participant refused to continue making stress remarks, the experimenter gave four consecutive verbal prods, just as Milgram did.

There was a control group in which the participants could choose when to make the negative remarks and could stop making them at any time during the test. When the participants in the control group stopped making negative comments, the applicant stopped making errors and his 'tension' level dropped.

Results of experiment 1

- Almost all (91.7%) of the participants were obedient and made all the stress remarks; the average number of stress remarks given was 14.81.
- Twenty-two of the 24 participants in the experimental group obeyed to the end.
- In the control group, no participant made the stress remarks.
- There was no real opposition from the participants in the experimental condition. Almost all had some discussion with the experimenter, but continued when ordered to do so.

Table 1.17 Stress remarks, apparent stress levels and the number of errors made by the applicant

Set of questions	Position of stress remark	Stress level	Number of errors
Set 1	0	n/a	0
Set 2	1	29	0
	2	33	0
	3	35	0
	4	41	1
	5	45	2
Set 3	6	41	2
	7	44	3
	8	48	4
	9	51	5
	10	52	6
Set 4	11	52	7
	12	53	7
	13	58	8
	14	60	9
	15	65	10

- Follow-up questionnaires showed that they did not like the experiment, so they were clearly upset by the procedure.
- Seventy-three per cent believed in the experiment, 23% were not sure and 4% thought it was a hoax.
- Participants were aloof with the applicant and shifted blame, acting as agents of the experimenter.
- In the experimental group, 45% blamed the experimenter, 33% thought they were to blame and 22% blamed the applicant.
- In the control group, 41% blamed the experimenter, 41% thought they were to blame and 18% blamed the applicant.

So in the control group, they felt that they and the experimenter were equally to blame; in the experimental group, they felt the experimenter was more to blame. This could be evidence for the agency theory explanation of obedience.

The level of obedience in this study is much higher than in Milgram's study. Therefore, it seems that, when obeying orders, it is easier to administer psychological violence than physical harm.

Procedure for experiment 2

Meeus and Raaijmakers (1986) wanted to look at variations on their experiment to compare with Milgram's variations. They carried out a second study with two conditions. In one condition, the experimenter was absent from the room; in the other, there were two peers who rebelled. Milgram (1974) found 22.5% obedience when the experimenter was absent and 10% obedience when two peers rebelled. Meeus and Raaijmakers (1986) wanted to see if their study found a similar drop in obedience.

There were 41 participants, 22 in the 'experimenter-absent' condition and 19 in the 'two-peers-rebel' condition.

'Experimenter absent' meant that the experimenter ordered the stress remarks to be made and then left the room. The procedure was then the same as for experiment 1.

'Two peers rebel' meant the real participant was in a group with what he or she thought were two other participants (actually confederates) and they were all instructed together. Thereafter, the procedure was similar to experiment 1, except that after stress remark 8, both peer-confederates started protesting. The experimenter gave them the usual prods. After stress remark 10, when the applicant withdrew his consent to the experiment, the first confederate ignored all the experimenter's prods. The second confederate then did the same. The experimenter ordered the participant to continue on his own. The procedure was subsequently the same as for experiment 1.

Results of experiment 2

In both variations, obedience dropped from the baseline. A Chi-squared test was carried out (Chapter 5) and the difference in the level of obedience was found to be significant.

The results are summarised in Table 1.18, in which the stress remark number is the position of that stress remark and N is the number of participants.

Table 1.18 *Results of the two variations (Meeus and Raaijmakers 1986)*

Stress remark number	Number of participants who stopped in the experimenter-absent condition (*N* = 22)	Number of participants who stopped in the two-peers-rebel condition (*N* = 19)
8	5	2
9	4	1
10	3	9
11	0	3
12	2	1
13	0	0
14	0	0
15	8	3

- In the experimenter-absent condition, 36.4% were fully obedient.
- In the two-peers-rebel condition, 15.8% were fully obedient.

Table 1.19 *Percentages of participants who believed in the experiment*

Belief level	Experimenter absent (%)	Two peers rebel (%)
Believed in the experiment	81	84
Had some doubts	14	16
Thought it was a hoax	5	0

Conclusions of experiments 1 and 2

The Meeus and Raaijmakers (1986) study, as in Milgram (1973/4), found that obedience dropped when variations were introduced. In all cases, obedience in Meeus and Raaijmakers's (1986) Dutch study was higher than in Milgram's USA study, in which participants thought that they were giving electric shocks to another person. It seems that administering psychological violence is easier than administering physical punishment. However, the different cultures, rather than the type of punishment, could have led to the difference in obedience.

The results are similar in the two studies in that there is a drop in the level of obedience when the experimenter is absent and an even larger drop when there are peers present who rebel. It appears that with the experimenter absent, the participants cannot defer responsibility to the experimenter and act as agents of the experimenter. They have to take more responsibility, which could be why obedience then drops considerably. When others are disobedient, the participant also disobeys. It is noticeable that nine of the 19 in the 'two-peers-rebel' condition stop at the same time as the two peer-confederates stop.

Meeus and Raaijmakers (1986) gave three explanations for the high levels of obedience in their studies:
- They considered the type of violence and concluded that psychological violence is different from physical violence. They suggested that physical violence has an immediacy that is not seen with psychological violence. The psychological distance is greater because the misfortune comes later, and although participants were aware that the psychological harm is real, they were distanced from it and so found it easier to obey.
- They considered the legitimacy of the contract between the experimenter and the participant. In the Dutch study, the participants knew that they were going to harm the applicant and they consented to this, so the consent carried more weight. In the Milgram studies, the participants did not agree to administer harm.

■ They pointed to the difference in dependency of the victim. In the Dutch study, the applicant had to continue in order to get the job so could object to the stress remarks, but could not refuse to complete the test. In Milgram's study, the victim could refuse to answer because there was no gain from continuing.

Meeus and Raaijmakers (1986) concluded that levels of obedience are as high as ever 'even in the Netherlands in the 1980s'.

Evaluation of the Dutch study of obedience by Meeus and Raaijmakers (1986)

Strengths

■ The study builds on Milgram's study by focusing deliberately on two areas that Meeus and Raaijmakers saw as needing attention. They used similar variations to Milgram to see if the levels of obedience fluctuated in the same way. Their study, therefore, is all the more useful because the findings can be compared with those of Milgram.

■ Due to the attention to detail, the study is replicable and can be tested for reliability. There are controls, which means that the details are clear and the study can be judged carefully. A study with good controls makes it easier to draw cause-and-effect conclusions.

Weaknesses

■ The study is an experiment and is, therefore, artificial. The need for controls, such as an applicant taking a test in a laboratory, means that the findings may not be valid. The situation is not very realistic and this might have affected the results.

■ Although the findings were compared with Milgram's findings, which is useful, there are differences between the two studies that make such comparisons difficult. One difference is that the studies were in different cultures (even though both are 'Western'); another is that the studies were 20 years apart, which could have affected obedience levels.

Table 1.20 *Strengths and weaknesses of the study by Meeus and Raaijmakers (1986)*

Strengths	Weaknesses
● Deliberately planned so that comparisons could be made with Milgram's studies, which means the results are more interesting and useful ● The controls and careful planning mean that the study is replicable and can be tested for reliability and cause-and-effect conclusions are more easily made	● The situation is not valid, in that the applicant is in a laboratory taking a test for a job, which is not a natural situation ● There are differences between the Milgram and Dutch studies, not only the planned differences (e.g. the studies are in different cultures and 20 years apart)

1

A comparison of the obedience studies by Milgram (1963, 1974) and Meeus and Raaijmakers (1986)

Percentage data for the three studies are shown in Table 1.21.

Table 1.21 *A comparison of the results of the studies by Milgram (1963 and 1974) and Meeus and Raaijmakers (1986)*

Type of study	Percentage of people obeying (Milgram 1963 and 1974)	Percentage of people obeying (Meeus and Raaijmakers 1986)
Main study	65.0	91.7
Experimenter-absent condition	22.5	36.4
Two-peers-rebel condition	10.0	15.8

Milgram (1963) found a disturbingly high level of obedience in his basic study — 65% obeyed him and gave up to a 450 volts 'shock' to a victim for answering questions wrongly, or for not answering at all.

Meeus and Raaijmakers (1986) found an even higher level of obedience when they asked participants to make negative comments while an applicant-victim was completing a test to try to get a job. Meeus and Raaijmakers called this psychological administrative punishment as opposed to Milgram's physical punishment and they thought that the different type of punishment had resulted in the higher level of obedience. They thought this happened because:

- the consequences of psychological punishment were more remote from the participant than the consequences of physical punishment, where screams could be heard
- the participants had agreed to harm the applicant-victim whereas Milgram's participants had not agreed to administer physical harm, i.e. the consent levels were different
- the applicant-victim had something to lose from stopping the study (the possibility of getting a job) whereas Milgram's victim did not

Milgram proposed the agency theory as an explanation for the levels of obedience. Meeus and Raaijmakers (1986) accept the agency theory and explain their finding that there is reduced obedience when the experimenter is absent by referring to Milgram's theory. They say that with the experimenter present the participants can transfer responsibility for the harm to the experimenter and act as his agents whereas with the experimenter absent they have to take more responsibility for themselves.

Drawing cross-cultural conclusions

It is not easy to draw cross-cultural conclusions because, although Milgram's studies were carried out in the USA and Meeus and Raaijmakers worked in the Netherlands, there were other differences between the studies. These differences were introduced deliberately — to try to address what the Dutch researchers saw as problems with Milgram's procedure. They thought that:

■ psychological administrative punishment is more acceptable in Western society
■ Milgram's participants did not really know they were causing harm to the victim
■ obedience studies would be more valid if the participants knew that they were causing real harm

Meeus and Raaijmakers seem to be saying that giving electric shocks was not realistic even at the time that Milgram did the studies. However, it could be thought that they used what they saw as a more modern punishment because their study took place more than 20 years later.

Meeus and Raaijmakers (1986) did not suggest that cultural differences would lead to a different level of obedience. They agreed with the agency theory explanation and did not have the aim of seeing if Dutch participants would show a different level of obedience from American participants. They concluded that obedience was found in both the studies and was just as prevalent in the 1980s as in the 1960s. They refer to Western societies when talking about type of punishment, so they appear to think that Dutch and US cultures are similar enough to have similar obedience levels. Therefore, it is concluded that cultural differences were not responsible for the higher level of obedience in the Dutch study.

> **Explore** Look up cross-cultural studies of obedience. Then consider whether differences in obedience are due to cultural differences or to other differences between the studies.

There are other cross-cultural studies of obedience, most of which show a higher level of obedience than did Milgram's study:

■ Shanab and Yahya (1977) asked children, aged 6–16, in Jordan to give 'shocks' to other children. The experimenter was female. Seventy-three per cent gave the maximum shock to same gender peers (higher than in Milgram's basic study but lower than in the study by Meeus and Raaijmakers). It was concluded that children are obedient, although it was mentioned that Jordan has a different culture from the USA, so there might be cultural differences.

■ Kilham and Mann (1974) asked first-year Australian psychology students both to order pain to be administered and to administer pain. They found there was a higher level of obedience when ordering pain than when administering it. They also found gender differences in obedience.

> **Study hint** Expect questions that ask you to compare studies and theories. When you are preparing for such questions, look for similarities and differences to use as evaluation points.

Ethical issues arising from obedience research

One criticism of Milgram's studies is that the procedure was not ethical for participants. There are also moral issues with regard to society.

Ethical problems for the participants in Milgram's studies

In the basic study, the participants showed distress — for example, sweating and shaking. Many showed signs of nervousness, including nervous laughter. Three participants had full-blown seizures, one of which was so convulsive that the experiment had to be stopped. One of the ethical guidelines is that participants should not be distressed.

The participants should be given the right to withdraw, which, in theory, they were. In practice, this was made difficult, which is against the guidelines. They should be reminded that they can withdraw, and this was not done. In fact, when they protested, verbal prods were used to encourage them to continue.

There should have been informed consent. Participants gave consent by volunteering for the study, but they did not know what it would entail, so their consent was not informed.

Milgram deceived the participants in a number of ways. He let them think that:
- the victim was receiving real shocks
- the experiment was about memory and learning, rather than about obedience
- the victim was also a participant
- they could have been victims

Ethical issues for participants that Milgram did address

However, there were ways in which Milgram was ethical:
- He debriefed all the participants. He let them meet the victim to see that no harm had been done. As far as possible, he made sure that the participants left the situation in a reasonable frame of mind. He gave them a questionnaire to complete so that he could judge their reactions to the study. In the main, the participants said that they were pleased to have taken part.
- He gave them the right to withdraw — if they objected after the fourth verbal prompt, he ended the study. They were then able to leave.
- He observed the participants, as did others, through a mirror. If the participant became unduly distressed, as one did, then the study was terminated.
- Milgram thought beforehand that the obedience levels were not likely to be high enough for the participants to become distressed. He asked colleagues and he also asked other people. Nobody thought the participants would go as far as they did, so the ethical issues were not anticipated. By asking colleagues, Milgram was checking his own competence, so he adhered to that guideline.

Ethical issues for participants in other studies of obedience

There have been other studies of obedience in other countries and similar ethical issues apply:
- Meeus and Raaijmakers (1986) put their participants under stress because the participants did not like making negative remarks when a job applicant was

taking a written test. They thought that the applicant might fail the test and they protested. They became distressed.

- Meeus and Raaijmakers did not give the right to withdraw until the participant had resisted their verbal prompts, which were designed to make the participant continue. This is not reminding participants of the right to withdraw, which is against ethical guidelines.
- The participants in the Dutch study were deceived into thinking that the applicant was really applying for a job, whereas he was an accomplice of the researchers.

So, the same criticisms can be made of the study by Meeus and Raaijmakers as are made of Milgram — unsurprisingly, as their study copied Milgram's study in order to be able to compare results.

Other studies of obedience have similar problems regarding ethics. It is difficult to set up a situation in which someone has to obey an order that will 'harm' another person unless there is some deception, because researchers do not want to actually harm anyone.

Ethical issues regarding obedience studies and society

It has been claimed (1994) that Milgram argued that it is important to carry out such studies, even though they involve deception.

There is the issue of society needing to know about obedience. For example, if it is known that the Nazis obeyed orders and that anyone is likely to do the same, then maybe society could take steps to try to make sure that this cannot happen.

It is also useful to consider issues such as whether certain societies have different obedience issues from others. So when the Dutch study concluded that people in the Netherlands in the 1980s were as obedient as people in the 1960s in the USA (and possibly Germany in the 1930s), then this is useful information. Meeus and Raaij-makers suggested that their study and that of Milgram were carried out within Western society ideas, which helps people to appreciate that there might be different levels of obedience in a different social structure.

The section on key issues within the social approach gives situations where knowing about obedience can be useful for society. For example:

- members of the armed forces apparently obeying orders and then subsequently having to stand trial to see if they were personally responsible for their actions
- people in authority, such as prison guards, may be seen by others as having overstepped the mark with regard to brutality
- in a trial, psychologists can use results from studies to show that some actions that go against society's moral code might still be carried out by someone under similar circumstances

> **Explore** Using the internet or other sources to find out how Philip Zimbardo has been involved in such issues.

1

What is meant by prejudice and discrimination?

Stereotyping means developing an idea about someone and carrying that idea forward to apply it to other similar people — for example, someone might see a woman as weak and then stereotype all women as weak. Stereotypes are common traits attributed to a large human group. Often the original idea comes from something read or heard, rather than from first-hand experience. Stereotyping leads to **prejudice** when it affects attitude — for example, not only saying that all women are weak but thinking badly (or well) of women because of this. Prejudice leads to **discrimination**, which is an act carried out because of prejudice.

> **Prejudice** is an attitude (usually negative); **discrimination** is an action that occurs because of prejudice.

Social identity theory as an explanation of prejudice

There are several theories of how prejudice develops. You are required to study the social identity theory. This is a good explanation of how prejudice can come about and is also helpful as an explanation of human behaviour in general.

Tajfel and Turner (1979) suggest that prejudice comes from the formation of two groups, without any other factor being present. The mere existence of two groups causes conflict. One of the studies in detail suggested for the social approach is the 1970, 1971 study of minimal groups by Tajfel et al., which shows clearly that the creation of two groups leads to prejudicial attitudes.

The social identity theory suggests that a person has several personal 'selves' and that these 'selves' link in with group membership. Different social situations might trigger an individual to act in different ways, perhaps linked to his or her person, family, or national membership. An individual also has several social identities (self-concepts).

> **Study hint** Even if you choose not to study Tajfel et al. (1970, 1971) in detail, read about it now because it provides useful evidence for describing and evaluating social identity theory (see CD-ROM). It was from such studies that the theory was developed.

Social identity comes from how people see themselves in relation to membership of their social groups. Belonging to a group creates in-group self-categorisation, which leads to in-group favouritism and hostility towards the out-group. To enhance self-esteem, people perceive their in-groups as better.

> **Social identity** is an individual's self-concept.

There are three processes involved in becoming prejudiced against out-group members:
- **Social categorisation** is seeing oneself as part of a group. Any group will do, and there does not have to be conflict with other groups.

- **Social identification** is the process of moving from categorising oneself as part of the in-group to identifying with the group more overtly. An individual is likely to take on the norms and attitudes of group members.
- There is **social comparison** with the out-group. The individual's self-concept becomes wrapped up with the in-group. People start to see their in-group as better than the out-group, which enhances their self-esteem. To see their in-group as better, there has to be comparison with the out-group.

There are three variables that contribute to in-group favouritism. These are:
- the extent to which the individuals identify with the in-group
- the extent to which there are grounds for making comparisons with the out-group
- the relevance of the comparison group in relation to the in-group

If an in-group is central to the individual's self-definition and it is meaningful to make comparisons with the out-group, then there is more likely to be in-group favouritism (which leads to prejudice against the out-group).

Therefore, the idea is that one group for a person is the in-group and that makes other groups out-groups. Tajfel et al. (1970, 1971) showed that there is in-group favouritism and that people identify with their in-group. They want to promote their in-group because it enhances their self-esteem.

Other studies have confirmed in-group favouritism and out-group prejudice. Crocker and Luhtanen (1990) showed that people who think highly of the group that they are in have a high collective self-esteem and show loyalty to their group. Even when a group is not performing well, there is strong group loyalty. Lalonde (1992) studied a hockey team that was not doing very well. The members of the team knew that other teams were doing better than they were, but said that they were 'dirtier' in their tactics. Thus, they claimed moral superiority, which was in-group favouritism. When Lalonde watched the matches, he decided that the other teams were not 'dirtier'. Therefore, he had found in-group bias.

There are different causes of prejudice — for example, race in the USA, religion in Northern Ireland and linguistic differences in Belgium. However, Tajfel suggested that there are two features of prejudice that are the same:
- attitudes of prejudice towards an out-group
- discriminatory behaviour towards the out-group

These are the features that Tajfel focuses on. He says that prejudice and discrimination can arise from genuine competition or can be to release emotional tensions. A vicious circle may be generated (Figure 1.4).

Children also learn such attitudes, so they may be perpetuated even without personal contact. In order to give society order, groups are classified into 'us' and 'them'. Any group someone belongs to is the in-group. There is often

Figure 1.4 *A vicious circle producing prejudice and discrimination*

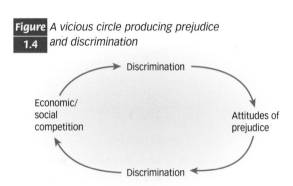

competition between in-groups and out-groups and usually people act to benefit their in-group and act against their out-group. Prejudice can arise even without competition between the groups.

Football supporters are an in-group and are likely to be prejudiced against another team, which will be the out-group

Evaluation of social identity theory as an explanation of prejudice

As an explanation of prejudice, the theory has strengths and weaknesses.

Strengths

- The amount of evidence that shows in-group favouritism, e.g. the studies by Crocker and Luhtanen (1990), Lalonde (1992) and Tajfel et al. (1970, 1971) (see CD-ROM). When there are different studies in different scenarios supporting a theory, it suggests that the theory has merit. Members of a group are willing to say that their group is better than another group (an out-group), even when this is not the case. The above studies looked at different groups, and found in-group identification and prejudice towards the out-group.

> **Explore** Search for more studies that find prejudice towards an out-group. Use these as examples when answering exam questions. What sort of groups are studied? Can you find any evidence to say that in certain in-group and out-group situations there is more prejudice and discrimination than in others?

- The theory has a useful practical application. There are many in-groups in society, from football teams to racial groups. Sometimes, problems that arise can be traced back to the existence of two opposing groups, perhaps two religions in a particular country. People identify with the in-group and are prejudiced towards the out-group, sometimes to the extent of being violent against another group of people, such as when genocide occurs. When a theory can explain such real-life events, it is particularly useful because it can suggest ways of solving social problems.

Weaknesses

- There is another theory that attempts to explain prejudice (realistic conflict theory) and social identity theory can be seen as being part of that. Rather than holding that it is just the creation of two groups that leads to prejudice, the realistic conflict theory says that the two groups are competing in some way. For example, the hockey teams (Lalonde 1992) were competing to win the tournament. Realistic conflict theory claims that two groups are prejudiced towards one another when there is a goal in sight or when there is the possibility of material gain.

It is often the case that two groups live side by side in reasonable harmony until there is competition for resources. This goes against the social identity theory as an explanation for prejudice.

- By focusing only on the groups, no other factors are taken into account. The theory does not measure how much prejudice there is, such as whether there are some situations in which there is greater prejudice against the out-group. In practice, in group situations there are often a number of factors involved. So having one theory to explain something as complex as prejudice is unlikely to be satisfactory.

Explore Look up the situation in Rwanda and see how two groups turned against each other. Was it over competition for resources, as realistic conflict theory suggests?

Study hint Even if you choose not to study Tajfel et al. (1970, 1971) in detail, read about it now because it provides useful evidence for describing and evaluating social identity theory. It was from such studies that the theory was developed.

Study hint One way of illustrating weakness in a theory is to show how another theory can explain the same events either as well as, or better than, the theory being evaluated. Only do this once, because putting forward an alternative theory when evaluating is a single weakness, however many alternatives you mention.

Examination-style questions

1   Describe the agency theory as an explanation of obedience.   *(5 marks)*

2   Evaluate Milgram's basic study in terms of ethical implications. In your answer consider where it could be said to be ethical and where it might not be.   *(8 marks)*

3   Compare Milgram's studies of obedience with one study from another country. In your answer, consider the methodology, ethics and findings (results and/or conclusions).   *(10 marks)*

Extension questions

1   Compare the social identity theory of prejudice with one other theory, e.g. the realistic conflict theory. In your answer, evaluate the social identity theory as an explanation of prejudice. (NB: for your course you do not have to know any theory other than social identity theory.)   *(12 marks)*

2   Discuss why Milgram carried out his basic study of obedience and also one of the variations. In your answer, consider issues such as why he set up the studies in the first place and why he made the methodological decisions that he did.   *(12 marks)*

Studies in detail

For the social approach, the study that you have to learn in detail is the study of nurses and obedience by Hofling et al. (1966). You then have to choose one of the following:

- the Robbers Cave study of prejudice (Sherif 1954, 1961, 1988)
- the study of minimal groups (Tajfel et al. 1970, 1971)
- the BBC prison study, *The Experiment* (Reicher and Haslam 2003, 2006)

Three studies are covered in detail and the fourth is summarised (it is covered in detail on the CD-ROM).

Hofling et al. (1966)

Hofling et al. (1966) studied the reaction of nurses to an order from a person they thought was a doctor. The question was 'How far would the nurses obey the doctor, and what would their reactions be?'

This is a **field experiment**, because it took place in the nurses' natural setting — a hospital.

> A **field experiment** takes place in a natural setting.

> **Study hint** Note that 'et al.' is a Latin abbreviation. It stands for 'and others'. It is used when there are a number of researchers involved and it saves you from having to remember all their names.

Aims

Hofling et al. (1966) carried out a practical study into the doctor–nurse relationship. They wanted to look specifically at health care and many of the researchers in the study were medical personnel. In particular, they wanted to investigate what happens when a doctor asks or directs a nurse to carry out a procedure contrary to her professional standards because they thought that this was an issue within the profession. They were interested in the response to an irregular order to administer a dose of medication, to see if the nurses would refuse to carry out the order.

Procedure

There were some clear procedural points that would make the order contrary to the nurse's professional standards:

- Ask the nurse to give an excessive dose of medicine (it would actually be a placebo).
- Transmit the order over the phone (against hospital policy).
- Use an unauthorised drug (one either not on the ward stock list or not cleared for use).
- Have the order given to the nurse by an unfamiliar voice.

The situation for the study involved 12 wards in public hospitals and 10 wards in private hospitals. Questionnaires were given to graduate nurses at another hospital as a matched control. The questionnaires asked the nurses what they would do in the same circumstances. Student nurses were then also given the questionnaire, to see what less experienced nurses would do.

The main study: giving the orders and observing the consequences

Pill boxes were central props in the study. Each was labelled: 'Astroten, 5 mg capsules. Usual dose, 5 mg. Maximum daily dose, 10 mg'.

The boxes, containing **placebo** capsules filled with glucose, were placed on the wards. A script was written for the phone conversations and a set of standard replies to possible questions was also prepared. The tone of the phone call was courteous, yet self-confident; researchers monitored the calls to make sure the tone was appropriate. Circumstances for ending the call were:

■ when the participant complied
■ when the participant refused
■ when the participant insisted on referring to someone else
■ if the participant became upset
■ if the participant could not find the medication
■ if the call lasted more than 10 minutes

There was an observer on each ward. The observer stopped the study if:

■ the nurse had the medication ready and moved towards the patient's bed
■ the nurse refused and ended the conversation
■ the nurse began to contact another professional person
■ 10 minutes had passed since the call and none of the other conditions for ending the study had occurred

The observer then interviewed the nurse to obtain more information. The observer also allayed any 'disquieting feelings' and 'offered psychiatric first aid'.

The experiment was run on medical, surgical, paediatric and psychiatric wards from just before evening visiting to just after it (between 7 p.m. and 9 p.m.). Administration of medication does not normally happen at those times and doctors are not normally present on the wards then, so the nurses would have to make their own decisions.

The observer made sure conditions on the ward were suitable and then phoned the office using the ward phone and a code sentence to start the experiment. After the incident, a nurse-investigator would follow up within half an hour and request a follow-up interview. The interviews were unstructured but the nurse-investigator would have heard the tape recording of the call and would also have the observer's report.

Information asked for was:

■ unguided narrative (What happened…?)

■ emotions (What were your feelings…?)

■ discrepancies (Are you sure it happened that way…?)

■ any similar naturally occurring incidents

■ retrospective view (What do you feel about it now…?)

■ biographical data (age, religion…)

The nurse-investigator also offered support and promised anonymity.

The questionnaire to graduate and student nurses

Questionnaires were sent to graduate nurses. The participants were closely matched for age, sex, race, marital status, length of working week, professional experience and area of origin. Twelve graduate nurses were involved and the questionnaires were administered in a large conference room. The nurses were given the imaginary scenario with a doctor explaining the whole situation. For example, they were told: 'You are the only nurse in the ward. Now, will you please give Mr Jones a stat dose of 20 milligrams — that's four capsules — of Astroten. I will be up within 10 minutes and I will sign the order then.' They were then given a copy of the written instructions and instructed to 'Please write down exactly what you would say and do'. There were also other questions, such as asking what they thought the majority of nurses would have done.

The questionnaire was also given to 21 degree-programme nursing students. The procedure was the same as for the graduate nurses.

Results

The main study

For the main study, the data from 22 nurses yielded the following results:

■ Twenty-one nurses would have given the medication as ordered.

■ Phone calls were brief, with no resistance to the order.

■ There seemed to be no delay during the call or afterwards.

■ Eleven nurses said that they were aware of the dosage discrepancy.

■ None said that they needed written confirmation, although several asked the doctor to appear promptly.

■ Eighteen said that they were generally aware that non-emergency phone calls were not appropriate, but that this sort of thing was not uncommon.

■ In 17 cases, there were general issues such as mishearing, misplacing things and temporary forgetting as in normal life, e.g. not seeing the Astroten, although it was clearly on display.

■ No participant was hostile to the caller or the observer, but the one nurse who refused said she did feel some hostility to the caller.

■ The nurses' reactions varied from mild scientific interest through mild confusion to guilt or anger.

■ Sixteen nurses felt that they should have been more resistant to the telephone order.

- Fifteen nurses said that they could remember similar incidents; several said that doctors were displeased if nurses resisted their orders.
- Only one nurse questioned the identity of the observer and why he was on the ward.

The questionnaires

The questionnaires to graduate nurses yielded the following results:

- Ten of the 12 graduate nurses said that they would not have given the medication; two said that they would have.
- When saying why they would not have given the medication, seven nurses mentioned the dosage discrepancy; some mentioned 'hospital policy' or 'necessity for written order'.
- Seven participants said that they thought most nurses would act as they would, two said that they thought nurses would act differently and three were unsure.

The questionnaires to student nurses yielded the following results:

- All 21 said that they would not have given the medication.
- Nineteen student nurses noticed the excessive dosage.
- Eight student nurses cited the excessive dosage as the reason they would not have given the medication.

Conclusions

The researchers drew the following conclusions:

- None of those asked thought that nearly all the nurses would obey in the experiment. However, the obedience showed the strength of the doctor–nurse relationship and how a patient can suffer as a consequence. The researchers say that instead of two 'intelligences' — the doctor and the nurse — working for the patient, one of these 'intelligences' seems to be non-functioning.
- The nurses were affected by the study. They were upset that they had been observed without their knowledge and also that their specific behaviour had been noted. Perhaps the slips — for example, the confusion and not noticing the pill box — showed that at a non-conscious level, the nurses had some doubts.
- Nurses think that they will defend their patients and are proud of being professionals. However, the reality seems different.
- The nurses appeared to trust the doctors, which may be a valuable trait. They were willing to act promptly and efficiently, again a valuable trait. However, this study suggests nurses need to be encouraged to use their own intellectual and ethical resources.

The researchers concluded that there was potential for nurses to be encouraged to question and think without being disloyal or discourteous to doctors.

Evaluation of the study by Hofling et al. (1966)

Strengths

- The study took place in the nurses' natural surroundings — the wards on which they were working. There is ecological validity because the setting is real.

There is also validity in that the task was apparently realistic, because the nurses who answered the questionnaire agreed that such situations did arise.

■ There were many controls, so the study could be repeated to test it for reliability. For example, the tone of the 'doctor' making the phone call had to be similar in each case; if it was not, then that trial was withdrawn. The pill-boxes were the same and were placed in similar positions.

Weaknesses

■ The nurses were upset that they had been observed without permission and that they had acted as they had. This is against ethical guidelines, which say that informed consent must be obtained and participants must not be distressed.

■ The study took place in 1966, when, as the researchers themselves point out, most doctors were male and most nurses were female. So some of the obedience found could have been due to gender differences. In the twenty-first century doctor–nurse relationships are likely to be different, so it is not easy to generalise the findings from the study to the situation 40 years later. The study's findings may have been useful at the time, but may no longer apply. Some changes in doctor–nurse relationships may have come about because of the study, so this was not a weakness of the study in 1966; it is a weakness of using the study now.

Table 1.22 *Strengths and weaknesses of the study by Hofling et al. (1966)*

Strengths	Weaknesses
● The study was carried out in the nurses' natural setting, so there was ecological validity	● There are ethical issues in the study because the nurses were upset that they had been observed and tested without their permission
● There were clear controls so the study could be replicated to test for reliability; the results could be said to be because of the situation as set up, rather than other factors	● The study was carried out in 1966, so the findings may not apply in the twenty-first century because doctor–nurse relationships are different

Sherif et al. (1954)

Sherif carried out research into groups, leadership and the effect of groups on attitudes and behaviour. The Robbers Cave study — so-called because it took place at a camp in Robbers Cave State Park, Oklahoma — built on his previous work and there were later records of the study too. He thought that social behaviour could not be studied by looking at individuals in isolation. He recognised that social organisation differs between cultures and affects group practices, citing, for example, that in America discussion is seen as a useful learning method but that this is not the case in India, where dependence on authority is more valued. So, he claimed that groups have to be understood as part of a social structure. The Robbers Cave study involved setting up two groups of similar participants (11-year-old boys) to find:

> **Study hint** The Robbers Cave study is an example of how the social approach focuses on interactions between people, rather than on individuals. It is also useful for answering questions about prejudice.

- how the groups developed
- if and how conflict between the groups arose
- how to reduce any such friction

The conflict could be seen as prejudice; reduction of friction would be reducing the prejudice. Therefore, the study has a practical application.

Three terms defined according to Sherif are:
- **small group** — individuals share a common goal that fosters interaction; individuals are affected differently by being in a group; an in-group develops with its own hierarchy and a set of norms is standardised
- **norm** — a product of group interaction that regulates the behaviour of members in terms of the expected or ideal behaviour
- **group** — a social unit with a number of individuals who are interdependent and have a set of norms and values for self-regulation; individuals have roles within the unit

Study hint

The definitions of small groups, norm and group are useful when answering questions about explanations of terms.

Aims

The aims of the Robbers Cave study were to use a field experiment to produce group norms and to measure their effects on the perceptions and judgements of those involved. The plan was to use a real-life situation to lead to group norms and values. The researchers wanted to see how in-group behaviour developed to include related out-group hostility and to see how such friction could be reduced. The study looked at relationships within each group and at how the two groups related to one another. It was a study of **inter-group** relations.

The researchers aimed to trace the formation and functioning of negative and positive attitudes of members of one group towards members of another group. They examined how attitudes and behaviours developed and changed as a result of controlled alterations in conditions.

'Inter-group' means between two (or more) groups; 'intra-group' means relations within a single group.

Procedure

Participants

The participants were 22 boys, aged 11 years who did not know each other before the study. The boys were matched as far as possible. They were all from Protestant families in Oklahoma and were screened to eliminate problems at home or other difficulties that might account for individual attitudes and behaviour. As part of the matching process, the boys were rated (including IQ) by teachers. When the boys were divided into two groups for the study, they were reassessed and also matched for the split, including issues such as sporting ability. In order to produce 'natural' groups, participants were not informed that they were part of a study and were kept unaware of the aims of the camp. A nominal fee was charged for the camp and parents were asked not to visit, ostensibly because it might make the boys homesick.

Data collection

One important feature of the study was the range of data collection methods:

- **Observation** — a participant observer was allocated to each group for 12 hours a day.
- **Sociometric analysis** — issues such as friendship patterns were noted and studied.
- **Experiment** — e.g. the boys had to collect beans and estimate how many each boy had collected.
- **Tape recordings** — adjectives and phrases used to refer to their own group members and to out-group members were examined.

The participant observers were trained not to influence the boys' decision making, but to help them once decisions had been reached. The researchers claimed that using different data-gathering methods, with similar results, meant that their results were valid.

The three stages of the study

There were three stages to the study:

- **Stage 1**: the two groups were formed and set up norms and hierarchies (to see how they became in-groups).
- **Stage 2**: the two groups were introduced and competition was set up in the form of a tournament (to see if this led to friction, name-calling and hostility to the out-group).
- **Stage 3**: the two groups were set goals that they needed each other to achieve (to see if **superordinate goals** led to the reduction of friction).

> **Superordinate goals** are goals in which the resources and energies of either single group are not adequate for the attainment of the goal. To achieve the goal, two groups have to work together.

Stage 1: in-group formation

The two groups were kept apart for 1 week to help the formation of group norms and relations. They had to work as a group to achieve common goals that required cooperation. Data were gathered by observation, including rating of emerging relationships, sociometric measures and experimental judgements. Status positions and roles in the groups were studied. There is much detail about how hierarchies within each group developed. The measurements were thought to be both valid and reliable because different data collection methods produced similar results. For example, in the bean-collecting task, the boys tended to overestimate the number of beans their own group members had collected and underestimate the number collected by the other group (the number of beans was, in fact, the same).

Stage 2: inter-group relations, the friction phase

After the first week, the two groups were told about one another and a tournament was set up with competitive activities. Points could be earned for the group and there were rewards. As soon as they heard about each other, the two groups became hostile. They wanted to play each other at baseball, so they effectively set up their own tournament, which was what the researchers wanted.

The aim behind the competition was to make one group frustrated because of the other group, to see if negative attitudes developed. Adjectives and phrases were recorded to see if they were derogatory and behaviour was observed as previously. The researchers introduced the 'collecting beans' experiment. The boys had to collect beans and then judge how many each boy had collected. This was to see if the boys overestimated the abilities of the in-group members and minimised the abilities of the out-group members.

Stage 3: inter-group relations, the integration phase

The researchers wanted to achieve harmony between the two groups, which they did by introducing superordinate goals (the resources and energies of either group were not adequate for the attainment of the goal; the groups had to work together).

First, they introduced tasks that simply brought the two groups together so they could communicate. They then introduced the superordinate goals, which included:

- fixing the water tank and pump when the water supply was threatened
- a truck that would not start, so they had to pull together to try to start it
- pooling resources so that they could afford a film that they all wanted to watch

The researchers measured the use of derogatory terms and used observation and rating of stereotyping.

The camp

The location was a 200-acre Boy Scouts of America camp completely surrounded by Robbers Cave State Park. The site was isolated and keeping the two groups of boys apart at first was easy because of the layout of the site (see Figure 1.5).

Results

Stage 1: in-group formation

Near the end of Stage 1 the boys gave themselves names — the Rattlers and

Figure 1.5 *General layout of the Robbers Cave camp and respective areas of the two groups*

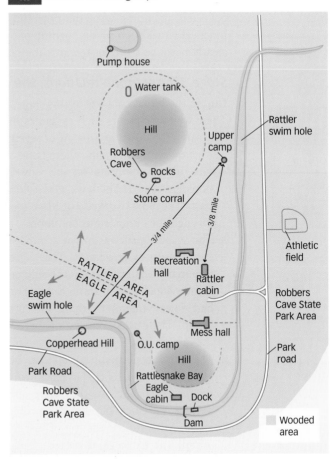

1

the Eagles. The groups developed similarly; they had been matched carefully, so this might be expected. However, there were some differences, partly because their cabins were situated in different places, which affected their decisions.

For both groups, status positions settled over the last few days of the first week and there was some stability; both groups had a recognised leader. The Rattlers discussed the existence of the other group frequently. For example, they said 'they had better not be in our swimming hole'. The Eagles did not refer to the Rattlers as much, but they started to become more competitive and asked to play a game against them. It seemed that the very existence of the out-group led to hostility.

Stage 2: inter-group relations, the friction phase

As soon as the groups found out about each other they wanted to compete at baseball, so they had naturally moved themselves on to Stage 2. The Rattlers were excited and discussed issues such as protecting their flag. The Eagles were not as keen as the Rattlers, but they made comments such as 'we will beat them'. The boy who was elected as baseball captain for the Eagles became their leader for all of Stage 2, although he was not the leader at the end of Stage 1. When the two groups first came into contact, there was some name calling. A great deal of evidence was collected, including what the boys did and said, who they were friends with and practical issues such as the burning of one of the flags. It was found that there were clearly negative attitudes towards the out-group members.

Stage 3: inter-group relations, the integration

During the initial contacts in this stage, hostility between the two groups remained. There were comments such as 'ladies first' and when they watched a film together, they sat in their own groups. After seven contact activities, the need to work together was set up with situations where there were superordinate goals:

- First, the staff turned off the valve to the water supply and placed two large boulders over it. The boys were told that vandals had damaged the system in the past. The boys worked together to restore the system. When the water came through they rejoiced in common.
- The second goal was to get a movie by chipping in to pay for it. They agreed eventually that both groups should contribute equally, even though one group had fewer members than the other group. There was cooperation between the two groups.
- The third goal involved all the boys going on a trip to Cedar Lake, which required transport. As they were about to leave, the truck 'developed' a problem and they had to use the tug-of-war rope to pull it to try to get it started.

Table 1.23 *Friendship choices of in-group and out-group members at the end of Stage 3*

	Rattlers	Eagles
In-group choices of friends	63.6%	76.8%
Out-group choices of friends	36.4%	23.2%

Table 1.24 *Friendships compared between the end of Stage 2 and the end of Stage 3*

	Rattlers	Eagles
Out-group friendship choices at end of Stage 2	6.4%	7.5%
Out-group friendship choices at end of Stage 3	36.4%	23.2%

There were other similar situations. The result was reduced friction and increased cooperation between the groups. At the end of Stage 3, friendship choices were still found more within the in-groups but had also increased between the groups.

It was noticeable how friendships differed between Stage 2 and Stage 3. More out-group members were chosen as friends by the end of Stage 3, which is evidence that friction was reduced.

Conclusions

The hypotheses put forward at the start of the study were largely confirmed. The conclusions include the following:

- Picking matched participants ruled out home background or individual factors that would explain the attitudes and behaviour of the boys.
- Groups developed status hierarchies and group norms, although they were not stable throughout the study.
- Each group had a leadership structure by the end of the first week.
- Leader–follower relations developed as a result of having to solve problems through combined action; as group structure stabilised, an in-group formed.
- When two groups meet in competition and in frustrating situations, in-group solidarity and cooperation increases and inter-group hostility is strong.
- Because of the various means of collection, the data were considered valid.
- People tend to overestimate the abilities of their own group members and to minimise the abilities of out-group members.
- Contact between two groups is not enough to reduce hostility.
- When groups needed to work together, exchanged tools, shared responsibilities and agreed how to solve problems, friction was reduced. One example of working towards a superordinate goal was not sufficient, however; they needed to co-operate more than once.

Evaluation of the Robbers Cave study (Sherif et al. 1954)

Sherif et al. (1954) pointed out the strengths of the Robbers Cave study, but they did not point out the weaknesses.

Strengths

- There was careful planning and controls. Previous studies were used to show what was necessary — for example, the need to enable the groups to develop as naturally as possible and to brief observers not to advise when decisions were being made. The participants were matched carefully so that individual differences would not affect their attitudes and judgements. The planning and controls enabled cause-and-effect conclusions to be drawn confidently.
- The validity of the findings. The researchers used participant observers because they knew from previous research that participants' behaviour is affected when they know that they are being watched. The participants did not know that they were part of an experiment, so their behaviour was natural. Several data collection

methods were used so that the findings could be compared to make sure that they were valid.

Weaknesses

■ Informed consent was not obtained — the boys did not know that they were part of a study, which meant that there was also deception. Parents were informed more fully, but they were asked not to visit and could not check whether the boys were happy at the camp. Debriefing is not mentioned and may well not have taken place. The researchers wrote a book about the study, but ethical issues are not considered. However, the account does not suggest that the boys were treated unethically or were unhappy.

■ It might be difficult to generalise the findings beyond the type of participants used because they were so carefully selected. They were 11-year-old boys from similar family and school backgrounds, and with fairly similar abilities. It might, therefore, be hard to say that findings would be true of others — for example, girls, those in other cultures, those with 'difficult' backgrounds and those with less sporting ability. Generalising is difficult when the sample is so restricted, even though the restriction was deliberate to help the study.

Table 1.25 *Strengths and weaknesses of the Robbers Cave study by Sherif et al.*

Strengths	Weaknesses
• There were controls, such as the careful sampling and the briefing of observers so that they followed the same procedures; this meant cause-and-effect conclusions could be drawn more justifiably than when observing naturally occurring groups • There were several data collection methods and the findings agreed, so validity was claimed — for example, observations showed derogatory behaviour and recordings found derogatory remarks against the out-group	• It was unethical in the sense that consent was not obtained, there was no right to withdraw and parents could not visit, so there was no check on the boys' welfare • It was hard to generalise to other situations because the sample was restricted to boys with a specific background

Tajfel et al. (1970, 1971)

Tajfel carried out studies to see if groups formed for experimental purposes for no 'real' reason would lead to discrimination of an out-group member by an in-group member. Laboratory experiments were carried out using groups of boys who were asked to make choices to either reward or punish (using money) another boy. The aim was to see if boys rewarded or punished differently according to whether the other boy was in their group or a member of the other group. In general, it was found that there was in-group favouritism.

This study is covered in more detail on the CD-ROM.

Reicher and Haslam (2006)

Background

Riecher and Haslam carried out a study in conjunction with the BBC in the UK. In May 2002, four 1-hour programmes showed what happened. The study involved 15 male volunteers who were either prisoners or guards in a set-up environment. Full details of the study were published in the *Psychologist* in 2006 and are summarised below.

Some background to the study is useful because it helps to link it to other areas of the social approach. The researchers point out that social psychology looks at the effects of groups and social organisation, including leadership, on the behaviour of individuals. Following the events of the Second World War, when 6 million Jews were exterminated, social psychologists turned their attentions to obedience and related areas, to try to understand how such horrific events could happen. These issues link to your course, for example:

■ Milgram's ideas about obedience, including the agency theory explanation, suggest that people act as agents of society and so follow orders.

■ Sherif's study of group behaviour shows how realistic conflict between groups can lead to prejudice between the groups, which can explain extreme behaviours such as genocide.

■ Social identity theory suggests that members of an in-group will turn against members of an out-group.

Reicher and Haslam's study tests the idea of social identification and the focus of their study is on how people come to condone tyranny or become tyrannical themselves.

This study may be seen as a replication of the Stanford prison experiment, carried out by Zimbardo and others in 1971.

However, Reicher and Haslam claim that it is more than a replication of that study. Zimbardo showed that when college students were set to control other college students who were their 'prisoners', they took on the role of guards. Brutality developed to such an extent that the study had to be stopped early. Reicher and Haslam could not replicate Zimbardo's work because his study was unethical. Since Zimbardo's research, studies into such areas have tended to be laboratory experiments, which Reicher and Haslam realised makes the findings invalid. They suggest that fieldwork is needed, so there is a need for a more ethical way than Zimbardo's of studying the effects of roles, social organisation, and being in groups.

> **Study hint**   This study illustrates key ideas in social psychology, e.g. that interactions between people, including power in groups, are important.

> **Explore**   Look up Zimbardo's Stanford prison experiment, written up as Haney et al. (1973). Also look up Philip Zimbardo. He has used the findings of Haney et al. (Zimbardo was part of the team) to show that when serving soldiers are charged with committing brutal acts, social structures must be considered. This is instead of holding such soldiers completely responsible for their actions — the soldiers are acting within a social role.

Aims

The aim of Reicher and Haslam's study is to investigate tyranny at a group level. They define tyranny as 'an unequal social system involving the arbitrary or oppressive use of power by one group or its agents over another'.

The researchers argue that groups work against tyranny and it is only when social systems fail that tyrannical forms of social organisation come into being. One aim of the BBC prison study, *The Experiment*, was to examine the effects of group behaviour on issues such as tyranny. Because of the real-world application of such work, it is an important area for society. More precisely, the aim was to investigate the behaviour of groups that were unequal in terms of power, status and resources. Another aim was to revisit the issues raised in the Stanford prison experiment, e.g. to study:

- whether participants accept their role uncritically
- whether those who have power use it without constraint
- whether those without power accept their subordination without complaint

The aims of the researchers were:

- to look at the unfolding interactions between groups of unequal power and privilege
- to see when people identify themselves as a member of a group and when they accept or challenge inter-group inequalities
- to look at social, organisational and clinical (regarding mental-health issues) factors to see how they affect, and are affected by, group behaviour
- to develop ways of studying such behaviours ethically

Procedure

To some extent, Reicher and Haslam's study is similar to an experiment because they manipulate variables and the study is carried out in the field: it takes place in a simulated setting that is supposed to resemble real-life. However, data come from observations, video and tape recordings, analysis of conversations, and from other measures such as psychological and physiological testing. Since so many different ways of collecting data are used, and the data are in depth, detailed and about a one-off situation, the study is more like a case study. Reicher and Haslam call it an experimental case study; you can think of it as a case study.

Reicher and Haslam carried out the study but the BBC was involved in setting up the situation, providing the taped evidence and organising it into the four programmes. This was a unique collaboration. The environment had to create inequality between two groups that was real for the participants. It was a study of the behaviour of groups in dominant and subordinate positions and the developing relations between them. It rested on the ideas of social identity theory and there were manipulated variables – interventions — based on the theory. 'Prisoners' were allocated in threes to lockable cells surrounding a central area and a lockable steel mesh separated the cells from the guards' more comfortable quarters.

Ethics

The inter-group inequality was set up to be ethical. Details were discussed with colleagues, a university ethics committee and the BPS ethics committee. The novelty of the study was given as a reason for it taking place and various safeguards were put in place:

- Participants went through detailed screening.
- They signed a comprehensive consent form, which informed them that they may be at risk of psychological discomfort, confinement and stress.
- Two independent clinical psychologists monitored the study and could contact participants at any time. They could ask for the withdrawal of a participant from the study.
- A paramedic was on standby throughout.
- On-site security guards were ready to intervene if behaviour became dangerous.
- An independent five-person ethics committee monitored the study throughout (and at the end said that it was exemplary).

Study hint Use the detail given here when discussing ethical issues concerning human participants in psychology studies. For each of the five main ethical guidelines listed for your course, use the above evidence to illustrate it including the guideline of competence, which is well illustrated in this study.

Participants

Male participants were recruited using an advertisement in the national press and through leaflets. Those who responded were screened thoroughly, including a full weekend assessment. Well-adjusted and prosocial participants were selected, both for ethical and practical reasons. For example, if antisocial behaviour was found in the study, it could then be claimed that this could be generalised to the whole population because the participants were not antisocial initially. Of 332 applicants screened, 27 men were chosen. Only men were used, so that there would be no issues of having males and females together in the cells and having to provide facilities for both sexes. Fifteen participants were then chosen, ensuring a spread of age, class and ethnicity. The 15 were grouped into threes that were matched as far as possible; from each 'three', one person was chosen randomly to be a guard. So there were five guards and ten prisoners.

Gathering data

Data were gathered using video and tape recordings. Tests were also carried out to investigate issues such as depression (a clinical factor), compliance with rules (an organisational factor) and right-wing authoritarianism (a social factor). Cortisol levels were measured because they link with stress and depression.

How the study was run

The evening before the study, five participants were invited to a hotel and were told they that would be guards. Their jobs were described to them. They had to:

- carry out a roll call
- allocate work duties to prisoners
- ensure the institution ran smoothly
- ensure that prisoners did all their tasks

The guards drew up rules and punishments for the violation of the rules. They were told that they could not use physical punishments and that they had to give the prisoners basic human rights, but they were *not* told how to do their jobs. The guards were taken to the setting in a van with blacked-out windows. They had better conditions than the prisoners, e.g. better quality uniforms and more comfortable quarters.

Nine 'prisoners' arrived singly (one came later) and each was given the prison rules and a list of basic rights.

Interventions

The experimenters wanted to examine the effect of **permeability** on group behaviour. Permeability meant that group boundaries were drawn loosely and members could pass between the groups. To set up permeability, the researchers told the guards that they should look for guard potential among the prisoners, as there would be a promotion because the researchers thought that they might have assigned the prisoners wrongly. A promotion was made on day 3 and after that the participants were told that there would be no more movement between the groups.

The researchers also wanted to look at the effects of **cognitive alternatives** on group behaviour. A cognitive alternative is when someone sees that there is a different way of thinking about something. A new prisoner who had been a trade union official was introduced on day 5. The experimenters thought that he would have ideas about getting better conditions and on how to negotiate, which would give cognitive alternatives for the prisoners.

Results

There were two phases to the study. The first phase lasted until the prisoners became stronger than the guards; the second phase began with a new social organisation.

Phase 1: rejecting inequality

The guards failed to identify with one another as a group. The prisoners did not identify as a group up to day 3, but after the promotion they became much more cohesive — so much so, that they became stronger than the guards and challenged them. There was a shift in power and a collapse of the prisoner–guard system. The observations showed the solidarity of the prisoners and the lack of identity within the guards; the quantitative data backed up the observational data. For example, prisoners were asked to rate their ties with other prisoners, their ties with guards and their solidarity with other prisoners.

After the promotion on day 3, the prisoners started to agree norms of behaviour, but the guards did not. So the participants did not see differences in qualities between the two groups because the guards did not seem to be stronger people. Therefore, the groups did not seem to be legitimate. Cognitive alternatives emerged, such as the prisoners envisaging changing the situation and the power structure. This happened before the introduction of the additional prisoner. When the new prisoner was introduced on day 5, he immediately questioned the legitimacy of the study, rather than of the groups, and suggested to his cell mates and to one of the guards that they challenge the experimenters.

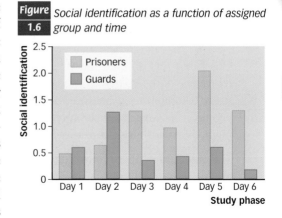

Figure 1.6 *Social identification as a function of assigned group and time*

At the start of the study, neither the guards nor the prisoners saw cognitive alternatives — these developed over time. Gradually, the prisoners started acting against the social inequality — for example, they started to be insubordinate during roll call. The guards remained reasonably compliant but after day 3, the prisoners did not. A shift in power began. Through planning and mutual support, the prisoners became progressively more dominant. No participant became very depressed but the guards, who were less depressed at the start, became more depressed than the prisoners. By late on day 6, the prisoners broke out of their cells and took over the guards' quarters.

Phase 2: embracing inequality

Participants agreed to continue as a self-governing commune. All but two prisoners wanted the commune, but those who had been more rebellious towards the guards started plotting against the commune and so confidence was lost. Some participants then wanted to impose a more authoritarian system. The others agreed because they had become despondent (partly because they thought the experimenters were disappointed in them and that they had failed). To achieve the aims of the study, a strong social system that worked was seen as desirable. At day 8, the experiment was stopped because the new tyrannical system was against the ethical rules, so the study had come to a natural conclusion.

Conclusions

It was concluded that groups create social order based on shared values and norms, and the prisoners formed a group on this basis. However, when groups fail, people are inclined to accept the imposition of social order, even if this goes against their own values and norms. So tyranny arises because of group failure, not because of the development of tyrannical group behaviour. People do not accept automatically roles that are assigned to them; other factors affect whether they identify with their social positions.

Social identity theory suggests that permeability affects how far people identify with groups. This study supports this conclusion because the prisoners formed a group after the promotion (when the groups became impermeable), rather than before.

One factor that affected social identification was the view of others, as seen by the reluctance of the guards to appear authoritarian. This was probably the effect of the study being televised because their behaviour would be seen and judged by many people. This suggests that surveillance affects behaviour. Making behaviour visible might avoid authoritarianism, which is a useful finding for society.

The researchers also found that mental state was affected by how effectively the groups performed, with a dysfunctional group leading to lower effectiveness with regard to mental health — again an important finding for society. Social support is known to help in improving mental health.

The study showed that understanding collective conflict and tyranny cannot be achieved by looking at individuals, it requires an analysis of group processes and relations between groups. Group behaviour can be antisocial or prosocial depending on the norms and values associated with the identity of the group members. Failing groups present problems for their own members and for others. It is not that group norms and values lead to antisocial behaviour, but that problems with the functioning of groups affect social organisation and mental health and so affect society. When people cannot construct a social system for themselves, they fall back on a more authoritarian ideology.

Evaluation by the researchers

The researchers discuss four problems they identify with the study and address the issues.

Were the results affected by the study being televised?

The researchers accept that the participants knew their behaviour would be shown on national television and that, to an extent, this would affect their behaviour. However, they felt that the participants could not 'act' over 9 days and also, as their behaviour changed in that time, it was not 'acting' but real. In any case, they argue, other studies where anonymity is guaranteed, are likely to be less valid. There is a way in which people think of themselves as being watched when in social roles in any case, so the study can be said to be valid because 'being watched' is a natural state in society.

Were the participants of a particular personality type?

Three prisoners had the strongest personalities of all the participants, so maybe their personalities could have caused the results. However, prisoners and guards were matched on several variables including racism, authoritarianism and dominance. Individuals changed throughout the study, which would not be accounted for by different personalities. If people were 'rebellious', it could be asked why they deferred to the experimenters and deferred in some situations but not others.

Was the inequality real for the participants?

The evidence suggested that the situation was real for the participants, for example:

■ From the start, the prisoners disliked their unequal status.

■ The prisoners did not like their food being of poorer quality than the guards' food.

■ The guards also engaged with their roles. They were concerned about using their power, but they accepted that they had power.

■ The guards tried to ease the inequalities – for example by offering the prisoners their leftovers.

■ The guards did not gel together as a group, seemingly because they were uncomfortable with their situation, which suggests that they identified with it.

Were they really measuring impermeability and cognitive alternatives?

The researchers admitted that there could be explanations other than their own for the changes that they found after their interventions. They felt that using different ways to collect data, including gathering both qualitative and quantitative data, helped to show both reliability and validity. However, there were problems in saying that the prisoners' group cohesion came when the groups became impermeable. It might have been that the participants distrusted the experimenters after the promotion or were uncertain about what might happen next.

General evaluation of Reicher and Haslam (2006)

Strengths

■ It is a case study that used many different means of collecting data. There are both qualitative and quantitative data and there can be triangulation when results from the different research methods are compared. If the data agree, then they would appear to be measuring the same thing and the findings are likely to be the same next time, which means that they are reliable. If when using different research methods data agree, it is more likely that the behaviour being measured is real and valid.

■ There was competence, in that different ethical committees were consulted and one was even set up especially for the study. There was informed consent and participants were warned, for example, about stress and confinement. There was no deceit, in that the participants knew exactly what the study involved and were told that it would be televised. There was the right to withdraw, in that even if the participants did not feel they could withdraw, there were people present who could ask for a participant to be withdrawn. There was a debrief after the study.

Weaknesses

■ There were a number of factors at work, rather than a single manipulated variable being studied. This means that although the complexity of group behaviour was being studied, it is not possible to draw firm conclusions about what causes which effect. For example, for the prisoners, strong identification with the group happened after the groups become impermeable, but it might not be the impermeability that caused the changes.

■ The study was televised and the participants' behaviour was likely to be affected by such surveillance. The researchers turned this into a positive by saying that in society people are watched anyway, so the television aspect makes the study valid. However, the guards may have behaved differently had they not been constrained by what others would think of them. For example, one guard was well thought of 'in the world outside' and the researchers suggest that this might have made him reluctant to be as authoritarian as a guard might need to be. He was made artificially into a guard with another life 'outside', which was not a valid situation.

Table 1.26 *Strengths and weaknesses of Reicher and Haslam (2006)*

Strengths	Weaknesses
• The study used multiple methods of collecting the data, so the data could be compared for reliability (if the same results were found by different means) and validity (if the same results were found it is more likely that behaviour was 'real life') • The study was set up to adhere to ethical guidelines — for example, with regard to competence, two ethical committees were consulted and one was especially set up for the duration of the study	• It was difficult to claim that the interventions caused the behaviour — for example, the prisoners may not have gained a group identity because of the impermeability of the groups but because of other factors, such as not knowing what would happen next; the researchers acknowledge this weakness • The study was televised, which probably affected the behaviour; this could be seen as a strength, because in society people are observedl; however, it could be what led to the behaviour, rather than the situation itself

Study hint When giving strengths and weaknesses, first explain the strength or weakness and then give an example to illustrate it (see Table 1.26). To gain marks you need to show knowledge with understanding. A good way of doing this is to give examples. So, for example, don't just say a study is ethical, show how it is ethical.

Examination-style questions

1 The following three studies were set up to investigate how two groups of people behaved towards each other:
- the Robbers Cave study (Sherif et al. 1954) was a field study of two groups of 11-year-old boys
- the BBC prison study (Reicher and Haslam 2006), in which a prison-like situation was set up with five participants who were given the role of guards and ten participants who were 'prisoners'
- the minimal groups study (Tajfel et al. 1970), which used teenaged boys

Choose one of the above studies and answer the following questions:

a Outline the procedure of the study, other than what is given in the question. *(3 marks)*

b Outline the findings (results and/or conclusions) of the study. *(4 marks)*

c You will have covered the study of obedience in nurses by Hofling et al. (1966) and either the Robbers Cave study (Sherif et al. 1954, 1961, 1988), the BBC prison study (Reicher and Haslam 2006) or the minimal groups study (Tajfel et al. 1970, 1971). In terms of the methodology, compare Hofling et al. (1966) with one of the other studies. *(6 marks)*

Compare Hofling et al. (1966) and one other study that you have covered in detail in terms of what they studied, the procedures and results/conclusions. *(12 marks)*

Key issues

You have to study one key issue in each approach and apply concepts and ideas from the approach to that issue. Concepts and ideas include research, studies and theories. Three of the five issues suggested for your course are covered here. The other two issues are summarised here and covered in more detail in the CD-ROM. However, you do not have to choose one of these issues — you can choose any issue. In the examination, you may be given an issue to read and then have to apply concepts and ideas from the approach to that issue. Studying all the issues will help you to learn how to apply concepts, ideas, theory and research to a new issue.

Blind obedience to authority in a prison setting

Different types of obedience have been studied and, in general, it has been found that people obey those in authority without question. This key issue is about obedience in a prison setting — for example, obedience by prison guards or soldiers acting as guards. A recent example is the torture of Iraqi detainees by US soldiers at Abu Ghraib prison in April 2004.

Describing the issue

There have been occasions when soldiers or prison guards have acted according to their role to an extent that is beyond many people's understanding. When someone breaks what is thought by most people to be a reasonable moral code, then questions are asked about how this could have happened. This sort of obedience is called 'blind obedience' precisely because it seems to ignore the person's own code of conduct and to be 'blind' to moral rules.

A shocking photograph of a tortured prisoner in the Abu Ghraib prison in Iraq

1

The Abu Ghraib prison in Iraq, built by the British and the size of a small town, was used by Saddam Hussein to keep and torture prisoners of all sorts, often people imprisoned for their political or religious beliefs. At the start of the twenty-first century, Saddam Hussein came under pressure from US and other forces and he released all prisoners by October 2002.

However, subsequent events at Abu Ghraib prison caused an outcry when Iraqi detainees were photographed being tortured by US army personnel. In general, public opinion is that the soldiers were brutal, rather than being ordinary soldiers doing their job. It is thought that this was not just a case of following orders and that such actions should be punished because they are crimes.

Application of concepts and ideas

- Zimbardo and colleagues carried out a study (Haney et al. 1973) in which they set up a prison situation, allocated volunteers to a prisoner or guard role and then observed the resulting behaviour. The guards became brutal towards the prisoners and the study had to be stopped.
- Zimbardo has been a witness in trials where, for example, soldiers have been charged with similar brutality to that found by Haney et al. His point is that the soldiers were acting according to their roles and that the situation is such that other people are likely to have done the same. However, courts usually find the soldiers guilty, rather than accepting this defence.

> **Explore** Zimbardo has written a best-selling book, *The Lucifer Effect*, about the issue of obedience. It is worth reading at least some of it because it explains psychological ideas about behaviour such as obedience.

- Milgram found that 'ordinary' volunteers were willing to give what they thought were powerful electric shocks to a victim, for no reason other than that they were ordered to do so.
- Real prison settings have led to brutality by guards, or soldiers acting as guards, in the way predicted by the studies of Milgram and Zimbardo. Since the participants in Milgram's and Zimbardo's studies were volunteers and not specially selected, it is thought that everyone is likely to behave similarly, i.e. act according to the role that they are in, blindly and without reference to their normal moral code. Milgram's participants were under orders but they did not enjoy giving the 'shocks' — they were under pressure. However, despite protesting, 65% continued to obey to the end.
- Milgram suggested agency theory as an explanation. He thought that because the guards or soldiers were acting as agents within society (it was their role), they did not see themselves as responsible and were more able to obey orders.
- Milgram's participants were clearly under moral strain and it is not suggested that such obedience is carried through lightly.
- Zimbardo's study was replicated to an extent when Reicher and Haslam worked with the BBC and carried out *The Experiment* to see what people would do in a prison-like setting when one group of people had power over another.

Obedience during conflict resulting in harm to others

Obedience is also found in war situations. This key issue considers obedience during conflict when one person obeys orders and, as a result, harms another.

Describing the key issue

There have been occasions when soldiers have obeyed orders and harmed civilians, which is not what their training would have led them to do. An example occurred at My Lai during the Vietnam War. On 16 March 1968, US army forces murdered over 350 unarmed Vietnamese civilians, mostly women and children (page 7). Some of the victims were tortured before being killed; some of the dead bodies were mutilated. This caused outrage around the world. Once again, as with Eichmann in the Second World War, the soldiers said that they were just obeying orders. When carrying out his 1963 study, Milgram had asked 'Would anyone in the same situation also have obeyed?'

Application of concepts and ideas

- Agency theory states that people obey orders because they are acting as agents in their society, so responsibility for their actions is seen as belonging to the person who gives the orders. Not having to take responsibility means that behaviour that goes against an individual's moral code is more likely to happen.

- According to agency theory, the tendency to be an agent in society and to obey orders might be a survival instinct. This is because a society in which members are willing to obey orders (even if obeying means going against what they would do normally) is likely to be beneficial to society as a whole. So where people had such an instinct, their genes may have been more likely to be passed on. This is an example of evolution and survival of the fittest.

> **Explore** Use the internet or other sources to research the My Lai massacre. There are a number of factors that are thought to have led to the level of violence exhibited. This was not an order given in an experimental situation, but an order given after a series of events and in particular circumstances. Reading about it should help to show you why experiments are often said not to be valid because they do not represent real life. The massacre horrified everyone; read about it in depth to understand the full story.

- When people are under orders to do something that they would probably not do as individuals, they are likely to obey. This is particularly true if their role as agents is clear — for example, if they are in the army or in a similar role, as people are when at war.

- Milgram showed that people obeyed orders to 'shock' someone else even when they showed symptoms of moral strain, such as sweating and trembling. He demonstrated the strength of the tendency to obey. Therefore, when under orders in a conflict situation, people are likely to obey — whatever the consequences.

- Such obedience has been found in other countries in different situations and experiments. This can be taken as evidence for such a tendency to be instinctive, as agency theory suggests.

- In My Lai, the soldiers were ordered to kill everyone in the village, which they did, mostly without question (there were exceptions). Soldiers are trained to obey orders without question; they are not trained to be autonomous. Therefore, it could be argued that it is not so surprising that such atrocities occur.

Football violence

One issue that is highlighted at certain times is football violence. This issue seems to be always present, but sometimes it is more severe than others. It is reported periodically, which makes it seem worse at those times.

Describing the issue

Sports teams tend to have very loyal followers. In football, team followers can be loyal to the point of rivalry escalating into violence. The police have searched through video and other records and identified people who they think are ring leaders of such violence. They may be banned from matches or prevented from travelling abroad to support their teams.

Rivalry between teams can spill over into violence after a match. The teams wear colours to identify them on the pitch; supporters wear the same colours, on shirts, scarves and hats. The two groups are, therefore, easily identifiable.

There is also an international dimension to football hooliganism. English fans travel abroad to support teams and there is sometimes quite a high level of disturbance. Examples occurred in Marseilles in 1998, in Charleroi in 2000 and in Stuttgart in 2006. Sometimes, English fans are attacked by local people or by fans of other teams, rather than causing the disturbances. However, the violence is usually reported to have come from the football supporters. The issue is what causes this sort of violence when those concerned are not usually violent on other occasions.

Application of concepts and ideas

- The two groups of supporters can easily identify each other. This makes identification with an in-group stronger, which is likely to mean that prejudice against the out-group is also strong.
- Social identity theory suggests that people identify with their in-group and think of their group as being superior because this enhances their self-esteem. There is, therefore, a need to see the members of the other group as inferior. This can lead to prejudice and violence against the out-group members.
- Tajfel et al. (1970, 1971) found that even minimal groups discriminate in favour of their in-group and against their out-group. Football supporters are members of a group for more solid reasons than the group members in Tajfel et al.'s study, so they could perhaps be more prejudiced and so discriminate more.
- There is also the issue of bad crowd behaviour. One explanation of this suggests that because members of a crowd cannot be identified as individuals, they are 'deindividuated'. **Deindividuation** is when individual people do not feel recognised

as individuals, which means they no longer feel responsible for their own actions. When there is deindividuation, behaviour that as individuals, people would not display, can occur. A group of football supporters can become a crowd quite quickly.

- Realistic conflict theory is another explanation for prejudice. It suggests that when teams compete, they are likely to be prejudiced against one another. Football is all about competition. The claim of social identity theory that just having two groups causes prejudice might not explain football violence — it could be just about competition.

- Realistic conflict theory suggests that one way of reducing prejudice is to have two groups work together towards a goal that they both aspire to. This could explain why supporters of two opposing UK teams might come together as supporters of their national team.

Race riots

Crowd behaviour is something that society wishes to control because any form of violence is usually considered harmful. When crowd behaviour becomes violent, and turns into a riot, there is a cost to society both in emotional and financial terms. When a riot is a race riot, and two or more races turn against one another, there is often a high cost to society. Social identity theory can help to explain why one racial group may turn against another.

The issue of race riots is explained in more detail on the CD-ROM.

Cult behaviour

Cult behaviour is of concern to Western societies. A cult is a group of people outside what society considers to be normal. Usually, the word 'cult' refers to a group led by a charismatic leader. The leader often has strong beliefs in his or her (often 'his') power and strong religious views with themselves in the chief role.

Social identity theory and theories of obedience can help to explain cult behaviour, which is covered in more detail on the CD-ROM.

Examination-style question

Read the following passage:

There had always been unrest in the country but now the two factions had turned from legal protesting to actual fighting, so something had to be done. It had got worse since the rebel had taken over as leader — they followed her no matter what she ordered them to do. And the other side was just as bad — as soon as the violence against them had escalated, they fought back even harder. You would have thought that after so long living together in the same country they would have learned to share it — but the one group of course claimed ownership of the land, and the other group saw themselves as having an equal right to be there too.

Using concepts and ideas from the social approach, explain how the situation outlined in the stimulus material above might have come about. *(9 marks)*

Practical: a semi-structured interview

In the social approach you have to carry out a practical that is either a questionnaire or an interview. Here, a semi-structured interview about obedience is worked through. It includes questionnaire-type questions together with information about carrying out an interview. You have to gather both qualitative and quantitative data in your practical, which is possible using a semi-structured interview.

Aim

The aim is to find out if people act in an obedient way in society because they feel that they are agents of those in authority, rather than that they have autonomy.

Brief background

Milgram's agency theory states that, in general, people in society are agents of others, rather than being in charge of their own decisions. If you have not already covered this theory of obedience, look at it now because it will help you to understand the practical.

Research method

The research method suggested is a semi-structured interview. You could carry out this practical alone, or work in a small group so that you can pool data. For the purposes of this section, it is assumed that you are working alone.

Design

Participants

Use opportunity sampling to find two people (interviewees/respondents) to interview. If you are working in a small group of four, you would need to gather data from eight people. This would mean more data to analyse, but working alone is fine.

Ethical issues

It is important for every practical that you address the **ethical guidelines**:

- competence
- debriefing
- informed consent
- right of withdrawal
- deception

Include written standarised instructions to give participants the necessary information. Standardised instructions are the same for everyone and are written so that the briefing the participants have had is recorded because it might affect the results.

Drawing up an interview schedule

A list of decisions to be made when drawing up an interview schedule is given below for you to work through.

- Find two participants and note the sampling method for your records.
- Write out instructions for the participants, including ethical issues.
- Plan when and where the interviews will take place.
- Decide on the length of the interview and how it will be recorded (e.g. taking notes or tape-recording).
- Decide what personal data you need (e.g. age and gender).
- Decide what closed-ended questions will be asked.
- Decide what open-ended questions will be asked.
- Decide how you will explore issues as they arise, particularly if there will be more than one researcher doing the interviewing (if you are working in a group).
- Construct the interview schedule, set out appropriately, so that quantitative data can be recorded accurately.

> **Practical** Do not proceed with your investigation until your teacher or supervisor has approved it in terms of ethics.

> **Study hint** When working through the list and making decisions, write notes explaining why you made those decisions. Recording how you progressed through the practical will help you to remember problems and how you dealt with them, in readiness for the examination.

An example interview schedule
Semi-structured interview on obedience and agency theory

Thank you for agreeing to be interviewed about how we obey people in authority. Please note that you can stop the interview at any time. It will take just under an hour and no longer. Your name is not being recorded and all details are confidential. I can let you have my findings at a later date if you would be interested and I will also tell you more about the study once the interview is over, if that is okay with you. I am going to make some notes, which you can see at any time. I am just writing down your answers. Is it okay to start?

For questions 1 to 7, please select the answer that most closely describes yourself. Only answer the parts that you are happy to answer.

(1) Gender:
    Male ☐   Female ☐

(2) Age group:

18–24 ☐   25–30 ☐   31–39 ☐   40–49 ☐   50–59 ☐   60+ ☐

(3) Type of work:

Mainly manual ☐
Self-employed ☐
Not working ☐
Mainly professional ☐
Clerical ☐
Other ☐

(4) Type of upbringing:

Very controlled ☐
Reasonably controlled ☐
Fairly free ☐
Uncontrolled ☐

(5) Type of schooling:

Grammar ☐
Secondary modern ☐
Comprehensive ☐
Private ☐
Mixture ☐
Specific religion ☐
Other ☐

(6) Would you say that you are law abiding?

Yes ☐   No ☐

(7) Would you say that you are a leader or a follower?

Leader ☐   Follower ☐

For questions 8 to 13, please select the answer that most represents your response to the statements below. Only answer the questions that you are happy to answer.

SA = strongly agree; A = agree; DK = unsure (don't know); D = disagree; SD = strongly disagree

Statement	SA	A	DK	D	SD
(8) I tend to do what I am told	☐	☐	☐	☐	☐
(9) I like to make my own decisions	☐	☐	☐	☐	☐
(10) I agree that a society needs strong rules	☐	☐	☐	☐	☐
(11) I obey the law at all times	☐	☐	☐	☐	☐
(12) I think some laws are wrong	☐	☐	☐	☐	☐
(13) I stick to my own moral code, even if it means breaking the law	☐	☐	☐	☐	☐

The following questions ask for more detail about you. Is it okay to continue?

(14) Please tell me about your parents' style when bringing you up. Of course, only give information you are happy to give. What was your upbringing like?

(15) Please give me an example of when you have not wanted to obey someone in authority.

(16) If you are a parent, please tell me about your own parenting style when bringing up your own children.

(17) What do you think about the need for rules and laws in society?

Thank you very much for taking part in this interview. It is generally thought that people in a society are agents of that society — they obey the rules because that is how society works best. However, most people like to think that they make their own decisions, rather than obey others. I am looking at how far we obey others and how much we make our own decisions. Are you happy that I use the information you have given me for my psychology course?

Study hint It is best to design your own schedule. You will learn a lot from making the decisions and you will enjoy the practical more if it is your own.

How to carry out the study

Gathering the data

Decisions have to be made about gathering the data. Some issues include:

- being on time
- dressing appropriately
- having the necessary equipment (e.g. notebook and interview schedule)
- remaining objective
- not taking too much of the interviewees' time
- sticking to good ethical practices, such as explaining everything to the participants before starting, frequently giving right to withdraw, debriefing, letting the interviewees know what will be done with their data and, at a later date, contacting them with the results.

Once you have planned everything, then the data can be gathered.

Transcribing the data

Once the data have been collected, a **transcript** of the qualitative data has to be produced. Make complete copies of both the interviews and, if appropriate, share them with the others in the group.

Analysis of the data

Analysis of the personal data, the quantitative data and the qualitative data has to be carried out.

Analysing the personal data

- Add up the numbers, such as those of each gender, or age group, and any other information you gathered.
- Personal data are useful when looking for trends though if you gather only two lots of data, you will not find trends. If you have pooled data you may need to note these, to see, for example, whether type of upbringing relates to agency score as found from the statement scores. The statement scoring is explained below.

Analysing the qualitative data

- Draw up themes from the data. Two themes are likely to be 'act as an agent' and 'be autonomous'. However, themes must come from the data not from what you expect. Read through the data and spot categories that are mentioned often. Those categories are your themes. Other categories might not be mentioned often but might be of relevance to the respondent. These are also themes. It will not be easy to generate themes from two interviews but there may be some common ideas. Pooled data would help to show trends.
- Make a note of quotes that illustrate the themes so that you have evidence.

Analysing the quantitative data

- Add up numbers according to the questions asked, for example if you used a Likert-type scale of strongly agree, agree, don't know, disagree, strongly disagree.
- If you wish, present graphs and tables, as appropriate, to display your data.

Analysing the data from the example interview schedule

The data from the example interview schedule can be analysed in the following way.

- Note gender, age group, type of work etc. for each person, using the answers to questions 1 to 5.
- If you have worked with someone else and have enough data, work out percentages for the answers to questions 6 and 7. Otherwise, just note this information alongside the other personal data.
- Score the six statements according to the table below. A high score is assigned to being in an agentic state (obedient). Note how the scores for some statements go in one direction and some in the opposite direction. This is to avoid response sets and bias. The highest obedience score is 30; the lowest is 6.

Statement	SA	A	DK	D	SD
(8) I tend to do what I am told	5	4	3	2	1
(9) I like to make my own decisions	1	2	3	4	5
(10) I agree that a society needs strong rules	5	4	3	2	1
(11) I obey the law at all times	5	4	3	2	1
(12) I think some laws are wrong	1	2	3	4	5
(13) I stick to my own moral code, even if it means breaking the law	1	2	3	4	5

- Analyse the qualitative data from questions 14 to 17. Look for themes if possible. Possible themes are 'obeying authority', 'society needs control', 'living together means having rules', 'having had strict parenting could mean being a strict parent'. However, it is important to let themes develop from the data and to have examples of such themes as evidence.
- Draw some conclusions by examining all the data. For example, separate the male and female 'obedience' scores arising from the Likert-type scale and see if there are differences. Does strict parenting mean a high agentic state (obedience score)? Does gender, age or job affect how autonomous someone feels? Are leaders more autonomous than followers? These are suitable questions to ask yourself. Drawing conclusions from limited data is difficult but practise how to analyse them.

Answers to the practice boxes

Practice 1.1 on p. 12

1 Quantitative data
2 Quantitative data
3 Qualitative data

Practice 1.2 on p. 18

Issues that might affect the results are:

- gender of researcher
- age of researcher
- day of the week
- questions asked personally or not
- shoppers or golfers

Chapter

The cognitive approach

The cognitive approach is about how information is processed in the brain. When information is taken into the brain through the eyes, ears, tongue and other senses, it is recorded, processed and then there is output. The cognitive approach examines how this occurs.

Study of interest Studies have shown that using a mobile phone when driving is distracting and dangerous because the individual is attending to two tasks at once. A recent study (Griggs et al., in *The Psychologist,* 2007) showed that when conversations are emotional, driving is affected to an even greater extent. The study used participants who were either frightened by spiders or not affected by them. During conversations about spiders the phobic participants made more driving errors and had a narrower range of eye movements. This study is about cognitive psychology and how information is processed and how it affects behaviour. It is useful because it warns people not to drive when having emotionally charged conversations.

Everyday example: USA Track and Field, the governing body for marathon runners in America, has banned the use of headphones and listening to music in races such as the New York marathon. The reason is that runners would not then hear safety announcements or vehicles behind them, nor would they hear fans cheering them on. Runners were going to defy the ban.

Studies have shown that using a mobile phone when driving is distracting and dangerous

Some said that they got bored and needed to listen to music; for some, music provided a rhythm to run to. Another runner said that she never ran without headphones, adding that it just helped. (From *The Times*, 2 November 2007, news section, p. 5.) The runners were used to running with headphones and music and they linked the two together, which provided a context to help them. A theory for why we forget is cue-dependent forgetting, which suggests that if a context as a cue is removed, recall is harder. Perhaps runners need the context that they run in to help them perform well because they need the same environment for performing as they had for learning.

Summary of learning objectives

For the cognitive approach you have to:
- be able to define basic terms
- know what the approach is about
- study the methodology used in the approach

You will study two theories of memory and two theories of forgetting. You will look at one key issue on which concepts from the approach shed light, and carry out a practical using experimental method.

Definitions
You have to able to define the terms:
- information processing
- memory
- storage
- retrieval
- forgetting

Methodology
You have to be able to understand about three types of experiment, including strengths and weaknesses, in terms of:
- independent and dependent variables
- hypotheses, including directional and non-directional
- three types of experimental design
- operationalisation of variables
- counterbalancing and randomisation
- order effects
- control in experiments
- evaluation, including: objectivity, reliability, validity; experimenter effects; demand characteristics

Content
You have to be able to describe and evaluate:
- the levels-of-processing theory of memory and one other theory of memory
- the cue-dependent theory of forgetting and one other theory of forgetting

Other suggested theories are explained to help your choice.

Studies in detail
You have to be able to describe and evaluate in detail:
- the Godden and Baddeley (1975) study of cue-dependent forgetting/memory

- one other study chosen from Peterson and Peterson (1959), Craik and Tulving (1975) and Ramponi et al. (2004)

Three of these four studies are described and evaluated in this chapter. *The other one is summarised here and covered in detail on the CD-ROM.*

Key issues
You have to be able to describe one key issue and apply concepts and theories from the cognitive approach to explain it. The issue can be any issue. However, three key issues are given in the specification and two are explained here, to help you choose. *The other one is summarised here and covered in more detail on the CD-ROM.*

Practical
You have to:
- devise and conduct an experiment within cognitive psychology, adhering to ethical principles
- comment on the research design decisions
- collect, present and comment on the data including measures of central tendency (mean, median, mode), measures of dispersion (at least range), bar graphs, histograms and frequency graphs

In this chapter, one practical is worked through, though you could choose a different experiment. The information is there to guide you.

Study hint

Make the above summary of learning objectives into a checklist. Table 2.1 gives a suggested list. However, you could add detail. This would help your learning.

Table 2.1 *A checklist of what you need to know for the cognitive approach and for your progress*

I need to know about	Done	More work	I need to know about	Done	More work
Information processing			Levels of processing		
Computer analogy			One other theory of memory		
Memory, storage, retrieval			Cue-dependent forgetting		
Forgetting			One other theory of forgetting		
Three types of experiment			Godden and Baddeley (1975)		
Evaluation of three types of experiment			One other study of memory or forgetting		
Objectivity, reliability and validity in evaluation			One key issue in the approach		
Three participant designs			One experiment as a practical		
Hypotheses, directional and non-directional			Measures of central tendency		
Counterbalancing, randomisation and order effects			Measures of dispersion		
Independent variable, dependent variable and operationalisation			Graphs etc.		
Controls					

Definitions

You have to be able to define:

- **information processing** — what the cognitive approach is about, including input, processing and output, and how these work
- **memory** — encoding, storage and retrieval, explained in different ways by different theories
- **forgetting** — not remembering, which has more than one explanation
- **storage** — how information is retained in the brain ready for retrieval
- **retrieval** — getting stored information out of memory

An introduction to the cognitive approach

Humans and chimpanzees have 98% of their genes in common, which makes them very similar. However, there are obvious differences, so the small number of different genes must be important.

An important difference between humans and other animals is language ability. It is not only humans that use language — other animals, for example dolphins and bonobo chimps, use language in some form. Many experimental studies of chimpanzees have been made. Some can use grammar and create new sentences, as well as name objects, which is impressive. However, they cannot speak. Keyboards or signs are used to 'talk'. The ability to talk makes humans different — the structure of the brain and larynx are linked to speaking and language use. Chimpanzees and other apes can use tools as humans do and can solve problems. However, the human brain allows us to be better at solving these.

Chimpanzees can use language but not as comprehensively as humans can

Using tools, solving problems, using language and speaking are all skills that have contributed to human society and interaction. All are areas studied in the cognitive approach. Humans rely on remembering things and on being able to take information into the brain via the senses — sight, hearing, touch, taste and smell.

Memory, forgetting, problem solving, perception, language and thought are all studied within the cognitive approach. The overall focus is on how humans deal with information, from taking it into the brain via the senses, through processing to producing the required output.

Key assumptions

Key assumptions of the cognitive approach include the focus on information processing and the idea that the brain might process information in a similar way to a computer.

Information processing

The cognitive approach assumes that information is processed in the brain (**information processing**). Processing is considered to be **linear**, i.e. information flows 'through' the brain in a way that seems logical.

'Linear' refers to a single straight line.

Information is taken in by the senses before being processed. It is thought that, when being remembered, information is encoded in the brain (translated into a manageable form). It is then stored. When remembered, it is retrieved from storage. This is a linear, logical process. In studies within the cognitive approach the information is mapped at each stage. The assumption that information is processed follows scientific theory. In a scientific experiment, materials are assembled (information flows into the brain), something happens (there is processing) and the result is recorded (there is an output). The cognitive approach uses scientific methods such as laboratory experiments. The idea of a flow of information being tracked and tested at different stages would appeal to those working within this approach.

Figure 2.1 *A summary of the multi-store model of memory to show the idea of information processing*

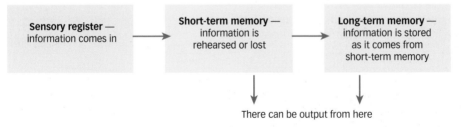

An example of a theory using information processing is the multi-store model (Figure 2.1). This is explained in more detail in the content section of this chapter (pages 107–132).

Brains work like computers

A computer has input, processing and output. It receives input via a keyboard or a voice-recognition device. Unlike a computer, the human brain receives information from the senses. Input into a computer is more limited whereas the human brain

receives masses of information all the time. The computer 'perceives' all the input whereas the human brain only perceives or pays attention to a small part of the information.

Once data have been input, the computer processes the data. The human brain processes the information it perceives, so in this way the two are similar. The computer uses memory and can solve problems. However, there are differences — the computer does not make mistakes whereas the human brain does. The computer will do the same processing repeatedly whereas a human brain might not repeat the same sequences for various reasons — for example interference from the environment.

Once the processing is complete, there is output. The computer produces output in the form of a printout or a screen display. A human being produces output using language or the written word. There are similarities between the two, but humans also use body language, emotions and other signals, so their output is more complex.

Figure 2.2 *A sick computer — humans are not really like computers because they really do get poorly, though they can both suffer from viruses*

The cognitive approach treats the brain as if it were a computer, albeit more complex (the **computer analogy**). Using ideas from a computer to explain human processing is useful because the brain is not yet well understood. It is also useful to clarify how the brain processes information.

Explore Use the internet or another source to investigate the computer analogy. Find out more about how the human brain works with regard to perception, problem solving, language or thought. Although not covered in your course, these areas are just as important in the cognitive approach as memory and forgetting. Look up the Necker cube, which is an illusion that helps to emphasise how the brain makes sense of what is seen.

Examination-style question

Outline two key assumptions of the cognitive approach and give one example for each. *(6 marks)*

Methodology

Study hint In Chapter 1, there is information about methodology and psychology. Surveys are explained in detail, focusing on questionnaires and interviews. Methodology issues are often common between research methods, so when terms are used again in this chapter refer back to Chapter 1 to compare their use. If you work hard on the methodology for the social and cognitive approaches, you will find the methodology for the Unit 2 approaches easier.

One research method used in the cognitive approach is the experimental research method. Cognition means thinking and the process of thinking cannot be measured easily by using an interview or a questionnaire. If questions were asked about thinking processes, a participant is not likely to be able to answer them.

Thinking is not easy to study. Early psychologists wanted to find out how information is processed in the brain and they used experiments to find out. A recent method of studying thinking processes is to scan the working brain. In the cognitive approach, you will look at older studies, before scanning was invented. Older studies were experimental, and modern studies still use experiments. Scanning is covered in Chapter 4.

Experimental research methods

Psychology uses experiments for the same reasons that they are used in other sciences. It is important for you to know something about psychology as a science and also about how science works. This issue arose in Chapter 1, underlining its importance. The experimental research method illustrates clearly how science works.

Psychology is a science

The way science works is outlined in Chapter 1. Science involves developing theories that explain events. For example, there is the theory that the Earth moves in a set pattern around the sun. As this theory explains all current measurements and findings, it is accepted as 'true'. Through the development of theories, psychologists want to claim certain 'truths'. For example, in the cognitive approach you will study a theory of memory that says remembering is about levels of processing:

- visual or structural processing (processing what something looks like, or its structure)
- auditory or phonemic processing (processing what something sounds like)
- semantic processing (processing the meaning of something)

You will also study a theory that forgetting occurs because the right cues are unavailable. These are tested theories that are accepted. They have been tested using scientific methods, which tried to show them to be false.

Explore Use the internet or other sources to read about Karl Popper's ideas about falsifiability and science. He said that there are many occasions when something is found to be true, but that there is no proof of the truth. This is because to show that the theory is not true there needs to be only one occasion when the theory is found to be false. It can never be known whether this is going to occur. For example, take the theory that 'all swans are white'. Lots of white swans can be found as evidence, but this does not prove that the theory is true. This is because it is impossible to know whether a black swan is going to be found. Once that black swan is found, it is certain that the theory that 'all swans are white' is not true. The only certainty is when something is not true.

Chapter 2

The cognitive approach

Science involves generating **hypotheses** (predictions) from theories and testing to see whether they are false or whether the findings support the prediction. A theory is an idea about why something happens, usually based on previous theories or research. A hypothesis is a statement of what the theory predicts. For example, there are studies about levels of processing, which is a framework or theory about how memory works. Levels of processing include:

- what something looks like
- what something sounds like
- what something means

Meaning is the deepest level of processing. A researcher tests participants by giving them tasks that involve different levels of processing and then testing their recall. The levels of processing framework says that the deeper the processing, the better the recall. A suitable hypothesis is: 'there is a difference in recall of words depending on the depth of processing required in a task, and words that have to be processed for their meaning are more readily recalled'. Craik and Tulving (1975) did a study based on this hypothesis (page 96). They found that if participants were asked whether a word was in capital letters (what the word looked like) they remembered fewer of those words than if they were asked whether the word belonged to a specific category (for which they needed to know the meaning of the word). When asked if a word was in a category (for example: 'Is red a colour?'), participants remembered more words of this type than if they were asked whether words rhymed or whether a word was written in capital letters.

When testing a hypothesis based on a theory, science uses controls to avoid bias, and concepts have to be measurable and produce quantitative data. Everything other than what is being studied must be controlled to keep it the same throughout, so that it does not affect the study. Quantitative data involve numbers. Therefore, mathematical analysis can be carried out. Science is objective; it is important not to let subjective (personal) opinions affect results.

If studies involve careful controls, objectivity and measurable concepts, then the results should be replicable. They can be shown to be reliable by repeating the study. Replicability means that a study can be repeated exactly. A study is said to be reliable if, when repeated, the same results are found. If findings are reliable and support the hypothesis, then the theory is supported and a body of knowledge is built. If, however, the findings do not support the hypothesis, then the theory is either abandoned or amended (Figure 2.3). Then further hypotheses are generated and in this way scientific knowledge is built up.

Figure 2.3 Processes involved in scientific testing

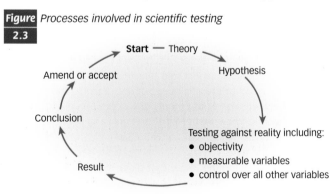

Features of experiments in psychology

Features of experiments in psychology mirror features of experiments in science.

Hypotheses

An **experimental hypothesis** is generated. This is a statement of what is expected. The experimental hypothesis is the alternative hypothesis (alternative to the null hypothesis). The **null hypothesis** states that any difference or relationship expected is due to chance — there is no relationship or difference as predicted. It is the null hypothesis that is tested when using statistical tests. For example, in the Craik and Tulving (1975) study, the experimental hypothesis could be 'there is a difference in recall of words depending on the depth of processing required in a task and words that have to be processed for their meaning are better recalled'. A null hypothesis could be 'any difference in recall of words depending on the depth of processing required is due to chance'.

Practice 2.1

Here are some suggested studies that you could carry out using the experimental research method. For each study, write out an experimental hypothesis and a null hypothesis.

Study 1 To see whether an interference task in short-term memory, such as counting backwards for 15 seconds after seeing a list of letters, affects recall of those letters.

Study 2 To see whether, after hearing a story read out, recall of that story is poorer over time, with less and less of the story being recalled correctly over a period of a few weeks.

Study 3 To see whether recall of a list of words is different depending on whether the setting for recall is the same as, or different from, the setting where the words are learnt.

Answers are at the end of Chapter 2.

Directional and non-directional hypotheses

A hypothesis may or may not predict the direction that the results will take. For example, if the experimental hypothesis is 'processing for meaning leads to better recall of words' then a direction is predicted — recall of words will be better if meaning is processed. However, if the hypothesis is 'processing for meaning affects

recall of words' then there is no direction. It is not clear whether recall of words will be better or worse. The first example is a **directional** (or **one-tailed**) **hypothesis**; the second example is a **non-directional** (or **two-tailed**) **hypothesis**.

Practice 2.2

Note down whether the following hypotheses are directional or non-directional.

Hypothesis 1 Divers remember more words when recalling in the same situation in which they were learnt than when recalling in a different situation.

Hypothesis 2 Counting backwards to provide interference in short-term memory affects recall of letters.

Hypothesis 3 Recall of a story is affected by the length of time since hearing the story.

Answers are at the end of Chapter 2.

The two main variables

Variables are whatever is likely to affect the experiment. They include:

- what is being tested
- what is being measured
- what else is likely to affect the results

There are two important variables in any study — the **independent variable (IV)** and the **dependent variable (DV)**. The independent variable is changed or manipulated by the researcher. This is to see the effect on the dependent variable. The dependent variable is measured by the researcher. It changes as a result of manipulating the independent variable. It is common practice to use the abbreviations 'IV' and 'DV' when referring to these variables, but you need to know the full terms. Both the independent and dependent variables have to be measurable; to make them measurable is to **operationalise** them.

These ideas can be better understood by using an example. The hypothesis of the Craik and Tulving (1975) study could be that there is a difference in recall that depends on the level of processing. However, the hypothesis suggested above was 'there is a difference in recall of words depending on the depth of processing required in a task, and words that have to be processed for their meaning are better recalled'.

There is an important reason for the hypothesis being the fuller version. The independent variable in this study could be said to be the level of processing and the dependent variable to be the recall. However, this is not accurate enough and does not give enough detail. The variables 'level of processing' and 'recall' have to be operationalised because they are not measurable directly, and experimental method requires measurable factors. Level of processing needs to be explained; it is about depth of processing — but this too requires explanation. Recall also needs explaining. The fuller hypothesis included that a deeper level of processing (meaning has to be understood) leads to more words from a list being recalled. The independent variable is whether or not meaning has to be understood in the task and the dependent variable is the number of words recalled from a list.

It is usually easy to identify what is being measured in a study, because that will be the scores and the data gathered (dependent variable). Once this has been identified it is usually easy to identify the independent variable.

> When you have to find the variables in a study, identify the dependent variable first.

Practice 2.3

Here are some alternative hypotheses. Identify the independent and dependent variables for each hypothesis.

Hypothesis 1 Divers will recall more words from a list that they learnt underwater when they recall underwater than when they recall on land.

Hypothesis 2 Students will score more marks in an examination if it is taken in the room where they learnt the material than if they take the examination in a different room.

Hypothesis 3 There will be more letters recalled from a list of 21 letters if the letters are grouped (chunked) into recognisable sets of three letters (such as CSI) than if the letters are presented randomly.

Answers are at the end of Chapter 2.

Other variables

There are other variables that might affect the results in a study. These are **extraneous variables**. A requirement in an experiment is to control to decrease the number of extraneous variables. Extraneous variables are those that might affect the results, as well as, or instead of, the independent variable. Examples of variables that have to be controlled in an experiment are:

- **participant variables** — for example age, gender, experience and mood of the participants
- **situational variables** — for example temperature, noise, interruptions and light

When extraneous variables are not controlled for and affect the results they are called **confounding variables**.

Controls

In any experiment, the researcher must control as many variables as possible (other than the independent variable). The aim is to show that the change in the independent variable causes the change in the dependent variable. Therefore, it is important to ensure that nothing else, including participant and situational variables, can affect the results. One aspect that is controlled is the information given to participants with standardised instructions so that each participant has the same information.

Experimenter effects

Another aspect that needs to be controlled as far as possible is the effect of the experimenter. **Experimenter effects** come from cues or signals from an experimenter that can affect the participant's response. Cues might be tone of voice or non-verbal cues such as gestures or facial expression. It is difficult to control such effects. The best way is to have someone else carry out the experiment, rather than the designer.

Experimenters must make sure that they do not affect the results

In a **double-blind technique** the participants are not aware which group they are in or what the study is about. The study is carried out by someone other than the person who knows who is doing what. Neither the participants nor the person running the study knows precisely what is expected.

In a **single-blind technique** the participants are not aware of what is expected but the person carrying out the study is. The single-blind technique stops participants' expectations from affecting the results but does not stop experimenter effects.

Explore Robert Rosenthal has studied experimenter effects and their power to affect experimental results. Use the internet or another source to find out what Rosenthal says about such effects and what should be done to try to avoid them.

The double-blind technique is the better of the two.

Conditions of a study

A study can have a different number of **conditions**. Conditions are aspects of the independent variable and there must be two or more conditions. For example, for the hypothesis 'divers recall more words when in the same situation in which they learnt them', participants are either in the same situation when recalling or in a different situation. This is to see whether words are better recalled in one condition (same situation recall) or another condition (different situation recall). There must be at least two conditions so that a comparison can be made. Sometimes there are more than two conditions for the independent variable. For example, the Craik and Tulving (1975) study involved participants:

- looking at the words (visual)
- rhyming the words (auditory)
- considering the meaning of the words (semantic)

Therefore, in this study there were three conditions.

Experimental (participant) design

When designing a study that uses an experiment or another research method, a decision has to be made about what design to use with regard to the participants.

The researcher can ask participants to partake in all the conditions of the study or in only one condition. When participants do all the conditions of the study this is called **repeated measures design** because the 'measures' or 'conditions' are repeated (participants do all parts). When participants do only one of the conditions, this is called **independent groups** because there are different participants in the groups and they do different conditions. There is one more experimental design — **matched pairs** — which is explained below.

Suppose that a researcher suggests the hypothesis that 'more words will be recognised if they have been processed for meaning than if they have been processed by sound'.

In a repeated measures design, the researcher would ask participants to look through a complete list of words, some of which have to be processed to see if they rhyme (auditory/sound) and some of which have to be processed for meaning (semantic). Then the participants see if they can recognise the words out of a list that also includes other words. If they recognise more of the words they processed for meaning, then it is said that processing for meaning gives better recall. This is a repeated measures design because the participants do both conditions of the study — they process for sound (one condition) and for meaning (the other condition).

In an independent groups design, the researcher would ask one group of participants to process words for meaning, perhaps by getting them to say whether something is true of a word or not, such as 'cat — has two legs' or 'dog — has four legs'. Then the researcher asks another group of participants to process the same words for sound, such as 'cat — rhymes with pop' or 'dog — rhymes with fog'. All participants are then given the list containing other words to see which words they recognise.

A **matched pairs design** uses different participants, as does an independent groups design. Here, the participants are paired up, one from each group, according to what the researcher thinks are important factors – for example age, gender, social class or ethnicity. Although there are different participants doing each condition, this design is treated as if it is a repeated measures design because the researcher is trying to get participants to be as similar as possible to control the participant variables. It is difficult to match participants and difficult to make sure they are matched in all important ways. For these reasons matched pairs designs are rare (unless perhaps using identical twins).

Practice 2.4

Decide which participant design should be used in each of the following studies.

Study 1 The aim is to look at the effect of gender on driving ability on a specially laid-out driving course.

Study 2 The aim is to look at whether recall of a story involves less and less detail over time.

Study 3 The aim is to see whether divers recall more words when recalling in the same conditions in which the words were learnt.

Answers are at the end of Chapter 2.

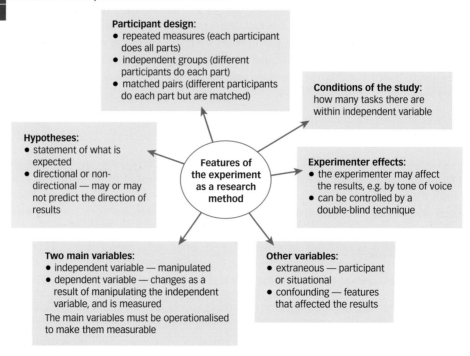

Figure 2.4 Features of the experimental research method

Participant design:
- repeated measures (each participant does all parts)
- independent groups (different participants do each part)
- matched pairs (different participants do each part but are matched)

Conditions of the study: how many tasks there are within independent variable

Hypotheses:
- statement of what is expected
- directional or non-directional — may or may not predict the direction of results

Features of the experiment as a research method

Experimenter effects:
- the experimenter may affect the results, e.g. by tone of voice
- can be controlled by a double-blind technique

Two main variables:
- independent variable — manipulated
- dependent variable — changes as a result of manipulating the independent variable, and is measured

The main variables must be operationalised to make them measurable

Other variables:
- extraneous — participant or situational
- confounding — features that affected the results

Strengths and weaknesses of participant design

Repeated measures

■ One strength of a repeated measures design is that the same participants do all the conditions, so participant variables — features of a participant that might affect the results — are controlled. Each participant does all the conditions, so any feature will affect both (or all) conditions and, therefore, will cancel out. For example, if age affects memory and all participants do all conditions, it does not matter how old the participants are provided that there is a range of ages overall.

■ Another strength is that more data can be gathered because each person does all conditions. If a different person is needed for each of two conditions, then double the number of people is needed. This could be inconvenient or costly and, possibly, less ethical.

■ One weakness of a repeated measures design is that there might be **order effects**. Whichever condition participants do first might be their best performance simply because they are less tired than when undertaking the task for the next condition. This is the **fatigue effect**. Participants might do the second task better, because, having already done the first task, they know what to do. This is the **practice effect**. An order effect will affect the results and, if not noticed, would mean drawing a wrong conclusion With a fatigue effect, the results of the first task will be better than the results of the second task; with a practice effect the results of the second task will be better. As a result of any one of these effects the results will not be due to manipulating the independent variable, so the study will not be useful.

- Another weakness is that there might be demand characteristics. These occur when participants' responses are affected by guessing what the study is about. They might either try to please the researcher or try to go against what they think is predicted. Either way the results are affected. For example, when participants are asked to decide whether words rhyme or not and are then asked to decide whether characteristics of a word are true or not, they might guess that the second task is harder, and so do worse. This is not true — they should do better — but their thinking may affect the results.

Independent groups

- One strength of an independent groups design is that there are no order effects because different people do the different conditions. This strength of an independent groups design is a weakness of repeated measures designs.
- Another strength of an independent groups design is that it is less likely that demand characteristics will affect the results. This strength of an independent groups design is a weakness of repeated measures designs.
- One weakness of an independent groups design is that participant variables might affect the results. For example, there might be more older people in one group than in the other, which, if age affects recall, might influence the results. This weakness of an independent groups design is a strength of repeated measures designs.
- Another weakness of an independent groups design is that more participants are needed because different people do the different conditions. This is a weakness for a number of reasons:
  - It might be more unethical.
  - It might mean that the sample takes longer to obtain.
  - It might mean that the study either takes longer or is more difficult to carry out because the participants have to be split into groups and do the study at a different time.

> **Study hint** Note that strengths for one design are often weaknesses for another and vice versa. Learn them in this way to help you to remember them.

Matched pairs designs

- One strength of matched pairs designs is that they are similar to repeated measures designs, so participant variables should not affect the findings. *If the important participant variables for a study have been matched, then the results should be the same as if the same participants had carried out the study.*
- Another strength is that, because different people are doing the different conditions, there will not be order effects.
- One weakness of matched pairs designs is that different people are used (even though matched in some ways) so there will *still* be participant variables that might affect the results. For example, it might be difficult to match type of education or background. Matching exactly will not occur even if identical twins are used.
- Another weakness is that more people are needed than for a repeated measures design, with the problems that this entails.

Counterbalancing and randomisation

When a repeated measures design is used, order effects can affect the results to such an extent that the findings are not useful. However, steps can be taken to minimise order effects.

In **counterbalancing**, the researcher alternates the conditions for each participant. For example, when there are two conditions, one participant does the first condition followed by the second condition. The next participant does the second condition followed by the first condition and so on. Order effects can still occur but should cancel out. If the participants get tired after the first condition, then the first participant will do less well on the second condition. However, the next participant will do less well on the first condition because that is carried out second.

The order in which the participants do the conditions can be randomised. This is called **randomisation**. For example, if a study has two conditions, a coin could be tossed to see which condition is done first. This should help to cancel out order effects.

> **Practical** When carrying out an experiment with a repeated measures design, make sure that you use counterbalancing or randomisation when allocating conditions to participants.

Table 2.2 *Strengths of the different participant designs*

Repeated measures	Independent groups	Matched pairs
Participant variables are controlled because all participants do all conditions	No order effects to affect results	Helps to control participant variables
Uses fewer participants, so so more efficient in terms of cost,convenience and ethics	Demand characteristics less likely	No order effects

Table 2.3 *Weaknesses of the different participant designs*

Repeated measures	Independent groups	Matched pairs
Order effects such as practice and fatigue effects can affect the results if there is no counterbalancing	Participant variables may affect the results	Different people are used, so there may be participant variables that affect the results
Demand characteristics are possible because participants could guess the aim(s) of the study	More participants are needed, so less efficient and less ethical	More participants are needed, so less efficient in terms of cost and less ethical

Three types of experiment

The three types of experiment are **laboratory experiments**, **field experiments** and **natural experiments**. The material outlined above about experiments applies, to a greater or lesser degree, to all three types. It is important, however, to know the differences between them.

Laboratory experiments

Laboratory experiments take place either in a laboratory or in a controlled setting, which is unnatural for the participants. Scientific experiments take place in laboratories and laboratory experiments in psychology are seen as the most scientific. This is because one variable (the independent variable) is manipulated and other variables are kept constant or controlled so that the effects of that manipulation can be seen on what is being measured (the dependent variable). A common design is to have an **experimental group** and a **control group** — the experimental group does something and the control group does not. Therefore, the control group provides a **baseline measure**, i.e. what the dependent variable would be like without manipulation. The results for the experimental group are compared against the baseline measure. This is important, because otherwise the 'normal' situation would not be known.

For example, consider the hypothesis 'there will be more letters recalled from a list of 21 letters if the letters are grouped (chunked) into recognisable sets of three letters (e.g. CSI, FBI, and CIA) than if the same letters are presented randomly (e.g. FIS, BIA and CIC)'. One group of participants — the experimental group — has the letters presented in groups (chunked); the other — the control group — has the letters presented randomly.

There are two groups of participants, so this is an independent groups design. If it were a repeated measures design the participants would have to learn the same list (albeit differently presented) twice. The two conditions would have to be carried out some time apart so that the participants forgot the letters.

Field experiments

Field experiments are experiments with as many controls as possible and a manipulated independent variable, but which are carried out **in the field**, rather than in a laboratory situation. Hofling et al. (1966) carried out a study into obedience (Chapter 1) that involved nurses in their natural setting (the hospital). This was, therefore, a field experiment. Apart from being in the field rather than in a laboratory, all other features of a laboratory experiment apply to field experiments.

In this context, **'in the field'** means in the participant's natural setting.

Natural experiments

Natural experiments usually take place in the field rather than in a laboratory because they involve finding a naturally occurring independent variable. For example, natural experiments have been carried out to investigate the effects of television on children. The children's behaviour (for example, their level of aggression) was measured before television was introduced into the area and then measured afterwards to see if there were any effects. The researchers did not themselves arrange for children to have no television and then to have it — that would be neither ethical nor practical. They found a community where television was going to be introduced and carried out measurments before and after the introduction. The situation is naturally occurring (television is going to be introduced anyway) and this is, therefore, a natural experiment.

Social and Cognitive Psychology

Natural experiments are **quasi experiments** because the independent variable is not manipulated by the researcher. Usually, natural experiments involve situations that are found rather than manipulated, so they take place in the participant's natural environment. However, gender is in a way not manipulated so experiments involving gender are quasi experiments, as are other experiments in which the participants 'naturally' belong in one group or another because of the independent variable.

Strengths and weaknesses of the different types of experiment

Laboratory experiments: reliability, validity and experimenter effects

■ Laboratory experiments are replicable, which means that they can be repeated. This is because of controls, such as standardised instructions. **Reliability** is tested by carrying out a study more than once. For there to be reliability, there must first be **replicability**. Similarity can be tested using statistical tests (Chapters 3, 4 and 5).

> **Study hint** It is often said that experiments are reliable when what is meant is that they are replicable. They are only reliable if they have been repeated and the same results have been obtained. Craik and Tulving's (1975) study about levels of processing is reliable because it has been successfully repeated. You should only say that experiments are reliable if they have been repeated and the same results found. It is safer to say that experiments are useful because they are replicable and can be tested for reliability.

■ Another strength of laboratory experiments is that a cause-and-effect relationship between variables can be shown. The laboratory experiment is the only way of doing this. This is because of the controls — if only the independent variable is altered, any change in the dependent variable must be due to the change in the independent variable.

■ A weakness of laboratory experiments is that the tasks that arise from manipulating the independent variable are not natural. Therefore, they might not be measuring 'real' behaviour. If the task is not natural, the results of the task lack validity, which means it is difficult to apply the results to the real world. This is a problem, because the idea is to find out about real behaviour *not* behaviour set up by a researcher. Consider the example of investigating whether recall of a list of 21 letters is affected by whether or not they are grouped — it is not often that we need to learn in this way in real life.

■ A second weakness is the unnatural setting. Not only are participants likely to be doing an unnatural task, they are in an unnatural environment. This means that there is no **ecological validity**. Occasionally, the laboratory experiment has valid findings because, even if the setting is not natural, the response is. This is true of some classical conditioning studies, for example measuring salivation in dogs. When food is brought in, a dog

Ecological validity is connected with the setting (ecology) of the participant/experiment.

will salivate to the same extent whatever the situation (Chapter 5). When the response is a reflex such as this, it is likely to be valid anywhere. However, laboratory experiments are not usually ecologically valid, particularly those in the cognitive approach.

■ A third weakness of laboratory experiments is that the strict control of all variables apart from the independent variable, and the use of experimental and control groups, mean that the experimenter will focus on the conditions of the independent variable and on which group participants are in. Everything else is equal, so the experimenter will focus on, for example, whether the participants are learning grouped (chunked) or randomised letters. That focus may be picked up by the participants. Something about the tone, gestures or facial expression of the experimenter might give them a cue or clue about what is expected and they could react accordingly. Such cues can lead to experimenter effects. One way to avoid this is to use a double-blind technique.

Field experiments: reliability, validity and experimenter effects

■ One strength of field experiments is that they take place in a more natural environment for the participant than do laboratory experiments. Therefore, field experiments are more likely to have ecological validity. The results relate more closely to situations in real life than those of laboratory experiments and may, therefore, be more valid.

■ Another strength is that they have most of the controls of a laboratory experiment. Cause-and-effect conclusions can often be drawn.

■ A weakness of field experiments is that it is harder to control the variables than it is in a laboratory because the setting is natural. Therefore, features of the setting can affect the results. So the results may not be valid with regard to the task; they may be caused by something other than the independent variable.

■ A second weakness is that they are more difficult to replicate than are laboratory experiments. The setting and circumstances are likely to have aspects that are unique even if, in general terms, the experiment can be set up again in a similar way. If a study is difficult to replicate then it is difficult to show that the results are reliable.

■ A third weakness is that field experiments can be affected by experimenter effects. With the setting not well controlled, it is even more difficult to make sure that participants do not react because of their expectations of the study, by deriving cues from the experimenter.

Natural experiments: reliability, validity and experimenter effects

■ One strength of natural experiments is that the independent variable is not manipulated, it occurs naturally. Therefore, the results come from a non-manipulated set-up and because of that are more valid with regard to the independent variable. For example, people either have television or not, whereas being allocated to one of two conditions to learn lists of words is not as valid ('real').

■ A second strength is that natural experiments often have ecological validity. Not only is the independent variable not manipulated but often natural experiments

are in a non-manipulated setting as well because the independent variable often involves the setting.

> **Study hint** Note that strengths and weaknesses of research methods are general, rather than specific. What is good or bad about a study might yet depend on the study, rather than the research methodology. When answering questions about strengths and weaknesses of research methods it is better, for example, to say 'A research method gathers more valid data than another method', than to say 'it gathers valid data'. Avoid statements that are too precise.

- One weakness of natural experiments is that there are often factors other than the independent variable that might affect the results. A natural experiment is likely to be in a situation that is going to happen anyway — for example the intro-duction of television. This could lead to other factors changing. It is difficult (perhaps impossible) to isolate the independent variable to find a cause-and-effect relationship.

- A second weakness of natural experiments is that because the independent variable is not manipulated by the researcher, the study might be difficult to replicate — for example, television can never again be introduced into a community for the first time. This does not apply to all natural experiments but it is the case that natural experiments are more difficult to replicate than labora-tory experiments, so reliability cannot be tested. If an experiment cannot be repli-cated, then reliability cannot be tested.

> **Study hint** Sometimes it is difficult to say whether a feature is a weakness or a strength. In your course you are asked to give strengths and weaknesses — in fact, these often depend on the study itself. It is easier for you to prepare clear strengths and weaknesses for a study and avoid discussion where there are 'it depends' factors. However, knowing the 'it depends' factors can be useful as it means that you understand the issues clearly.

- Another possible weakness is that, although a natural experiment may be less affected by experi-menter effects because the independent variable is naturally occurring, it is more difficult to use a double-blind technique because of the uncontrolled situation. It is possible that in the presence of experimenters, participants have expectations of what is wanted and that this could affect the results. On the other hand, it could be said that a double-blind technique is easier because people within the naturally occurring situation, rather than the experi-menter, may be able to collect the data. It rather depends on the actual study.

Table 2.4	*Strengths of the different types of experiment*	
Laboratory	**Field**	**Natural**
Good controls; replicable; reliability can be tested	More ecologically valid than laboratory experiments because they take place in natural settings	Independent variable occurs naturally, so valid because not artificially set up
Good controls; cause-and-effect relationship can be established	Fairly replicable because of experimental features	Tend to take place in a natural environment so likely to be ecologically valid

| Table 2.5 | Weaknesses of the different types of experiment |

Table 2.5 *Weaknesses of the different types of experiment*

Laboratory	Field	Natural
So controlled that tasks may not give valid results because they are not natural/real	Natural setting, so hard to control all factors, which means results may be less valid	Difficult to control variables because the independent variable is naturally occurring, making it difficult to isolate all factors that might affect results
Environment unnatural and controlled, so not ecologically valid	Hard to control because of natural setting, so may not be replicable	Hard to control for experimenter effects; using a double-blind technique is not straightforward because most are carried out in natural settings
Experimenter effects can mean results are not valid because there may then be bias	Experimenter effects can mean results are not valid because there may then be bias	

Examination-style questions

1a Outline the three types of experiment. *(9 marks)*

b For each type of experiment, explain one strength and one weakness. *(12 marks)*

2a Outline the three types of participant designs. *(9 marks)*

b For each design, explain two strengths and two weaknesses. *(12 marks)*

3a Give three studies that are laboratory experiments. For each experiment, identify the independent and dependent variables and whether the hypothesis is directional or non-directional. *(12 marks)*

Extension questions

1 Discuss when each type of experiment should be used and the relative values of each type of experiment to society and/or psychology. Use examples of studies in your answer. *(12 marks)*

2 Explain the links between a particular participant design and psychology as a science. In your answer, consider aspects of control and the aim to establish cause-and-effect relationships. *(12 marks)*

3 Discuss whether experiments are more valid or more reliable and why this is important. *(12 marks)*

Content

For the cognitive approach you have to know:

■ the levels of processing (LOP) model of memory and one other theory of memory of your choice

■ the cue-dependent theory of forgetting and one other theory of forgetting of your choice

Some other theories of memory and forgetting are suggested in the specification. Four of these theories are given here, to help you choose. *The fifth, the spreading-activation theory, is summarised here and covered in detail on the CD-ROM.*

First, five theories of memory are explained. These are:
- the multi-store model
- the levels-of-processing framework
- reconstruction theory
- the working-memory model
- the spreading-activation theory (*covered in detail on the CD-ROM*)

Second, four theories of forgetting are explained. These are:
- the theory of trace decay
- the cue-dependent theory
- interference theory
- displacement theory

The theories are evaluated by identifying strengths and weaknesses.

The multi-store model of memory

The multi-store model of memory is one of the choices in your course. It is explained here because some central ideas in other models have developed from it. The multi-store model explained here is based on Atkinson and Shiffrin (1968), but the basics of the other models from the same era are the same.

Capacity, duration and mode of representation

Three areas are studied in the multi-store model of memory. Researchers investigate:
- **capacity** — the size of the store
- **duration** — how long information remains in the store
- **mode of representation** (mode of storage) — the form in which information is stored

Encoding, storage and retrieval

Researchers investigate:
- **encoding** — how memories are encoded, which means how they are registered as memories
- **storage** — how memories are stored, which means how they remain as memories after they have been registered
- **retrieval** — how we retrieve memories when the output is needed

The concept of retrieval is important. We may have memories but, if we cannot access them, perhaps they are not true memories.

Explore Is a memory a memory if it cannot be accessed? We are likely to say, in that case, that we cannot remember. In cognitive psychology memory is studied as a separate topic from forgetting. Explore ideas around 'memory' and 'forgetting' and discuss whether these are two different ideas or not. For your course, however, treat 'memory' and 'forgetting' as being different.

The three main stores

The central idea of the multi-store model is that there are three stores of memory, which involve a flow of information. The model focuses clearly on information processing. First, there is the **sensory register**, which is where the information comes into the brain from the senses and is held for a short time. The information is in the store in the same format as it is received — for example, what is heard is stored as sound.

All the information from the senses goes into the sensory register but only a small amount is attended to. The rest is not registered. The information lasts in the sensory register for up to 2 seconds (see Figure 2.5). Perception can be thought of as seeing something *as* something; in the sensory register there is no attempt to perceive information *as* something, merely to receive it. From the sensory register, information that has been attended to passes to the short-term store. Any information not attended to is lost.

> When information is in the same form as it is received, it is said to be **modality specific.**

The second store is the **short-term store** (STS), often called short-term memory (STM). Short-term memory stores information in auditory form — by sound. Information can stay in the short-term memory for up to 30 seconds. From experiments, it seems that short-term memory can hold between five and nine items or chunks. If information is rehearsed in short-term memory, it passes into the long-term store (LTS) or **long-term memory** (LTM). Any information that is not rehearsed is lost from the short-term store.

The third store is long-term memory. Information can stay (potentially) in the long-term memory forever. Information is held largely in **semantic** form, which means it is held according to meaning. It can also be visually or acoustically stored. There can be a infinite amount of information stored in long-term memory.

Table 2.6 *The multi-store model summarised (adapted from Craik and Lockhart 1972)*

Feature	Sensory register	Short-term store	Long-term store
How information enters	Before attention is paid — comes from senses	To go to short-term store, needs attending to	Needs rehearsing to go to long-term store
How information is maintained	Not possible	Continued attention; rehearsal	Repetition; organisation
The form information is in	Literal copy of input	Phonemic (sound); probably also visual and maybe semantic	Mainly semantic; some auditory and visual
Capacity	Large, but only a small amount is attended to	Small	Limit not known
Information loss	Decay	Displacement; possibly decay	Possibly no loss; loss of accessibility by interference
Duration of trace	Up to 2 seconds	Up to 30 seconds	From minutes to years
Retrieval	Readout (can only read back what is received at that moment in time)	Probably automatic; items in consciousness can be retrieved	Needs retrieval cues; possibly uses a search process

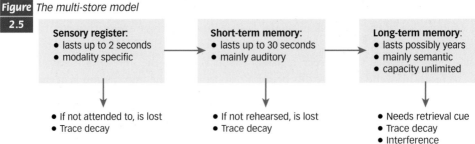

Figure 2.5 *The multi-store model*

Sensory register:
- lasts up to 2 seconds
- modality specific

Short-term memory:
- lasts up to 30 seconds
- mainly auditory

Long-term memory:
- lasts possibly years
- mainly semantic
- capacity unlimited

- If not attended to, is lost
- Trace decay

- If not rehearsed, is lost
- Trace decay

- Needs retrieval cue
- Trace decay
- Interference

Evaluation of the multi-store model of memory

There has been a great deal of experimental work based on the multi-store model of memory. From these studies, strengths and weaknesses of the model can be found.

Strengths

- The evidence supporting it has been found by experiment. Such studies are reliable because they have been repeated often and, being well controlled, they are replicable. The experimental research method is scientific and so a sound body of knowledge can be built up. So when studies such as that by Glanzer and Cunitz (1966) provided evidence for the model, this was strong evidence — because it was scientifically based. Glanzer and Cunitz (1966) carried out a study using word lists. They found that the first words in a list were recalled well, as were the last words, but that the middle words were not remembered well. They claimed that the **primacy effect** (the good recall of the first words) was because those words had been rehearsed and so were in long-term memory and accessible. The **recency effect** (the good recall of the last words) was because those words were still in consciousness in the short-term memory, so were recalled easily. The middle words were neither well rehearsed and in long-term memory nor in consciousness in short-term memory. Therefore, these words were the most easily forgotten.
- There is evidence for it from case studies that give physiological support. For example, the case study of Clive Wearing (Blakemore 1988) showed that there is an area of the brain (the hippocampus) which, if damaged, prevents new memories from being laid down. It appears that the hippocampus holds the short-term memory because a person with a damaged hippocampus can no longer build long-term memories. If there is no rehearsal, no new long-term memories, and a particular area of the brain is damaged, this suggests that when undamaged, this area of the brain fulfils that purpose.

Weaknesses

- Although case studies like Clive Wearing have suggested an area of the brain for short-term memory, another case study (Shallice and Warrington 1970) showed that a victim of a motorbike accident was able to add long-term memories even though his short-term memory was damaged. This goes against the multi-store model.

- It is hard to say what capacity means. Craik and Lockhart (1972) ask whether it is limited processing capacity or limited storage capacity. Short-term memory tends to take limited capacity as limited storage and holds that capacity is five to nine items. However, if words, rather than letters, are used in a span test, 20 items can be recalled. This shows that capacity needs to be defined more rigorously.
- Experiments used to test the multi-store model tend to employ artificial tasks — for example testing short-term memory using letters or digits. The findings may not be valid because, in real life, processing is rarely as isolated as these tasks suggest. The levels-of-processing theory holds that deeper processing gives better recall. Letters and digits would not involve deep processing, so are likely to give rise to 'short-term' recall.
- Craik and Lockhart (1972) suggest that the idea of primacy and recency effects being evidence for the multi-store model can be criticised because these effects can also be explained by the levels-of-processing framework. The primacy effect could be due to rehearsal and deep processing, because individuals know that they have to learn the words in the list. The recency effect could be because those words are in consciousness and rely on phonemic processing, which is Type 1 processing, which means processing in the same format as the information is 'received' in, in this case sound. The participant repeats those last words at the same level and although there is no trace, the words can be repeated back if this is carried out immediately. According to Craik and Lockhart (1972), this explanation fits the findings just as well as does the multi-store model.

Table 2.7 *Strengths and weaknesses of the multi-store model*

Strengths	Weaknesses
• Experiments such as the one by Glanzer and Cunitz (1966) support the model because the primacy and recency effects are explained by it	• The experiments that give evidence for the model use artificial tasks, which means that the results might not be valid
• Case studies such as that of Clive Wearing support the model; they give physiological support, e.g. the hippocampus may be an area for short-term memory	• Craik and Lockhart (1972) say that their levels-of-processing framework explains the primacy and recency effects just as well as the multi-store model does

The levels-of-processing framework

The model of memory specified for your course is the levels-of-processing framework for memory. This model arose because of what were perceived to be problems with the multi-store model. Craik and Lockhart (1972) presented the idea that memory depends on the **level of processing** of information, rather than being in different stores with different features.

Selective attention

Selective attention involves examining what we pay attention to, and why and how. Models of memory can draw on ideas about selective attention. The multi-store model states that the first store is a sensory register that receives information from

the senses ready for processing. Theories of selective attention also start at the point where information comes in via the senses. The theories continue by looking at how information is selected and attended to and what information is lost.

One feature of selective-attention models is that they require a limited-capacity central processor. This idea is important in the levels-of-processing framework for memory. No theory holds that humans have unlimited capacity for processing information. It is clear that theories of selective attention and theories of memory are not as separate as it might at first appear. The levels-of-processing framework suggests that information is either processed by repeating it in the same format (Type I processing) or is processed in different depths (Type II processing). It is the idea of depth of processing that is explored in Craik and Lockhart's framework. Type 1 processing is referred to as **primary memory**.

Explore Investigate theories of selective attention, but not in too much depth. This will help you to understand the levels-of-processing framework and also the spreading-activation model of memory (on CD-ROM). Broadbent's work is the best place to start. He looked at selective attention to help work in the field of aviation, so that important information, such as that needed by air-traffic controllers, was not missed.

The levels-of-processing framework for memory

Craik and Lockhart (1972) developed a framework for memory, rather than a theory. They explored what they saw as problems with store models and then linked their ideas to theories of selective attention. They held that memory is a by-product of the processing that occurs when attending to information, rather than that memory is a 'thing'.

Most models of memory agree that perception involves rapid analysis of information, that lines and angles and so on have to be detected and that there is then some sort of matching against 'stored abstractions from past learning' (Craik and Lockhart 1972). These are processing stages that are hierarchical in that there are different depths involved, with matching being the deepest level of processing. Elaboration coding is adding enrichment from experiences and previous understanding to something that is recognised. This is an example of deep processing.

The levels-of-processing framework is summarised in Figure 2.6. Note that the flow of information is not necessarily linear, even though it appears to be so in the diagram. For example, analysis may come first.

Figure 2.6 *The levels-of-processing framework*

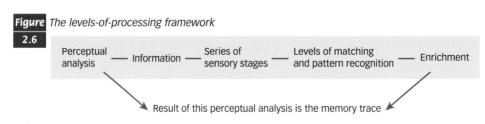

Coding, duration and persistence of the memory trace come from depth of analysis. Deeper analysis gives elaborate, longer-lasting and stronger traces. The depth of analysis is not hierarchical because it is a spread.

One argument is that existing cognitive structures allow the more meaningful material to be rapidly processed to a deep level and that meaningful material is also better retained. Depth comes from familiarity with the material, the processing time available and how the information fits with existing cognitive structures. There is a limited capacity processor, so if information is being recycled in the same form, there is little capacity left for other processing. Type I processing (maintaining the information in the same form) does not leave a trace, so there is no memory of this material. For it to be retained, material must be more deeply processed. Type II processing can improve study techniques; Type I processing cannot. Therefore, simply repeating the information in the same format without any further attention does not lead to learning. Only Type II processing, deeper analysis and rehearsal at this level improve memory performance.

| Table 2.8 | Summary of the levels-of-processing framework |

Feature	Explanation
Memory trace	Comes with depth of processing or degree of elaboration. No depth of processing means no memory trace
Deeper analysis	Leaves a more persistent memory trace
Rehearsal in primary memory	Holds information but leaves no memory trace
When attention is diverted	Information is lost at a rate that depends on the level of analysis

Evidence for the levels-of-processing framework

Hyde and Jenkins (1971) found that when participants carried out different tasks there was different recall. They asked participants to cross out vowels, to copy words or to judge something about the meaning of words. People remembered four times as many words when judging meaning.

It has been found in other studies that if participants are specifically asked to remember words, they do not do any better than participants who do not know that they will be asked to recall the words. The first type of task, in which participants are told that they will have to remember, is **intentional learning**. The second type of task, in which participants do not know that they will have to recall, is testing **incidental learning**. Participants were asked to carry out a task that involved using the meaning of words and they then had to recall the words without prior knowledge that this was a requirement. They did just as well as participants who knew that they were going to have to recall the words. This suggests that deeper processing, involving the meaning of words and/or past experience, leaves a memory trace that is as good as when people deliberately learn. This is evidence for the idea of levels of processing.

> **Practical** The study by Hyde and Jenkins (1971) could be adapted and carried out as your practical.

Craik and Tulving (1975) carried out a study to test the levels-of-processing framework (page 96). They found, amongst other things, that:

- having to process the look or structure of a word leads to the worst recall or recognition
- having to process what a word sounds like leads to better recall than when processing the structure of the word
- having to process the word for meaning leads to the best recall or recognition

This study, therefore, provides evidence for the levels-of-processing framework.

Study hint When making notes or learning material, add meaning for yourself — it will help you to recall. For example, the levels-of-processing framework could be 'LOP', the multi-store model could be 'MSM' and the spreading-activation model could be 'SAM'. Make up your own links so that you are adding meaning and are, therefore, likely to recall the material better.

Evaluation of the levels-of-processing framework

There are so many experiments in the area of memory research that one way of evaluating an idea is to put forward one of the other ideas as an alternative explanation. Here, some strengths and weaknesses of the levels-of-processing framework are suggested.

Practical The Craik and Tulving (1975) study could be adapted and carried out as your practical for the course.

Study hint In an exam, you can often give one weakness of a theory by saying that there is an alternative. For example, you could say that a strength of the levels-of-processing framework is that it explains the primacy and recency effects. You could go on to say that a weakness is that the multi-store model offers an alternative explanation for the findings of Glanzer and Cunitz (1966). Only use the 'alternative explanation' idea once, for 1 mark. If you use other alternative explanations you would be giving a list and would not be explaining the theory or framework given in the question. Similarly, do not explain the alternative explanation — you would be then answering a question about the alternative explanation, rather than the one set.

Strengths

- Evidence has shown it to be a useful explanation. Studies such as that of Hyde and Jenkins (1971) show that adding meaning when processing information does mean better recall or recognition. Craik and Tulving (1975) carried out a study to test the framework and found what was predicted by the model — that deeper processing gives better recognition.
- The framework links theories and studies of selective attention and perception with theories and research about memory. The cognitive approach examines the way that information is processed in the brain. The levels-of-processing framework looks at the whole process, rather than looking only at storage. In this way, the framework is more useful than, for example, the multi-store model. However, the spreading-activation model also takes into account the processes involved.

Weaknesses

- Craik and Lockhart (1972) pointed out that, when testing the framework, the longer time for the processing involved must be separated from the depth of processing. Often, using existing experience and elaboration takes longer. It is then difficult to conclude whether it is time taken or meaning added that leads to improved recall.
- Not only might the processing take longer, but it is also likely to require more effort from the individual. Therefore, depth of processing has to also be separated from effort used. Craik and Lockhart agree that 'depth' is hard to define; they talk about spread and elaboration as being 'depth'. If the term is not clear then the framework will not be clear, which is a weakness. Problems such as these indicate why the idea of levels of processing is, according to Craik and Lockhart, a framework and not a theory. This is perhaps a weakness when trying to make predictions from the concept.

Table 2.9 *Strengths and weaknesses of the levels-of-processing framework*

Strengths	Weaknesses
• There is evidence for the framework: Hyde and Jenkins (1971) and Craik and Tulving (1975) • It links research into memory with research into perception and selective attention; it focuses on information processing and the whole process; this means it is a stronger explanation than the multi-store model, because more studies can be explained by it	• Depth of processing also tends to mean more time spent processing; it might be that the time spent makes the memory stronger, not the depth of processing • There may be more effort involved in 'deeper' processing and the greater effort might account for the better recall; the term 'deep' is not well defined by Craik and Lockhart (1972); it could be time spent processing, effort involved or using past experiences and adding meaning

The spreading-activation theory of semantic processing

The spreading-activation theory of semantic processing is about memory, but as the name suggests it is mainly about processing, just as the levels-of-processing framework is about processing. The term 'semantic' refers to meaning, so the model is about processing meaning. The spreading-activation theory is explained by Collins and Loftus (1975) and came from a theory developed by Collins and Quillian (1969). 'Spreading' means that, as a search starts from one concept to find another, the search spreads out further and further until the answer is found. 'Activation' means that as the search spreads, it moves from one concept to another and activates them.

This theory is covered in more detail on the CD-ROM.

Reconstructive memory (Bartlett 1932)

Three models or frameworks for how memory might work have been covered. Your course suggests two more — **reconstructive memory** and **working memory**.

These are not covered in as much detail as the others. This does not mean that they are less interesting or less important. You have to study the levels-of-processing framework and one other theory, so you do not need detail for all five theories. However, if you choose reconstructive memory or working memory, then there is enough information given here.

Bartlett's idea that memory is reconstructive

Bartlett (1932) maintained that memory is not like a tape recorder. This idea has been taken up by other researchers — for example, Elizabeth Loftus agrees with Bartlett. The idea is that a memory is not perfectly formed, perfectly encoded and then perfectly retrieved. The levels-of-processing framework shows that coding and retrieval depend on how well an event is processed. The spreading-activation model suggests that memory depends on tracking down a concept and identifying it. The multi-store model suggests that memories are retrieved after a short time only if they are in the long-term store, and that that only happens if the material is attended to and rehearsed. With so many studies illustrating these sorts of processes, you can see that it is unlikely that a memory that is retrieved is exactly what was originally perceived. Bartlett's view starts from this idea.

Bartlett thought that the past and current experiences of individuals would affect their memory for events. There would be input, which would be the perception of an event. Then, there would be processing. This would include the perception and also the interpretation. Interpretation would involve previous experiences and **schemata**.

Schemata are ideas and scripts about the world — for example, you might have an 'attending a lesson' script or a 'going to the cinema' script. These scripts or schemata give you expectations and rules about what to do. You know, for example, that before you go in to watch a film you have to buy a ticket and you also expect to watch advertisements.

Schemata is the plural of schema.

Memory of an event involves information from specific traces encoded at the time of the event and ideas that a person has from knowledge, expectations, beliefs and attitudes. Remembering involves retrieving knowledge that has been altered to fit with knowledge that the person already has.

Evidence for memory being reconstructive

Bartlett thought about memory being reconstructive as when engaged in a game of Chinese whispers. In this game, someone invents a short story and whispers it to the next person, who whispers it to the next and so on. The story becomes changed along the way, often for it to make more sense to the person telling it. The final retelling can be completely different from the original.

Bartlett carried out a study using the idea of Chinese whispers. He used a Native American folk story, the *War of the Ghosts*. This story was unfamiliar to the participants and came from a different culture, so it did not fit in well with their existing schemata. He read the story to participants and then asked them to recall it. There were several recalls — soon after the telling, some time later and after a year. As time went on, the participants were able to recall less of the story, but it tended to make more sense.

The story became shorter and shorter — after about six recall sessions it was reduced from 330 words to 180. Participants altered the story. Bartlett found that people rationalised the parts that made no sense and filled in their memories so that they were recalling what was, to them, a sensible story.

This means that they reconstructed their memories of the story. Bartlett concluded that memory is reconstructive, rather than reproductive. Loftus has taken this idea and used it to show that eyewitness testimony is unreliable (page 147). She claims that eyewitnesses reconstruct their memories of an event to make it make sense. She showed how leading questions, such as using a particular verb, can manipulate memory. For example, if people are asked about two cars smashing into each other they 'remember' the cars going at a faster speed than if they are asked about two cars hitting each other. The verbs 'smash' and 'hit' lead to different memories of the same event because they mean different things to people. This study was carried out by Loftus and Palmer (1975).

> **Confabulation** means making up bits to fill in a memory so that it makes sense.
>
> **Rationalisation** means making something make sense.

> You will come across the Loftus and Palmer (1975) study again if you choose the criminological application in the second year of the course.

Evaluation of the reconstructive theory of memory

The evidence for the theory can be criticised, which means that the theory can be criticised.

Strengths

■ The evidence for the theory, first from Bartlett and his *War of the Ghosts* study and from Loftus who has carried out many studies on the unreliability of eyewitness testimony (page 147). Backing up the evidence is the idea of Chinese whispers, which many people have found works — people do change the story to make both more sense and different sense.

Practice 2.5

Try a game of Chinese whispers involving six to eight people. Make up a short story that is hard to make sense of and pass it round. See how it comes out. Then make up a story with a clear structure involving people or objects. At the end, examine how the people or objects were changed. Compare the outcomes of the two stories.

■ It can be tested by experimental method because the independent variable can be operationalised and measured. A story can have features that can be counted each time the story is recalled and the changes recorded. So, up to a point, the theory can be tested scientifically.

Weaknesses

- The study providing the evidence involves an unusual story that does not make sense to the participants. Therefore, it could be argued that they will alter it to make it make sense because they are being asked to retell the story. There could be demand characteristics, where the participant guesses what is intended. Therefore, the results of the study might not be reliable.
- It does not explain *how* memory is reconstructive. It takes one part of memory and describes what happens, rather than explaining it. The theory holds that memory is an active process, which is a useful contribution to the debate. However, it does not explain what that activity is, other than saying that schemata are used. The spreading-activation model attempts to explain the activity and how it works, which is more thorough and, therefore, perhaps more useful.

Table 2.10 Strengths and weaknesses of the theory of reconstructive memory

Strengths	Weaknesses
• There is much evidence for the theory: Bartlett (1932) and the work of Loftus on eyewitness testimony	• Bartlett's (1932) story did not make sense so participants may have altered it because of demand characteristics
• The theory can be tested experimentally	• The theory describes memory as reconstructive but does not deal with the processes

Working memory (Baddeley and Hitch 1974)

This modern model of memory is probably the most dominant model today. Referring back to the multi-store model (page 108), will help you to understand the **working-memory model**. The multi-store model suggests that there is a short-term store and a long-term store. The working-memory model focuses on the short-term store and on providing more information about short-term remembering than is given by the multi-store model.

The working-memory model

Baddeley and Hitch's (1974) original model of memory has the following components:

- a central executive that supervises the system and controls the flow of information
- a phonological loop that holds sound information
- a visuospatial scratch pad that deals with visual and **spatial information**

> **Spatial information** is about where things are situated in physical space. Doing a jigsaw and reading a map require spatial awareness.

The reason the original model has separate phonological and visuospatial systems, is that, according to Baddeley, if participants in an experiment are asked to do two tasks simultaneously that involve sound, they cannot do it. Similarly, people find it difficult to do two visual tasks at the same time. However, they can carry out simultaneously a visual task and a task involving sound. Therefore, the model was developed to say that the two systems are separate. The central executive is necessary to explain how tasks are allocated and how the systems are controlled. A test that requires an individual to perform two tasks simultaneously to compare performance with single-task conditions is called a **dual-task paradigm**.

Figure 2.7 *The working memory model*

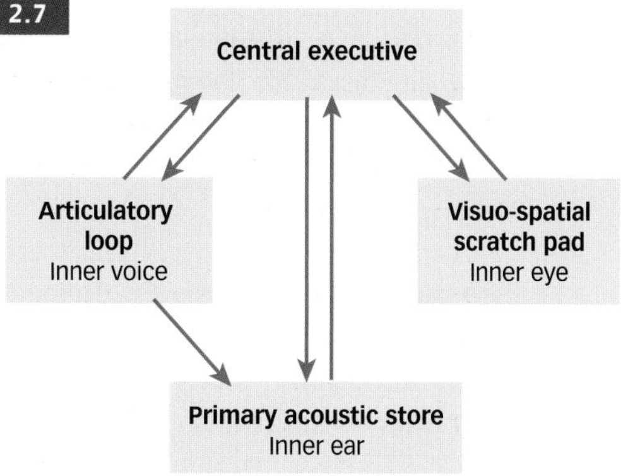

The central executive

The central executive puts information from different sources into one episode. It also coordinates other parts of the working memory. It moves between tasks, operates retrieval strategies and controls selective attention. It is a supervisory system that controls cognitive processes. Using the idea of information processing, the model suggests that there must be a system to control the flow and the processing.

The phonological loop

The phonological loop deals with auditory information:

- The short-term phonological store, or **primary acoustic store**, holds auditory memory traces. These decay rapidly.
- The articulatory rehearsal part, or **articulatory loop**, revives memory traces by rehearsing them.

Sound information goes directly into the primary acoustic store. This has been called the 'inner ear' and remembers sounds in their order. The articulatory system has been called the 'inner voice' because information is repeated to maintain the trace. Information in the phonological loop is assumed to last for about 2 seconds before it decays. Word lists and other items are stored as sound.

If you have studied the multi-store model, compare it with the working-memory model. The multi-store model maintains that information in the short-term store is mainly auditory and is held as sound and suggests that information in the short-term store does not last more than 2 seconds. So, the working-memory model is an expansion of the multi-store model and, in some ways, they support each other.

The visuospatial scratchpad

The visuospatial scratchpad:

- holds the information we see
- is used to manipulate spatial information, such as shapes, colours and the position of objects

Anything to do with spatial awareness, such as finding your way through a building or doing a jigsaw uses the visuospatial scratchpad. The visuospatial scratchpad could be called the 'inner eye'. The pad is divided into visual, spatial and perhaps kinaesthetic (movement) parts. It is thought that the pad is in the right hemisphere of the brain.

Social and Cognitive Psychology

The visuospatial scratchpad is divided into two parts:

- The visual cache stores information about form and colour.
- The 'inner scribe' deals with spatial and movement information. It also rehearses information and transfers it to the central executive.

The episodic buffer

In 2000, Baddeley added the episodic buffer to the working-memory model. The buffer provides time sequencing for visual, spatial and verbal information — for example, the chronological order of words or the sequence of pictures in a film. The episodic buffer might also bring in information from the long-term store.

Evidence for the working-memory model

Evidence for the phonological loop is that lists of words that sound similar are more difficult to remember than lists in which the words sound different. It is claimed that whether the words have similar meaning or not has little effect compared with whether they sound alike.

If participants are asked to learn a list of words, and at the same time to say something aloud, then they find the learning difficult. This is said to be because they are already using the phonological loop, so cannot do both the tasks simultaneously. The articulatory loop is being used to say something aloud and is not available for repetition of the words being learnt.

Evidence for the two parts of the visuospatial scratchpad — the visual cache and the 'inner scribe' — is that when two spatial tasks are carried out they are found to be more difficult than when undertaking one visual task and one spatial task There is also neurophysiological evidence. Scans show that tasks involving visual objects activate an area in the left hemisphere and tasks involving spatial information activate areas in the right hemisphere.

Evidence for an episodic buffer is that people with amnesia who could not lay down new memories in the long-term store could recall stories in the short-term store that contained a lot of information. This information was more than could be retained in the phonological loop.

Evaluation of the working-memory model

The working-memory model has strengths and weaknesses.

Strengths

- The model expands on the multi-store model, giving more information and refining it. Studies showed, for example, that some dual tasks were more difficult than others, which needed an explanation. The working-memory model explains such features of the memory system, introducing the ideas of an 'inner ear', an 'inner voice' and an 'inner eye'.
- The amount of research it has generated and is still generating. Studies within the model have led to refinements of the model. Research has not only been experimental; there is neurophysiological evidence for the model from brain scans. The model has been expanded, but still helps to explain the data.

Weaknesses

- The model has had to be added to as new findings are made. This means that the model itself was inadequate and was not a valid explanation of memory. The episodic buffer, which draws information from long-term memory, was an addition to the model and needs further explanation.
- The experiments tend to be artificial tasks, such as learning word lists and remembering stories. Such tasks depend heavily on either visual or sound information. In real life, tasks tend to involve many of the senses. It could, therefore, be said that the tasks mean that the findings lack validity.

Table 2.11 *Strengths and weaknesses of the working-memory model*

Strengths	Weaknesses
• There is evidence for the model — for example, simultaneously carrying out two tasks involving sound is difficult • The model has generated research, including linking with neuropsychological research	• The model has been added to to take account of results from new studies — for example, adding the episodic buffer; therefore, the original model was inadequate • Studies testing the model use experiments with artificial tasks, so results may lack validity

The trace-decay theory of forgetting

Memory is about what is remembered and forgetting is about what is not remembered.

You have to study the cue-dependent theory of forgetting and one other from interference theory, trace-decay theory and displacement theory. All the theories are covered, to help you choose. The **trace-decay theory of forgetting** is explained first, because it is relevant to the cue-dependent theory.

> **Study hint** Theories of memory and forgetting must link — for example, when forgetting is explained, the theory relies on what memory is thought to be. Be careful not to confuse the two topics. If you are asked about a theory of memory, do not provide a theory of forgetting. In psychology, the two topics are considered separately.

Introduction to the trace-decay theory of forgetting

The trace-decay theory of forgetting is best understood by recalling the multi-store model of memory in which there is a short-term store and a long-term store. Trace decay is a theory of forgetting that applies to both the short-term store and the long-term store.

The main point is that memories have a physical trace. Over time, this trace deteriorates until finally it is lost. It is thought that memories are stored in the brain, which means a structural change must occur. This is called an **engram**. Engrams are thought to be subject to neurological decay. As an engram decays, the memory disappears and forgetting occurs. One way of renewing the trace is to repeat and rehearse information, which reinstates the engram. It is thought that when something is first learned the trace is fragile, but that after further learning the engram becomes more solid and is less likely to be destroyed. The change from a cognitive process to an engram is a neurochemical one. In the biological approach you will study how neurochemicals work.

> **Explore** In 1949, Hebb set out the idea of an engram and what a memory is. Penfield (1891–1976) tried to help patients with epilepsy and during surgery identified places where memories are stored, which is evidence for the existence of engrams. Look up Hebb and Penfield and find their contribution to the trace-decay theory.

Evidence for the trace-decay theory of forgetting

Reitman (1974) and McKenna and Glendon (1985) carried out studies into trace decay. In one study, focusing on the short-term store, male students were shown a list of five words for 2 seconds and then had to listen for a faint tone over headphones. The tone was given after 15 seconds. The participants had to then try to recall the words. Word recall fell by 24% in the 15-second period before recall, when recall rate was compared with no 15 second gap.

The passage of time led to forgetting. This suggested that forgetting came about because of the decay of the trace. Listening for the tone prevented rehearsal and stopped new information from being thought about. Therefore, there was no rehearsal of the current material to renew the trace and no displacement by new material, so the trace in the short-term store must have decayed.

In a study focusing on the long-term store, shop and office workers volunteered to take part in a task to learn how to resuscitate someone (restart the heart). Their performance was measured up to 3 years later. After 3 years, recall of the technique was poor. The conclusions were that such skills need renewing to be remembered and that the memory trace in the long-term store had decayed. Since memory worsens over time, it is time that causes the trace to decay.

Evaluation of the trace-decay theory

The trace-decay theory of forgetting has both strengths and weaknesses.

Strengths

■ Physiological evidence supports the idea that there is a physical trace in the brain. This does not, however, prove that such a trace will decay. Hebb put forward the idea of an engram; Penfield provided evidence when he probed the brains of epileptic patients who were awake and found areas of the brain that held particular memories.

■ The focus on the physical aspects of memory. People with Alzheimer's disease seem to lose memories, rather than not being able to retrieve them. This seems to be a physical process. Therefore, the theory helps to explain forgetting in real-life situations, which suggests that it may be valid.

Weaknesses

■ In studies of memory loss in the short-term store, it is difficult to know whether new information has been attended to. Therefore, it is difficult to test only the trace-decay theory, without any suggestion that displacement could have caused the forgetting. So in the short-term store, it is difficult to test whether the trace has decayed or whether the memory cannot be retrieved for some other reason.

■ Although there is evidence that memories in the long-term store become inaccessible, there are some memories that are resistant to being forgotten and can be recalled after a long time. Flashbulb memories are those that are remembered clearly. Therefore, some memories seem to retain the trace. Bahrick and Hall (1991) do not agree that forgetting is caused by decay of the trace. They found that people can remember algebra that they learned at school and after practice can improve their algebraic skills. Therefore, the traces could not have been lost.

Table 2.12 *Strengths and weaknesses of the trace-decay theory of forgetting*

Strengths	Weaknesses
● It is backed by physical evidence — for example Penfield's work with epileptic patients ● It helps to explain forgetting in real situations such as in Alzheimer's disease, which means that it may be valid	● It is difficult to measure trace decay in the short-term store because there is the possibility that new information has displaced the material or that there has been interference ● Some memories are resistant to being forgotten and it is difficult to see why some traces would be more resistant to decay

The cue-dependent theory of forgetting (Tulving 1975)

The cue-dependent theory of forgetting applies to long-term memory, not to the short-term store. The theory states that forgetting occurs if the right cues are not available for memory retrieval. This suggests that memory depends on cues being available and that forgetting occurs when the cues are absent. This theory was put forward by Tulving (1975).

The main ideas of the cue-dependent theory

Tulving claims that there are two events necessary for recall:

■ a **memory trace** — information is laid down and retained in a store as a result of the original perception of an event

■ a **retrieval cue** — information present in the individual's **cognitive environment** at the time of retrieval that matches the environment at the time of recall

The argument of the cue-dependent theory is that a memory trace could only be activated selectively if there is a retrieval cue. Tulving says 'we remember an event if it has left behind a trace and if something reminds us of it'. He defines **forgetting** as 'the inability to recall something now that could be recalled on an earlier occasion'. For Tulving, forgetting is about the trace being intact but memory failing because the cognitive environment has changed — there is no appropriate cue to activate the trace. This is different from the trace-decay theory of forgetting, which holds that the trace itself has been lost. Tulving provided studies as evidence that the cue-dependent theory of forgetting is the most appropriate.

> **Study hint** When learning material, particularly when revising, provide yourself with cues to use when retrieving the material. For example, when making notes use headings; when testing yourself, give yourself the headings and try to recall the material. Keep the headings short so that they are clear cues.

Some studies as evidence for the cue-dependent theory

Study 1: Tulving and Watkins (1975)

Tulving and Watkins presented participants with pairs of related words. Some of the pairs were words with strong associations (e.g. bark–dog) and some were rhyming words (e.g. worse–nurse). The participants knew that they had to recall the right-hand word of the pair. In condition (1), participants were given the left-hand word and had to recall the right-hand word. Of the words in the associative condition 74% were recalled; 56% of the words in the rhyming condition were recalled. In condition (2), the researchers gave a different cue for the same words — for example, 'rhymes with grog' for 'dog' or 'doctor associated with' for 'nurse'. In condition (2), the participants recalled words that had been forgotten in condition (1). In condition (2), rhyming words obtained 22% of the words forgotten in condition (1); the associative condition resulted in recall of 30% of the forgotten words. Therefore, new cues were effective in obtaining 'forgotten' words. Even when an obvious cue fails (e.g. bark–dog), a new cue (e.g rhymes with grog) can retrieve the memory. The information was not lost in the sense of the trace having decayed.

Study 2: Tulving and Watkins (1975)

Participants were shown 28 five-letter words. Recall was tested without a cue or using two, three, four or five of the letters of the word (in the correct order). Suppose the target word had been 'grape'. Recall was tested without a cue, or with 'gr', 'gra', 'grap' or 'grape' as cues. It was found that the longer the cue, the better the recall. It seems that the trace is present, but the cognitive context is what helps recall. This is taken as evidence for the cue-dependent theory of forgetting.

Study 3: Light et al. (1972)

Light et al. (1972) carried out a study to see if forgetting is linked to cues at retrieval. They showed participants either words alone or words as part of meaningful sentences, one sentence at a time. Participants had to recall words with or without cues. There were three types of cue:

- homonyms, which are words that sound like the target words
- synonyms, which are words that mean the same as the target words
- words identical to the target words

The participants did not know that they would be tested, so that they would all learn the words in the same way. This acts as a control. The results are shown in Table 2.13. The numbers in the table are the proportion of words recalled from the list.

Table 2.13 Results of the study by Light et al. (1972)

	Identical-word cues	Homonyms	Synonyms	No cues
Single words	0.92	0.81	0.51	0.32
Words in sentences	0.92	0.83	0.40	0.18

It can be seen that when the cue for recall is the word, recall is very good (although it seems strange that it was not perfect). The next best cues are homonyms, followed by synonyms. The worst recall was when there were no cues. This suggests that forgetting might be because the cues relating to the cognitive environment are absent, as the cue-dependent theory of forgetting suggests. The probability of recall decreases down to 'no cues' in both conditions. With no cues and with synonyms as cues, recall of words in sentences is worse than recall of single words. Therefore, it is not just that cues about the cognitive environment help recall, but that different cues have different effects. If forgetting were due to trace decay, then whether or not the cues were different would have no effect.

Cues have been differentiated into:

- **context-dependent** cues — the situation or context is different from that at encoding
- **state-dependent** cues — the person's state or mood is different from that at encoding

Other studies that show cue-dependent forgetting

Godden and Baddeley (1975) examined the effect of cues in the environment on forgetting. The study and the results are explained in detail on pages 133–36.

Other studies of cue-dependent forgetting include those by:

- Smith (1985), who examined music as a cue to memory
- Schab (1990), who examined the smell of chocolate as a cue
- Eich et al. (1975) , who examined the effect of marijuana as a cue

The studies by Godden and Baddeley (1975), Smith (1985) and Schab (1990) were of context-dependent forgetting; that of Eich et al. (1975) was of state-dependent forgetting.

Unit 1

Smith (1985)

The results of the study by Smith (1985) are shown in Table 2.14. The numbers in the table are the average numbers of words recalled.

Table 2.14 Results of a study of context-dependent forgetting using music as a cue (Smith 1985)

Music at study	Mozart at test	Jazz at test	No music at test
Mozart	18.2	12.7	13.3
Jazz	11.2	20.8	8.5
No music	16.3	15.3	11.7

The highest recall (18.2 and 20.8) is when the music at study is the same as the music at test, which is what the cue-dependent theory of forgetting would predict.

Schab (1990)

The results of the study by Schab (1990) are shown in Table 2.15. The numbers in the table are the proportions of words recalled.

It can be seen that the highest recall (0.21) is when the cue at study is the same as the cue at recall.

Table 2.15 Results of a study of context-dependent forgetting using the smell of chocolate as a cue for retrieval (Schab 1990)

Study cue	Test cue: smell	Test cue: no smell
Smell	0.21	0.17
No smell	0.13	0.14

Eich et al. (1975)

The results of the study by Eich et al. (1975) are shown in Table 2.16. The numbers in the table are the averages of the number of words recalled.

Table 2.16 Results of a study of state-dependent forgetting using marijuana as a cue (Eich et al. 1975)

At study	At test: drug	At test: no drug
Drug	10.5	6.7
No drug	9.9	11.5

It can be seen that the higher numbers are when the study matches the test, either with a cue or without a cue.

Experimental procedures, showing that forgetting depends on lack of cues

Tulving explained many different experimental techniques and studies that show that forgetting is cue dependent. Some of his examples are covered here.

Studies of free recall

Free recall means that participants are allowed to recall the material in any order. Free-recall tests can mean giving participants a single word and asking them to recall it immediately (test 1). Or, a list can be given and the participants asked to recall the words in any order (test 2). This time some words will be forgotten. The question is why? According to the multi-store model (called the dual-store model by Tulving) the words go into the short-term store, which has limited storage capacity. The words can be recalled easily from the short-term store until displaced, or they can be transferred into the long-term store. With a list of words, forgetting is caused by displacement as new words arrive in the short-term store. A third type of free recall uses a retrieval cue when recall is required (test 3). This improves recall. The multi-store model does not explain this idea. For information not in the long-term store, cues would not help retrieval.

According to Tulving, the cue-dependent theory explains all three types of free-recall tests (tests 1, 2 and 3). The memory trace for each word is created rapidly when the word is perceived and encoded and the information present helps to retrieve it. The first test is easy because the information present at encoding is still there, so retrieval is guaranteed. The second test is more difficult because new information is present and retrieval information has gone. The third test replaces the retrieval information with cues, so recall is easier.

Retroactive interference tasks

Retroactive interference (see page 130) occurs when something that is learned gets in the way of previously learned material and inter-feres with those earlier memories. One study by Tulving and Psotka (1971) used lists of 24 words, with four words in each of six different categories.

Words in each category were grouped to encourage encoding by that category. The first group of participants learned one list, the second learned two lists and so on up to the sixth group, who learned six lists. All the lists were structured in the same way, but with different words and categories. Each list was shown three times in succession, at 1 second per word.

> **Practical** One list used by Tulving and Psotka (1971) was:
> - hut, cottage, tent, hotel
> - cliff, river, hill, volcano
> - captain, corporal, sergeant, colonel
> - ant, wasp, beetle, mosquito
> - zinc, copper, aluminium, bronze
> - drill, saw, chisel, nail
>
> You could replicate this study for your practical. You would also need to generate other lists.

A non-cued recall test was given (free recall: test 2) for each group of participants after each list had been presented.

After the last test and the last list, participants were asked to recall all the words from all the lists they had seen (test 2a). No cues were given. They then spent 10 minutes on another task and were asked to recall the words (test 2b), again with no cues. In the final test, they were given the names for the categories on their lists (cues) and were asked to list all the words (test 3).

The results were that the number of words forgotten from a list is related to the number of other lists shown between learning and recall. With non-cued recall, the number of words recalled fell from 15 words after one list to about eight words after five lists. With cued recall, the fall was less — for example, from 18 words after one list to 16 words after five lists.

It seems that with free recall and no cues there is interference from the other lists. However, with cued recall, the effects of interference are cancelled. This suggests that forgetting is reversible — it is not just that a memory trace is lost. The cue-dependent

theory suggests that as the number of lists grows, the retrieval environment is being moved away from. Using the category headings as cues reinstates the retrieval environment, so there is less forgetting. Therefore, this study supports the theory that forgetting is cue dependent.

Failure of recognition

Other studies suggest that lack of retrieval cues explains forgetting. For example, in the study by Tulving and Thomson (1973) there were four different tasks:

(1) Participants were shown pairs of words and asked to remember the second word in the pair — the target word.
(2) Participants were given a word close to the target word and asked to generate four words with similar meaning. Their generated words often included the target word.
(3) Participants looked at the list they had generated and identified the target word.
(4) Finally, they were given the cue word — the first in the pair — and asked to recall the target word (the second word of the pair).

Participants did better with cued recall (the fourth task) than they did in recognising the word that they were supposed to remember from the lists that they had generated. Cued recall helped with recognition.

Evaluation of the cue-dependent theory of forgetting

There are strengths and weaknesses of the cue-dependent theory of forgetting.

Strengths

■ The theory accounts for many instances of forgetting and there is much evidence to support it. Tulving points out how the cue-dependent theory explains forgetting better than do, for example, trace decay and interference.
■ The idea is testable in a way that trace decay is not. Cues can be given in experiments to see if they aid recall. If they do, it is assumed that lack of cues is what causes forgetting. Experiments can be set up easily to test this idea because cues are tangible and measurable. The memory trace is not measurable in the same way; neither is interference nor displacement.

Weaknesses

■ The experiments use artificial tasks. Even though there are some tasks more related to real life, for example the diving study by Godden and Baddeley (1975), the tasks usually involve learning lists of words and categories. This can be criticised as lacking validity.
■ Although it might be accepted that retrieval cues are necessary for remembering, Tulving agrees that there is also a memory trace. The theory may only account for some types of forgetting that occur when words are being learned. There might be other types of forgetting associated, for example with the memory trace.

Table 2.17	Strengths and weaknesses of the cue-dependent theory of forgetting	
Strengths	**Weaknesses**
• This theory accounts for forgetting in different tasks. There are many supporting studies • The idea is testable because the retrieval environment can be replicated	• Tasks are artificial, so the results might lack validity • It may only account for some forms of forgetting

Displacement as a theory of forgetting

The theory that displacement causes forgetting can be understood by reference to the multi-store model of memory. The idea is that there is a short-term store where information is held for a short time (up to about 30 seconds). It is either rehearsed there, so that the information goes into the long-term store, or is lost. The theory of displacement as a reason for forgetting is that the rehearsal loop in the short-term store has a limited capacity — perhaps nine items or fewer. If material is being rehearsed in the short-term store it is possible that, before a bit of information has gone into the long-term store, it could be displaced in the rehearsal loop by a new bit of material. The old bit of material is lost — in other words, it is forgotten.

Evidence for displacement as a theory of forgetting

The ideas of the primacy and recency effects come from the multi-store model of memory:

■ The primacy effect is that information learned first is quite well remembered, probably because it has gone to the long-term store through the rehearsal loop.
■ The recency effect is that information that is learned last is quite well remembered, probably because it is still in the rehearsal loop and so is available for immediate recall.
■ Information from the middle is not well recalled. This is probably because it did not go from the rehearsal loop into the long-term store, but was displaced by new material in the loop and was lost, i.e. forgotten. This is evidence for the idea of displacement in the short-term store.

Waugh and Norman (1965) tested this idea. They read a list of letters to participants. After hearing the list, the participants were told one of the letters and they had to try to remember the subsequent letter. For example, if the list was 'B P S T J F A O N' and the researchers called out 'T', the participants had to say 'J'. They found that displacement did seem to occur. However, Glanzer et al. (1967), although they thought that displacement was a factor in forgetting, also thought that decay caused forgetting. This was because there is a time delay in experiments — the longer the time before recall, the greater the forgetting. This forgetting could not be displacement alone because displacement would cause the same degree of forgetting, whatever the time delay between learning and recall. Therefore, displacement alone does not explain forgetting.

Evaluation of the displacement theory of forgetting

There are strengths and weaknesses of the displacement theory.

Strengths

- The theory fits with the multi-store model of memory and the working-memory model. This is because both these models suggest a loop where information is rehearsed before being stored in the long-term store. If there is a loop with limited capacity (the multi-store model suggests up to nine items) then it makes sense to say that new material displaces material already in the loop. This theory of forgetting supports two models of memory that are themselves supported by a great deal of evidence. This, in turn, is support for this theory of forgetting.
- It is tested by experiments that are well controlled and, therefore, yield information about cause and effect. The experiments are replicable and can be tested for reliability. Therefore, displacement is tested scientifically, which is a strength.

Weaknesses

- The theory is difficult to operationalise. What is taken to be displacement could be interference. The information in the rehearsal loop could be written over, which is displacement. However, it could be that the incoming new information interferes with the information being rehearsed. This would be interference, rather than displacement.
- It is tested using artificial tasks, such as lists of letters. This means that what is being tested may not be valid because it is not a real-life task.

Table 2.18 *Strengths and weaknesses of the displacement theory of forgetting*

Strengths	Weaknesses
• It suggests that there is a rehearsal loop in the short-term store, which is a feature of both the multi-store model and the working-memory model; it links with those memory models, which are supported by much evidence	• It is difficult to measure displacement. The idea of new items replacing old ones in the rehearsal loop could also be explained by interference
• It has been tested by experiment, giving cause-and-effect relationships. Experiments have been replicated and appear to be reliable	• Tasks used in experiments are artificial and may lack validity

Interference theory of forgetting

The theory that interference causes forgetting differs from the theory of displacement in that it says that an item gets in the way of another item, rather than displacing it. Peterson and Peterson's (1959) study (pages 136–39) investigated interference in the short-term store. However, the interference theory of forgetting is usually focused on the long-term store.

There are two types of interference:

- **Proactive interference** is when something learned earlier interferes with current learning.

- **Retroactive interference** is when something learned later gets in the way of something learned previously.

For example, suppose you learn Spanish and subsequently French. If learning French stops you remembering the Spanish word for something, then that is retroactive interference. If your knowledge of Spanish interferes with your ability to learn French, then that is proactive interference.

Study hint Think of 'pro' as 'before' — what was learned before gets in the way. Think of 'retro' as 'back' — what is learned now gets in the way (interferes going backwards).

Evidence for the interference theory of forgetting

To find out if interference is a cause of forgetting, **paired associate tasks** are used. These are also used to test cue-dependent forgetting. Participants have to remember pairs of words. For recall, they are given one word from the pair and are asked to recall the other. When testing interference, participants are given one set of pairs to learn, followed by a second set. The first word of each pair in each set is the same. For example, one set could include table–chair and the other set could include table–stool. Participants become confused between the two lists. It is said that this is caused by interference.

Jenkins and Dallenbach (1924) carried out an experiment to test the idea that interference causes forgetting. They thought that what is learned later will interfere with what people have already learned. Participants were given ten nonsense syllables (for example, BOH or INJ) to learn. Some participants slept after the learning and others carried on with their everyday routines. Those who stayed awake did not remember as much as those who slept — there was more forgetting. The researchers claimed that this was because sleeping had not caused interference whereas the day's activities had and that interference had caused forgetting.

Study hint When evaluating a theory, research evidence can be used to support or refute it. Therefore, Jenkins and Dallenbach's study can be used as a strength of the interference theory of forgetting because its findings are consistent with the theory.

Evaluation of the interference theory of forgetting

As with all theories of memory and forgetting, there are strengths and weaknesses of the interference theory.

Strengths

- There is much evidence to support the theory. Different lists of words are used with participants and what they learn first does interfere with what they learn second. Jenkins and Dallenbach (1924) found that when participants had a normal day after learning, their daily activities interfered with their learning. They concluded this because the control group of participants, who slept rather than being active, remembered more.
- The evidence comes from experiments, which are controlled and so yield cause-and-effect conclusions. This scientific approach to study is rated highly because

firm conclusions can be drawn. It also means that studies are replicable and can be tested for reliability.

Weaknesses

- The theory describes a feature of forgetting in memory experiments, where similar tasks make remembering difficult, and it is thought that this is because of interference. However, it does not explain *how* this happens. The problem is separating the idea of interference from displacement or trace decay. It is difficult to show that displacement causes the loss of recall from the short-term store and not that the memory trace has simply decayed or that interference from a new set of information (rather than displacement by that new information) has caused the memory loss.

- The studies tend to use word lists and artificial tasks. In real life it is not usual to do only one thing at once and many tasks are carried out quickly. It is not likely, therefore, that interference accounts for all forgetting, so the conclusions may not be valid. Solso (1995) says that the tasks carried out to test interference theory, for example learning nonsense syllables, would not occur in real life.

- The effect of interference disappears when participants are given cues. Therefore, it seems that the memory trace was present, but could not be retrieved. This goes against the idea of interference as an explanation for forgetting.

Table 2.19	*Strengths and weaknesses of the interference theory of forgetting*

Strengths	Weaknesses
• There is much evidence to support the theory, e.g. Jenkins and Dallenbach (1924) • It has been tested by experiment, giving cause-and-effect relationships. Experiments have been replicated and appear to be reliable	• It is hard to separate interference from displacement and trace decay; it can be shown that interference seems to happen but not why this happens or what occurs • Tasks used in experiments are artificial and may lack validity

Examination-style questions

1   Describe two theories of memory.   *(10 marks)*

2   Compare two theories of forgetting.   *(8 marks)*

3   Evaluate one theory of memory.   *(5 marks)*

4   Explain why revision works best if strategies are used to add meaning to the material.   *(6 marks)*

5   Explain why people forget more as time passes, but can still remember some events very clearly.   *(6 marks)*

Extension questions

1   Discuss why people forget.   *(12 marks)*

2   In your opinion, which of the theories of memory that you have studied explains memory best? Give reasons for your answer.   *(12 marks)*

Studies in detail

The main study for the cognitive approach is that by Godden and Baddeley (1975) of divers and cue-dependent forgetting. You then have to choose one other study from:

- the role of interference (Peterson and Peterson 1959)
- levels of processing (Craik and Tulving 1975)
- levels-of-processing effects on age (Ramponi et al. 2004) (*covered in detail on the CD-ROM*)

> **Study hint** When studying the levels-of-processing framework in the content section you are likely to have covered Craik and Tulving's (1975) study and when studying the cue-dependent theory of forgetting you are likely to have covered Godden and Baddeley's (1975) study. For the studies in detail section you have to examine further the Godden and Baddeley study. You could choose to study Craik and Tulving (1975) in detail and not cover Ramponi et al. (2004) or Peterson and Peterson (1959). However, it is useful to explore beyond just what you need. It is recommended that you read through the other studies even if you do not learn them in detail for the exam.

Godden and Baddeley (1975)

Godden and Baddeley (1975) is the main study for the cognitive approach and connects with the cue-dependent theory of forgetting. You must know this study.

Aims

The aim of the Godden and Baddeley (1975) study was to investigate the effect of environment on recall. In particular, they wanted to examine the role of retrieval cues. They looked at **context cues**, which are cues about the environment, rather than cues within the individual, which are **state cues**. Their aim was to see if recall was better when the learning context was present at recall. They chose the underwater environment and compared it with an on-shore environment. This was because these two natural environments differ strongly. Their aim was also to carry out a study about context-dependent forgetting that was not a laboratory study, but had more ecological validity.

Procedure

Divers were asked to learn words both on land and underwater. The words were then recalled both on land (dry) and underwater (wet). There were four conditions:

- 'dry' learning and 'wet' recall
- 'dry' learning and 'dry' recall
- 'wet' learning and 'dry' recall
- 'wet' learning and 'wet' recall

The hypothesis was that 'wet' learning and 'wet' recall and 'dry' learning and 'dry' recall would both result in more words being recalled than in either of the other

conditions. This was because it was thought that when learning and recall were in the same context, recall would be better because of the presence of context-dependent cues.

There were 18 diving-club participants, 13 male and five female. The lists each had 36 unrelated words of two or three syllables chosen at random from a word book.

The word lists were recorded on tape. The researchers used two Diver Underwater Communication (DUC) devices, so that the divers could hear the taped words and instructions. There was a practice session because the divers had to learn to breathe out, breathe in and hold their breath before each group of three words, because otherwise their breathing would have hampered their hearing of the words. When the divers were learning a list, the lists were presented twice. After the second presentation of the list, the divers heard 15 numbers that they had to write down. This was to stop words remaining in short-term memory. All participants experienced all four conditions, so it was a repeated measures design. There were at least 24 hours between conditions.

The experiment was carried out in Scotland. In all sessions, the participants were wet and cold because each condition was at the end of their diving day (they were on a diving holiday). The dry environment was when they were sitting by the water with their gear still on (face masks up). The wet environment was when they were 20 feet below the surface, with weights helping them to sit on the bottom.

Results

Words learned underwater were recalled best underwater and words learned on land were recalled best on land. Those who recalled words on land recalled 37% of the words learned on land compared with 23% of the words learned underwater. Those who recalled words underwater recalled 24% of words learned on land compared with 32% of words recalled underwater. The results are shown in Table 2.20. The numbers in the table are the average number of words recalled from the list.

The mean values for 'dry' and 'dry' (13.5 words out of 36) and the mean average for 'wet' and 'wet' (11.4 words out of 36) are much higher than the means obtained when the context for recall differed from the learning context.

Table 2.20 Results of the study by Godden and Baddeley (1975)

Study environment	Test environment: dry	Test environment: wet
Dry	13.5	8.6
Wet	8.5	11.4

Conclusions

Godden and Baddeley point out some problems with the study. Issues include:

- The divers were on holiday and were volunteers, so it was not possible to use the same setting each time because each day's diving was in a different place.
- They could not control either the time of day or the weather. Therefore, the study was not carried out on four consecutive days as originally planned.

There were other difficulties:

- In the underwater condition, there could have been cheating because the researchers could not observe the participants. However, the researchers thought that cheating did not occur because:
  - the underwater recall would then have always been better, and it was not
  - the diving partner would have been aware of any cheating
  - the participants were medical students who understood the importance of instructions and procedures
- When the divers were in a different context for recall than for learning, they had to change situation. This did not happen when they remained in the same context for both learning and recall. Moving from one situation to the other could have led to the poorer recall.

Godden and Baddeley wanted to examine the latter possibility, so they carried out a second study, with similar procedures, involving 18 participants. This time, for the condition when the learning and recall contexts were both on land:

- the divers went in and out of the water between learning and recall — the disrupted condition
- the divers did not go in and out of the water between learning and recall — the non-disrupted condition

The results of this study were that the mean number of words recalled was 8.44 for the non-disrupted condition and 8.69 for the disrupted condition. These recall figures are so similar that it was concluded that the disruption of moving context would not have caused the difference in results in the first experiment. It is interesting that in the first experiment the mean number of words recalled when the learning and recall both took place on land was 13.5, whereas in the second experiment it was only 8.44. Godden and Baddeley thought that this was because there was more background noise in the second experiment and because these participants were less used to testing.

They concluded that the environment in which recall takes place is important, possibly because cues from that environment help the recall by linking to cues at the time of encoding. It was thought that context acts as a cue and that when forgetting occurs it is because the context was absent. Recall is better if the original learning environment is reinstated and the results are not likely to be due to disruption between learning and recall. They also emphasised that these results were found in a real environment, not in a laboratory situation.

Evaluation of the Godden and Baddeley (1975) study

The study needs to be evaluated in terms of strengths and weaknesses.

Strengths

- The study is an experiment with strong controls, including the times of the learning and the recall, and the intervals between the conditions. The situation is set up clearly and the context cues are clear. Therefore, the study is replicable and

the findings are reliable. They themselves replicate the study to an extent, although it is noticeable that different results were obtained. The study is detailed.

■ Even though it is an experiment and so rather artificial, the participants were actual divers, who were used to diving and carrying out tasks underwater, if not learning lists of words. The environment they were in was not unfamiliar, so there might have been some ecological validity. This strength was pointed out by Godden and Baddeley and was a deliberate choice.

Weaknesses

■ The two environments — land and underwater — are so different and the task was unnatural. We do not normally perform such a task in such different environments. The conclusions, therefore, may not be valid. The situation was fairly natural, so there was ecological validity, but the tasks were not natural. So, in this sense, perhaps the study was not valid.

■ The results show a large percentage of forgetting even when the context for recall was the same as the context for learning. Therefore, there must be some other explanation for forgetting. This is not so much a weakness of the study as a weakness of the conclusions.

Table 2.21 *Strengths and weaknesses of the Godden and Baddeley (1975) study*

Strengths	Weaknesses
• It was an experiment with clear controls, so replicable; this means it can be tested for reliability and is a scientific study	• The situation was artificial and the contexts were very different; this means the results may not be valid
• The environment was familiar to the participants, who were divers, so there was some ecological validity	• The results showed a lot of forgetting even when the context for encoding and recall were the same; therefore, context dependency cannot be the only reason for forgetting

Peterson and Peterson (1959)

Peterson and Peterson (1959) is a useful study because it relates to the multi-store model of memory, which you may have chosen as your second memory theory.

Aims

The study is about how information is acquired by the long-term store. In particular, it examines the time that passes between repetitions. The multi-store model suggests that, if there is rehearsal, material passes into the long-term store from the short-term store. Peterson and Peterson (1959) aimed to look at the effect of passage of time on rehearsal to see if this affects whether material is in the long-term store or not. So their aim is to look at the effect of passage of time on the retention of items.

Procedure for experiment 1

Experiment 1 tests recall of individual items after several different short time intervals. There were 24 participants, who were all students on an introductory psychology course. The materials were 48 consonant syllables not associated with each other and 48 three-digit numbers from a random-numbers table. A number was given to the participants after each presentation of a syllable and they had to count backwards from it. This meant there was continual verbal activity, which would minimise rehearsal. The numbers were given to prevent any other interference.

- The experimenter spelled out a syllable and then gave a three-digit number.
- The participant counted backwards from the number.
- A signal flashed and the participant had to then try to recall the syllable.
- The timer was activated from the moment the three-digit number was given. The timer generated the signal to recall.
- The time between the signal and recall — the **latency period** — was recorded. This was the time it took for the participant to respond.
- The time between when the participant started counting backwards and the signal being given for recall is the **recall interval** and is the **independent variable**.

There were standardised instructions for the participants. There were two practice trials and the experiment was then carried out eight times at each recall interval. The recall intervals were set at 3, 6, 9, 12, 15 and 18 seconds. Each syllable was used only once with each participant. There were other controls — for example, no two successive syllables had a letter in common.

Results of experiment 1

The data showed that the longer the latency period — up to about 8 seconds — the more syllables were recalled. If the latency period was any longer, recall did not improve. The 3-second recall interval led to the best recall, followed in order by the other recall intervals. The longer the recall interval, the lower the recall.

Procedure for experiment 2

When the researchers examined the results of experiment 1, they concluded that repeating the stimulus would improve recall, because a shorter time between learning and recall leads to the best recall. It seemed that 'forgetting should proceed at differential rates for items with different numbers of repetitions'. Repetition either strengthens the memory trace or postpones the onset of decay of the trace. This is tested in experiment 2.

There were 48 student participants. Half had to repeat the stimulus aloud, until stopped by being given the number from which to count backwards. This was the 'vocal' group. The others were not told what to do in the gap between the presentation of the syllable and the instruction to recall. This was the 'silent' group.

- Both groups had the same recall intervals, during which they either rehearsed (the vocal group) or had the choice of rehearsing or not (the silent group). If there was different recall for the two groups, this would be taken to mean a failure to rehearse by the 'silent' group.
- Both groups were given a number to count backwards from to give the time to stop rehearsing (or at the end of the silent period).
- Recall intervals were 3, 9 and 18 seconds.

- A third of the occasions they were given no rehearsal time, a third of the occasions they had 1 second to rehearse and a third of the occasions they had 3 seconds to rehearse. A rehearsal was taken to be 1 second.
- Participants were assigned in order of appearance to a randomised list of conditions.
- There were six practice presentations.

Results of experiment 2

The results are summarised in the Tables 2.22 and 2.23. For all the participants, the shorter the recall interval, the better was the recall. This was expected from experiment 1. However, those in the 'vocal' group had better recall than those in the 'silent' group for the 3-second rehearsal, but not when there was either no rehearsal time or 1-second rehearsal time. Comparison of zero rehearsal time with 3-seconds rehearsal time for the 'vocal' group has a $p \leq 0.01$ significance level, indicating a significant difference. However, for the silent group, there is no significant difference between the zero-second gap and the 3-second gap.

Table 2.22 *Proportions of items correctly recalled by the vocal group in experiment 2 of the study by Peterson and Peterson (1959)*

Rehearsal time (seconds)	Recall interval: 3 seconds	Recall interval: 9 seconds	Recall interval: 18 seconds
3	0.80	0.48	0.34
1	0.68	0.34	0.21
0	0.60	0.25	0.14

Table 2.23 *Proportions of items correctly recalled by the silent group in experiment 2 of the study by Peterson and Peterson (1959)*

Rehearsal time (seconds)	Recall interval: 3 seconds	Recall interval: 9 seconds	Recall interval: 18 seconds
3	0.70	0.39	0.30
1	0.74	0.35	0.22
0	0.72	0.38	0.15

Some differences may have occurred because the study used independent groups, so there could be participant variables. However, it seems that there is a differential rate of forgetting, with the 18-second recall interval producing the poorest recall for both groups. Every time there was a 3-second gap in which to either rehearse or not, the vocal group did better. The longer the recall interval, the poorer was the recall.

> **Study hint** You will learn about significance levels later in your course. A probability of $p \leq 0.01$ means that 1 in 100 times it might be wrong but 99 times of out 100 it is likely to be right. Therefore, this is a very positive result.

Conclusions

The results provide evidence that repetition aids recall. This could be evidence that a rehearsal loop is used, as predicted by the multi-store model. The study worked within the short-term store and found evidence of forgetting, which could show either trace decay or interference. Repetition may have improved recall or what happened during the 'silent' period may have led to forgetting.

Evaluation of the study by Peterson and Peterson (1959)

As with any study, results should be evaluated with strengths and weaknesses in mind.

Strengths

- Careful controls were used. For example, the same letters were not repeated in consecutive trials and the recall intervals were the same for all participants. The study is repeatable, so it can be tested for reliability.
- Two experiments were carried out and the results reinforce each other. This means that the results are likely to be reliable, because they have been repeated and the same results found. In both experiments, the longer the recall interval, the lower was the recall.

Weaknesses

- It was an experiment so the independent variable had to be operationalised. This means that 'real' recall is not represented. The participants recalled syllables, not real words. It is not often that something as clear as this is done, repeated and then recalled. Therefore, the validity of the study can be questioned.
- The conclusion is not clear. What did the 'silent' group do in the time before they had to count backwards? They may have rehearsed, although the difference in the results suggests that they did not, because their recall was not as good. However, it means that the conclusion is either that repetition helped recall or that whatever the 'silent' group did made recall worse. It is not possible to know which of these is the case.

Table 2.24 *Strengths and weaknesses of the study by Peterson and Peterson (1959)*

Strengths	Weaknesses
• The controls mean that the study can be replicated, so reliability can be checked • By doing two experiments the researchers replicated their own study and the results show that the longer the recall interval, the poorer is the recall; the results are likely to be reliable	• The experiment operationalises the task, which is artificial, so its validity can be questioned • The conclusion is not clear; it might be that repetition helps recall or it might be that what the 'silent' group did made recall worse

Craik and Tulving (1975)

Craik and Tulving (1975) is a useful study because it connects with the levels-of-processing framework, which is the main theory of memory. The levels-of-processing framework looks at the processes of memory and information processing, not at the structure. It examines attention, encoding, rehearsal and retrieval, not duration, capacity and mode of representation.

Aims

The main aim of the study was to test the levels-of-processing framework, which claims that the best recalled material is that which has been processed for meaning.

The general aim of the study was to see if the **durability** of a memory trace comes from the depth of processing.

> **Durability** of a memory trace is how long the memory trace lasts.

Forgetting occurs when the memory trace has gone. If the levels-of-processing framework is correct, then the memory trace is an automatic by-product of cognitive operations. More specifically, the aim is to see whether material that is more deeply processed is recalled better. Depth of processing means a greater degree of semantic (meaning) involvement.

In order to operationalise depth more clearly, a further aim was to see if deeper processing meant processing for a longer time. This is because 'deep' means 'meaningfully processed' and 'meaningfully processed' means 'deep'. Craik and Tulving (1975) recognise that this is not helpful and they suggest that, unless the material is very familiar, deep processing means a longer time spent processing.

Therefore, the aims of the study are:

- to see if semantic processing leads to better recall and recognition
- to see if deeper processing means a longer time processing

Procedure

In the experiments that make up the main study, participants were put into situations where they used different depths of processing:

- For **shallow encoding**, they were asked questions about the script itself. This is **structural analysis**.
- For **intermediate depth** encoding, they were asked questions about rhyme. This is **phonemic analysis**.
- For **deep level encoding**, they were asked whether a word fits into a particular semantic category. This is **semantic analysis**.

The tasks involved are summarised in Table 2.25.

| Table 2.25 | A summary of the tasks in the study by Craik and Tulving (1975) |

Level of processing	Explanation
Shallow encoding	Structural (what it looks like) analysis of a word, such as judging the script in some way (e.g. is the word in capital letters?)
Intermediate encoding	Phonemic (sound) analysis of a word such as whether it rhymes with another word (e.g. does dog rhyme with hog?)
Deep encoding	Semantic (meaning) analysis of a word such as whether it fits into a certain category (e.g. does a dog have two legs?)

After the encoding phase, there was an unexpected recognition or recall task.

All ten experiments used the same basic procedure. Participants were tested individually and were told that the experiments were about perception and reaction time. A **tachistoscope** was used. This device allows an image to be displayed on a screen. The experimenter can flash words,

> Researchers used **tachistoscopes** before computers were available.

letters or other stimuli onto the screen for a short time in sequence. The time the stimulus is exposed and the time between stimuli can be controlled.

Different words were shown, one at a time, for 200 **milliseconds**. Before the word was shown, participants were asked a question about the word. The question led to different processing of the word, from shallow (the appearance of the word) to relatively deep (the meaning of the word). In some experiments, the participant read the question on a card; in other experiments the question was read out to the participant. Then the participant looked into the tachistoscope.

A **millisecond** is one-thousandth of a second.

Answers to the questions were given using a 'no' response key with one hand and a 'yes' response key with the other. There was a 'ready' signal, then the word, followed by the response. For example, participants were asked: 'Is the word an animal name?', then shown the word 'tiger'. They then pressed a response key. After some trials, participants were unexpectedly given a recognition test. The hypothesis was 'memory performance on a recognition test would vary systematically with depth of processing'. A more detailed hypothesis was that it would take longer to answer deeper level questions but there would be a more elaborate memory trace and, therefore, higher recognition and recall. Therefore, the reaction time from question to answer was also measured.

Three types of questions were asked at encoding:
- The structure of the word was tested by asking if the word was printed in capital letters.
- The phonemic structure asked about sound (e.g. does the word rhyme with…?).
- Semantic analysis was activated by asking 'category' or 'sentence' questions (e.g. whether the word fits into a particular category or whether it fits into a particular sentence).

Half the questions should have yielded 'yes' answers and half should have yielded 'no' answers.

To summarise, the study involved explaining the idea, carrying out the tasks and giving an unexpected retention or recall test:
- free recall (all the words were requested in any order)
or
- recognition (including distractor words)

A number of experiments used this procedure. One experiment is given in detail, so that results can be presented.

Details of an experiment

Experiment 1 measured structural, phonemic and semantic processing and also whether or not a particular word was present. A tachistoscope was used and words were presented at 2-second intervals. The 'yes' and 'no' responses were voice activated. There were 40 trials (40 words) and ten conditions. Five questions were asked:
- Do the words rhyme?
- Is the word in capitals?

- Does the word fit into this category?
- Does the word fit into this sentence?
- Is there a word present or not?

The five questions had both 'yes' and 'no' responses, so there were ten conditions. Each condition had four words. There were 80 words in the recognition task because there were 40 distractor words (words that the participants had not seen).

Results of the experiment

The results of experiment 1 are given in Table 2.26. Results showed that when there had to be deep processing, response time was longer.

Table 2.26 *The response time (milliseconds) depends on the level of processing*

Response type	Level of processing from least deep (1) to deepest (5)				
	1 Is there a word?	2 Is the word in capitals?	3 Does the word rhyme?	4 Does the word fit the category?	5 Does the word fit the sentence?
	Response in milliseconds				
Yes	591	614	689	711	741
No	590	625	678	716	832
	Proportion of words recognised correctly				
Yes	0.22	0.18	0.78	0.93	0.96
No	N/A	0.14	0.36	0.63	0.83

- Different encoding questions gave rise to different response times.
- The responses to the questions about meaning took longer.
- Semantic processing led to the best recognition.
- Response times rise (it takes longer) as the level of processing is deeper. The times are similar, whether the answer to the question is 'yes' or 'no'.
- The proportion recognised rose with depth of processing. The 'yes' answers were recalled better than the 'no' answers.

One issue is whether the better recognition was because of the depth of processing or because of the longer study time: 200 milliseconds of extra study time gave 400% improvement in recognition.

Conclusions

Deeper encoding (when the participants had to consider whether a word fitted into a particular category or sentence) took longer and gave higher levels of performance. Questions leading to a positive response (such as 'Yes, the word does fit into the sentence') produced a higher level of performance than if there was a negative response (such as 'No, the word does not fit into the sentence').

It was concluded that the enhanced performance was because of qualitatively different processing, not just because of extra study time. Craik and Tulving (1975) say 'manipulation of levels of processing at the time of input is an extremely powerful determinant of retention of word events'. It is interesting that 'yes' and 'no' responses took the same amount of time but that 'yes' answers led to better recognition of those words. This does not seem to be just about levels of processing, so it needs to be further investigated.

Evaluation of the study by Craik and Tulving (1975)

The Craik and Tulving (1975) study needs to be evaluated to judge its strengths and weaknesses.

Strengths

- The experiments were designed carefully with controls and clear operationalisation of variables. For example, the time for which the words were exposed was controlled by the tachistoscope. The number of words in each category, including whether answers are 'yes' or 'no' was also controlled. The study can, therefore, be replicated and the findings are likely to be reliable. In fact, by carrying out so many experiments, Craik and Tulving (1975) have replicated their own work.
- The framework is clear and the study takes the ideas and tests them directly, subsequently feeding back to the framework. For example, the researchers recognised that deep processing being measured as meaningful processing is a circular argument, so they focused on depth of processing needing longer processing. Focusing on a criticism of the framework strengthened the framework.

Weaknesses

- One weakness is how to test 'depth', when the idea is vague. A problem is the circular argument that 'deep' means 'meaningfully processed' and 'meaningfully processed' means 'deep'. This is recognised by Craik and Tulving who say that deeper processing means a longer processing time, which can be tested. However, there is still the problem that the material might be recognised better because of the study time, not because of deeper processing.
- The tasks are artificial. They involve processing words in artificial ways and then trying to recognise them. This is not something that is done in real life, so the study could lack validity.

Table 2.27 *Strengths and weaknesses of the study by Craik and Tulving (1975)*

Strengths	Weaknesses
• The experiments were controlled carefully, so the study is replicable; replication occurred within the study so the findings are reliable	• Even if 'deeper' means longer processing, it might still be that the improved recognition is due to the length of processing time, not the depth of processing
• The study reinforces the levels-of-processing framework; the study looks at depth meaning longer processing time	• The tasks are artificial, so the study could lack validity

Ramponi et al. (2004)

Ramponi et al. (2004) is a useful modern study that connects with the levels-of-processing framework, which is the main theory of memory for the AS course. The

study tested whether older participants find it harder to make new associations between words whereas they are not affected by age when dealing with strong associations. An example of a strongly associated pair of word is 'table–chair' and a weakly associated pair of words is 'table–meal'.

They also looked at levels of processing to see if having to carry out 'semantic' processing leads to better recall of words. They found that age affected weak associations more than strong ones. They also found that semantic processing led to better recall. Younger participants always did better than older ones, and the worst recall was always in the phonemic condition for older participants.

This study is covered in more detail on the CD-ROM.

Examination-style questions

1 Describe two studies from the cognitive approach. *(12 marks)*
2 Evaluate one study from the cognitive approach. *(6 marks)*
3 Compare two studies from the cognitive approach in terms of their methodology. *(8 marks)*
4 Discuss the procedure of the study by Craik and Tulving (1975). *(6 marks)*

Extension question

With reference to two studies from the cognitive approach, discuss how successful the experimental method is in obtaining information about the processes involved in either memory or forgetting. *(12 marks)*

Key issues

You have to study one key issue in each approach and apply concepts and ideas from the approach to that issue. Concepts and ideas include theories, studies, assumptions and terminology. Two of the three issues suggested for your course are covered here. *The other one is summarised here and covered in more detail on the CD-ROM.* However, you do not have to choose one of these — you can choose any issue. In the examination, you may be given an issue to read and then have to apply concepts and ideas from the approach to that issue. Studying all the issues will help you to learn how to apply concepts, ideas, theory and research to a new issue.

Study hint When reading newspapers, keep your course in mind. If an event seems to connect with what you are learning, for example an article about old age and memory loss or about someone forgetting when they have had a car accident, cut that article out and keep it. It could be the basis of a key issue — you might like to start collecting such items as a class. You could then get used to applying ideas from the approach to new situations.

Flashbulb memory

Describing the issue

A flashbulb memory is when an event is so powerful that people see it as if they have taken a photograph of it and they can relive the whole event in great detail for a long time afterwards. Researchers used the phrase 'now print' to explain such memories because it was as if the whole episode was a snapshot and imprinted in memory as such. Features of flashbulb memories are that they are vivid and can last potentially for the person's lifetime. They tend to be about events that have an emotional significance. Some national and international events, for example Princess Diana's car crash and the events of 9/11, are remembered by many as flashbulb memories. Researchers would like to explain how flashbulb memories are stored, partly because this is of interest and partly to see if this helps to explain how we remember. This issue is what leads to 'flashbulb' memories and how they can be explained.

> **Study hint** It is not easy to describe the key issue without giving concepts and ideas from the relevant approach. However, that is what you are asked to do. Do not give research evidence until asked to explain the issue using concepts from the approach. You may find that you have to use terms, such as 'leading questions' if you are looking at the issue of how reliable eyewitness testimony is, but as far as possible do not use concepts and ideas from the approach when describing it. You also need to say what the issue is — how to explain flashbulb memory. It is a good idea to think of the issue as a question.

Application of concepts and ideas

Here is a list of ideas that you can use when applying concepts and ideas from the cognitive approach to explain what flashbulb memories are:

- Brown and Kulik (1977) described the idea of flashbulb memory and pointed out that such memories are special and long lasting.
- Brown and Kulik (1977) found that 75% of black people who were asked about the assassination of Martin Luther King (who was black) could recall it, compared with only 33% of white people asked.
- Robinson (1980) carried out a study using cues to compare the memory of words that had an emotional connotation with words that were 'non emotional'. It was found that recall was quicker for 'emotional' words. This suggests that emotion is part of what makes a flashbulb memory.
- Colgrove (1899) found that most people could remember what they were doing when Abraham Lincoln (president of the USA) was assassinated.
- Niesser and Harsch (1986) asked 106 people about the *Challenger* crash, within 24 hours of its occurrence. Three years later, when they asked 44 of them again, their memories of the crash were nowhere near as vivid. This goes against the idea of flashbulb memory.
- Williams (1994) investigated whether people who had been victims of abuse when younger could remember it when they were older; they found that many could not. This goes against the idea of flashbulb memory because, in theory,

such strongly emotional events should be remembered clearly. This lack of memory is taken by the psychodynamic approach as evidence of repression.

- It may not be that flashbulb memories are encoded in a different way and so never forgotten. It may be that such memories are rehearsed more often and are also talked about, so they are renewed and, therefore, remembered.
- The trace-decay theory of forgetting suggests that a trace can be renewed, which will preserve the memory. Flashbulb memories might just be renewed often.
- Cue-dependent forgetting suggests that retrieval is better if the right environmental cues are present. Perhaps a flashbulb memory occurs when environmental cues are remembered clearly, which helps with retrieval of the memory.
- Flashbulb memory goes against the idea of reconstructive memory because flashbulb memory is supposed to be clear and not allow for any reconstruction of the event(s).

How reliable is eyewitness testimony?

The reliability of eyewitness testimony is an important issue because there have been cases where people have been found guilty of crimes purely on the basis of eyewitness testimony.

Describing the issue

Eyewitness testimony comes from someone who has seen a crime. An eyewitness gives a statement, might identify a suspect from a line of others and may have to testify in court. Eyewitnesses can give evidence in civil cases as well as in criminal cases. This can have important consequences, such as deciding who was at fault in a car accident. If eyewitness testimony is unreliable, then someone may be convicted or blamed wrongly.

> There is also **'earwitness' testimony** — people testify from what they have heard.

One case of how perception can be faulty is described by Elizabeth Loftus, who has carried out many studies in the area of eyewitness testimony. Two men in Montana had been hunting all day for bears. When they were returning, the light was bad and they were tired and hungry. They had been thinking about bears all day and were talking about bears. When they heard a noise just off the road in the woods, they thought it was a bear. They fired at the noise, but what they had heard was a couple making love. The woman was killed. The jury found it hard to understand what Loftus calls 'event factors', such as the state of mind of an individual and how it affects processing.

Eyewitnesses will be in an emotional state, perhaps thinking about their own lives, so eyewitness testimony is not likely to be exact like a tape recorder. So, how reliable is eyewitness testimony? Witnesses can be swayed by identity line-ups. This is because they want to help and are likely to assume that the criminal or person to be identified is present in the line-up. They are looking for the person they saw and could just look for the nearest match, which is not the same as identifying the person. If a black suspect was in a line-up with five white men, and the eyewitness had seen someone black at the crime, then the black person is likely to be chosen.

A real case is that of Bobby Joe Leaster. In 1970, he was picked up by police and accused of murdering the owner of a shop. The police drove him to the shop and the murdered man's wife came out and identified him while he was sitting in the police car. He was convicted and sentenced to life in prison. In 1986, the bullet from the murder victim was matched to a gun linked to two men who had been arrested for robbery just after the murder. Bobby Joe Leaster was released after 16 years in prison. Borchard looked at 69 cases of wrongful conviction; in 29 cases (42%) mistaken eyewitness testimony was responsible for the convictions.

Application of concepts and ideas

Here is a list of concepts and ideas from the cognitive approach to help explain the issue, 'How reliable is eyewitness testimony?':

- Bartlett (1932) discussed the idea that memory is reconstructive and that schemata are used when 'remembering', so memory is not like a tape recorder.
- Loftus (1979) carried out a study in which participants acting as jurors judged a 'defendant' accused of robbery. When they were given only circumstantial evidence, 18% found the defendant guilty. In another condition, the 'jurors' were given the evidence of an eyewitness who identified the 'defendant' as the robber; 72% found the defendant guilty. Just having one eyewitness, with all other factors constant, swayed a large percentage of the jurors.
- Loftus and Ketcham (1991) suggest that, when eyewitness testimony is used in a case, innocent individuals are convicted wrongly 45% of the time.
- Chartier (1997) suggests that the memory of an eyewitness will be vague and to make sense the witness will fill in the gaps. This is consistent with Bartlett's (1932) theory.
- Sadava and McCreary (1997) found that interviewing could sway the results. This is partly because both the police and the witness want to solve the crime and partly because the witness is likely to believe the police and think that they know who the criminal is. Witnesses will often comply with what they think interviewers want to hear.
- There can be a self-fulfilling prophecy because the interviewer may ask questions that only elicit the desired answer and may ignore other information (Sadava and McCreary 1997).
- To interview witnesses more successfully the cognitive interview has been encouraged. This includes, for example, reinstating the cognitive environment at the time of the incident that was witnessed. Cue-dependent forgetting says that this will help with recall.

The cognitive interview

Cognitive psychology looks at issues to do with information processing, including input, processing and output. When interviewing takes place the questions are

input, processing occurs and the answer is the output. It is possible that the processing might distort the answer.

An area where this has been studied is police interviewing. Rather than merely asking a sequence of questions, cognitive interviews use the experiences, emotions, thoughts and situations of witnesses in order to obtain witness statement. However, police in the field say that it takes too long. If there is another crime to deal with and they want information quickly, they are likely to use other techniques. If they do not want too much information, because there is no one to follow it up, they will not use the cognitive interview. The issue is whether the technique is useful, which depends on the accuracy of the generated information, together with the practical issues of time and quantity of information.

This issue is covered in more detail on the CD-ROM.

Examination-style questions

1 Describe one key issue within the cognitive approach. *(6 marks)*

2 Using concepts and ideas from the approach, explain one key issue within the cognitive approach, *(8 marks)*

3 Explain why the key issue you have studied for the cognitive approach is important in today's society. *(5 marks)*

Extension question

Discuss one key issue within the cognitive approach and relate it to at least one of the key assumptions of the approach. *(12 marks)*

Practical: a laboratory experiment

In the cognitive approach you have to carry out a laboratory experiment. Here a laboratory experiment looking at interference in short-term memory is worked through, but in your particular course you may do a different experiment.

Study hint In the examination you will be asked questions about your practicals. Keep a notebook, so that you have information that you can revise for each examination.

Aim of the practical

The **aim** is to partly replicate the study by Peterson and Peterson (1959) and to see if repetition improves recall.

Brief background

You may have studied the Atkinson and Shiffrin (1968) multi-store model of memory. Issues within short-term memory, such as the need for rehearsal, are also important in other models of memory and forgetting. The multi-store model suggests that short-term and long-term memory have different features. Short-term memory lasts for up to 30 seconds and we remember in short-term memory by sound. Long-term memory can last a lifetime and is in different forms, e.g. pictures, sound and meaning. This suggests that if information is rehearsed in the short-term memory it can go into long-term memory. If it is not rehearsed, it is lost. Findings from studies such as Peterson and Peterson (1959) suggest that rehearsal leads to better recall. This backs up the model and supports the idea that rehearsed information is transferred into long-term memory and non-rehearsed information is lost.

The experiment replicated partially here is the second experiment from the Peterson and Peterson (1959) study. Some of Peterson and Peterson's (1959) results are in Table 2.28. The scores are the proportions of items correctly recalled.

A greater proportion of items was recalled after 9 seconds than after 18 seconds. In each case, a greater proportion of items was recalled when there was more repetition time. This study looks at the effect of repetition time, to see if rehearsal aids recall.

Table 2.28 *Proportions of items correctly recalled after two different times for repetition of items and two different times of interference*

Repetition time (seconds)	Proportion recalled after a time interval of 9 seconds	Proportion recalled after a time interval of 18 seconds
1	0.34	0.21
3	0.48	0.34

Research method

The research method suggested is a **laboratory experiment**. You could carry out this practical alone or work in a small group so that you can pool data.

Experimental hypothesis

The basic **experimental hypothesis** for this study is 'in short-term memory the more participants rehearse an item the better their recall'.

- Recall is the number of three-letter nonsense syllables correctly repeated at the end of the trials. Three-letter nonsense syllables are three-letter 'words' without meaning, e.g. POK.
- Rehearsal is repeating the nonsense syllables aloud.
- 'More rehearsal' is set up (**operationalised**) as the number of times the nonsense syllables are repeated aloud increases — the more times participants repeat the material, the more they are said to have rehearsed it.

A complete hypothesis is 'in short-term memory participants correctly recall more three-letter nonsense syllables the more times they repeat the material aloud before recall'.

Directional or non-directional hypothesis

The hypothesis is **directional** because it is saying that the more the participants rehearse the better their recall will be. Thus the direction of the results — being clear when participants will do better — is given.

Variables

The **independent variable** is what is manipulated — in this case, how many times the participant repeats the stimulus. This is how 'more rehearsal' will be **operationalised**. It is difficult to measure 1 and 3 seconds. Therefore, one repeat of the nonsense syllable is taken as allowing 1 second and three repeats of the nonsense syllable is taken as allowing 3 seconds.

The **dependent variable** is what is measured as a result of the manipulation of the independent variable. In this case it is the number of three-letter nonsense syllables correctly recalled.

Conditions in the experiment

There are two **conditions** in this experiment:
- the participant repeats the stimulus material aloud once
- the participant repeats the stimulus material aloud three times

Design

This is a **repeated measures design**, because the same participants are doing the two conditions.

Participants

Use **opportunity sampling** to find ten people to take part in the study. Note down their age group, gender and any features that might affect the results. For most people, gender and age should not affect the results of this study. Avoid asking anyone who has memory problems or people old enough to feel that they have memory problems.

Ethical issues

It is important for every practical that you address the **ethical guidelines**:
- competence
- debriefing
- informed consent
- right of withdrawal
- deception

> **Practical**
>
> Do not proceed with your investigation until your teacher or supervisor has approved it in terms of ethics.

Include written **standarised instructions** to give participants the necessary information. Standardised instructions are the same for everyone and are written so that the briefing the participants have had is recorded because this might affect the results.

Preparing the apparatus

For a laboratory experiment, **apparatus** is usually needed. In this study, the dependent variable is recall of three-letter nonsense syllables. Peterson and Peterson (1959) used nonsense syllables rather than 'real' words so that each participant had an equal chance of remembering them. This removes any advantage due to familiarity with the words. Adding meaning to words also means using other cognitive processes, rather than 'pure' memory. Therefore, meaningless materials are better for carrying out such a task.

> **Apparatus** means the materials used in the study.

Prepare ten sets of three-letter nonsense syllables. Suggested items are given below.

Decisions about the study

In this experiment, the remaining decisions are based largely on the Peterson and Peterson (1959) study. However, other decisions could be made. Here, the decisions are:

- The participants are asked to repeat the nonsense syllable aloud either once or three times. This is to represent Peterson and Peterson's (1959) measures of 1 second and 3 seconds for rehearsal.
- The time that the participants count backwards for before recalling is 18 seconds (which replicates Peterson and Peterson, 1959).
- Ten three-letter nonsense syllables are prepared for the task. Eight are needed, but it could be useful to have two more in case of stumbling over a syllable in one of the trials.
- Participants will take part in two practice trials, to make sure they understand the instructions, followed by six actual trials. Three of the six main trials involve repeating the nonsense syllable aloud once; three involve repeating the nonsense syllable aloud three times.
- Data are to be recorded for each participant from the six trials (not from the practice trials). Record the letters recalled, the nonsense syllable itself and whether the recalled nonsense syllable is complete.
- Use **counterbalancing** so that one participant does the 'once aloud' condition first and the next participant does the 'three times aloud' condition first. This will help to control **order effects**.
- Ten numbers from which the participants will count backwards need to be written down, so that the same number is used for each participant as a **control**. Use numbers in the hundreds and ask them to count backwards in ones so that the task is not too difficult. Eight numbers are needed, but ten are prepared in case of difficulties arising.

Suggested three-letter nonsense syllables are:

BUH   VID   FOM   REL   DUS   WOV   QIY   RIH   PEB   KEC

Suggested sets of three numbers are:

475   396   259   639   502   489   326   843   740   582

How to carry out the study

The main points about carrying out the study are listed below. Copy the list so that you can use it to remind you of the steps that have to be followed:

- Give out the standardised instructions (see below) and check that all is in order.
- Carry out two practice trials, one using the 'once aloud' condition and the other using the 'three-times aloud' condition.
- Check all is well and start the main study.
- Inform the participant that the first trials are the 'once aloud' trials.*
- Read one of the nonsense syllables out to the participant.
- Wait for the participant to repeat it *once*.
- Read one of the numbers to the participant.
- Wait 18 seconds while the participant counts backwards from that number.
- Ask the participant to recall the nonsense syllable.
- Note down the letters recalled and whether the nonsense syllable is complete or not.
- Repeat this twice more (i.e. do three 'once aloud' trials).
- Inform the participant that the next trials are the 'three-times aloud' trials.*
- Repeat the steps for the 'once aloud' trials, but wait for the participant to repeat the nonsense syllable *three times* before reading out one of the numbers.
- Thank the participant and debrief him or her.

*If possible, use counterbalancing — ask one participant for the 'once aloud' condition first and ask the next participant for the 'three-times aloud' condition first.

Instructions

When a participant has been chosen, find somewhere comfortable to carry out the experiment.

An example of standardised instructions for the study

Thank you for taking part in this study. Please note that you can stop at any time.
I am looking at memory to see how we process information and I will explain what this particular study is about once you have taken part. Is that all right? This is not about you as an individual but about how we all remember. The study will take about 20 minutes.
I hope that is all right.

I am going to read out three letters. You then repeat them out loud to rehearse them briefly. Then, when I ask you to, I would like you to start counting backwards in ones from a number that I will give you. Finally, I will ask you to recall the three letters I read out at the start. I would like to do this eight times altogether. The first two times are for practice. Then, I would like to do six trials, and each time I will note down what you recall of the letters. For some of the trials, I will ask you to repeat the letters once and for other trials I will ask you to repeat the letters three times.

Carry out the study

Start with the two practice trials, answer any questions, and then carry out the six proper trials, recording what the participants recall each time.

Debriefing participants

Once the experiment is over the participants have to be debriefed. This means telling them what the study is about and how their results will be used. Explain the two conditions and inform them of their results. Tell them that rehearsal is meant to aid recall and to help transfer memories into the long-term memory. Ask them if you can use their results and explain it is for your AS psychology course. Debriefing should be done individually, after each participant has completed the experiment.

Recording results

You should record your results in a table. Table 2.29 could be used to show the letters recalled by each participant in each of six trials and the total number of complete nonsense syllables recalled correctly.

Table 2.29 A table for recording results

Repeat 'once aloud' condition					Repeat 'three times aloud' condition				
Participant	Trial 1	Trial 2	Trial 3	Total of correct syllables recalled	Participant	Trial 1	Trial 2	Trial 3	Total of correct syllables recalled
1					1				
2					2				
3					3				
4					4				
5					5				
6					6				
7					7				
8					8				
9					9				
10					10				

Analysing the data

Use the raw scores table, which is your completed table once the ten participants have been tested. You could use the total number of letters recalled correctly by each participant for each condition or you could use the total number of nonsense syllables recalled correctly. Work out a mode, median, mean and range for the data. If you use the number of syllables recalled correctly there are only three possible scores, which limits the data; if you use the letters recalled then there might be an element of guessing. Decide which you think is best for your data.

You should also represent your data in graphical form. This experiment is a repeated measures design, so you should be able to compare the scores from the two conditions.

Work out the proportion/percentage of recall for the two conditions. Then compare your results with those of Peterson and Peterson (1959). They found a proportion of 0.21 for the 1-second repetition condition and 0.34 for the 3-second repetition condition when they used an 18 seconds' interference task (counting backwards).

Suggestions about presentation of data

Some possible data are shown in Table 2.30.

Table 2.30 Possible data

Repeat 'once aloud' condition					Repeat 'three times aloud' condition				
Participant	Trial 1	Trial 2	Trial 3	Total of correct syllables recalled	Participant	Trial 1	Trial 2	Trial 3	Total of correct syllables recalled
1	R	DUS	WV	1	1	BUH	VID	FOM	3
2	REL	DUS	WOV	3	2	BUH	VID	FOM	3
3	REM	DUH	OV	0	3	BS	VID	FOM	2
4	RM	DUS	WOV	2	4	BUH	VID	FOM	3
5	REL	DUS	WOV	3	5	BUH	VID	FOM	3
6	REP	DUS	VW	1	6	UH	VD	FOM	1
7	TL	DUS	WV	1	7	BUH	VID	FOM	3
8	REP	DUS	OV	1	8	BUH	VID	FOM	3
9	REL	DUS	WOV	3	9	BUH	VID	FOM	3
10	PEP	VUS	WOV	1	10	BUH	VID	FOM	3
			Mode	1				Mode	3
			Median	1				Median	3
			Mean	1.6				Mean	2.7
			Range	3				Range	2

Descriptive statistics

- The raw scores are the actual scores of the participants.
- The **measures of central tendency** are the mode, median and mean.
- The **mode** is the most usual score, the one that appears most often. There can be more than one mode. If there are two, the data are bi-modal.
- The **median** is the middle score. If there is an even number of scores, there are always two points in the middle. For example with 10 sets of scores, the median is the average of the scores ranked 5 and 6. Here, both sets of scores have the same number at 5 and 6, so there is no problem. However, if the fifth score was 2 and the sixth score was 3, then the median would be 2.5.
- The **mean** is the average. It is calculated by adding up the set of scores and dividing by the number of scores in the set.
- The **range** is a **measure of dispersion.** It is worked out by subtracting the lowest score from the highest score. You could also work out the standard deviation.

Levels of measurement and measures of central tendency

It is not always correct to work out the mode, median and mean for all data. It depends on the **level of measurement** of the data. In psychology, three levels of measurement are used:

- **nominal data**, which are data in categories — the mode is suitable
- **ordinal data**, which are data in ranks such as rating scales — the mode and median are suitable
- **interval/ratio data** — mathematical scores and all three measures of central tendency are suitable

> For this course, **interval** and **ratio data** are taken to be the same.

That the mean is not suitable if the scores are not 'real' measurements.

One way to remember levels of measurement is to think of temperature:

- Sorting days into hot and cold days is a nominal level of measurement because the data are in categories.
- Rating days according to how cold, warm and hot they are is an ordinal level of measurement because a rating scale is used to rank the days.
- Recording the temperature in degrees Celsius is an interval/ratio level of measurement. This is a 'real' mathematical measurement and the mean could be used.

Summary table

When presenting data, it is usual to give the measures of central tendency and dispersion, not the raw scores. This makes it easier to compare the scores. The results calculated from the suggested data for this experiment are summarised in Table 2.31. The data are for the number of complete nonsense syllables (out of three) recalled correctly in each condition.

Table 2.31 Summary of results

Repeat 'once aloud' condition		Repeat 'three times aloud' condition	
Statistic	Value	Statistic	Value
Mode	1	Mode	3
Median	1	Median	3
Mean	1.6	Mean	2.7
Range	3	Range	2

Graphs

You need to be able to interpret graphs. It is also useful to know how to produce them, because this aids understanding. Here are some rules about drawing graphs:

- A computer-generated graph may not help when comparing data because the computer tends to adjust the scales. You must adjust the scales if you use a computer but this requires the necessary skills. If you do adjust this correctly a computer-generated graph is fine. When comparing graphical data the scales have to be the same.
- If the experimental design uses independent groups, you should not compare the data for one person directly with the data for their opposite number. At least one of the sets of data should be in rank order to make comparisons worthwhile. Or, present the two sets of data on separate sets of axes, but using the same scale.
- A simple graph is used to present the two means for comparison. Make sure that the scale is sensible.

- There may be so many raw data that it is not useful to present them graphically. However, this is done here (Figure 2.8) as an illustration and because there are only ten sets of data.
- In a frequency graph, the number of times each score is achieved is recorded. Frequency graphs are useful because they show clearly the differences between data (Figure 2.9).

Figure 2.8 *The effects of rehearsal on recall*

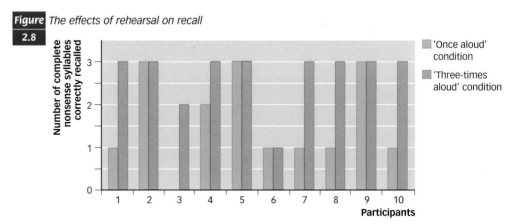

Table 2.32 *Frequency data for the two conditions*

Scores	Repeat 'once aloud' condition	Repeat 'three times aloud' condition
0	1	0
1	5	1
2	1	1
3	3	8
Total	**10**	**10**

Figure 2.9 *Frequency graph to show the number of complete nonsense syllables recalled correctly after 1 second rehearsal and 3 second rehearsal*

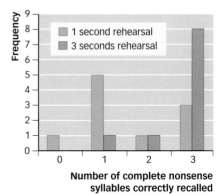

Figure 2.9 shows that more syllables are recalled correctly with rehearsal for 3 seconds than with rehearsal for 1 second.

Consider your findings

Decide how far your findings support the idea that the more we rehearse the better we recall.

Some ideas from the suggested data are as follows:
- The mean, median and mode all show that repeating three times gives better recall than repeating once.
- The ranges are similar. This shows that the scores are similarly distributed. However, with only four possible scores, this is not a useful measure.

- Some nonsense syllables are recalled better than others. For example, FOM is always recalled correctly. It may be that the ones better remembered were remembered as words. One participant remembered VW, which suggests that people may search for meaning when trying to learn.
- Some of the mistakes show that short-term memory uses sound, because the mistakes show letters replaced with similarly sounding letters, such as REM for REL.
- Three participants remembered all six syllables.
- In general, rehearsal for 3 seconds gives better recall than rehearsal for 1 second. which is what is predicted, given the findings of Peterson and Peterson (1959).

Record your study

The notes in your practical notebook should provide you with enough material for exam revision. Now that you have carried out a practical you should have a better understanding of the methodological terms.

> You could make your own glossary of terms, using your own words. This would help your revision.

Examination-style question

This question is about the experiment that you carried out within the cognitive approach.

1 Describe the procedure. *(5 marks)*

2 Explain how you chose the participants. *(5 marks)*

3 Discuss ethical issues that affected or might have affected the experiment. *(6 marks)*

Extension question

Explain what you found out from the experiment that you carried out within the cognitive approach. In your answer, consider:
- learning about methodology, including ethical issues
- the background research that gave rise to your study
- your findings in relation to the background research and theories you have studied *(12 marks)*

Answers to the practice boxes

Practice 2.1 on p. 95

Study 1 Experimental hypothesis: there is a difference in recall of a list of letters, i.e. counting backwards for 15 seconds after seeing the letters will lead to poorer recall than if there were no counting backwards.

Study 1 Null hypothesis: there is no difference in recall of a list of letters, i.e. counting backwards for 15 seconds after seeing the letters will not lead to poorer recall than if there were no counting backwards.

Study 2 Experimental hypothesis: there is a difference in recall of a story depending on the length of time after hearing the story the recall takes place, i.e. the longer the time after the story is heard the less well the story is recalled.

Study 2 Null hypothesis: there is no difference in recall of a story depending on the length of time after hearing the story the recall takes place, i.e. the longer the time after the story is heard it is not the case that the story is recalled less well.

Study 3 Experimental hypothesis: there is a difference in recall of words depending on whether the setting for recall is the same as, or different from, the setting where the words are learnt.

Study 3 Null hypothesis: there is no difference in recall of words depending on whether the setting for recall is the same as, or different from, the setting where the words are learnt.

Practice 2.2 on p. 96

Hypothesis 1 Directional (one-tailed)

Hypothesis 2 Non-directional (two-tailed)

Hypothesis 3 Non-directional (two-tailed)

Practice 2.3 on p. 97

Hypothesis 1 The independent variable is whether the diver is recalling underwater or on the surface. The dependent variable is the number of words recalled from the list.

Hypothesis 2 The independent variable is whether the examination is taken in the same room or a different room from that in which learning took place. The dependent variable is the marks scored.

Hypothesis 3 The independent variable is whether the letters are grouped (chunked) into recognisable sets of three letters or presented randomly. The dependent variable is the number of letters recalled.

Practice 2.4 on p. 99

Study 1 Independent groups — the independent variable is gender and people can only be male or female.

Study 2 Repeated measures — the same person has to keep recalling the story. (You could possibly use different people and an independent groups design. However, the thoroughness of reading the story and the memories could be different.)

Study 3 Repeated measures — they have to learn and recall words; abilities are kept the same by using the same people.

Unit 2

Understanding the Individual

Chapter

The psychodynamic approach

This chapter is about Sigmund Freud's theory and the ideas that make up the psycho-dynamic approach.

Study of interest   Williams (1994) examined medical records to find young women who had been treated for sexual abuse when they were children. The question was: 'Would these women remember their experiences from 17 years previously?' Freud's theory suggests that repression would lead them to forget. Indeed, 38% had forgotten the experiences. This study shows motivated forgetting to prevent such memories becoming conscious. It is an example of the use of defence mechanisms. Defence mechanisms, repression and the role of the unconscious are explained in this chapter.

Everyday example   In 2007, a girl fell 10 metres from a window, apparently after an argument over a 'love triangle'. She was in a coma but was set to make a full recovery. However, she has no memory of what happened. This seems to be an example of motivated forgetting and repression. She is protected from traumatic memories. Motivated forgetting and repression are concepts that are explained by the psycho-dynamic approach.

Summary of learning objectives

Definitions

You have to be able to define the terms:

- id, ego, superego
- oral, anal, phallic, latency and genital stages of development
- defence mechanisms and repression
- conscious, preconscious and unconscious
- Oedipus complex

Methodology includes:

- case studies, including strengths and weaknesses and Freud's special case studies
- analysis of qualitative data
- correlation designs, including strengths and weaknesses
- longitudinal and cross-sectional studies
- ethics and credibility of Freud's work
- sampling techniques

Content covers:

- Freud's five stages of psychosexual development and the Oedipus complex in the phallic stage (including how Freud explains gender development)
- Freud's three-part theory of personality (id, ego, superego)
- the conscious, preconscious, and unconscious
- defence mechanisms, including repression and one other mechanism
- Freud's idea about gender development compared with the explanations of the biological and learning approaches

Studies in detail

You have to be able to describe and evaluate in detail:

- Freud's study of Little Hans (1909)
- one other from Axline (1964/1990), Bachrach et al. (1991) and Cramer (1997)

Three of the studies are described and evaluated in this chapter, *one is summarised here and covered in detail on the CD-ROM.*

Key issues

You have to be able to describe one key issue of your (or your teacher's) choice and apply concepts and theories from the psychodynamic approach to explain it. Two of the key issues suggested in the specification are covered in this chapter, *two are summarised here and covered in detail on the CD-ROM.*

Practical

You have to:

- carry out one practical of your (or your teacher's) choice, which must be a correlation, using self-report data and rating scales
- use a scattergram and a Spearman's test to analyse the results

- know how to write up the procedure, apparatus, sampling and results sections of a report
- be able to evaluate using strengths and weaknesses of correlations

One suggested practical is given in this chapter.

Study hint Make the above summary of learning objectives into a checklist, as suggested in Table 3.1. You could include more detail. For example, instead of correlations, list negative and positive correlations, and strengths and weaknesses of correlations.

Table 3.1 *A checklist of what you need to know for the psychodynamic approach and for your progress*

I need to know about	Done	More work	I need to know about	Done	More work
Case studies			Conscious, preconscious, unconscious		
Freud's case studies			Defence mechanism		
Qualitative data			Repression		
Correlations			Another defence mechanism		
Cross-sectional studies/designs			Little Hans study		
Longitudinal studies/designs			One other study		
Ethics and credibility of Freud			One key issue		
Sampling techniques			One practical: a correlation		
Id, ego and superego			Strengths and weaknesses of a correlation		
Oral, anal, phallic, latency, genital stages			Spearman's test		
Oedipus and Electra complexes			Scattergraphs		
Gender development					

Definitions

The following terms are defined in this chapter:
- id, ego and superego — the three parts of the personality according to Freud
- conscious, preconscious and unconscious — three parts of the mind according to Freud
- oral, anal, phallic, latency and genital stages — the stages of psychosexual development according to Freud
- Oedipus complex — occurs in the phallic stage
- defence mechanisms — repression and one other

An introduction to the psychodynamic approach

This chapter is about Freud's psychodynamic theory. The methodology also examines other issues, but the main focus is on Freud's psychosexual approach. Case studies are central to his approach and correlations are a good way of testing his theory. The studies in detail explore the theory in more depth, as does the key issue, which should help you to relate the theory to everyday concerns. The practical is a chance for you to test some aspect of Freud's theory for yourself.

The methodology used by Freud is not easily separated from his theory. The ideas of dream and symbol analysis are outlined in the methodology section, together with his other research methods of free association and slips of the tongue. Freud's therapy — psychoanalysis — is also mentioned. The content section covers the theory in some detail.

Study hint It is useful to study the approach as a whole rather than the methodology, content, studies in detail, key issue and practical as separate sections. Read the chapter as a whole, taking in some of the information but without taking notes or learning the terms. For this approach, the Little Hans study is the main study. It is mentioned in the methodology section, it features in the content section and is described and evaluated in the study-in-detail section. After reading the whole chapter, you can then start learning in earnest.

Background to the psychodynamic approach

Freud made some basic assumptions about human nature that have to be appreciated in order to understand his theory. Information about his life is included, with a suggestion that you research further to find out what sort of person he was. Freud used cocaine, which almost certainly did him physical harm. However, as his theory was developed over his lifetime, it is probably not true to say that what some call his 'rather fantastic ideas', were drug-induced.

A brief background of Freud

Freud was a medical doctor. He saw people in hospitals with severe mental health problems getting either very little treatment or no treatment at all. We would consider any treatment given to be barbaric — for example trying to shake the madness out of them or giving them cold baths.

He was an ambitious man who wanted to develop a theory applicable to all people. He had what he thought of as interesting dreams and could remember that as a child he had strong feelings for his mother, the relevance of which becomes clear once you study his ideas. His world was upper-middle class, mixing with people in Viennese

3

'high' society. He married, had children and lived a comfortable existence. However, he was also Jewish at a time of persecution of Jews. He experienced hatred, his books were burned and he eventually left his home country of Austria.

He seems to have been a compassionate man, who believed in his own ideas. These changed throughout his life as he continued to develop his theory. His training as a medical doctor made him scientific in his approach and, although he has been criticised strongly for being unscientific, he did make an effort to be scientific in his studies. For example, Little Hans was a small boy whose development was relayed by the boy's father to Freud over quite a long time. When studying Little Hans, Freud says that he tried hard to consider only data that came directly from Little Hans and to discount interpretations by Little Hans's father. The story of Little Hans provided evidence for some of Freud's ideas and is detailed on page 196.

Sigmund Freud

TopFoto

is detailed on page 196.

Explore In developing his theory and treating patients with neuroses, Freud studied individuals in detail. This type of approach to developing a theory is called **idiographic**. When scientists look for general laws, it is called a **nomothetic** approach to developing a theory. Freud, though working in an idiographic way, claimed to have found a general theory for all mankind and claimed to be working in a nomothetic way. Exploring the issues of idiographic and nomothetic approaches is a useful way of evaluating Freud's work.

Explore The Freud museum website (**www.freud.co.uk**) has lots of information about Freud himself and some original letters. There are Freud museums in London and Vienna. The one in Vienna is in the house where he lived, which is itself of interest.

Key assumptions underlying Freud's theory

The first key assumption is the importance of the first 5 years. Freud thought that the first 5 years of life were the most important time for forming a personality. Unsolved problems that arose in those years would affect development.

The second key assumption is that development occurs through stages that all children pass through. According to Freud, in the first 5 years there are three important psychosexual stages. If all is well and the child resolves any issues that arise within those stages, then the child will develop a stable personality and be able to form good adult relationships. If, however, there are problems in one or more of those stages, then the adult will not have a stable personality and will have problems to resolve.

A third key assumption is the importance of the unconscious. For Freud, the unconscious part of the mind is the largest and the most powerful — and almost inaccessible.

A fourth key assumption is that everyone has an amount of energy that does not decrease or increase and that some of that energy is **libido**, which is sexual energy. This assumption is what leads to Freud's theory being called 'psychosexual'. It is a theory of the mind and a theory of instinctive energy and innate (inborn) drives. He thought that the basic drives of hunger, thirst and need for shelter were catered for in the Viennese society he moved in, so he focused on the sexual drive.

Examination-style question

Outline two assumptions of Freud's approach. In each case, give an example from the approach. *(6 marks)*

Extension question

Discuss what is meant by a theory belonging to the psychodynamic approach. Include the expected features of the theory. In your answer, draw on examples from the approach to illustrate your argument(s). *(12 marks)*

Methodology

For the psychodynamic approach you need to look at case studies in general, case studies as used in the approach, correlation design, cross-sectional and longitudinal studies and sampling techniques.

The case study research method

The case study is a research method that allows data to be gathered in both depth and detail. It is either a study of an individual or of a small group of individuals connected in some way, such as a group of children brought up together and deprived of parenting. Some case studies involve a particular programme, e.g. a government-funded programme of health promotion.

The individual, small group or programme becomes the focus of a case study. Within that study, different research methods are used. Since depth and detail are required, the researcher can use interviews, questionnaires, and observations, among other research methods, to gather as many data as possible. A central research tool is the case history, in which details of the case are described. The case history provides qualitative data. If appropriate, tests and experiments can be carried out.

It is important to note that a case study is a research method in itself. However, other research methods are used to gather the data. Data are not gathered *by* a case study but *within* or *for* a case study, which makes it different from other research methods. Case studies provide mainly qualitative data, but some research methods, for example tests and questionnaires, do gather quantitative data.

One way of using the different research methods within a case study is to see them as ways of gathering data and then to use **triangulation** to work out themes and to generate the final results. A researcher will pool data about one person or event from different sources and then look for common themes. A piece of information from one source can thus reinforce data from another source.

> **Triangulation** is the term for analysing data gathered by different means and developing themes.

> **A study using the method** The story in a case study is usually interesting because it is details of a life that is different from one's own. One such case study is that of Genie (Curtiss 1977), a child who had not been cared for and who was found at the age of 13. The study is explored in detail in the child psychology option in Unit 3.

> **Explore** Use the internet or other sources to research two different case studies. You could choose the study of Genie and the study of Clive Wearing, who suffered memory loss with grave consequences. These very different case studies show the variety of what is studied within this research method. You could, of course, find studies of your own that are of personal interest.

Case studies and science

Whether or not case studies are scientific is arguable — there are points for and against. One argument goes further and says not only are case studies not scientific, but that they should not be scientific.

It can be argued that case studies are not scientific because they tend to use qualitative data, which means that the aim is for an understanding of meaning. There is an argument that meaning is found within the data but is not a 'thing' that will be found repeatedly, because it depends on the person interpreting the data as well as on the time, place and culture (amongst other things) within which the data were gathered. If the results are relative to the time, place, culture and interpretation rather than being 'facts' then the data are not 'scientific' and they do not help to build an indisputable body of knowledge. However, their value is in the detail and richness, which is perhaps what real meaning is about.

> **Explore** Social constructionism is the idea that, within a particular society, inventions and culture of that society are found. These inventions are not 'real' in the sense of existing and are only real to those within that culture and society. In another culture, a different reality might be found. This is what is meant in the argument that qualitative data are not 'scientific'.

There is a counter-argument that case studies are scientific. The researcher has to gather information systematically and make sure that evidence for any claim is available in, for example, the form of quotations or percentages. Any tools such as interview schedules or questionnaires must be well constructed and, where possible, show validity and reliability. To be valid, they must measure what they claim to measure (for example, what someone thinks, not what they feel they ought to think). To be reliable they must, when repeated, produce the same results. Validity and reliability can be shown by finding the same results by different means. The more the data are valid and reliable, the more they can be said to apply to other similar situations. This means that they are then, to an extent, **generalisable** (although not being generalisable is often given as a weakness of case studies).

Generalisability means that results from one study can be said to apply to other similar situations.

Another way that case studies can be scientific is when researchers deliberately look for evidence that goes against their predictions. Researchers recombine data and try to build different categories to test the value of their results. If the results remain the same, then it is claimed that the study is reliable and valid. One way of confirming validity is to carry out shorter repeat interviews, for example, asking relevant participants whether the results from the main study are appropriate. If the interviewee thinks the conclusions are appropriate, this suggests that the study is valid.

Analysing qualitative data

Qualitative data are analysed by generating themes and categories. If more than one case is involved in a case study, there can sometimes be cross-case analysis. Triangulation can also be used.

Generating themes

Case studies contain a great deal of qualitative data and it is useful to look at how qualitative data are analysed. In order to develop categories and themes, data are sorted into arrays and tables and, possibly, flow charts. Frequencies of events can be calculated; repeating patterns can be identified. The quantitative data that are often gathered for a case study can reinforce the analysis of the qualitative data — for example, by using statistics and figures to reinforce the themes. Sometimes more than one researcher analyses the data. If the same themes are found, this increases the level of confidence in the data.

Cross-case analysis

If there is more than one case within a case study, for example when studying a programme with more than one contributor such as a preventive medicine programme run by more than one NHS department, then the cases can be divided up for analysis. The different types of data can be divided up across the cases for analysis, rather than case by case. So, for example, all the interview data from the different cases could be analysed by one person and the questionnaire data by another. Themes can be found more readily in this way.

Analysis of qualitative data and validity issues

In general, qualitative data are valid because they are in depth and detailed and tend to measure what they claim to measure. They are not collected in an artificial setting, so there is no lack of validity in this regard.

However, it could be claimed that the presence of a researcher means that the situation is not natural, so the data are not valid. It could also be claimed that people will not divulge everything and if there are data missing, there is less validity.

However, in general:
- qualitative data are said to be valid
- the research methods for gathering such data are said to give valid data

Analysis of qualitative data and reliability issues

In general, qualitative data are not reliable. This is partly because they cannot be tested for reliability because gathering qualitative data tends not to be replicable. Qualitative data are gathered from an individual (or small group) and are in depth and rich. The focus is on that individual (or group) and it would be difficult to repeat the data gathering in precisely the same way and, therefore, difficult to obtain the same results again. Situations and people change, so data gathered a second time might be different. If a study is difficult to replicate, then its results are said to be unreliable.

To assess the issue of reliability and qualitative data, it could be said that sometimes similar case studies can be carried out or a particular case study can be replicated, so some qualitative data could be reliable. For example, case studies of brain-damaged patients have shown that damage to the hippocampus causes a problem with short-term memory, so the case of Clive Wearing has in a way been replicated. More than one of Freud's case studies showed that hysteria could cause physical problems, so it could be argued that these case studies have been tested for reliability.

Analysis of qualitative data and issues of generalisability

In the main, case studies are not generalisable. If the study is of a particular individual (or small group} and data are focused on that individual (or group) and are in depth and detailed, then the data are likely to be valid for that individual (or group). They might not, however, have relevance to other individuals or groups. This is particularly true of Freud's case studies because they focused on such things as an individual's dreams and early experiences. The early experiences of other people would not be the same.

To assess the issue of generalisability in case studies, it can be argued that people with similar experiences might produce similar data, and so to that extent case studies could be generalisable. For example, Freud claimed from his case studies that symbols in dreams had meaning and that they helped to uncover unconscious thoughts. The content of the dream and the symbols themselves might be different, but the idea of symbol and dream analysis was generalised.

Analysis of qualitative data and issues of subjectivity and objectivity

In general, case studies are said to involve subjectivity and to lack objectivity. Whatever research method is used, qualitative data are recorded as thoroughly as possible. However, data gathering could involve subjectivity because the methods might require a choice of data — for example, when observing or interviewing. There can also be subjectivity when analysing data. The difficulty is that large amounts of data must be summarised, perhaps by generating themes and categories. The researcher chooses the themes, albeit having to take them from the data and having to provide evidence. Since the researcher is active in summarising the data, objectivity might be compromised.

To assess the claim that case study data are analysed subjectively, it could be said that this is not the case because of the efforts to gather both valid and reliable data. There are arguments that case studies are scientific; these arguments hold that there is objectivity.

There is an argument that subjective analysis of case-study data is a good thing. Meaning from the data comes from the participant and the researcher because each study is in a particular context and data are socially constructed. Therefore, subjectivity becomes part of the data. Thus the argument is that scientific research methods are not appropriate for case studies.

Summary of issues when analysing qualitative data

Validity

In general, qualitative data are valid because:

- they are detailed, rich and in depth
- information comes from a person in a real situation and is about his or her own life

However, qualitative data:

- may be influenced by the researcher
- are a snapshot of a certain time and situation

Reliability

In general, qualitative data are not likely to be reliable because:

- case studies are not easily replicated to test for reliability
- if repeated by another person, a case study may not yield the same results (at a different time of life or with a different participant)

However:

- similar situations can be found
- data from different case studies can be compared and conclusions drawn

Generalisability

Data from case studies are not normally generalisable because they come from one individual (or small group) and are, therefore, specific rather than general. However, Freud generalised from his case studies because he thought that they provided evidence for his general theory.

Unit 2

Subjectivity/objectivity

Case studies are usually subjective because, for example, they involve interpretation by a researcher to develop themes. However, many case-study researchers aim to use scientific method. They aim for objectivity by using triangulation, valid measures, several methods, cross-case analysis, finding evidence to support theories and by testing for reliability.

Freud thought that given his aims, his interpretation was appropriate. He thought that his conclusions were objective.

Evaluation of case studies as a research method

Strengths

- The detail of the information gathered. The researcher finds out as much as possible about the individual (or small group), often using a variety of methods. Therefore, a large amount of data is gathered for analysis. When Milgram carried out his laboratory experiment, he noted that many participants were distressed by their actions. However, he was not able to investigate further to find out why some were more distressed than others. The missing data could have been useful. A case study gives as complete a picture as possible and much more detail than a laboratory experiment does.
- Valid data are produced. The researcher includes the setting and environment of the individual as part of the data, and data are gathered in a natural setting. As far as possible, the findings are about 'real' situations. The setting is natural so there is ecological validity. There are no unnatural tasks (such as in an experiment) or restricted questions (as when data are gathered by questionnaire only). Therefore, there is validity with regard to what is measured. When saying that what is measured is valid, in that it is about 'reality', this is **construct validity**. Valid means measuring what it is claimed has been measured, and can be taken to mean relating to 'real life'.

> **Study hint** Milgram is studied within the social approach. If you are not already familiar with it, look at his study now.

Weaknesses

- Only one person (or small group) is studied and the data are about that person. The in-depth study, which looks at the uniqueness of that individual, means that it is difficult to generalise the results to other people and situations. Case studies tend to lack generalisability because most are about a specific individual.
- Case studies cannot easily be shown to be reliable because it is not easy to repeat them. They are in-depth studies at one particular time with one individual. Those exact circumstances cannot be repeated. If a study is not reliable, or cannot be shown to be reliable, it is difficult to test whether it provides useful knowledge. The research method is, therefore, said to be unscientific.

Table 3.2 *Strengths and weaknesses of case studies (other than Freud's)*

Strengths	Weaknesses
• Data are valid because they are in depth, detailed and focus on real experiences in a real situation • A valuable research methodology because a case study may be the only way to gather rich, detailed qualitative information in context and with meaning for those concerned	• Lack generalisability because they are about one individual (or small group) only, so they are specific rather than general and data cannot be applied fairly to others • Hard to replicate, so cannot be tested for reliability, which means data may be subjective and cannot be used to build up a body of knowledge

The case study as used in the psychodynamic approach

Freud used case studies in order to investigate each individual case fully. Each of his cases analysed one individual. Little Hans was such a case study.

Freud used case studies slightly differently from the way outlined earlier; nevertheless, there are similarities. Freud gathered qualitative data, but he did not use questionnaires or tests to gather quantitative data. He used his own methods to access the data he required. He wanted to access the **unconscious** mind, which is not possible by standard means. According to Freud, the unconscious mind is hidden and inaccessible, so he could not ask direct questions about it. He had to 'trick' the people into revealing their unconscious thoughts and he found unusual and special ways to do this.

Freud's case studies were written up using data gathered by means of various research methods, but not those used in other types of case study. Freud used case studies both to build a body of knowledge and as a research method. At the same time, he used them to help cure his patients. Therefore, Freud's case studies are both research methods and therapy. The people in Freud's case studies are patients, clients or analysands (patients undergoing analysis), rather than participants, and they are referred to as such in this section.

Research methods used by Freud in case studies

One research method that Freud used was **free association**. This is the idea of associating ideas, things and feelings by saying what is in one's mind without censoring one's thoughts. As one thing follows another, the analyst listens to find connections, which can reveal unconscious thoughts.

Another method that Freud used was **dream analysis**. Dream analysis involves listening to the content of the analysand's dreams and applying concepts from the psychodynamic approach to the dreams to explain them. The content that is described by the dreamer is the **manifest content**, and the underlying meaning is the **latent content**. These concepts are outlined elsewhere in this chapter, as is the process of dream analysis. **Symbol analysis** takes place when trying to uncover the unconscious through dream analysis as the manifest content is symbolic of the latent content. Symbol analysis can also be carried out not just on dreams, but on other content, for example literature.

Explore Symbol analysis in literature is worth investigating. You can find websites where such analysis is explained. For example, nursery rhymes are analysed because they have the 'bad' person, the 'good' person and the struggle between them. According to Freud, we all have the id (the 'I want' part of the personality), the superego (conscience) and the ego (reality trying to balance the id and the superego). The 'id' could be the bad person, the 'superego' could be the good person and the 'ego' is dealing with the struggle — though there is more to it than that. These parts of the personality are explained in detail later.

Another research method that Freud used was to look for **slips of the tongue**. These are when a person says one thing and means another — for example saying 'erection' when meaning 'rejection' or 'orgasm' when meaning 'organism'. These are often called Freudian slips. Repressed thoughts are revealed by the mistake or slip that is made. The examples here are clearly sexual, but other errors can include calling someone by someone else's name. Freud, however, was often looking for underlying sexual meaning.

Freud's therapy was psychoanalysis. This could also be called a research method because he built his case studies using psychoanalysis. His main purpose was to cure the patient, but alongside this he was gathering data to reinforce or amend his theories. Psychoanalysis involves gathering data by, for example, dream analysis, symbol analysis, free association and slips of the tongue, and then talking with the

Figure 3.1 *Methods used by Freud in his case studies*

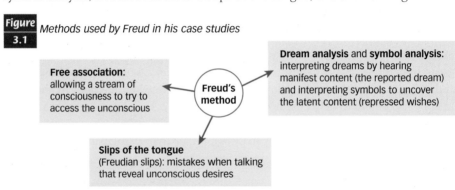

Free association: allowing a stream of consciousness to try to access the unconscious

Freud's method

Dream analysis and **symbol analysis:** interpreting dreams by hearing manifest content (the reported dream) and interpreting symbols to uncover the latent content (repressed wishes)

Slips of the tongue (Freudian slips): mistakes when talking that reveal unconscious desires

analysands about the data in order to reveal their unconscious wishes and desires. Once understood, those desires would be released and the patient would be cured.

Comparing case studies as used by Freud with case studies used in other approaches

It is clear that the case study research method as used by Freud differs from the case study research method used in other approaches.

Differences include:

- the special research methods within Freud's case studies
- that he was both using a therapy and researching his theory

Similarities include:

- the focus on qualitative data
- the gathering of in-depth rich data from one person

<table>
<tr><td>

Practice 3.1

Draw up a table with two columns and two rows. Use the two columns in the first row and allocate one for similarities between the two styles of case study and one for differences. For the two columns in the second row, give strengths and weaknesses of each style. Complete these rows of the table as fully as possible.

Suggested answer at the end of Chapter 3.

</td><td>

Study hint In the exam, you are likely to be asked to compare theories, studies or methods. You cannot *learn* every answer you need for the examination, so you have to make sure that, as well as the knowledge, you have the necessary skills to compare, analyse, assess and explain your knowledge. It is useful to practise these skills, as you are asked to do here when comparing the two types of case study.

</td></tr>
</table>

Evaluation of Freud's case study research methods

Strengths

- The data are qualitative and have depth and detail. The depth means that an individual's differences can be studied and focused upon. The data are valid because they come directly from the individual, so in that way they are 'real'. The strength, therefore, is that in-depth detailed and valid data are gathered that are difficult to gather in any other way.
- Freud's style of case study can be used as a therapy as well as a research method. It was intended as therapy, which makes it different from other research methods, which is a strength. The unconscious is not measurable in other ways, and this is a way of uncovering repressed memories and releasing them, so is therapeutic in itself.

Weaknesses

- There are failings of particular research methods within Freud's style of case study. For example, Freud himself recognised the weakness of free association. However hard patients tried to allow a stream of conscious thoughts 'out', they could not

Understanding the Individual

do so because their unconscious blocked them. Freud concluded that there would always be a block on such thoughts and that the unconscious was not easily accessed by free association.

■ Probably more than with any other research method the therapist has to interpret the data. Symbols have to be analysed and each symbol is unique to the individual. Therefore, the therapist is interpreting the data from the individual, which is likely to be subjective. A scientific approach requires objectivity if the 'truth' is to be uncovered. However, this subjective interpretation might yield valid data, so although 'being subjective' is a weakness, there are also strengths.

■ Freud's case studies were aimed at accessing the unconscious and the unconscious is not measurable in a scientific way. This means that any research method is going to be unscientific, which, if the aim of psychology is to build a firm body of knowledge, is a criticism.

Case studies in general are summarised in Table 3.3; Freud's case studies are summarised in Table 3.4.

Table 3.3 Case studies in general

Description	Analysis
● Study of individual or small group	● Generation of themes
● In-depth rich data	● Use tables of categories
● Mainly qualitative data	● Cross-case analysis
● Use many research methods such as questionnaires, case histories and observation	● Some quantitative data
● Uses triangulation	

Table 3.4 Freud's case studies

Description	Analysis
● Study of individual	● Suggesting interpretation to analysand
● In-depth, rich data	● To help to reveal unconscious repressed thoughts, emotions and memories
● Qualitative data	● To make the unconscious conscious
● Uses different techniques such as slips of the tongue, dream analysis and free association	● To release the energy to aid the symptoms
	● To give evidence for Freud's ideas

Strengths and weaknesses of Freud's style of case study are summarised in Table 3.5.

Table 3.5 Strengths and weaknesses of Freud's style of case study

Strengths	Weaknesses
● Uses different methods to uncover unconscious wishes which are impossible to access by conventional means	● Involves subjective interpretation by the analyst, so it is not scientific
● Acts both as a research method and a therapy and allows the analysand to be cured	● Cannot be replicated to test for reliability because it focuses on the unique unconscious desires of an individual and the analysis is carried out by one therapist

Ethical issues in case-study research

The British Psychological Society (BPS) and other professional bodies outline ethical guidelines that must be followed in research. Five main ethical principles are emphasised for your course, but there are others. Whatever the research method, the guidelines must be adhered to; case studies are no exception.

Study hint Ethical issues were outlined in Chapter 1. Review the issues there and be clear about the meaning of the participant giving informed consent, having the right to withdraw data, being debriefed fully, and not being deceived — and about the researcher being competent to carry out the study.

Not only was Freud's style of case study different, there are also ethical differences. The main reason is that Freud's case study is also a therapy, so ethical guidelines for practitioners must also be followed. Case studies gather in-depth data about one individual (or small group), so it might be possible to identify the individual. The detail will include more personal data than that from other research methods. This has ethical implications for confidentiality of data and the rights of the individual.

The BPS Code of Ethics and Conduct, 2006

The BPS published a new Code of Ethics and Conduct in March 2006. The code defines ethics as 'the science of morals or rules of behaviour'. Within the code, the main areas of concern include multiple relationships, competence, personal relationships, confidentiality, falsifying data or plagiarism, and bringing the profession into disrepute. It is clear that the BPS code of conduct addresses more than the five main issues focused on for this course.

The four main areas within the Code of Ethics and Conduct are respect, competence, responsibility and integrity. Other ethical principles, such as privacy, come under these four headings — for example, privacy is part of respect. Ethical issues are important for all research methods, but they are particularly important for case studies because they examine an individual's differences in ways that experiments and surveys do not. The BPS has also published Ethical Principles for Conducting Research with Human Participants and you will find details of the five ethical guidelines covered in your course there as well as others (**www.bps.org.uk**).

The five ethical issues focused on for AS psychology are deceit, consent, competence, debriefing and right to withdraw.

Explore Go to the BPS website (**www.bps.org.uk**) and look up the Code of Ethics and Conduct, March 2006. Make notes about issues of privacy and confidentiality, and explore the rest of the code.

According to the BPS website's summary of the Ethical Principles for Conducting Research with Human Participants:

> In all circumstances, investigators must consider the ethical implications and psychological consequences for the participants in their research. The essential

principle is that the investigation should be considered from the standpoint of all participants; foreseeable threats to their psychological well-being, health, values or dignity should be eliminated. Investigators should recognise that, in our multi-cultural and multi-ethnic society and where investigations involve individuals of different ages, gender and social background, the investigators may not have sufficient knowledge of the implications of any investigation for the participants. It should be borne in mind that the best judge of whether an investigation will cause offence may be members of the population from which the participants in the research are to be drawn.

Confidentiality of data and privacy

One of the BPS guidelines is that all data should be confidential and that participants should not be identifiable. There are occasions when confidentiality is waived, such as the case of Clive Wearing. His brain was damaged by a virus (which is rare) and he is now unable to lay down new memories. However, it is rare for real names to be used in case studies. For example, Genie is not a real name, and you may have read about the case studies of either HM or KF when studying memory. Both had damage to their hippocampus and both are only referred to by their initials to protect their privacy. Individuals have the right of privacy, unless they, or those close to them, choose otherwise.

To assess the ethical issue of privacy, which states that the rights of the individual with regard to confidentiality and privacy should be respected, it could be argued that the data might be valuable enough to warrant invasion of such privacy. The code, however, does not support this argument, other than some discussion of costs and benefits when deciding on a course of action and the ethical issues involved.

Ethics for practitioners

Other than competence, the ethical guidelines for practitioners are not part of your course. However, it is useful to know that there are strong guidelines for practitioners, including issues of competence, obligation, informed consent, personal conduct, access to health records, confidentiality, responsibility, safeguarding fitness to practice, teaching training and supervision, publications, private practice and relations with the public and media.

The issue of credibility with regard to Freud's theory

Credibility is an important issue in scientific research. As you investigate Freud's theory further, you will see why the question of credibility is raised. You may find aspects of Freud's theory incredible, such as the idea that a boy has sexual feelings for his mother (although it is not quite so straight-forward as this). Freud's work was controversial in his lifetime

> **Credibility** refers to how believable the findings of research are.

and remains controversial. He has been criticised for overemphasising sexual development. A later theorist, Erikson, followed Freud's ideas but developed them to focus on social development and on an individual's whole life span. His views are considered more credible because of this.

Masson (1984) criticised Freud on a number of issues. He says that Freud originally thought that what he was hearing from his patients was about child abuse, but he then dismissed this and came up with the **Oedipus complex** theory to explain his patients' stories. Freud thought that child abuse could not be so widespread, so the stories must be fantasies. Masson claims that the stories were about real child abuse and, therefore, Freud's theory is not credible.

> The **Oedipus complex** is the idea that a boy has sexual feelings for his mother, but that he feels guilty because he hates his father for being a rival for his mother's affections.

Masson (1989) criticised Freud's work again and thought there were three flaws:

- First, Masson emphasised that the power of the analyst who was interpreting the patient's thoughts and dreams could lead the patient to accept the interpretation.
- Second, Masson claimed that Freud's theory shows gender bias because he focused mainly on boys in the phallic stage and claimed that boys identified with their father more thoroughly than girls identified with their mother, so girls are said to have a less strong moral code. If a theory emphasises one gender over another, it is called **alpha bias**. If a theory does not emphasise gender differences, this is **beta bias**. Freud's theory shows alpha bias. Alpha bias is often 'against' females and there is a feminist argument that Freud's theories are biased against women.

> A key issue described in this chapter is the problem that recovered memories may be false memories. This key issue examines the power of the analyst.

- Third, Masson claimed that Freud's theory overemphasised sexual matters, which was a sensitive issue for patients. It is claimed that, in psychoanalysis, feelings that the patient has for others can be transferred to the analyst. Those feelings can be feelings of love. This is, therefore, a sensitive issue that can lead to problems for the analysand.

Power, gender bias and sensitivity are important issues and possible problems with psychoanalysis that bring its credibility into question.

Correlation designs

In Chapter 2, three participant (experimental) designs were outlined:
- matched pairs
- independent groups
- repeated measures

Another type of design, though not an experimental one, is **correlation design**. Correlation design involves comparing data from the same participants. Two measures

are taken from one individual and recorded. Once the two scores are obtained from enough participants, the relationship between the scores is tested. Possible relationships are:

■ scoring highly on both measures
■ scoring highly on one of the measures and having a low score on the other

There are two types of correlation:

■ A **positive correlation** is when one score rises as the other rises, e.g. as age increases so does the time it takes to react to a stimulus.
■ A **negative correlation** is when one score rises as the other falls, e.g. as age rises, average driving speed falls.

The main points in a correlation are that the same person produces the two scores and that both measures have numerical data. In psychoanalytic theory, it has been claimed from studies that as length of time in analysis increases, benefits of the therapy rise — a positive correlation. It could also be claimed that as the level of worrying dreams rises, the ratings of a good early relationship with parents falls — a negative correlation. However, this is only speculative, rather than being derived from studies. It is just an idea for a negative correlation based on Freud's theories.

Important features of correlation design include:

■ There is no independent or dependent variable. There are two variables of equal importance. For example, one variable might be length of time in analysis and the other might be the measured benefit of therapy.
■ The hypothesis will not be about a difference between two conditions, it will be about a relationship between the two variables.
■ The hypothesis could be directional because it could predict a positive or negative correlation. For example, a directional hypothesis for a correlation might be that 'there is a positive relationship between length of time in analysis and the benefit of therapy'. The direction is predicted — the hypothesis mentions a positive relationship rather than 'a relationship'.

Evaluation of correlation designs

Strengths

■ Initial relationships can be discovered which might not have been realised previously. Whenever there are two scaled measures and the same people are producing both sets of data, a correlation test can be carried out. Therefore, this is a flexible design, which, if an unexpected relationship is indicated, can lead to new research. A study investigating the relationship between troubling dreams and the early relationship with parents would be new and a relationship might be uncovered. The relationship would be only partly unexpected because it is suggested to an extent by Freud's views.
■ The same people are providing both sets of data, so the data will not be affected by individual differences. To be scientific, a research method must include controls to ensure that results are not affected by participant variables. Scores for a correlation are not affected in this way.

Weaknesses

- Correlation designs only indicate a relationship. To be scientific, a research method should be strong enough, with controls and no bias, to show a cause-and-effect relationship between the independent and dependent variables. A correlation cannot show a cause-and-effect relationship. For example, length of time in analysis and benefit of therapy could be connected, but it might not be the length of time that causes the benefit. It might be that the person staying in analysis for a long time has insight whereas a person who leaves does not have such insight. It could be that it is the ability to have insight that gives the greater benefits, not the length of time in analysis. A correlation shows a relationship but does not show that one of the variables depends on the other.
- The measures might not produce valid data. Time in analysis is a clear measure but the benefits of therapy are not easy to quantify. Some variables are more valid than others, but a correlation can use data from unnatural measures.

Table 3.6 *Strengths and weaknesses of correlation design*

Strengths	Weaknesses
• Good for finding relationships at the start of an investigation; also unexpected relationships; once two sets of data are collected from the same participants, a test can be carried out to see if there is a correlation between them • There are no participant variables, so yield more secure data	• Only suggests a relationship; this does not mean that the two variables are causally related; they may only show a relationship by chance or because of some other factor • Data may not be valid because the measures may be artificial or unconnected

Analysing a correlation

Table 3.7 contains some artificial correlation data in order to show how such data can be analysed.

Table 3.7 *Correlation data (artificial) to show the relationship between months in analysis and therapeutic benefit*

Participant	Months in analysis	Improvement in health score (therapeutic benefit)	Months in analysis (ranked from low to high)	Therapeutic benefit (ranked from low to high)
1	65	35	10	9
2	34	41	4	10
3	20	15	1	1
4	24	22	2.5	3
5	24	26	2.5	5.5
6	58	28	8	7
7	52	18	7	2
8	46	26	6	5.5
9	38	23	5	4
10	63	30	9	8
	Mode = 24 Median = 42 Mean = 42.4	Mode = 26 Median = 26 Mean = 26.4		

Table 3.7 shows the ranking of time in analysis and therapeutic benefit measured by improvement in health score (out of 100). The ranks can be compared to show if there is a relationship between the two variables (months in analysis and improvement in health score).

If a participant's ranks are both low, middle or high, then there is a pattern:

- Participant 1 is ranked 10 for 1 months in analysis and 9 for improvement in health score. Both ranks are high.
- Participant 3 is ranked 1 for months in analysis and 1 for improvement in health score. Both the ranks are low.
- Participant 4 is ranked joint second for months in analysis and third lowest for health score — again, a close match.
- Seven of the ten participants have ranks that are either the same or within 1 of each other, which shows a strong relationship.
- Three participants (2, 5 and 7) have ranks that do not match, which shows that the correlation is not perfect.

> **Study hint** By examining the data, patterns may emerge. You should familiarise yourself with drawing conclusions from the data in this way. A statistical test can be carried out, but it is useful to know beforehand what sort of result one might expect.

Using a scattergraph to display the results of a correlation

Correlation data are displayed graphically by using a **scattergraph**. The two scores from each participant generate a point on the graph, so in this example there are ten points. A line of best fit is drawn. If there is a relationship, the line of best fit is close to most of the points. A scattergraph of the data in Table 3.7 is shown in Figure 3.2.

> **Scattergraphs** are used only for correlations.

The line of best fit, with five scores on each side, is in a positive direction. The three scores that do not fit well are clear.

Overall, this graph suggests that there is a positive correlation between time in analysis and improvement in health score.

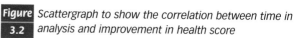
Figure 3.2 Scattergraph to show the correlation between time in analysis and improvement in health score

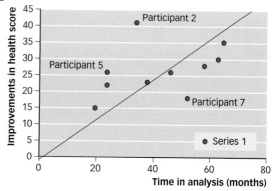

When does a correlation indicate that a relationship exists?

An 'eyeball' test — looking at data sets to see how they compare — is useful, but is difficult to draw firm conclusions from. Table 3.7 shows that, for seven out of ten participants, there seems to be a relationship between time spent in analysis and health benefit. A statistical test (Spearman test) can be carried out to see if the relationship is real for the group as a whole.

First, it is important to know how to interpret the results of the test:

- If both scores rise, there is a positive correlation. A result of +1 means a perfect positive correlation. There is a perfect relationship between the two scores.
- A result of 0 means that there is no correlation. The two scores do not relate to each other.
- If one score rises and the other falls, there is a negative correlation. A result of −1 means a perfect negative correlation. There is a perfect relationship between the two scores.

For example, a test result of +0.70 or higher shows a positive relationship; a test result of −0.70 or lower shows a negative relationship. That is not to say that a result of a +0.45 does not show a relationship (see page 178).

Carrying out a Spearman test

Table 3.8 Data for a Spearman test, based on Table 3.7

Participant	Months in analysis	Improvement in health score (therapeutic benefit)	Months in analysis (ranked from low to high — Step 1)	Therapeutic benefit (ranked from low to high — Step 1)	Difference between ranks (Step 2)	Differences squared (Step 3)
1	65	35	10	9	+1	1
2	34	41	4	10	−6	36
3	20	15	1	1	0	0
4	24	22	2.5	3	−0.5	0.25
5	24	26	2.5	5.5	−3	9
6	58	28	8	7	+1	1
7	52	18	7	2	+5	25
8	46	26	6	5.5	+0.5	0.25
9	38	23	5	4	+1	1
10	63	30	9	8	+1	1
	Mode = 24 Median = 42	Mode = 26 Median = 26				Total (Σ) = 74.5 (Step 4)

How to rank data

- Start with the lowest score. Give it a rank of 1.
- Allocate ranks as the scores rise.
- If there are two or more scores that are the same, allocate all those scores to the same rank by finding the middle rank. For example, if there are two scores of 20 that would be ranked 3 and 4, give them both the rank of 3.5. If there are three scores of 20 that would be ranked 3, 4 and 5, give them all a rank of 4.

How to calculate Spearman's coefficient of rank correlation

Refer to Table 3.8. The formula for the calculation of Spearman's coefficient of rank correlation (R_S) is:

$$R_S = 1 - \frac{6\Sigma d^2}{N^3 - N}$$

Step 1: Rank both sets of data.
Step 2: Work out the difference (d) between the ranks for each participant.

Step 3: Square (multiply by itself) the difference found in Step 2 for each participant. This gets rid of the minus signs.

Step 4: Add up the squared differences (the numbers worked out in Step 3). For the data given in Table 3.8, the total is **74.5**.

Step 5: Find N, which is the number of scores. (Here, $N = $ **10**.)

Step 6: Multiply the sum of the squared differences (from Step 4) by 6. (Here, $74.5 \times 6 = $ **447**.)

Step 7: Square N and subtract 1. (Here, $10 \times 10 - 1 = $ **99**.)

Step 8: Multiply the answer found in Step 7 by N. (Here, $99 \times 10 = $ **990**.)

Step 9: Divide the answer to Step 6 by the answer to Step 8. (Here, $447/990 = $ **0.45**.)

Step 10: Subtract the answer to Step 9 from 1. (Here, $1 - 0.45 = $ **+0.55**.) This is the result of the test. It is in Step 10 that a minus or plus sign is allocated. If the answer to Step 6 is larger than the answer to Step 8, the result of Step 10 will be negative and any correlation will be negative. If the answer to Step 6 is smaller than the answer to Step 8, the result of Step 10 will be positive and any correlation will be positive.

Step 11: Look up the result of the test in statistical tables to see if it is significant. (Statistical tables for the various statistical tests, including Spearman's, can be found in a statistics textbook or using the internet.)

For $N = 10$ and 0.05 level of significance, the result has to be greater than 0.56 for it to be significant.

The scores given here as an example seem to show a positive correlation from the eyeball test and from the scattergraph. However, the Spearman test shows that the result of +0.55 is not quite significant.

Cross-sectional and longitudinal types of study

Even with different research methods, if a study is looking at developmental trends, it can be carried out either cross-sectionally or longitudinally.

Cross-sectional studies

A cross-sectional study takes one moment in time and compares different groups at that time. Most experiments are cross-sectional because they are usually only used to test the participants once. For example, experiments to test memory are cross-sectional if they compare the memory of a list of words by a control group and an experimental group. However, if the study is about how memory changes with age, in other words if developmental trends are the focus of the study, then the choice of a cross-sectional or longitudinal design is important. One could choose a cross-sectional design and test, for example, 20-year-olds and 70-year-olds and compare the findings. The other way would be to choose a longitudinal design and wait 50 years for the participants to age. This would be rather impractical.

In the study by Bachrach et al. (1991) (on the CD-ROM), there were times when a longitudinal study was used — researchers went back to patients to see if therapeutic benefit had continued. Cramer (1997) (page 207) used data from a longitudinal study when investigating a possible link between personality and the use of defence mechanisms. She used data already collected for an ongoing **longitudinal study** of developmental issues studying people from the age of 3 years onwards. They were 23 years old when Cramer (1997) used the data.

The psychodynamic approach is about development and uses **longitudinal studies**. The cognitive approach is about information processing, so cross-sectional studies are more likely to be used.

Strengths of cross-sectional studies

- They do not take as long to carry out as longitudinal studies, so they are cheaper and easier. The study is manageable and the results can be analysed more quickly. Cost, time and ease of use are all useful factors when research is being planned. For these reasons, cross-sectional studies are more practicable than longitudinal studies.
- It is easier to find participants because they take part for only a short time compared with longitudinal studies.
- Cross-sectional studies are more ethical than longitudinal studies, which may put pressure on participants.

Weaknesses of cross-sectional studies

- Because they take place at one time only, they do not gather such rich data as longitudinal studies. At some other time, the participants might have responded differently. If a matched pairs or independent groups design is used, the participants may be different. Therefore, the data are less focused on the individual and less detailed.
- They cannot find trends in data or find out what would happen at a later date if the study were repeated. Cross-sectional studies are scientific if there are good controls, but they are snapshots of a situation and there is no opportunity to follow up on the findings.

Study hint When giving strengths or weaknesses, be sure to make the point fully. If you just say that a strength of cross-sectional studies is that they are easier or cheaper, you will not score the marks. You have to explain why this is the case.

Table 3.9 Strengths and weaknesses of cross-sectional studies

Strengths	Weaknesses
• They are reasonably cheap, quick and practical because there is no follow-up and participants are only tested once	• There is not as much detail as in a longitudinal design with regard to individual differences
• Participants are found more easily because there is no follow-up; this makes the studies more ethical because there is less pressure on participants than there is in longitudinal designs	• They are snapshots that gather data at one moment in time; they cannot easily gather data about trends in development

Longitudinal studies

Longitudinal studies follow one particular group over a period of time. A test or observation is repeated at intervals over the length of the study, which usually lasts quite a long time. The aim is to compare the data gathered each time to see the effects of the passage of time. For example, to study language development it would be useful to follow a group of children from babyhood through to perhaps 5 years and check their language ability at milestones along the way.

It is hard to say exactly how long a study has to be for it to be longitudinal. A study run over a few weeks is probably not longitudinal; a study run over a few months probably is. However, it depends on what is being studied.

Practice 3.2

Here are some suggested studies. Decide whether they should be cross-sectional or longitudinal.

Study 1 To examine the effect of upbringing on social class in adulthood.

Study 2 To see if participants will conform to a group even when an answer is obviously wrong.

Study 3 To examine the effect of smoking on health.

Study 4 To see if participants recall a story in less detail over time, checking the recall over the period of a year.

Answers are given at the end of Chapter 3.

Strengths of longitudinal studies

■ Longitudinal studies follow the same participants over the time of the study, so participant variables are controlled. This means that when comparing the data, any differences or similarities can be taken to come from the measure itself. For example, if the language development of some children follows the same developmental pattern from birth to 3 years, then individual differences in the participants will not cause a problem in drawing conclusions.

■ Detailed developmental trends can be found. In a longitudinal study the same people are tested over time and differences and similarities in the data can be taken to be due to developmental factors. For example, if language development of some children is followed from birth to 3 years, this is a better way to find out about language stages than a cross-sectional study because the patterns and trends in language development can be identified.

Weaknesses of longitudinal studies

■ Some participants may drop out because they no longer want to continue, or for some other reason. This can affect the findings because there will be fewer

Table 3.10	Strengths and weaknesses of longitudinal studies	
Strengths	**Weaknesses**
• The same participants are followed, so there are no participant variables to be considered and conclusions can be stronger than in an independent groups design	• The participants may not want to continue or may move away; those remaining may share characteristics that mean the findings are biased
• They are probably the best way of studying developmental trends because they repeat the tests or tasks over time and comparisons can be drawn	• There are practical difficulties; they can be expensive, time consuming and the researchers may change

participants from which to gather results and draw conclusions There could also be a bias because those that drop out may share characteristics, leaving those remaining sharing other characteristics, so the results may be affected.

■ Longitudinal studies are time consuming and expensive, and the researchers may change during the study.

Sampling techniques

Sampling techniques are important for all research methods. They are described in detail in the Chapter 1. The sampling techniques you need to know are:

■ **random sampling** — each person in the population has an equal chance of being chosen to be in the sample

■ **stratified sampling** — ensuring representation from certain groups

■ **volunteer** or self-selected sampling — people offer to take part

■ **opportunity sampling** — taking whoever is available at the time

> **Study hint** Use the information in Chapter 1 to make sure that you understand the strengths and weaknesses of sampling techniques.

Examination-style questions

1 Outline the features of a correlation design. *(4 marks)*

2 Evaluate both cross-sectional and longitudinal studies in terms of both strengths and weaknesses. *(8 marks)*

3 Explain two similarities and two differences between general case studies and Freud's style of case study. *(8 marks)*

Extension questions

1 Discuss the value in psychology of using case studies compared with using experiments. *(12 marks)*

2 Compare the use of cross-sectional and longitudinal designs by looking at their strengths and weaknesses. *(12 marks)*

Content

Freud's psychosexual theory

This section covers the five stages of psychosexual development, the three parts of the personality, the three parts of the mind, the Oedipus complex, defence mechanisms and how Freud explained gender development.

Concepts from Freud's psychosexual theory

This section covers the basic ideas that you need to understand Freud's theory. Remembering that his theory was developed over his lifetime, what is explained here is necessarily brief, but it is sufficient for an understanding of his views.

Freud dealt with neuroses not psychoses

Freud focused on adult patients with neuroses and looked for problems in their early lives to explain these. **Neuroses** are mental health problems in individuals who are aware that they have difficulties and, to an extent, are capable of having insight into these problems to help themselves get better. At first, Freud thought of neuroses as neural problems (problems to do with the nerves) rather than mental ones. Examples of neuroses are phobias and some types of depression. **Psychoses** are mental health problems in individuals who are not aware of their problems and do not have the insight to help themselves to get better because of the nature of the problems. An example of a psychosis is schizophrenia.

Freud's 'cure' needed patients who could gain insight into their problems, so he treated only neuroses. One particular neurosis that Freud thought interesting was hysteria. Hysterical symptoms are physical symptoms that have no physical cause (although Freud thought there was a physical cause to do with the nerves). An example is Anna O, whose case helped the development of Freud's theory. Anna O had some difficulties in speaking and listening and some minor paralyses, with no apparent physical cause. Freud thought that the symptoms were hysterical and that the problems came from the unconscious. Some desire in the person's unconscious was solved or granted by such hysterical symptoms. For example, if someone cannot see but there seems to be no physical reason for the blindness, perhaps there is something that he or she does not want to see.

Explore Look up the case of Bertha von Pappenheim (Anna O) who was a patient of Breuer (a colleague of Freud). She had typical symptoms of hysteria and when she talked about forgotten memories she seemed to get better. One symptom was that she could not drink out of a glass. After remembering an incident where a dog had licked a glass, she was able to drink from a glass again. Anna O said that Breuer and Freud's therapy was a 'talking cure'.

The role of the unconscious

Freud thought that the mind was made up of three parts:
- The **conscious mind** holds the thoughts, ideas, emotions and other aspects of thinking of which the individual is aware.
- The **preconscious mind** holds thoughts and ideas that can be accessed and are ready to be known about, but are not actually conscious at that time.
- The **unconscious mind** is the main part. It is where all thoughts originate, with some becoming conscious and some being allowed into the preconscious.

It is common to use an iceberg analogy — the conscious mind is the part of the iceberg above the surface, the preconscious is a small part below the surface and the unconscious is the remainder of the iceberg, below the surface, largely inaccessible, yet very important for the individual. Thoughts in the unconscious mind are active and trying to find a means of expression. According to Freud, the unconscious can only be accessed through research methods such as free association, slips of the tongue, dream analysis and symbol analysis.

Figure 3.3 *Freud's model of personality structure*

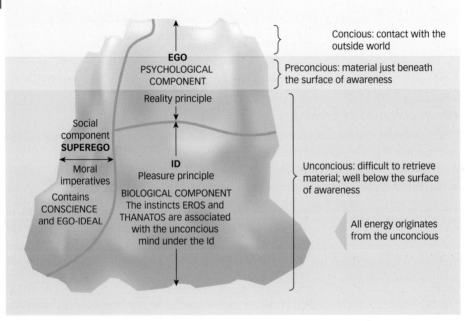

Repressed memories may cause neuroses

In the case of Anna O, Freud suggested that repressed memories were causing problems. For example, after remembering seeing a dog lick a glass, she had no problem drinking from a glass whereas she had been unable to do so before recovering the memory.

So Freud had the idea of repressed memories being inaccessible, but still guiding behaviour. He thought that if such memories were made conscious, then they would no longer guide behaviour inappropriately. From this idea, Freud built the therapy of **psychoanalysis**. The aim of psychoanalysis is to make unconscious thoughts conscious, thus releasing the thoughts and the energy that the individual was using to keep those thoughts unconscious. With that energy released, the individual can progress.

> The idea of energy being important is the 'dynamic' part of psychodynamic; the 'psycho' part is because it is a theory of the mind.

Hypnosis will not help the patient

Breuer, who worked in the same field as Freud, used hypnosis and Freud thought originally that this would be a useful method to find the cause of neuroses. However, Freud came to believe that the cure occurred when the patient understood the

unconscious urges and thoughts, and they were made conscious. Hypnosis does not enable such insight, so Freud rejected the use of hypnosis in psychoanalysis.

Life and death instincts

For repression to take place, energy must be used to keep thoughts unconscious. According to Freud, the energy that we possess is focused into a life instinct (**eros**), which is an instinct for both self-preservation and sexual energy. His idea was that urges and wishes from the life instinct in the unconscious lead to arousal, and that one of our drives is to reduce arousal. One way to reduce arousal is death, so Freud put forward the idea of the death instinct, which he called **thanatos**. Thanatos provides energy for the ego to inhibit the sexual instinct; eros provides the energy to inhibit the instinct that leads to death. With aggression the death instinct is channelled into something more productive, for example sport.

The importance of dreams

Freud suggests dream analysis as a way of finding out what is in the unconscious and needs to be released. In dream analysis:

- the manifest content is the actual dream that the dreamer relates
- the latent content is the underlying meaning of the dream

The dreamer relates the manifest content and the analyst analyses that content to reveal it as symbols hiding the latent content. The latent content comes from the unconscious because, in dreaming, the unconscious thoughts that are trying to make themselves known break out. Freud saw a dream as 'the royal road to the unconscious' because, when analysed, the latent content reveals the unconscious wishes.

The analyst's job during psychoanalysis is to explain the symbols and the meaning behind a dream so that the analysand can have insight. Once that has happened, the unconscious wish is made conscious and is then no longer a problem.

The three parts of the personality

According to Freud, there are three parts to the personality:

- The **id** is the part of the personality we are born with. It is the demanding part (id is 'it' in Latin, i.e. not yet a rational person). The infant is all 'I want' and demands to be satisfied. The id is in the unconscious in that the demands are not conscious — a baby knows what it wants, but unconsciously. The id works on the pleasure principle.
- The **ego** is the rational part of the personality. It works on reality principles, and tries to obtain for the id what the id wants. Ego is Latin for 'I' and the ego is the part of the personality that works out how to satisfy the person. The ego develops from the age of about 18 months.
- The **superego** develops during the phallic stage, at around 4 years of age. The superego (Latin for 'above I') works on the morality principle. The superego is made up of the conscience, given to individuals by their parents and by society indicating what is right and wrong, and the **ego ideal**. The ego ideal is the idea people have of what they should be like, again given by parents and society. The superego is the 'you can't have' part of the personality.

The ego has to pacify the id and the superego and find a balance between their conflicting demands. If two conflicting things are desired, the id also makes conflicting demands. The ego has to find a course of action that maintains a balance. The ego might do this is by repressing memories or using other defence mechanisms.

Figure 3.4 *The id, ego and superego*

The id wants satisfaction   The ego juggles demands   Superego = conscience

Defence mechanisms

Anna Freud, Freud's daughter, talked about defence mechanisms. These are sometimes called ego-defence mechanisms because their role is to enable the ego to keep the peace between the id ('I want') and the superego ('you can't have'), or between conflicting demands from the id. Defence mechanisms can either push a desire out of conscious thought or can transfer a desire onto something safer.

You have to study repression and one other defence mechanism. Denial, projection, displacement and regression are suitable examples. Repression and denial both involve pushing a desire out of conscious thought; projection and displacement both involve transferring a desire onto something safer. Regression involves going back to an earlier stage of development to avoid the conflict.

- **Repression** is when thoughts are kept in the unconscious mind and are not allowed into the conscious mind. It is as if they are forgotten — or at least not remembered. It is more a case of motivated forgetting. This is not done consciously. An example of repression is when something traumatic happens (e.g. abuse) and subsequently people cannot remember anything about it. They do not deny that something has happened; they just do not remember.
- **Denial** is when there is something traumatic happening but the individual 'denies it' (acts as if it has not happened). This protects the individual from unhappy or unacceptable thoughts. An example might be the denial of having inappropriate sexual feelings.
- **Projection** is when unacceptable thoughts are dealt with by saying that they are someone else's thoughts. Perhaps this is so that the ego can deal with the feelings, without problems from the superego. Not loving one's father, for example, might be projected onto a brother or sister.
- **Displacement** is when urges that are unacceptable to the individual concerned are dealt with by turning them into something else. For example, anger might be turned into aggression in a sport. So unacceptable aggression towards someone close to you can be turned into acceptable aggression.

■ **Regression** is when, to cope with something stressful, a person reverts to childhood behaviour. Examples are thumb sucking and not accepting responsibility.

Practice 3.3

The following situations show defence mechanisms at work. Identify a defence mechanism for each situation.

Situation 1 Someone close to a person has died, yet the person seems to be carrying on as usual and is not particularly upset.

Situation 2 Someone is told that he/she is seriously ill but does not remember the conversation.

Situation 3 Someone who is not happy at work asks suddenly why the boss is angry all the time.

Situation 4 Someone whose wife is having an affair takes up kick-boxing.

Situation 5 Someone starts eating more than previously and stops making decisions.

Answers are given at the end of Chapter 3.

Study hint You need to be able to describe repression and one other defence mechanism. You should prepare an answer worth up to 4 marks for a description question about each defence mechanism. If you think you have not written enough for the mark allocation, a way of gaining a mark is to give an example.

Strengths of the idea of defence mechanisms

■ There are everyday examples of such things occurring. Repression is a well-known phenomenon. Victims of crimes, accidents or other traumas often cannot remember anything about the event. Denial is in everyday language — people are told that they are 'in denial' about something that has happened. Therefore, there is validity in the concept.

■ When defence mechanisms are revealed to people and they understand that a mechanism is at work, they feel better. Anna O is an example. Freud says that after she remembered the incident of the dog licking the glass, she was then able to drink out of a glass. Evidence supports the claim that defence mechanisms keep urges in the unconscious and that once revealed to the conscious, the problems stop.

Weaknesses of the idea of defence mechanisms

■ It is difficult to test the idea of defence mechanisms scientifically. They are not measurable. It is possible to find examples in real life, such as repression, but this is not the same as scientific testing.

■ They need interpretation because they are about individuals. One person might be using projection when saying his or her sister hates their father; another might just *know* that the sister hates their father. Freud understood that his case studies were unique studies of individuals. He did not agree with general comments about features like defence mechanisms. The weakness is, therefore, that there may be subjectivity.

The stages of psychosexual development

Freud thought the first years of a child's life were important in personality development. In these first years, there are three psychosexual stages:

- the **oral stage** — birth–18 months
- the **anal stage** — 2–3 years old
- the **phallic stage** — from 4 years old

These are followed by the **latency period** and the **genital stage**. The stages have ages associated with them. However, different age ranges are suggested in sources, so the ages are just a guideline.

Freud focused on sexual energy, which for him is present from birth. At each stage, this energy is focused on a different body area. If the stage is resolved, there is no energy remaining to protect the individual from lack of resolution of the stage. If the stage is not resolved, then energy remains behind and can cause problems in adulthood. When a stage is not resolved, the individual is said to be fixated at that stage. People can be fixated at any or all of the stages. **Fixation**, therefore, is not resolving the issues arising in one stage and this means that energy is needed to maintain a balanced personality.

The oral stage

- The oral stage is the first psychosexual stage.
- The focus for energy and sexual pleasure is the mouth.

The newborn infant gets pleasure from the mouth, from nursing (which means feeding) and from sucking. This stage takes place from birth to around 18 months. The id and the pleasure principle are in control. The stage lasts for varying lengths of time because in different societies children are nursed for different lengths of time.

Adult characteristics, if fixated at the oral stage

Oral fixation means being obsessed with stimulating the mouth (e.g. smoking, pen sucking). If a baby is weaned too soon, or too late, conflicts at this stage may remain and cause maladaptive behaviour. If children are underfed, they might, as adults, become orally dependent and obsessed with achieving oral stimulation. This might involve manipulating others to fulfil these needs. If children are overfed or indulged, then instead of 'growing up', they might, as adults, demand help and be needy. Oral fixation can lead to over-eating, talking too much, being addicted to smoking, and chewing a lot. The person might be sarcastic or have a 'biting' personality. So, an oral character can be dependent, sarcastic, focused on the mouth and needy.

The anal stage

- The anal stage is the second psychosexual stage.
- It occurs from around 2–3 years or when potty-training is completed.
- The focus for pleasure and sexual energy is the anus.

The child focuses on faeces and potty-training or control is the issue. If the stage is not resolved, it leads to an anal character. Parents may be too strict or too lenient, leading a child either to be messy or to hold back. Either could cause fixation, holding back energy that is then not available for the adult to move forward.

Adult characteristics if fixated at the anal stage

When fixated at the anal stage there are two types of **anal character** in an adult:

- An **anal-expulsive character** is messy and might have a job or hobby that reflects this such as building or pottery.
- An **anal-retentive character** can be stubborn and obstinate. Anal-retentive people tend to be overly tidy and obsessively clean. They can also be mean with money, which is another way of holding back. They might hoard possessions or be obsessive about their property and rights.

> **Explore** A study investigating the relationship between parenting style and anal character is suggested for the practical. So, if you decide to do that practical, you can explore these issues.

> Usually by 'anal', people mean **anally retentive**.

The phallic stage, including the Oedipus complex and gender development

- The phallic stage is the third psychosexual stage.
- It occurs from the age of about 4 years.
- The focus of pleasure and sexual energy is the genitals.

During the phallic stage children develop their gender behaviour. Important features of the phallic stage are that:

- gender identity develops
- the superego develops
- the conscience and ego ideal develop

> **Gender development** is a theme that runs through the psychodynamic approach, the biological approach and the learning approach.

The **development of gender**, the superego, the conscience and the ego ideal all occur because of the Oedipus complex, so the Oedipus complex is explained first.

Oedipus is a mythical figure who killed his father and married his mother, although he was unaware of the relationships. Freud used this myth to explain his idea about the relationship between boys and their parents during the phallic stage.

> **Study hint** It is important that you understand the Oedipus complex and to understand it, it is best to try to accept it. So, keep an open mind. Learn about it before making a judgement. If you grasp this idea, the rest of the approach becomes simpler — you will understand and evaluate the Little Hans study better, you will be able to address the key issues more thoroughly and you will be able to compare Freud's ideas about gender development with other related ideas.

Freud found that there was often a problem with parents when children were about 4 or 5 years old and that this seemed to be a sexual problem. (Freud could have been hearing about child abuse, but he decided that this was not the case because it could not be that common.) He concluded that the sexual references he was hearing from his patients had to be wishes and urges from the unconscious. With sexual pleasure focused on the genitals, he thought it natural that a boy would focus those feelings on his mother. Therefore, because of the father's relationship with the mother, the boy would see his father as a rival. Alongside this, the boy would learn at about this age that his mother did not have a penis. He would hate his father as a rival and would be afraid that his father would punish him — a fitting punishment would be castration. **Castration fear** is the boy's fear that his father will castrate him because of his feelings for his mother. The father is hated and feared, and the son has to resolve such feelings, which are unconscious and powerful. One way to resolve the problems is to identify with the father and 'become' him. In this way, the boy can possess the mother (because he 'is' the father) and also not have to fear his father. The **Oedipus complex** is how the boy learns his gender, develops a conscience and learns his ego ideal when he identifies with his father in order to possess the mother, without feeling guilt about hating his father.

Identification is a key concept in the phallic stage. By identifying with his father, the boy takes on the father's beliefs and values. The boy develops a superego with a conscience and an ego ideal, all learnt from his father. He also develops his gender identity, doing what his father does because he 'is' his father. So boys learn male-gender behaviour by identifying with their father in order to resolve the Oedipus complex.

The **Electra complex** was developed (not by Freud) to explain what happens to girls in the phallic stage. It holds that girls also focus on their genitals at this stage and that they have feelings for their fathers. They understand that they do not have a penis and they develop **penis envy**. Penis envy is not as strong as castration fear, so the Electra complex does not bring such strong feelings as the Oedipus complex. This means that boys are seen to identify with their fathers more strongly than girls identify with their mothers.

A girl has no penis and feels less worthy than her father. So, she focuses on her father because she thinks that he can help her get a penis or a substitute. There has been a suggestion that this substitute is a baby. Others say that a girl wants male power, rather than a penis, which explains somewhat differently the attraction to the father. By becoming the mother, the girl can have her father, so the girl identifies with her mother. The girl then develops a superego with the conscience and ego ideal, and takes on her gender behaviour.

Adult characteristics if fixated at the phallic stage
If fixated at the phallic stage, there may be problems due to inappropriate learning of gender behaviour. The **phallic character** can develop, which is self-assured, reckless, vain and proud. A person fixated at the phallic stage might be incapable of loving another person.

The latency period

The fourth stage of psychosexual development is not really a stage — it is the latency period. As far as sexual energy is concerned, there is no focus on a part of the body from the resolution of the phallic stage to the start of the genital stage. In this period, children prefer friends of the same sex and focus on sport and school.

The genital stage

- The **genital stage** is the fifth stage of psychosexual development.
- It starts with puberty.
- The focus of sexual pleasure is the genitals.

If the Oedipus complex was successfully resolved in the phallic stage then, at the genital stage, friendships start to be between the two genders, rather than being same-sex friendships. Heterosexual friendships and relationships develop. If little energy was used up because of fixation in the oral, anal or phallic stages, there is sufficient energy in the genital stage for normal relationships to develop. If the person did not successfully resolve the Oedipus complex, and is fixated in the phallic stage, then problems can occur with relationships, including development of homosexuality.

Evaluation of Freud's theory and the psychodynamic approach

It is easier to evaluate Freud's ideas as a whole than to evaluate different aspects of his theory. This is because the same criticisms apply. If it is an overall criticism that his concepts are not measurable, then his personality theory can be evaluated by saying that the concepts (id, ego and superego) are not measurable. Consider the evaluation presented here and use these points when evaluating aspects of his theory.

Strengths

- Freud's new ideas about treating mental health problems provided solutions that at the time were otherwise unavailable. Psychoanalysis addressed neuroses, such as hysteria, whereas previously the only treatments were what we would think of as barbaric. So people were helped who would otherwise not have been helped.
- Freud generated his theory from in-depth case studies in which he looked at many aspects of a person's background and mental state. His theory was built from valid data and it focused on the dreams and problems of each individual.

Weaknesses

- Freud's approach does not use scientific method. Data are qualitative and personal, so an overall theory should not be generated from such individual data. The findings are not generalisable.
- The concepts are not measurable and so cannot be rigorously tested. For example, the unconscious is unreachable by normal means, and the id, ego and superego cannot be measured.
- The case studies had to involve some element of interpretation of symbols in dreams or of free-association data. There is, therefore, going to be subjectivity, whereas science requires objectivity.

- Freud worked in middle-class Vienna, mostly with women, so the sample is limited to this group. It is difficult to then generalise to the whole population, although Freud did so. The sample is biased, which makes generalisation difficult.
- Freud looked only at development up to puberty and adolescence. Later, others within the approach looked at development over the whole lifespan. Erikson developed the 'eight stages of man' and looked at different stages including old age. He also focused on social development rather than sexual development. A weakness of Freud's theory is that it is limited by not examining development later in life and for just focusing on psychosexual aspects.

However, these weaknesses show only that Freud's theory cannot be proved correct, they do not show that it is wrong.

Table 3.11 *Strengths and weaknesses of Freud's theory*

Strengths	Weaknesses
• It allowed treatment for mental illnesses that were untreated at the time	• The findings are not generalisable because the data are about individuals and are specific to them; the methods are not scientific
• The use of case studies allows valid data to be gathered and in-depth analysis to take place	• The method requires interpretation and it is difficult to achieve objectivity, so the theory is not scientifically based
	• The sample is biased; this bias means lack of generalisability
	• The theory is limited because the study stops at adolescence, and focuses only on psychosexual development

Comparison of the explanations of gender behaviour

The explanations of gender development given by the psychodynamic, biological and learning approaches are compared in Chapter 5.

Examination-style questions

1 Describe two defence mechanisms. In your answer, use an example for each defence mechanism. *(6 marks)*

2 Describe what is meant by the Oedipus complex. *(5 marks)*

3 Evaluate Freud's theory as an explanation for gender development. *(6 marks)*

4 Describe and evaluate Freud's explanation of personality. *(8 marks)*

Extension questions

1 Discuss how Freud explained mental health problems and explain how Freud thought they could be resolved. *(12 marks)*

2 Discuss the role of defence mechanisms in Freud's theory. Include examples of two defence mechanisms in your answer. *(12 marks)*

Studies in detail

For the psychodynamic approach, you have to know, in detail, Freud's case study of Little Hans and one other study from a choice of three:

■ Virginia Axline's 1964 case study of Dibs, from which she developed the idea of play therapy
■ an overall analysis of whether psychoanalysis works (Bachrach et al. 1991)
■ a study looking at young people and how identity develops, and whether there is a link to the use of defence mechanisms (Cramer 1997)

Three studies are given in detail here. *The other is summarised below and covered in detail on the CD-ROM.*

Freud's case study of Little Hans (1909)

The Little Hans study is one of Freud's best-known studies. Little Hans (not his real name) was the son of a couple who were followers of Freud and knew about his ideas. They wrote to Freud regularly, telling him of Little Hans's progress, so the study was a story of his development, which means that there are a lot of data. For the studies in detail section, you need to know the aims, procedure, results and conclusions, as well as the evaluation. However, for case studies such as this, it is difficult to separate procedure and results as the results are the story. Therefore, it is useful to give aims, background/procedure, case description (similar to results) and case analysis (involves conclusions).

Aims

The aim of the Little Hans study was to monitor the development of a child up to the age of about 4 or 5 years. The parents simply kept in touch with Freud, but the background aim was for Freud to have detail about 'normal' child development. Freud used the detail of the case study as evidence for the Oedipus complex.

Background/procedure

The case study did not involve different methods in the usual sense because the data came from either the letters that Little Hans's father wrote to Freud or from the few times that Freud met Little Hans. Little Hans himself also asked his father to tell Freud things. However, it could be argued that different methods *were* used because, for example, Freud analysed Little Hans's dreams and tried to use only the data that came from Little Hans, even though through his father. One of the main areas of the study is Little Hans's phobia of horses and his fear of going out into the street in case he saw a horse. There is more to the study but the phobia is the area of focus when summarising the study, because this is where Freud found evidence for the Oedipus complex.

Freud understood that the parents were followers of his and knew about his theories, so they might only notice, remember and report features of Little Hans's development that fitted the theory. Freud therefore tried to take only the evidence that came from Little Hans, even if reported by the father. Freud was particularly interested in Little Hans's conversations when he was resisting what his parents or Freud were saying. The flowing conversation could be like free association, and the times when he was resistant could be repression or the unconscious protecting itself.

Freud realised that readers of the case study might not agree with the analysis, but he thought that sometimes you have to be present at the time to understand. This is often true of work with young children. For example, you might watch a baby searching for something and know that the searching is deliberate, but this is difficult to convey in writing.

The parents of Little Hans were caring, cheerful and well educated and Little Hans appears to have had no developmental problems. This is important, because Freud takes his story and uses it as evidence for a universal theory of child development.

Case description

This section gives some themes and issues that Freud thought were important.

Hans appears to have had an early interest in 'widdlers', which is what he called penises. He noticed widdlers on animals and that his mother and baby sister did not have them. At one stage, when he had his hand on his penis, his mother threatened to cut his penis off. Hans had a dream where he wanted a friend of his (a girl) to share in his widdling. He also dreamt about his bottom and having children and wiping their bottoms. Hans denied thinking these things and said that they only came to him in dreams. This is the sort of detail that Little Hans's father relayed and that Freud thought was important.

Little Hans's father was away a lot, leaving Hans with his mother. He seems to have wanted his father to go away. When the family moved house and the father was not away as often, he wished his father was dead. Little Hans had dreams that his mother had gone away. He was close to his mother and, when his father was away, spent nights in her bed. His mother bathed him but worked round his penis when washing him and he had been told not to masturbate. All of this Freud thought was relevant.

Little Hans developed a phobia that horses would bite him. Eventually, he became afraid that a white horse would bite him. He had an anxiety attack in the street and stopped going out.

At one point, he said that he was afraid that a horse would come into the room. He later said that he was afraid of white horses with black things on their mouths and things over their eyes. He was afraid particularly of horses pulling laden carts. He did, after some time, recall a real experience of seeing a horse, that was pulling a bus, fall down.

This fear of horses was a real phobia because it limited Little Hans, making him scared to go out.

Unit 2

Little Hans had heard the father of a little girl who was staying with his family, tell her not to put her finger on the white horse that was pulling the cart that was to take her to the station. The father said the horse would bite her.

When he was around three-and-a-half years old, Little Hans's mother had a baby girl. Hans was jealous of his sister from the start. He also said that he was afraid of going underwater in the bath and that he was afraid of water. Little Hans dreamt about a plumber taking his bottom and 'widdler' away and bringing him new ones.

There is a dream about giraffes that Freud also found interesting. One giraffe was crumpled and Little Hans sat on it; the other giraffe just stood to one side.

There was also a time when Little Hans was playing with dolls and at 'having children'. Hans said that mummy was the children's mummy, he was their daddy and Hans's own father was their grandfather.

Case analysis

Freud thought that Little Hans's focus on 'widdlers', including his mother's threat to cut his off, may have been repressed into his unconscious and may have affected him later, in the phallic stage. When Hans talked about 'widdlers', asked to see his mother's and father's, and talked about widdlers of horses, Freud thought this indicated that Hans was making comparisons and trying to understand himself by comparison with others.

Freud thought that the dream about wiping bottoms and helping other children to widdle occurred because Hans had had this done to him and he had derived pleasure from it. This links to Freud's ideas about the anal stage. Hans denied this focus, which Freud interpreted as an example of repression.

The focus on wanting to be with his mother and wanting his father out of the way was interpreted by Freud as being Hans's desire to possess his mother. This was part of the Oedipus complex. The phobia of horses was really a fear of his father because of hating him and wanting him out of the way.

Freud thought that Hans was jealous of his sister because her birth and the attention paid to her brought back to Hans the pleasure that he himself had had at that age. Freud and Hans's father discussed the fear of going under the water in the bath. Freud thought this meant that Hans wanted his sister to fall under the water and drown. He wanted his mother to let go of his sister's head when she was in the bath. When Hans was asked about this by his father, he said 'yes'. Freud and Hans's father concluded that he wanted his sister to drown. Freud thought that Hans wanted both his father and his sister out of the way, so that he could have his mother to himself.

Freud thought that when Hans heard the father tell the little girl staying with them not to put her finger on the horse, Hans connected this to the instruction not to masturbate. Therefore he connected this with horses — hence his fear of horses. Freud thought that this, taken with his mother's threat to cut off his penis, linked to **castration fear**. The dream about the giraffes was interpreted as being a bedroom scene with the sex act and the giraffe watching. Freud also linked this with Hans's fear that a horse would come into the room.

At this stage, Freud told Hans's father to let Hans know that the white horse was Hans's father. The things in front of the horse's eyes were the father's glasses. The black on the horse's mouth represented the moustache of an adult man. So, Hans was afraid of his father and the horse represented his father.

The dream about the plumber seemed to suggest that Hans wanted a bigger 'widdler'. When this was put to him, he agreed. Freud thought that Hans was now overcoming his castration fear and was identifying with his father. Freud considered that the therapy had been successful; Hans's phobia did seem to go away (although this was not very clear). The claim was that his unconscious fears had been made conscious and, therefore, had gone away. Freud and Hans's father thought that when playing with dolls and making himself their father and his father their grandfather, with his mother as the mother, Hans had got around the problem of wanting his father dead.

Hans grew up to produce operas and was apparently completely normal. It is said that he could not remember the analysis but was not upset by it.

Conclusions

Knowing about the anal stage and Freud's ideas of the focus on the anus and pleasure, you can see how some of the evidence from the Little Hans study contributed to those ideas. Much of the case study is focused on the Oedipus complex; there are the ideas of castration fear and the boy desiring his mother and wanting his father out of the way. There is evidence that Little Hans had those feelings. The dreams, such as the dream about giraffes, seem to be about these confused feelings, which supports the idea that the unconscious can find a way of expressing itself through dreams.

Explore Look up Herbert Graf, who was Little Hans, and see what you can find out about him.

Evaluation of the Little Hans study

Strengths

- The amount of detail and its depth. The material is thorough and there is information from the parents and from Little Hans himself. Freud is able to draw on detail about dreams, thoughts, feelings, activities and friendships. Because of the information provided, the study can be re-analysed.
- A case study is one of the only ways to obtain this amount of detail about these sorts of issues. Experiments, observation, surveys or other research methods would not yield these data. Such a study can gather information about dreams and what is actually said, whereas other methods cannot.

Weaknesses

- The parents were followers of Freud and interpreted the detail before passing it on to him. There is, therefore, subjectivity from the parents and, perhaps, also from Freud. He did say that he tried to use only data that came from Little Hans

more directly, but this would not have been easy. Both the parents and Freud would have been noticing anything to do with sexual feelings and thoughts. In reality, these may not have had the importance they seem to have from the case study story. The parents even agreed to bring their son up with Freud's ideas in mind.

■ There are other possible explanations. Bowlby (e.g. 1949) suggests that attachments between mothers and children are very strong. At one point, Little Hans's mother threatened to leave. Hans would have been worried about this, and this might have caused his fears. An alternative explanation for the horse phobia comes from learning theory. Little Hans saw an incident in which a horse, pulling a bus, fell down. He may have connected the horse with his fear of the incident and so come to fear horses.

■ The concepts, such as the Oedipus complex and castration fear, are not measurable and so cannot be studied scientifically. There is nothing to test or measure and any interpretation could be said to be speculative.

Table 3.12	Strengths and weaknesses of the Little Hans study	
Strengths	**Weaknesses**
• The study has much detail and can be re-analysed; it is an in-depth study using qualitative data, which suggests validity • No other method could have gathered the data	• The parents would have been attuned to certain things that Little Hans said and did because they were aware of Freud's theories; Freud would also be looking for certain things, so there is likely to be some subjectivity in interpretation • There are other possible interpretations of the data, such as attachment theory (Hans would be concerned that his mother would leave him) and learning theory (the phobia of horses may have been learned) • The concepts are not measurable so it is not scientific

Axline's case study of Dibs (1964)

Axline's (1964) case study of Dibs is easy to read and is published by Penguin. The best way to understand the study is to read the full version. The book is interesting because it addresses issues for everyone. For example, it suggests that difficulties in life can lead to better self-awareness. The following quotation helps to show that this is not just a case study of a 5-year-old child, but sheds light on how to search for the self:

> Dibs has his dark moments and had lived for a while in the shadows of life. But he had had the opportunity to move out of those dark moments and discover for himself that he could cope with the shadows and sunshine in his life. Perhaps there is more understanding and beauty in life when the glaring sunlight is softened by the patterns of shadows. Perhaps there is more depth in a relationship that has weathered storms. Experience that never disappoints or saddens or stirs up feelings is a bland experience with little challenge or variation in colour. Perhaps when we experience the confidence and faith and hope that we see materialize before our eyes this builds up within us a feeling of inner strength, courage and security.

Aims

Axline's (1964) aims were to help Dibs, a small child who was locked in his own world. His behaviour troubled his teachers at the private school he was attending and they asked Axline, a clinical psychologist, if she could help. Her aim was to help Dibs to find a way to express himself and to 'unlock' his personality. The teachers thought that Dibs might have low mental ability. However, there were patterns in his behaviour that suggested he was very able. The aim of the study was to find out more about Dibs in order to help him, although neither the teachers nor Axline knew if this would be possible. Although it is not stated in the case study, another aim was to see if play therapy would help Dibs to find his 'self'.

Explore Try to get a copy of *Dibs: In Search of Self* and read it. A library should be able to obtain a copy for you. Reading the book will give you a much better understanding than any summary can.

Background/procedure

The case study starts with Dibs at school, where he did not interact with either the children or the teachers. The teachers felt that he needed help and asked Axline to watch Dibs, meet his parents, and see if she could help him.

First, Axline watched Dibs in the classroom. She took him once to a playroom at the school to see how he reacted. Then she obtained permission from his mother to carry out some observations and to work with him. At this stage, Dibs's mother made it clear that she would not be interviewed or asked about him. However, she gave permission for the study and took him to a weekly play-therapy session with Axline, where Dibs's behaviour was observed and notes were taken. The data that are analysed come mainly from those play-therapy sessions. However, Dibs's mother also visited Axline, who then had other data to draw upon. In the main, Axline did not ask questions, she waited for input — from Dibs, from the school and from the parents.

The play-therapy room was set up with a variety of toys, including a doll's house, a sandpit, toy soldiers, other doll figures, paints, crayons and clay. Dibs could play as he liked and what he said and did was recorded. There was a one-way mirror in the playroom so that other researchers could make comprehensive notes and tape-record the sessions. Dibs's parents gave consent to both this and to publishing the case study. Where possible, Dibs's actual words are used in the book, although any references that would identify the family were removed and the words were changed a little to help the flow of the story.

Axline was Dibs's therapist. She was not carrying out a study as a researcher, but responding to him in order to help him. She did not ask direct questions, but allowed Dibs to say and do whatever he was comfortable with. She did not interpret what he said or wanted, to ensure that she did not push his thoughts or actions in a direction dictated by her. She wanted Dibs to discover his own personality. This is quite different from carrying out a study to find the reasons for behaviour or to find a personality theory.

Case description

Dibs was 5 years old when the study started and 6 years old when it ended. He had a younger sister and lived with her and their parents. They also had servants, including a gardener who befriended him. Dibs had many toys and books — all the material things he could want. Dibs also had a grandmother whom he loved but did not see often, because she did not live nearby. Dibs's parents were professional people. His father was said to be a brilliant scientist and before Dibs was born his mother had been a surgeon. Dibs's parents had not wanted children and they thought that his birth had, in many ways, ruined their life together. Neither seemed to know about bringing up children — either that or their resentment of his birth led to a lack of communication (or both). There seemed to be no problems with his sister, however, although she was sent away to school at a very young age, apparently because of Dibs's problems.

When the therapy started, Dibs's behaviour was difficult for the family and for the school. He frequently fought (physically) when something was asked of him, such as taking off his coat or visiting the doctor. His behaviour was unmanageable and he would talk only rarely. He would say 'no go home', for example, but did not communicate in any other way. Not wanting to go home was one of the main difficulties. At school, he hid under desks or crawled around the edge of the room and did not mix with the children or teachers. He looked at books and turned the pages at a speed that suggested he might be reading them, but the teachers could not tell if he could read or not.

Through the therapy it became clear that Dibs was a gifted child. His speech was mature and he could read, write and spell well in advance for his age. It took the duration of the therapy for Dibs to reveal his hidden abilities. Eventually, he moved to a school for gifted children, where he thrived. The journey from non-speaking non-interacting to showing himself to be a gifted and intelligent child is the story of the therapy.

Throughout the therapy, Axline simply repeated to Dibs what he was saying or asking for. She tried not to interpret what he wanted. She allowed him to do what he wanted, without fear, and she did not put pressure on him by asking him questions.

As it turned out, the main problem for Dibs seemed to be excessive testing and teaching by his mother, who expected him to always answer correctly and to learn the order of things. Another problem was his father's apparent lack of love for him and his pressure on him not to be 'stupid'. So Axline had done the opposite of testing and asking questions, she had let Dibs find himself, which was the purpose of the therapy (although she did not know about the excessive testing at the start of the therapy).

There were interesting episodes in the play-therapy room that could be given as evidence for the importance of the relationship between Dibs, his mother, his father and his sister. Two examples are given here. Dibs buried a toy soldier he referred to as 'Papa' in the sand and built a mountain of sand over it so that soldier would remain buried. In a similar episode, Dibs locked the 'Papa' soldier away. Dibs talked a lot about not liking locked walls and doors.

Case analysis

The analysis is found within the case study, as the story is presented mainly as Dibs's comments and actions in the play-therapy room. Since Axline is presenting the story, she also makes comments. She avoided interpreting Dibs's words and explained that she did this because she wanted him to work through his feelings himself. For example, when Dibs was talking about some toy soldiers he said 'they are not shooting at you' and she replied 'I understand, they are not shooting at me'. She felt that it was important for Dibs to say what was important to him, and for her to stay in the background providing the opportunities. This was how he could find a way out of his confusion and anger. Although Axline does not mention the psychodynamic approach, one way of interpreting this is to suggest that the id part of Dibs's personality, which was demanding and needed gratification, was overpowered by the superego, which was controlling. The ego, which should have been balancing these demands, was overwhelmed and unable to do so. Therefore, Dibs was full of anger and confusion. His refusal to talk or interact with others was a result of this confusion.

Axline always told Dibs the truth and she felt that this was important. For example, the therapy lasted for 1 hour every Thursday. She tried to let him know when there were 5 minutes to go. At first, Dibs did not want to go home, just as he did not want to go home from school. However, Axline felt that as he *had* to go home, she should make that clear from the start, however upsetting it was. She says in the case study, that when Dibs had to go back into the classroom after his short visit to the school playroom, before the therapy itself began:

> I didn't ask him if he wanted to go. There was no real choice for him to make. I didn't ask him if he would like to come back again. He might not want to commit himself. I didn't say that I would see him next week, because I had not yet completed the plans with his mother. This child had been hurt enough without my introducing promises that might not materialise. I didn't ask him if he had had a good time. Why should he be pinned down to an evaluation of the experience he had just had? If a child's play is his natural way of expressing himself, why should we cast it in a rigid mould of a stereotyped response? A child is only confused by questions that have been answered by someone else before he is asked.

Axline does not interpret Dibs's behaviour from a psychodynamic viewpoint. However, her desire not to ask questions or impose any ideas on Dibs could be seen as an attempt to allow his personality — the id, ego and superego — to find a way through the confusion and anger. He did not need any more input into his superego by Axline imposing rules.

The focus on not liking to be locked away refers to when his father used to lock him in his room, so it is real, rather than symbolic. Burying the 'Papa' toy soldier, seems to mean Dibs getting rid of his father. He frequently showed anger towards his father and this anger was real. He was also angry with his mother and sister but, according to the situations he placed them in when using dolls as symbols, this anger was less extreme. Dibs called the dolls 'the mother, father and sister dolls', so the symbolism was not hidden. It was interesting, however, that he almost always rescued the 'family' dolls from whatever dangerous situation he had placed them in.

There is no suggestion that this is about the Oedipus complex, even though Dibs was around 5 years old when the study took place. It would be possible to use the Oedipus complex to analyse Dibs's feelings and, for example, his burying of the father doll. However, Axline does not do that. It is clear from the case study that Dibs's father is severe in his dealings with his son and frequently refers to his son's chatter (when there is any) as 'stupid'. Dibs's difficulties with his parents seem to be real, not symbols of unconscious desires. Indeed, it is clear from the case study that part of the solution to Dibs's problems came about when his parents realised that they had had a part to play in his problems and they then took an active part in the 'healing'.

Dibs's mother visited Axline once during the therapy (and again to thank her after-wards). The mother had been frightened that Dibs was not mentally able, so she started to teach him to read, which he could do from the age of 2 years. Dibs appeared to be overstimulated, which was part of the problem. When his mother showed him that she loved him and did not test his abilities all the time, their relationship was better. When his father started to show him love and started to listen to him, their relationship also improved.

Freud's theory suggests that revealing unconscious desires to the conscious self is cathartic in that the desires disappear and the individual can move on. Dibs's problems seem to be more real than the representation of unconscious desires, but the idea of **catharsis** does help to explain how the play therapy worked. As Dibs played out situations involving himself and his family, he seemed to go home a happier child and to find the balance that he needed. The case study starts by suggesting that Dibs has things locked away. This could be interpreted as having desires locked in the unconscious that need to be revealed. So even though the problems seem more real than symbolic, they are inaccessible until released through play.

> **Catharsis** means bringing repressed ideas into consciousness.

Conclusions

The case study is helped by an analysis that uses the three parts of the personality suggested by Freud, but is not helped by interpreting Dibs's feelings of hostility towards his parents and sister using the Oedipus complex. The idea of the problems being locked away in the unconscious and being revealed through play therapy seems to be a useful explanation.

Play therapy allowed Dibs to act out his fears and frustrations. By acting them out, he seemed to get rid of them. This cathartic effect seemed to be effective because Dibs went home happier and found a balance. Axline refers to this as Dibs finding his 'self'.

Dibs's 'ego' might not have managed to find a balance between the demanding 'id' and the controlling 'superego' that came from his serious-minded and perhaps confused parents, but, through play therapy, the 'ego' was helped. His parents also helped by working through some of their fears about Dibs's abilities and their own problems.

Evaluation of the study of Dibs by Axline (1964)

There are strengths and weaknesses of the Dibs case study, both individual strengths and weaknesses and those of case studies in general.

Strengths

- The play-therapy sessions were recorded and observed carefully and comprehensive notes were taken, so the book is full of real comments and actions. The therapist did not have to stop to take notes, so all the detail is there, and, mostly, the actual words are used (although there are some changes to protect identities and to help the flow). Other people made the recordings, so they are unaffected by the researcher. This makes the data more valid.
- Many different methods were involved, so the data have greater validity in that sense also. Others observed the play sessions and Axline also observed a great deal, rather than interacting with Dibs. She is a participant observer who tried to participate as little as possible so that Dibs was free to act as he chose, which gives the data validity. Axline also interviewed his mother and observed his interactions with his father. She obtained information from his teachers too. There is more than one source so the data can be validated.

Weaknesses

- Axline was a participant observer and so could have affected Dibs's play. It would be impossible to repeat the study using a different therapist because Dibs would not be the same. So the study cannot be tested for reliability. Axline says that, wherever possible, she used only Dibs's own words and she responded without interpretation. However, this cannot be tested, so the study may lack reliability.
- Axline's (1964) study is difficult to analyse theoretically. Axline presents the study as a story of one boy undergoing play therapy to help him unlock his problems. She shows how Dibs became stronger as a result. However, she does not use theories or concepts to explain the success of the play therapy. Her aim was to help Dibs. She appears to have succeeded and her approach of using play therapy and a supportive non-judgemental attitude appears to work. Therefore, it is difficult to criticise the study because of its lack of theoretical underpinning. However, the study is largely descriptive rather than explanatory, which can be seen as a weakness when looking at the study as a way of building a body of knowledge.

Table 3.13 *Strengths and weaknesses of the study of Dibs by Axline (1964)*

Strengths	Weaknesses
• Qualitative, detailed, rich, in-depth data, including Dibs's actual words, are provided • Uses many different methods (e.g. interviews, observations and play therapy) so there is an opportunity to test for validity	• Difficult to test for reliability as Dibs will never be the same again, so the study cannot be repeated • It is difficult to apply theory to the study, although there are links to psychodynamic theory (e.g. the role of the unconscious, the need to allow catharsis and the appropriateness of the id/ego/superego model of personality)

Bachrach et al. (1991)

The 1991 study by Bachrach et al. aimed to look at the effectiveness of psychoanalytic therapies by examining other studies into the effectiveness of the therapies. They wanted to compare the findings of many different studies and to draw conclusions from the comparison. The research method was meta-analysis. Many studies were reviewed and their methods and conclusions compared in order to draw overall conclusions. They then carried out an overall anaysis of these (other people's) data.

One conclusion that Bachrach et al. (1991) drew was that patients deemed suitable for analysis did benefit. Those who benefited most were those with the highest level of pre-treatment functioning (so they could bring more insight to bear on the issues raised). Sometimes, those judged as likely to benefit did not and those thought of as more severely impaired did.

Another conclusion was that it was difficult to predict outcomes from initial evaluation. There were also methodological weaknesses in the studies, including lack of consistent definition of terms. Finally, it was concluded that the quantitative studies gave trends rather than information about specific individuals, but that the trends were useful because they suggested areas for further research.

This study is covered in more detail on the CD-ROM.

Evaluation of the study by Bachrach et al. (1991)

Strengths

- As part of their findings, Bachrach et al. (1991) evaluated the studies from which they were gathering data. For example, they pointed out that definitions of factors were different, which would affect validity, as the studies were then not measuring the same thing. They pointed out that the patients were carefully selected, which is likely to mean there were biased samples. Their study is stronger because, as they draw conclusions, they recognise problems with their data.
- The study used data from so many other studies, at different centres, with different analysts, using different methods to choose patients and using both quantitative and qualitative data. In spite of these differences, there were common findings — for example, that the longer the time in analysis, the more likely there was to be therapeutic benefit. The strength is that reliability is shown, because similar results are given in different studies and circumstances.

Weaknesses

- Using data from many different studies, with different methodology, definitions and analytical techniques, means that there is likely to be low validity. Each study may not have been measuring the same thing. Bachrach et al. (1991) acknowledge this problem. This important weakness of meta-analysis must be recognised.
- Many of the quantitative data were gathered from the 1960s to the 1980s and analytical techniques have changed since then. Meta-analyses have to use published studies, the results of which might be out-dated.

Table	Strengths and weaknesses of the study by Bachrach et al. (1991)

3.14

Strengths	Weaknesses
• The study is strong because the meta-analysis evaluates as part of the analysis; they are able to point out strengths and weaknesses of the studies on which their evaluation is based • There is reliability because even though the studies are different, they show similar findings, which makes those findings reliable	• There is low validity because the different studies operationalise the features differently; it is difficult to compare the studies and to conclude that they are measuring what they claim to measure • Many studies that they analysed took place 30 years previously and psychoanalysis has changed since then

The study of defence mechanisms by Cramer (1997)

Cramer's (1997) study is given here in depth to help understanding. The headings (aims, procedure, results, conclusions, evaluation) should help you to structure your learning. You should use these headings when preparing for the exam.

Aims

Cramer (1997) carried out her study to see if the findings of a previous study (Cramer, 1995) would be replicated and also to see if, by having a different sample (aged 23 instead of a mean age of 18), different results would be found. She also used different methods to gather the data. A specific aim was to look at the relationship between identity, defence mechanisms and self-esteem. She wanted to test the idea that the greater an identity crisis, the more the person would use defence mechanisms. A further aim was to see if those who had made a commitment in terms of goals and values by young adulthood would continue to use defence mechanisms to protect against anxiety and low self-esteem.

Procedure

Cramer's (1997) hypotheses rested on the idea that times of crisis require defence mechanisms and that when people have made commitments to goals and values they will have higher self-esteem and have less need of defence mechanisms.

An important feature of this study is the use of the concept of dimensions of identity personality. The idea is that when identity is developing in adolescence:
■ there might be a crisis period during which the person is questioning and unsure
■ there will be a commitment period, when young people know their goals and beliefs

There are four ways in which crisis and commitment can go together (Table 3.15), which are the four identity personalities that Cramer (1997) tests. The identity personalities are from Marcia (1980).

Table 3.15 *Four identity personalities*

Identity personality	Crisis/questioning	Commitment/values agreed
Diffusion	There is no crisis yet	There is no commitment
Foreclosed	There has been no crisis	Commitment is based on views of others
Moratorium	A crisis is on-going	There is no commitment
Achieved	A crisis is resolved	Commitment is based on one's own values

- **Diffusion** is at the start of the process. There is no crisis and no commitment.
- A **foreclosed identity** means commitment without a crisis. Goals are those of parents or others in society. If young adults do not develop a foreclosed identity, they move from diffusion to the moratorium period.
- In the **moratorium period**, they are in crisis before they find a way to make a commitment.
- **Achieved identity** occurs when they are no longer in crisis and achieve commitment based on their own values.

Personality types are connected with these dimensions (Table 3.16).

Table 3.16 *Identity personalities and personality types*

Identity personality	Some aspects of personality type
Diffusion	Anxiety, low self-esteem, low autonomy, external locus of control
Foreclosed	Very low anxiety, high self-esteem, low autonomy, external locus of control
Moratorium	High anxiety, moderate self-esteem, autonomy, internal locus of control
Achieved	Low anxiety, high self-esteem, high autonomy, internal locus of control

Anxiety can be controlled by defence mechanisms. **Projection** and **denial** are used typically by adolescents. Identification is also used, before they develop their own identities. These are the three defence mechanisms that Cramer(1997) examines in relation to identity crises. Anxiety occurs in the diffused and moratorium identity states, so it is likely that defence mechanisms will be used more by people in those situations. Alternative hypotheses are listed in Table 3.17.

An **internal locus of control** means internal events cause behaviour. An **external locus of control** points to external events causing behaviour. **Autonomy** is when people are in charge of their own lives.

Table 3.17 *Alternative hypotheses of the study by Cramer (1997)*

Alternative hypotheses	
1	Moratorium and diffused statuses will show more use of defence mechanisms
2	Achieved and foreclosed statuses will show fewer defence mechanisms
3	Achieved and foreclosed statuses will show high self-esteem
4	Moratorium and diffused statuses will show low self-esteem

The participants were 46 females and 45 males, who were part of a longitudinal study. Data had been collected from the age of 3 years. They came from a mixture of backgrounds and were all 23 years old.

The identity personality (diffused, moratorium, foreclosed or achieved) was tested using the Q-sort Prototype for Ego Identity Status. Understanding of ego identity status was used to sort items into the characteristics likely, less likely, least likely and so on for each of the four dimensions. The Q-sort was set up to include cards with statements on them, and the participants were asked to sort the cards/statements according to what they felt applied to them. The statements were planned to 'match' the four personalities, for example, asking about anxiety and self-esteem, so the researcher could see from the statements what participants felt about their state of mind.

Participants did the Q-sort (they sorted characteristics into how they thought the characteristics applied to them) and a score was found for them for each of the four dimensions. Validity was high because the researchers were able to look for consistency between the dimensions — for example, to see if two dimensions both gave commitment as was expected. There was consistency.

Defence mechanisms were measured by using six **TAT** stories, which are pictures with objects, people and so on. One picture in this study showed a country scene, a young woman carrying books, a man ploughing a field and an older woman looking on. Another picture showed one woman with her hands around the throat of another woman. The individual has to 'tell' the story, which is then analysed. In this study, each story was scored by a trained coder looking for three defence mechanisms — denial, projection and identification. Examples of what the coders were looking for are shown in Table 3.18.

TAT stands for thematic apperception tasks.

| Table 3.18 | Examples of what is looked for in TAT stories with regard to defence mechanisms |

Defence mechanisms	Features of story from TAT that represent the defence mechanism
Denial	Omission of major characters or objects; mis-perception; reversal — and other features
Projection	Attributing hostile feelings or intentions to a character; adding ominous people; concern for protection from a threat — and other features
Identification	Emulation of skills; work — delay of gratification; regulation of motives and behaviour — and other features

| Figure 3.5 | A scene that could be used in a TAT test |

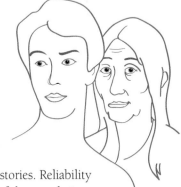

Other coders scored independently a random selection of 100 of the stories. Reliability was found when the two interpretations were correlated. The results of the correlations were: denial 0.80; projection 0.85 and identification 0.78. The nearer a correlation statistic is to 1 the better the correlation, so all three statistics show at least a good correlation.

Self-esteem was measured using the sort items and comparing a person's self-description with his or her ideal self-description. The more they matched, the higher their self-esteem.

Results

The main results are given in Table 3.19. Any result with an asterisk shows a significant correlation. The symbol p stands for probability; $p \leq 0.05$ is significant, $p \leq 0.01$ is a better level of significance, $p \leq 0.001$ is a very high level of significance. When there is an acceptable level of significance, it means the alternative hypothesis is taken as being 'true'.

Significance levels are explained in Chapter 4.

Table 3.19 *Correlations between identity prototypes and defence mechanisms*

	Diffusion	Foreclosure	Moratorium	Achieved
Denial	0.20*	−0.34***	0.30**	−0.17
Projection	0.12	−0.29**	0.27**	−0.06
Identification	0.03	−0.08	0.13	−0.15
Self-esteem	−0.94***	0.61***	−0.22*	0.92***
Significance levels	* = $p \leq 0.05$ Note that any figure with * is a significant one ** = $p \leq 0.01$ *** = $p \leq 0.001$			

In Table 3.19, the asterisks indicate the significance levels of the results:
- * = $p \leq 0.05$
- ** = $p \leq 0.01$
- *** = $p \leq 0.001$

It was found that the personality correlations were the same for both sexes. In summary:
- Moratorium identity status correlated positively with denial and projection.
- Diffusion identity status correlated positively with denial.
- Achieved identity status was unrelated to the use of defence mechanisms.
- Foreclosed identity status showed negative correlations with denial and projection.
- Identification did not correlate with any of the identity states.
- Self-esteem was high in both the achieved and foreclosed identity states.
- Diffused identity status gave rise to very low self-esteem.
- Moratorium identity status gave rise to fairly low self-esteem.

Conclusions

Identity personalities are arranged in order according to experience of crisis, from lowest crisis (foreclosed) through achieved and diffused to moratorium. The use of defence mechanisms increases as crisis is experienced.

Where a commitment has been made (achieved and foreclosed) there is high self-esteem. Diffused identity status gives the lowest self-esteem; moratorium gives fairly low self-esteem. These conclusions are predicted in the hypotheses and they reinforce the findings of Cramer (1995).

The study helps to show to what level each personality characteristic relates to the use of defence mechanisms. For example, people with clear and consistent personalities are less likely to use defence mechanisms. Unpredictability and changeability link with a high use of defence mechanisms. Diffused and moratorium statuses link to immaturity, which may be what leads to the use of defence mechanisms.

Evaluation of the study by Cramer (1997)

Strengths

- The care taken to measure the concepts. The interpretation of the TAT stories was carried out by experienced coders. Other coders worked on a random sample of 100 stories. There was a high level of correlation between the two sets of coding, which means high reliability.
- The tests for validity when considering the measures of identity personality. The researchers were able to check that the Q-sort measured what it was meant to measure because they could look at factors that should go together. Achieved and foreclosed identity statuses both showed commitment; diffused and moratorium statuses did not. This was as expected.

Weaknesses

- An assumption about the measures and their validity has to be made because defence mechanisms are unconscious processes and are, therefore, not measurable. It is assumed, for example, that omitting major characters in a story shows denial, but this may not be the case.
- There were differences between people in the four categories (diffused, foreclosed, moratorium and achieved) yet they were put into one of four identity personality categories. Categorising people in this way means ignoring differences in data. Therefore, the conclusions may not be valid.

Table 3.20 *Strengths and weaknesses of the study by Cramer (1997)*

Strengths	Weaknesses
• Careful operationalisation of variables means the measures were reliable	• Even though carefully measured, the concepts are still difficult to test scientifically
• Careful measurement means that internal validity was high; in the Q-sort it was possible to check that what should go together did go together	• Participants were categorised into one of four groups, even though they often showed characteristics from more than one group; this suggests a lack of validity

Examination-style questions

1 Describe the findings (results and/or conclusions) of the Little Hans study. *(5 marks)*

2 Outline the aim of two studies within the psychodynamic approach. *(4 marks)*

3 Evaluate two studies within the psychodynamic approach. In your answer compare the two studies at least once. *(8 marks)*

Extension question

1 Describe two studies within the psychodynamic approach, one of which must be Little Hans. *(8 marks)*

2 Compare the two studies in terms of their methodology and conclusions. *(6 marks)*

Key issues

You have to examine one key issue that can be both described and explained using concepts from the approach. The idea is:

- to find issues that can be found in newspapers or in general conversation
- to describe the issue itself and what interests people about it
- to apply ideas from the approach to explain the issue, perhaps giving answers to questions about it or suggesting why an event occurs

The skill that you are asked to develop is to be able to understand the approach sufficiently to apply it to current topics of conversation. In the examination, you may be given an issue to read and then have to explain the issue using concepts from the approach. Therefore, it is a good idea to learn all the key issues presented here in order to practise the skill of applying concepts. There are four issues suggested for your course, two of which are described here. *The other two are summarised below and covered in detail on the CD-ROM.* You can, however, choose any issue.

> **Study hint**   When you are describing an issue or debate, make sure that you describe both sides of the debate. Often an issue is a question, so it is a good idea to describe it in the form of a question. Avoid giving concepts from the approach when you are describing the issue. Keep those for the explanation.

How effective is psychoanalysis in treating abnormal and normal clients?

You may have studied the meta-analysis by Bachrach et al. (1991) that examined evidence for the effectiveness of psychoanalysis as a therapy. The key issue here, however, is about how effective the therapy is in treating both normal and abnormal clients.

Describing the issue

The issue is how good psychoanalysis is and whether it works. If it does work, is it good for both abnormal and normal clients? This issue arises from the amount of psychoanalysis and related therapies there are and the number of people who are 'in analysis'. These people are not just those with mental health problems. 'Normal' people, including celebrities, undergo analysis. Are they having analysis because they are abnormal, or mentally ill, or are they having analysis to improve their lives, just as they might go to the gym? Is psychoanalysis effective for those who do not have a neurosis or mental health problems? After all, it was developed to cure mental health problems.

Application of concepts and ideas

A list of concepts and ideas is given here to help you to apply concepts, ideas, studies and theories from the approach to the issue:

- Freud was interested in curing neuroses by revealing unconscious desires that were using energy and holding back development, so people with neuroses should benefit more from psychoanalysis. He focused on abnormality and problems such as phobias, with the intention of helping people overcome their phobias. So, people with abnormal mental health problems should be the ones to benefit.
- Bachrach et al. (1991) carried out a meta-analysis examining the effectiveness of psychoanalysis and found that the therapy is effective for 60% or more of those whom it suits. The patients in the studies had only limited problems and were chosen because the analysts were students. Some of the patients were helped, so it could be claimed that psychoanalysis can help 'normal' people.
- However, only 50% of those for whom psychonalysis is effective developed the insight that Freud thought led to the cure. Therefore, some of the patients were cured, but not by the 'psychoanalysis' as Freud saw it.
- If it is more effective for those with insight, then perhaps it would be effective for 'normal' clients because they would presumably have more insight than people who are mentally ill.
- Freud did not think that hypnosis was useful because people had to have insight into what was revealed about their unconscious. Under hypnosis, this insight would not be possible. This would apply both to 'normal' people and to those with abnormal functioning.
- Freud's general theory about the development of personality suggests that psycho-analysis could help anyone because it is not only the mentally ill who develop a fixation at a certain stage.
- Freud's theory is said to be unscientific because the concepts, for example the id and the unconscious, are not measurable. If it is not scientific, it cannot be evaluated easily because it is difficult to measure its effectiveness.

The question of whether psychoanalysis is effective, and whether it helps 'normal' people is therefore not easy to answer.

The debate concerning the issue of false memory and repression

You have learnt about repression and motivated forgetting. The idea is that, for the ego to maintain a balanced personality, traumatic memories are pushed into the unconscious. This repression is a defence mechanism.

Describing the issue

False memory is a memory that has been recovered during psychoanalysis and is found to be false. This is a relatively new concept. It has arisen because of some high-profile cases in which people undergoing analysis have 'recovered' memories, usually about their parents, and often about sexual abuse, that have turned out to be false. The debate is whether they are actually false. One side of the debate holds that they are recovered memories from childhood events that were so traumatic that the

memories only resurfaced during analysis; the other side holds that they are false memories and are simply not true. The argument is that they arise from the analysis as the analyst interprets issues such as dreams and the client accepts the interpretation as the truth. This is clearly an important issue. Families have claimed to be traumatised by such 'recovered' memories, which, if they are not true, can be extremely harmful. On the other hand, if they are true, they are harmful to the sufferer.

Applying concepts and ideas

Some ideas and concepts from the approach are listed here to help you apply them and explain the issue:

- According to Freud, one of the main purposes of psychoanalysis is to uncover repressed memories that are in the unconscious and are affecting the individual.
- However, Masson has pointed out that power is in the hands of the analyst and an analysand might agree with the analyst that what is being suggested is a real memory, simply because the analyst has the power.
- The case of Beth Rutherford illustrates why it is said that memories recovered while undergoing analysis can be false. She was sent into analysis by her father who thought that it might help her to cope with her work as a nurse on a stressful ward. The analyst asked her about abuse. This made her think about abuse, she then dreamt about abuse and, at that stage, the analyst suggested that the abuse was real. Under analysis, she 'remembered' sexual abuse by her father and an abortion of a baby that he had fathered. It was only when it was found out that her father had had a vasectomy and that she was a virgin that it was realised that the recovered memory was a false one. This is strong evidence that false memories can be 'remembered' while undergoing analysis.
- Symbol analysis does mean that subjective interpretations of dreams are possible, which could have happened in the case of Beth Rutherford.
- Repression is a defence mechanism. It is often found when something traumatic has happened, so it was understandable that the analyst thought that Beth Rutherford was repressing the abuse. However, it highlights the problem that concepts are not measurable and cannot be scientifically studied.
- Freud built his ideas on a small sample of middle-class Viennese people, mostly women. This is a biased sample, yet he generalised his theory to all people. Given this, perhaps it is understandable how false memories could come about, when the analyst is working with psychosexual stages and abuse might be something that would 'fit'.

The debate concerning the issue of how early childhood experiences may guide later sexual orientation

According to the psychodynamic approach, gender behaviour is taken on when a boy resolves the Oedipus complex and identifies with his father or a girl resolves the Electra complex and identifies with the mother. So early childhood experience (the Oedipus complex is in the phallic stage) guides later gender behaviour. Early experience guides sexual preference because one aspect of resolving the Oedipus complex is that in the genital stage boys and girls get together, whereas in the latency stage children prefer to be friends with those of their own gender.

This debate is covered in more detail on the CD-ROM.

The debate about whether dreams have meaning

Freud saw dreams as 'the royal road to the inconscious'. However, there are other theories about dreaming, e.g. the biological theory that dreams sort out the day's events ready for the next day. The debate is about whether dreams have meaning, as Freud claimed, or whether they have some other function.

Freud used dream analysis and symbol analysis in case studies and to try to uncover unconscious urges. He thought dreams could reveal these urges and, once revealed to the patient, then energy held back to deal with these repressed wishes would be released and the person would be freed from the issues involved.

This debate is covered in more detail on the CD-ROM.

Examination-style questions

1a Describe one key issue that can be explained by concepts and ideas from the psychodynamic approach. *(4 marks)*

b Use concepts, ideas, theories, or studies to explain the key issue from the point of view of the psychodynamic approach. *(8 marks)*

2 In each of two families, there is a young boy. They are discussing with their families what they want to be when they grow up. One boy wants to be an engineer, like his father. The other wants to be a gardener, like his father. The families agree that the first boy would be a wonderful engineer because he has an enquiring mind and enjoys making things. They also agree that the second boy will make a wonderful gardener as he helps his father in their garden and knows the Latin names of plants.

Use concepts, ideas, theories or studies from the psychodynamic approach to explain why the boys have chosen these career paths. *(8 marks)*

Extension question

Find some newspapers or magazines from a single week and choose one story that seems to fit with the psychodynamic approach. Issues about gender development, sexual orientation, the role of dreams, or any neurosis, such as a phobia, would be suitable. If the week you choose does not provide any suitable material, look these issues up on the internet. Summarise one suitable story and apply concepts from the approach to explain how the story and the approach fit together. *(12 marks)*

Practical: a correlation design

With a correlation design, you can sometimes develop an idea that comes only briefly from existing studies.

In the psychodynamic approach you have to carry out a correlation using self-report data and rating scales. Here a correlation is worked through, but in your particular course you may carry out a different study.

Self-report data and rating scales

Self-report data are data obtained by participants reporting on their own feelings and circumstances. For example, you could report that you have a good relationship with your parents or that you have few friends. You could report that you are a tidy person or that you are generous.

Self-report data often include **rating scales**. The participants rate themselves on a scale of, say, 1 to 5. A Likert-type scale uses categories such as 'strongly agree', 'agree', 'don't know', 'disagree' and 'strongly disagree', which are chosen by the participants and then scored on the scale of 1 to 5. This type of scale is outlined in Chapter 1.

The practical for the psychodynamic approach must use self-report data and must generate data suitable for a correlation, so rating scales are suitable.

Aim

The practical suggested here examines the relationship between the tidiness of the participants, as rated by themselves, and their parents' strictness, again rated by the participants. A correlation test is carried out to see if the perceived level of tidiness correlates with the perceived level of strictness of their parents. However, you could choose a different aim.

Brief background

This practical is based on psychodynamic ideas, particularly those about Freud's second psychosexual stage — the anal stage. This is characterised by reaction to potty-training and focus on faeces. According to Freud, fixation at the anal stage comes from either too severe or too lenient potty training. Fixation is indicated in the adult by meanness/generosity, tidiness/untidiness and being stubborn/easy-going. Meanness, tidiness and being stubborn (anal retentive) may be the result of over-strict training; generosity, untidiness and being easy-going (anal expulsive) may be the result of too loose a parenting style. It is, however, possible that both strict and lenient parenting lead to either anal retention or anal expulsion, and only 'middle' or democratic parenting leads to successful resolution of the anal stage.

Research method

The research design suggested is a **correlation** using self-report data and rating scales. You could carry out this practical alone or work in a small group so that you can pool data. The self-report data is collected by questionnaire and there are rating scales to provide scores that can be correlated. Note that yes/no answers are not scores and so cannot lead to a correlation test.

Alternative hypothesis for the suggested practical

The alternative hypothesis for this study is 'there is a positive relationship between self-reported tidiness as an adult and self-reported strictness with regard to upbringing'.

Directional or non-directional hypothesis

The above hypothesis is directional because the relationship expected is positive. This means that as strictness of parenting increases, it is expected that the level of tidiness (as reported by the individuals) will increase.

Design

Drawing up the questionnaires

The data should be collected by means of two questionnaires:

- One will ask about an individual's tidiness.
- The other will ask about parental strictness.

The scores from the questionnaires have to be correlated. It is, therefore, a good idea to write them on either side of the same sheet of paper, so that you are certain to match the correct scores for each participant.

Just asking for a rating of tidiness and then a rating of parental strictness would be one way of gathering data. However, it is better to devise more than one way of measuring tidiness and more than one way of measuring parental strictness.

For this practical there is no need to gather personal data such as age, gender or other information.

Examples of questionnaires

Examples of possible questions are given, but it would be more interesting and useful for you to design your own. Suggested standardised instructions are:

> Thank you for taking part in this study. Although the questions are about you, please note that your name will not be recorded. I am interested in how parenting style affects later characteristics in general, rather than in analysing your particular situation. Are you happy to continue? Please remember that you can stop taking part at any time. There are two short questionnaires, one about how tidy or messy you think you are and one about the parenting style of your upbringing. I will explain fully after you have completed both questionnaires. I hope that is all right.

A questionnaire about tidiness

(1) In general, would you say that you are a tidy or messy person? Please tick the appropriate box.

Tidy ☐   Messy ☐

(2) Please rate each statement in the table, as it applies to you, by ticking the appropriate box

SA = strongly agree; A = agree; DK = unsure (don't know); D = disagree; SD = strongly disagree

Statement	SA	A	DK	D	SD
I am proud of how organised I am.	☐	☐	☐	☐	☐
I am more comfortable with my things spread about.	☐	☐	☐	☐	☐
I keep my bedroom tidy most of the time.	☐	☐	☐	☐	☐
I would not be able to show anyone my room, it is so messy.	☐	☐	☐	☐	☐

(3) Please tell me *why* you think you are a messy or a tidy person.

A questionnaire about parental strictness

(1) In general, would you say your parents were strict or lenient with you? Please tick the appropriate box.

Strict ☐   Lenient ☐

(2) Please rate each statement in the table, as it applies to you, by ticking the appropriate box

SA = strongly agree; A = agree; DK = unsure (don't know); D = disagree; SD = strongly disagree

Statement	SA	A	DK	D	SD
My parents were mainly strict with me.	☐	☐	☐	☐	☐
My parents let me do what I liked.	☐	☐	☐	☐	☐
My parents let me make my own decisions but helped me make them.	☐	☐	☐	☐	☐
My parents were nowhere near as strict as those of my friends.	☐	☐	☐	☐	☐
I was not able to make my own decisions.	☐	☐	☐	☐	☐

(3) Please tell me *why* you think you had a strict or lenient upbringing.

Note The questions on upbringing are not as direct as those on tidiness. This is because upbringing is a more sensitive area. The statement that indicates that the parents were democratic (they let the person make decisions, but helped), is there to make the statements a little less harsh and will not be scored for the correlation, as explained later.

Ethical issues

The subject matter of this study might cause anxiety for some participants. It is important to allow people not to take part if they do not wish to. If people have been brought up strictly, remembering details may distress them.

If this is a class practical, it might be difficult to allow some class members not to take part. One way round this is to work on the questionnaires as a group and to make sure that everyone understands the practical. Then, ask the members of the group to take the questionnaires away with them and return them next lesson. If the questionnaires are on either side of a sheet of paper (i.e. they are linked) there is no need for names to be on them. It would, therefore, not be known which class members did not complete the task. Ethical issues should take precedence over other issues and all class members should be allowed to share the data. Remember to:

- give the right to withdraw
- get informed consent
- maintain confidentiality
- debrief afterwards

How to carry out the practical

You need to gather at least ten sets of data. If you are working on a class practical you can complete the questionnaires yourselves and pool the data. If you are working alone or in a small group you will need to ask other participants to help you. An opportunity sample will be sufficient.

Analysing the data

The questionnaires have to be analysed to obtain a score for each participant. One score is a 'tidiness' score and one score is a 'parental strictness' score. It is best to give high scores to 'tidy' and 'strict' and low scores to 'untidy' and 'lenient'.

The first and last questions on each questionnaire are checks to make sure that the data seem appropriate. For example, if someone gets a high 'tidy' score but says they are not tidy, then the data might not be valid. Similarly, answers given to the open question should help to see if the data are valid. These two additional questions (the one that asks directly about tidy/messy and strict/lenient and the open question) also check for reliability because in a way they are asking the question again to see if the same results are found.

Remember to check the questionnaires for validity and reliability. If the answers do not match up for the same person, you might consider not using that set of data.

The middle questions for the two questionnaires, where ratings are given to statements, are where the scores come from for the correlation.

Scoring for the questionnaire about tidiness

Statement	SA	A	DK	D	SD
I am proud of how organised I am.	5	4	3	2	1
I am more comfortable with my things spread about.	1	2	3	4	5
I keep my bedroom tidy most of the time.	5	4	3	2	1
I would not be able to show anyone my room, it is so messy.	1	2	3	4	5

Scoring for the questionnaire about parental strictness

Statement	SA	A	DK	D	SD
My parents were mainly strict with me.	5	4	3	2	1
My parents let me do what I liked.	1	2	3	4	5
My parents were nowhere near as strict as those of my friends.	1	2	3	4	5
I was not able to make my own decisions.	5	4	3	2	1

The data

- Both questionnaires have two statements where strongly agree gets 5 points and two questions where strongly agree gets 1 point.
- Calculate two scores for each participant, one for their 'tidiness' and one for 'parental strictness'.
- A person whose perception was 'very tidy' could score a maximum of 20 points. A person with a perception of 'very strict' parenting could score a maximum of 20 points. The lowest possible score is 4 (either 'very untidy' or 'very strict' parenting).

> The scores from self-report data are only perceived.

Writing up the results

- For a correlation, you need to show the actual scores, so that the rankings are clear and can be judged before the scattergraph and statistical test.
- The results section of a report should include a results table. The raw scores usually go in an appendix, but for this correlation, as there are few data, they are all displayed in Table 3.21. The table should be followed by a commentary, explaining what it represents.
- The graph for a correlation is always a scattergraph. The graph should be followed by a commentary.
- A statistical test is carried out. The actual calculations go in an appendix. The result of the test is given in the results section, with a commentary explaining what it means, such as whether it is significant or not.

A table of possible results

Some possible results are given in Table 3.21, but you should draw up your own table with your own results. The scores come from self-rating, so are **ordinal data** and the mean is, therefore, not calculated. Ordinal data are ranked data, not necessarily with real mathematical scores.

> **Study hint** Review the practical section in Chapter 2. Check that you understand about measures of central tendency, measures of dispersion and levels of measurement. Write out your own definitions of these terms, including mode, median, mean, range, standard deviation, nominal data, ordinal data and interval/ratio data.

Edexcel AS Psychology

	Table
Table 3.21	*The relationship between perception of tidiness and perception of parental strictness*

Participant	'Tidiness' score (self-report data on rating scale)	'Parental strictness' score (self-report data on rating scale)	Ranking for 'tidiness' score	Ranking for 'parental strictness' score
1	15	12	8	4.5
2	9	7	3.5	1
3	18	16	10	9.5
4	10	15	5	8
5	6	8	1	2.5
6	14	13	7	6
7	11	16	6	9.5
8	8	8	2	2.5
9	9	12	3.5	4.5
10	17	14	9	7
	Mode = 9 Median = 10.5	Mode = 8/12/16 Median = 12.5		

The 'eyeball' test

Now carry out the 'eyeball' test to see if there seems to be a relationship between the two sets of scores for each participant. If there is a relationship then a high rank for one score will go with a high rank for the other score; low ranks will also go together.

Participants 3, 6, 8, and 9 have two rankings that are within 1 unit of each other, which is a good match that shows a relationship. Participants 5 and 10 have ranks up to 2 apart, which is a fair relationship. Participant 2 has two reasonably close ranks. However, participants 1, 4 and 7 have ranks further apart, which suggests no relationship.

A scattergraph

A scattergraph can help to show whether there is a relationship present.

The line of best fit, with five scores on each side, is in a positive direction, although some scores are quite a distance from the line. The graph, together with the 'eyeball' test, seem to suggest that there is a positive correlation between tidiness and parental strictness. A statistical test will show whether this is the case.

Figure 3.6	*A scattergraph to show the relationship between reported 'tidiness' scores and reported 'parental strictness' scores*

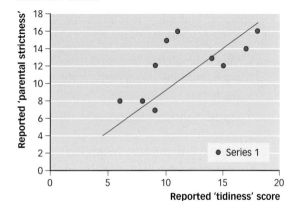

Understanding the Individual

221

Unit 2

Spearman's rank correlation coefficient test

A Spearman's test is carried out on the data because it is the correct test for a correlation with ordinal data.

> Levels of measurement are nominal (categories), ordinal (ranks), and interval/ratio (real measurements, such as time).

Table 3.22 Calculations for the Spearman's test

Participant	'Tidiness' score (self-report data on rating scale)	'Parental strictness' score (self-report data on rating scale)	Ranking for 'tidiness' score (Step 1)	Ranking for 'parental strictness' score (Step 1)	Difference between ranks (Step 2)	Differences squared (Step 3)
1	15	12	8	4.5	+3.5	12.25
2	9	7	3.5	1	+2.5	6.25
3	18	16	10	9.5	+0.5	0.25
4	10	15	5	8	−3	9
5	6	8	1	2.5	−1.5	2.25
6	14	13	7	6	+1	1
7	11	16	6	9.5	−3.5	12.25
8	8	8	2	2.5	−0.5	0.25
9	9	12	3.5	4.5	−1	1
10	17	14	9	7	+2	4
	Mode = 9 Median = 10.5	Mode = 8/12/16 Median = 12.5				Total (Σ) = 48.5 (Step 4)

How to calculate the Spearman coefficient

Refer to Table 3.22.

Step 1: Rank both sets of data.

Step 2: Work out the difference between the ranks for each participant.

Step 3: Square (multiply by itself) the difference found in Step 2 for each participant. This gets rid of the minus signs.

Step 4: Add up the squared differences (the numbers worked out in Step 3). For the data given in Table 3.22, the total is **48.5**.

Step 5: Find N, which is the number of scores. (Here, $N = 10$.)

Step 6: Multiply the sum of the squared differences (from Step 4) by 6. (Here, $48.5 \times 6 = 291$.)

Step 7: Square N and subtract 1. (Here, $10 \times 10 - 1 = 99$.)

Step 8: Multiply the answer found in Step 7 by N. (Here, $99 \times 10 = 990$.)

Step 9: Divide the answer to Step 6 by the answer to Step 8. (Here, $291/990 = +0.29$.)

Step 10: Subtract the answer to Step 9 from 1. (Here, $1 - 0.29 = +0.71$.) This is the result of the test. It is in Step 10 that a minus or plus sign is allocated. If the answer to Step 6 is larger than the answer to Step 8, the result of Step 10 will be negative and any correlation will be negative. If the answer to Step 6 is smaller than the answer to Step 8, the result of Step 10 will be positive and any correlation will be positive.

Step 11: Look up the result of the test in statistical tables to see if it is significant.

Statistical tables show that for $N = 10$ and a significance level of 0.05, the critical result is 0.56. As +0.71 is greater then 0.56, the result is significant. Therefore, there is a positive correlation between strict parenting and tidiness.

Writing up a psychology study

A study in psychology is written up in a specific format:

- **Abstract** — an initial summary, to enable people to grasp what the study was about and what was found.
- **Introduction** — detail of background research, the aims and hypotheses, and why the study is being carried out.
- **Procedure/method** — details of the study, such as the participant design, procedure, apparatus and sampling method.
- **Results** — with tables and graphs to describe the data.
- **Discussion** — which considers what was found.
- **References and appendices**.

For your course you do not have to write up a full report. However, you are asked to write up some of the sections, so that you know how this is done. For this practical, you are asked to write up procedure, sample, apparatus and results.

Short report on procedure, sample, apparatus and results

The procedure, sample, apparatus and results are parts of a full report.

Procedure

The procedure of a study is what was carried out. In this practical, it involved drawing up the two questionnaires and asking participants to complete them. The procedure should cover what questions were asked and why (see Box 3.1).

A pilot study would have been useful to check that the questionnaires gathered the required data.

Sample

For the study suggested here:

- You may have carried out a class study, in which case you did not use a sampling method because you did not choose participants.
- If you gathered data using family or friends, you used an opportunity sample.
- If you put up a notice about the study at school or college, you may have used a volunteer sample.

Your report should detail your sampling method (see Box 3.1).

Apparatus

The apparatus section of a report details the materials used and justifies their choice.

In this study, the apparatus is the questionnaires and a pen or pencil for the participant to complete them. If they were posted, there would be the need for envelopes and stamps. The main point is to detail everything (see Box 3.1).

Box 3.1 **Suggested procedure, sampling and apparatus sections for the study**

Apparatus: copies of two questionnaires, one for rating parental strictness and one for rating perceived tidiness, and pens or pencils to complete them.

Sample: opportunity sampling of ten participants was carried out by asking the first person available in the student common room of a Sixth Form College. When one person had completed the questionnaire, the next was approached. There were six males and four females in the sample, all aged 16 years. They were all students in the sixth form and none was studying psychology.

Opportunity sampling was chosen because it was convenient and quick, while still being ethical. There was no need to access registers, as for a random sample, and no need to select certain sorts of people as for a stratified sample. The students were asked clearly if they would like to participate or not, so were able to volunteer. They were told it would take around 15 minutes.

Procedure: the two questionnaires were drawn up making sure that there were two rating scales and that the scores were sufficient to see if there were a correlation. There were also some checking questions to see if the ratings matched the other data. Qualitative data were requested, so that information could be found to see if the ratings were valid and reliable. The questionnaires were short, so that participants were not inconvenienced for a long time. It was decided that opportunity sampling would be used and that questionnaires would be completed with the researcher present. A pen was taken for the participant to use. It was decided to have the questionnaires completed one-by-one, rather than in a group to make sure that each participant was not affected by the others in order to get data that were more valid. One researcher collected the data. The participants were asked if they had 15 minutes to help with a psychology study. Standardised instructions were read out (see the appendix to this report). When the participant was happy to start, the questionnaires were handed out, with the pen. At the end, the participant was thanked and debriefed by telling him or her the aim of the study and that the data would be kept confidential.

Results

For the results for this study, see page 222. You should draw together the details of your results (e.g. table, graph, statistical test) into a single section of the report, so that they are presented clearly and are easy to understand.

Advantages and limitations of correlation designs

- One advantage of a correlation design is that it can show a relationship that is difficult to show by other methods. This practical has shown how to gather data about people's habits (tidiness) and upbringing (parental style), which are not easy to gather other than by interview or questionnaire. The statistical test shows whether or not there is a significant relationship.

- Another advantage is that results of a correlation design are comparatively easy to analyse. Two scores are compared and an 'eyeball' test can give a quick indication of whether or not the two sets of rankings are related. The statistical test is straightforward to carry out and the result is easy to assess. For example, a result approaching +1 or −1 is a significant correlation; the sign indicates whether the correlation is positive or negative. A result near zero means that there is no relationship.

- One weakness of a correlation design is that it only *suggests* a relationship; it cannot show that the two variables are linked causally. There could be a chance relationship, or the two variables being measured might be linked by some other variable. So although from this practical you might claim that being tidy links with strict parenting, it could be that some other variable (e.g. a genetic tendency to tidiness linked to a genetic tendency to liking rules) connects them.

- Another weakness of a correlation design is that it is only as useful as the measures taken. For example, the data gathered for this practical are **self-report data**. The problem is, for example, that you might say that you are tidy, but your friends might disagree. You might say that you had strict parenting, but your friends (or parents) might disagree. So self-report data, though valuable, might not be valid. However, you could argue that you are the best person to say what you are like, which, if true, would make the data very valid.

> **Study hint** You need to revise the practicals because there will be questions about them in the exams. Keep your written-up procedure, results and so on in a practical file so you can revise from it. Strengths and weaknesses of your study are also useful because you could be asked questions about your conclusions.

> This practical tests one of Freud's stages. **Self-report data** are suitable because individuals' perception of themselves has value from the psychodynamic viewpoint.

Examination-style questions

1 You will have carried out a study using a correlation design and self-report data. Describe how you gathered the self-report data. *(4 marks)*

2 Outline the aim of a study you carried out yourself as part of your course using self-report data and a correlation design. *(2 marks)*

3 When you carried out your correlation design study, outline two controls that you used to make sure the data were either reliable or valid. *(4 marks)*

Extension question

Explain the aim(s), procedure and findings (results and/or conclusions) of the practical you carried out within the psychodynamic approach. Give two criticisms of your study.

(12 marks)

Answers to the practice boxes

Practice 3.1 on p. 173

A comparison of Freud's case studies and general case studies:

Similarities	Differences
• Both use more than one research method • Both involve qualitative data • Both focus on the individual • Both look for in-depth data; detailed	• They use different research methods (e.g. questionnaire v free association) • Freud's case studies are also used for therapy • Freud used only qualitative data; general case studies also use quantitative data • Freud focused only on revealing the unconscious mind, general case studies have much wider application

Strengths	Weaknesses
• Case studies are carried out largely in the natural setting; the data are from that setting so tend to have ecological validity • In case studies, if triangulation and other research methods are used and the same data are found, there may be reliability • Freud's research methods are the only way to uncover unconscious thoughts, so unique and useful in that sense • The richness of the data in both Freud's and general case studies allows insight that is not possible any other way and real meaning is uncovered (another form of validity)	• Both Freud's and general case studies tend to focus on individuals in detail and are therefore not generalisable • Both are difficult to replicate, being so individual, and so it is difficult to show reliability • Both need interpretation because the data are qualitative, so could be subjective • Freud's case studies, using research methods such as symbol analysis, tend to lack credibility

Practice 3.2 on p. 184

Study 1 Longitudinal
Study 2 Cross-sectional
Study 3 Longitudinal
Study 4 Longitudinal

Practice 3.3 on p. 190

Situation 1 Denial
Situation 2 Repression
Situation 3 Projection
Situation 4 Displacement
Situation 5 Regression

Chapter 4

The biological approach

Psychology is the study of the brain and behaviour. The brain can be explained according to its biological functioning; behaviour can also be explained in terms of biological and chemical actions and interactions. People act according to their inherited characteristics, which is an explanation that draws on biological understanding. The biological approach in psychology tends to focus on the effect of genes on behaviour and on the effect of the nervous system (brain, spinal cord and nerves). In your course, you will look at both the influence of genes and the nervous system, and you will also look in depth at gender development and behaviour, and biological aspects of how we acquire our gender behaviour.

Study of interest *The Times*, 15 November 2007 covered a story about research being carried out which suggests that implants into the brain could restore speech to those who can no longer speak because of paralysis. A man who was paralysed after a car accident and who is completely aware but not able to speak has received such implants. He can communicate through eye movements. The researchers have asked him to think of vowel sounds (such as 'oh', 'ee', and 'oo') so that they can examine the patterns of activity. If the separate sounds he thinks of can be identified, then they can translate the patterns into speech. The electrodes take readings from the neurones that generate movement in the mouth and tongue during speech. The man will be able to let researchers know how accurate the speech is so that they can refine the system. They are some way from anything like full speech but are encouraged that this will be possible.

Everyday example Cancer is a disease that has more than one cause; studying it can help to show how biology, the environment and social issues can come together. All cancers involve damage to DNA and this damage promotes cell division. One example cancer of is leukaemia, where almost every white blood cell carries an unusually small chromosome 22. The bone marrow produces damaged cells, which reproduce more quickly than undamaged cells. Research suggests that in leukaemia, chromosome 22 is smaller because part of it has broken off and transferred to chromosome 9. This transfer leads to production of a new protein and this leads to the abnormal cell division. Another example is a cancer caused by a virus that damages the genes controlling cell growth. People can be born with a genetic structure that makes them vulnerable to developing cancer, but requires something to trigger it. Some factors can damage the natural system, such as smoking and other life-style decisions. This example shows that academic disciplines such as biology, psychology and sociology can work together in explaining problems such as disease. This is why in your psychology course there is a large section that appears to be about biology, and why there is a focus on genes and the brain.

Summary of learning objectives

Definitions
You have to be able to define the terms:
- central nervous system (CNS); synapse; receptor; neurone; neurotransmitter
- genes
- hormones
- brain lateralisation

Methodology
You need to cover:
- twin and adoption studies and evaluate them
- PET and MRI scanning techniques
- three types of hypotheses; one- or two-tailed testing of hypotheses; levels of significance; the Mann-Whitney U test and critical and observed values; dependent and independent variables; the use of control groups; experimental procedures such as sampling and randomising; levels of measurement
- strengths and weaknesses of using animal experiments
- ethics, practical issues and credibility when using animals in experiments
- evaluation of laboratory experiments in terms of validity, reliability and generalisability

Content
The topics covered are:
- the roles of the central nervous system and neurotransmitters, and the role of genes, in behaviour
- the nature–nurture debate
- gender development
- a comparison of the explanation of gender development given by the biological approach with those of the psychodynamic and learning approaches

Studies in detail

You have to describe and evaluate in detail:

- the Money (1975) study of a normal male infant reassigned as a girl
- one other study chosen from Gottesman and Shields (1966), Raine et al. (1997) and De Bellis et al. (2001)

Three of the studies are described and evaluated in this chapter. *The other study is summarised below and covered in more detail on the CD-ROM.*

Key issues

You have to be able to describe one key issue and apply concepts and theories from the biological approach to explain it. Two of the three issues suggested by the specification are covered here to help you choose. *The other suggested key issue is summarised below and covered in more detail on the CD-ROM.* However, you can choose any key issue.

Practical

You have to:

- carry out one practical, which must be a test of difference using ordinal or interval/ ratio data and an independent groups design
- carry out a Mann-Whitney U test and interpret the results
- write up the hypothesis, results and analysis of the study, using graphs and tables as appropriate
- draw brief conclusions and consider the validity, reliability, credibility and generalisability of your practical

> **Study hint** Make the summary of learning objectives into a checklist. Table 4.1 gives a suggested list. However, you could add detail, which would help your learning.

One suggested practical is given in this chapter. However, you (or your teacher) could choose a different practical.

Table 4.1 *A checklist of what you need to know for the biological approach and for your progress*

I need to know about	Done	More work	I need to know about	Done	More work
Central nervous system, synapse, receptor, neurones, neurotransmitters			Levels of measurement		
Hormones			Strengths and weaknesses of using animal experiments		
Genes			Ethics, practical aspects and credibility when using animals in the approach		
Brain lateralisation			Evaluation of using experiments in terms of validity, reliability and generalisability		
PET and MRI scanning			The role of the central nervous system and neurotransmitters in behaviour		
Three types of hypothesis			The role of genes in behaviour		
One- or two-tailed testing			The nature–nurture debate		

I need to know about	Done	More work	I need to know about	Done	More work
Levels of signficance			Gender behaviour in terms of hormones, genes and brain lateralisation		
Mann-Whitney U test			Evaluation of the biological approach when explaining gender behaviour		
Critical and observed values			Comparing biological, psycho-dynamic and learning approaches and their explanations of gender behaviour		
Dependent and independent variables			Money (1975) and evaluate the study		
The use of control groups			One from Gottesman and Shields (1966), Raine et al. (1997) and De Bellis et al. (2001)		
Sampling and randomisation			One key issue		

Definitions

The following terms are defined in this chapter:

- central nervous system (CNS)
- synapse
- receptor
- neurone
- neurotransmitter
- genes
- hormones
- brain lateralisation

An introduction to the biological approach

The biological approach focuses mainly on genes and characteristics that have been inherited, and how the brain works. Other aspects of biology, such as how the body works, are less involved in psychology, although issues such as phantom limb pain and body dysmorphism are part of the biological approach.

Explore Look up body dysmorphism and phantom limb pain to broaden your understanding of the biological approach.

The biological approach as a whole examines in detail the structure and function of the brain. However, you will study brain lateralisation only, which is how the two halves of the brain work together.

Study hint It is useful to study the approach as a whole rather than the methodology, content, studies in detail, key issues and practical as separate sections. Read the chapter as a whole, taking in some of the information but without taking notes or working hard to learn the terms. After reading the whole chapter, you can then start learning in earnest.

Key assumptions

Psychology is about people and includes aspects of how the brain works as well as how social and environmental influences affect our behaviour. The biological approach looks at chemical activity in the brain, including how neurotransmitters act at synapses to enable messages to be transmitted. Another way that messages are transmitted is by hormones. The biological approach includes an evolutionary perspective, which examines how characteristics are inherited via genes. The function of the various parts the brain is touched on, but the main focus in your course is on brain lateralisation.

Functioning of neurotransmitters

One way that messages are passed within the brain is by neurotransmitters, which are chemicals that pass from neurone to neurone. Between neurones there are gaps, called synapses. If the receptors of one neurone are set to receive the neurotransmitters of another, then the message continues. This process is explained in more detail on page 264.

Hormonal transmission

Another way that messages are passed is through hormones. These send messages more slowly that neurotransmitters and are used for different purposes. This process is explained in more detail on page 272. Hormones have a large part to play in our development as either male or female — for example, androgens are 'male' hormones and oestrogen is 'female'.

Genetic influences

The biological approach also looks at how genes are passed on from parents to children and how they govern behaviour as well as physical characteristics. Children receive half their genes from their fathers and half from their mothers. The human genome has recently been decoded, which means that all the genes have been identified. However, this does not mean that the function of each gene is known because it is often the combination or the position of genes that leads to certain characteristics, rather than one particular gene.

Parts of the brain and their functions

The brain has many parts, for example:
- The limbic system is linked to aggression and was examined by Raine et al. (1997) (page 283).
- The hippocampus is thought to be where short-term memory occurs.
- The brain is in two halves, joined by the corpus callosum.

In general, it is said that females use both halves of the brain more than males, and males are more right-brain dominant. **Brain lateralisation** is the term for considering the two halves of the brain separately. This is explained in more detail on page 274.

Methodology

The biological approach in psychology is a scientific approach in that the research
methods are those used when looking for scientific truths, e.g. experiments,
scanning to study the brain, and the use of animals in experiments. However, some
studies — for example twin and adoption studies — are not as scientific as might at
first be thought, because variables are not manipulated; twin and adoption studies
look at naturally occurring events.

Twin and adoption studies as research methods

Twin and adoption studies are used to study the influence of **genes** on behaviour.
How genes influence behaviour is described in detail on page 265. Genes and DNA
give the biological blueprint for each person's development; they interact with the
environment as the person grows. Identical twins have identical genes; non-identical
twins share 50% of their genes. By comparing identical and non-identical twins
with regard to a certain characteristic, it can be seen what influence genes have.

A problem is that twins tend to share
much of their environment as well as
their genes, which is why adoption
studies are important. Adopted children
are brought up in different families and
do not share their environment with their
biological family (see page 235).

Twin and adoption studies relate to the
nature–nurture debate (page 238) which
is about how far a characteristic comes
from nature and how far it comes from
our nurture:

> **Explore** How much of 'you' do you think is
> due to inherited characteristics (50% from
> your father, 50% from your mother) and
> how much is due to your own character
> and experiences? Does it feel strange
> thinking of yourself as 'just' your parents'
> son or daughter? This is why people
> discuss the nature–nurture debate. Most
> people like to think they make their own
> decisions and are not slaves to their genes.
> Ask some of your friends what they think.

- Nature is what we are born with and is controlled by our genes.
- Nurture is what we experience from the environment as we develop. Environment includes influence from parents, culture, interactions with others and all other experiences.

Twin studies

Identical twins are **monozygotic (MZ)** twins — they come from one fertilised egg (mono = one). There is one sperm and one egg and one product of fertilisation, so MZ twins have identical genes. Their DNA is 100% the same and they are always the same sex. If a characteristic is genetic, then MZ twins should both show that characteristic. For example, if the cause of schizophrenia is totally genetic, then if one MZ twin has schizophrenia, the other must also have it. If IQ is genetic, then the IQ of one MZ twin should exactly match the IQ of the other. In practice, no characteristic connected with behaviour is shared completely by MZ twins — there is always some influence from the environment.

Some important points include:
- MZ twins do not share the same environment, even in the womb, so they tend to develop differently, despite their DNA being the same.
- From the start, there are some small physical differences between MZ twins, such as their fingerprints.
- Some characteristics that are genetic are triggered by the environment, so identical twins can become less identical over time, although, of course, their DNA does not change.
- **Epigenetic modification** is the term for how, over time, different environmental influences affect which genes are switched on and off. Young MZ twins have few epigenetic differences. However, 50-year-old MZ twins have over three times the epigenetic differences of young MZ twins.
- Some characteristics, such as IQ and personality, might become more alike as the twins age.

Non-identical twins (left) and identical twins (right)

This shows the importance of both genes and the environment on development. It is useful information when discussing the nature–nurture debate because it shows that it is unlikely that any characteristic comes wholly from either nature or nurture.

Non-identical twins are **dizygotic (DZ)** twins, which means that they come from two fertilised eggs (di = two). Since they develop from different eggs, the DNA of DZ twins is only as similar as that of any siblings; it is not 100% the same, as it is in identical twins. This means that if a characteristic is genetic, DZ twins would be expected to share that characteristic to an extent but not as much as MZ twins would share it.

Twin studies compare MZ and DZ twins on certain characteristics to see if there are differences between the MZ twins and the characteristic and between DZ twins and the characteristic. If there are quite strong differences then that characteristic is said to have a genetic basis, at least to an extent. When both twins share a characteristic there is said to be a **concordance rate**. Characteristics that have been studied in this way include schizophrenia, IQ, alcoholism, depression, personality and anorexia.

Studies involving the methodology One well-known study that compares MZ and DZ twins is that by Gottesman and Shields (1966), who investigated schizophrenia. They obtained data from five studies about twins and traced whether, if one twin had schizophrenia, the other also had it or some similar mental health problem. They looked at both MZ and DZ twins. They thought that if both twins had schizophrenia or some similar mental health problem more often and were MZ twins than if they were DZ twins, then this suggested a strong genetic basis for schizophrenia. When both twins share a characteristic there is a concordance rate for that characteristic. In MZ twins, there was a concordance rate for schizophrenia and similar illnesses of between 35% and 58%; in DZ twins, the rate was between 9% and 26%. This means that for MZ twins, around 42% of the time when one twin has schizophrenia, the other has it or a similar illness. For DZ twins, the average figure is around 17%. When only the most severe cases of schizophrenia were considered, the concordance rate for MZ twins was between 75% and 91%. The study strongly suggests that there is at least some genetic basis for schizophrenia.

Explore It is interesting to look further at twin studies and schizophrenia. For example, there is a study (Boklage 1977) that shows that there is more to it. When the researchers looked at left- and right-handedness in MZ twins they found that when the MZ twins were right-handed there was a concordance rate for schizophrenia of 92% — in almost all cases, when one MZ twin had schizophrenia, the other did too. However, when one MZ twin was right-handed the other was left-handed, the concordance rate for schizophrenia was 25%. This suggests a genetic link, and also a genetic link with handedness. It also shows that percentages can hide facts and need to be used carefully. Explore this issue using the internet or other sources.

Evaluation of twin studies: strengths

■ Both MZ and DZ twin babies are born at the same time and share a similar environment, but MZ twins have exactly the same DNA as each other whereas DZ twins share 50% of their genes. So twin studies are the main way that the influence of genes on behaviour can be studied — there is no other way of having identical DNA.

■ Both MZ twins and DZ twins share their environments and are treated as twins. For the most part, people treat twins as twins, whether they are MZ or DZ twins. So although there are differences between an MZ and a DZ set of twins in terms of their shared genes, for either type of twin there should not be environmental differences between the twins themselves.

> **Study hint** In an exam, avoid giving a strength that merely says something does what it does. It is so easy to say, for example, that twin studies are 'good because they study identical twins'. This is unlikely to score a mark. You should expand your answer to say that they are good because identical twins have DNA that is 100% the same and that there are no other types of people with identical DNA. Twin studies, therefore, control for the effects of genes.

Evaluation of twin studies: weaknesses

■ MZ twins, being of the same sex and likely to look identical, will be treated more alike than DZ twins, which means that their environments are not the same. MZ twins may share the same environment to a greater extent than DZ twins.

■ Although the genetic differences between MZ and DZ twins are what makes twin studies useful, there is epigenetic modification to take into account. From the moment of conception for MZ twins, there are differences — for example, some share the placenta and some do not. Many genes need an environmental switch; if environments are different, then, over time, MZ twins may become more different. So, even though MZ twins have identical DNA (100%) and can be compared with DZ twins that do not have identical DNA (only 50%), neither share their environment completely. Therefore, it is difficult to say that a characteristic is caused by genes just because MZ twins share it and DZ twins do not share it to the same extent. No study has found any behavioural characteristic that is 100% shared by MZ twins, so environment is bound to play a part.

Table 4.2 *Strengths and weaknesses of twin studies*

Strengths	Weaknesses
● There is no other way to study genetic influences so clearly because only MZ twins have 100% of their DNA in common	● MZ twins have identical DNA, but epigenetic modification has to be taken into account and they may grow and develop differently because of environmental influences
● MZ twins and DZ twins share their environments, so there is a natural control over environmental effects	● MZ twins may be treated more alike than DZ twins because they are the same sex and look identical; so their environments may not be as controlled as might be thought

Adoption studies

Adoption studies are carried out because the environment of adopted children is not the same as that of their biological families, yet they have genes in common with them. For example, if the effect of genes on schizophrenia is being studied, a researcher might want to find out whether children of a parent with schizophrenia

Unit 2

are more likely to develop schizophrenia than children without a family history of it. The problem is that children usually have both genes and the environment in common with their biological parents. If researchers study children who have a parent with schizophrenia and compare them with children without a parent with schizophrenia and choose all adopted children, then the issue of environment is controlled. Adopted children do not share their environment with their biological families. Therefore, if there are similarities with their biological families, it is likely to be because of genes not environment.

> ### Studies involving the methodology
> Kety et al. (1994) carried out an adoptive family study in Finland and found evidence for a genetic cause of schizophrenia. Out of a sample of 155, schizophrenia was diagnosed in nine adopted children, eight of whom had biological mothers either with schizophrenia or diagnosed as having spectrum psychoses.

Studies have found more evidence of schizophrenia amongst adopted children whose biological mothers had schizophrenia or a similar diagnosis than amongst other adopted children, whose mothers did not have schizophrenia. However, the problem with such studies is that the adoptive family might be matched closely to the biological family, so the environments of the two families might not have been as different as first thought.

Adoption studies do not all look at schizophrenia. However, it is a useful example and it is a mental health issue studied in the clinical psychology application in A2 psychology.

Evaluation of adoption studies: strengths

- Adoption studies are a way of separating genes from the environment. They keep the genetic link because they compare children with their biological parents; they control for the environment because the children are in a different environment from their biological families, so similarities cannot be because of environmental or learning factors. Using children who are brought up away from their biological families removes that influence, so if the children are similar to their biological families then it is their genes that cause the similarity and not the environment. Adoption studies remove this 'environment' issue from the study.
- Developmental trends can be studied because the studies can be **longitudinal**. The same child or group of children can be followed as they develop, so characteristics that come about as genes are triggered (e.g. schizophrenia) can be studied. The longitudinal approach means that the same children are studied at different times during their development, so trends can be found. Trends can then be linked to genetic influences.

Evaluation of adoption studies: weaknesses

- The environment may not be as different as at first thought. Adoption is an official process and only certain types of people are allowed to adopt. This might mean that adopted children are brought up in a similar way, so environmental factors could, after all, affect the findings.

- Children requiring adoption are often placed with families similar to their own. Therefore, environmental factors might not be so very different from those of their biological families.

Table 4.3 *Strengths and weaknesses of adoption studies*

Strengths	Weaknesses
• They control for environment because the children do not share the environment with their biological parent; therefore, similarities with biological parents are genetic • Studies can be longitudinal, so developmental trends can be studied	• Families that adopt are similar to each other, so there may be something in that similarity that is causing the results • Families that adopt tend to be chosen to be as similar as possible to the biological families, so the environment may not be very different

Studying MZ twins reared apart

Another form of adoption study is to look at MZ twins who have been separated at birth and brought up apart (usually adopted). This is a way of controlling the fact that MZ twins, as well as having 100% of their DNA in common, are usually brought up in a very similar environment. If MZ twins reared apart share characteristics, it can be more certainly claimed that those characteristics have a genetic basis. If the twins were reared together, their shared environment might have caused the characteristics, rather than their genes.

Studies involving the methodology Bergemann et al. (1988) carried out a study of identical twins with non-shared environments. The study of non-shared environments can include twins reared together but who have differences in their environments, such as attending different schools. In this study, the twins had been separated all their lives, so were 'reared apart'. Therefore, because they did not share the same environment, their characteristics would come from their identical genes. Two factors covered by the study were personality traits and how impulsive the twins were. The findings were that the way in which the environment affects individuals depends on their genetic make-up as well as on the type of environment. For example, those who scored low on extraversion genetically also showed low extraversion in a highly controlled organised environment; those that scored high on extraversion did not show high extraversion in an organised environment. So, interaction between genetic make-up and the environment depends on the match between them. This suggests that nature and nurture are not separate, but act on one another in all situations.

Evaluation of studying MZ twins reared apart: strengths

- Environmental conditions are controlled. Therefore, because their environments are different, if the MZ twins are similar in a characteristic, this is likely to be due to their identical DNA. When looking for causes of behaviour it is not easy to control for environment. The strength of studying MZ twins reared apart is that it does this, as do adoption studies.
- Rearing MZ twins apart is a unique research method controlling for genetic differences. There is no other way of finding identical human DNA and having two different environments, other than carrying out an experiment, which would not

Unit 2

be allowed for ethical reasons. Adoption studies do not have the advantage of comparing individuals who have identical genes; they compare adopted children with their biological parents, which is not the same thing.

Evaluation of studying MZ twins reared apart: weaknesses

- There are not many MZ twins who have been reared apart, so there are not large numbers from which to draw conclusions. It is difficult to find them, and they or their families may not want to take part in a study.
- When it is claimed that MZ twins are reared apart, this may not be entirely true. Up to the second half of the twentieth century (and later) when an unmarried girl gave birth, the girl's mother often brought up the child as her own and the biological mother acted as the child's sister. In the case of twins, sometimes another member of the family, such as an aunt or the biological mother's grandmother, brought up one of the twins. So they were reared apart, but in the same family. They may even have gone to the same school and played together. In such cases, they would have shared much of their environment, so the purpose of using MZ twins reared apart would have been lost.
- Although in theory it should be clear whether twins are MZ or DZ, in practice it is not always the case. Sometimes twins have had to be excluded from a study because it was not clear whether they were identical (MZ) or non-identical (DZ). Mistakes can be made.

Table 4.4 *Strengths and weaknesses of studies of twins reared apart*

Strengths	Weaknesses
• When MZ twins are reared apart, they do not share their environment, so any similarities are likely to be genetic • It is a unique method; there is no other way of studying MZ twins (which are rare) with a different environment unless they have been separately adopted and both can be traced and accessed (which is even rarer)	• There are not many MZ twins reared apart who can be accessed for study and if numbers are small it may be hard to draw meaningful conclusions • MZ twins may be reared apart but this has often meant within the same family and attending the same school, so their environments may not be very different, and they might even play together

Practice 4.1

For the three studies outlined below, explain whether you would use a twin study, a study of twins reared apart or an adoption study and explain briefly why.

Study 1 To look at whether depression is inherited.

Study 2 To look at the nature–nurture issue.

Study 3 To look at IQ and how far it might be inherited.

Suggested answers are at the end of Chapter 4.

The nature–nurture debate

Nature refers to what people are born with; nurture refers to what is learned through interaction with various environments, such as family, school, society and media.

It is an important debate in psychology, particularly for the biological approach. You should use the ideas about, and data from, the research methods using twins and adopted children to present arguments for and against claims about whether characteristics arise from nature or nurture, or both. Table 4.5 shows how such arguments might be used to discuss the nature–nurture debate.

Table 4.5 *Using twin and adoption studies in the nature–nurture debate in psychology*

Argument	Nature	Nurture	Interaction (both)
Definition	Characteristic given by genes	Characteristic given by environment	Genes need environmental trigger
Schizophrenia	Around 50% genetic (from twin studies)	Some instances caused by environment	If 50/50, then might be different causes or different types
Twin studies	MZ twins have identical DNA, so when a characteristic is the same, it is probably genetic	MZ twins share their environment	MZ twins become more different over time — epigenetic modification
Twins reared apart	MZ twins have identical DNA, so when a characteristic is the same, it is probably genetic	Environment is controlled (different), so if a characteristic is the same, it is probably genetic	Environment might be more similar than thought — it might be same family
Adoption studies	Compare adopted children with biological parents to see similarities — said to be genetic	Environment is controlled (different from biological family) so if a characteristic is the same, it is probably genetic	Environment might be more similar than thought, because might be matched when adopted
Environment	People are responded to according to the type of person they are (genetic)	Genes (personality) shape the environment, rather than the other way around	If personality (temperament) is genetic and environment responds, there is interaction
Genes	Each person is unique, with 50% of genes from each parent	Each person has a particular environment from conception	From the start there is interaction; nature and nurture are never separate

Unit 2

Study hint Make notes on the nature–nurture debate and how material about genes can inform the debate. Keep the notes ready for the learning approach, which is about the influence of the environment.

Explore Schizophrenia is used in this section to explain how twin and adoption studies are used in psychology. Choose another characteristic that interests you and do some research into whether it is controlled by genes or the environment, or a combination of both. Depression, anorexia, alcoholism, drug taking, addictive behaviour, temperament (personality), autism and IQ are all possible characteristics that you could explore. Alternatively, you might like to choose a characteristic according to your interests.

Explore Plomin et al. (1997) investigated the effects of genes and drew conclusions that should help your understanding of this area and the use of twin studies in the nature–nurture debate. Plomin is an important researcher in this area, so use the internet or another source to look up his work.

Study hint You might be asked to choose a characteristic that is examined within the nature–nurture debate — schizophrenia, depression, anorexia, alcoholism, drug taking, addictive behaviour, temperament (personality), autism and IQ. Be ready to use at least one of these characteristics in an argument.

PET and MRI scanning techniques as research methods

Twin and adoption studies are research methods used in the biological approach to look mainly at the causes of characteristics that might be genetically controlled. Scanning is a research method used for other purposes. There are different types of scanning, which give different types of information. Some scans are used to study biological, rather than psychological, aspects of an individual — for example, looking for diseases and tumours. Psychology is interested in scans that examine all aspects of the brain and information processing (thinking, remembering, using language, attending to information, forgetting and problem solving). The information that is needed guides the type of scan that is chosen.

> **Study hint** The AS course only requires you to be able to describe PET and MRI scanning techniques. However, it is also useful to be able to evaluate them because it aids understanding. This is why strengths and weaknesses are given in this section. You will be able to use this information when discussing such issues as, for example, whether psychology is a science and 'how science works', which is a theme throughout the course.

> PET and MRI scanning techniques are being refined constantly, so you are likely to find more up-to-date information than is given here. However, the ideas presented are sufficient for your course.

Scans used to be used solely for medical purposes. However, scans are now also used for research purposes. Much information is being gathered, although the machines are still expensive and relatively hard to access.

PET scanning techniques

PET (positron emission tomography) can be used to study the brain. It picks up 'hot spots' in the brain enabling us to find out which parts are working at a particular time. A radioactive tracer is added to a chemical (usually glucose) that the body uses and is injected into a vein in the arm. The tracer provides small, positively charged particles called positrons, which give signals that are recorded. As the glucose is used in the brain, this shows up as an area of activity. The recordings can be displayed as images, which are then interpreted.

Images from a PET scan, showing activity in the brain

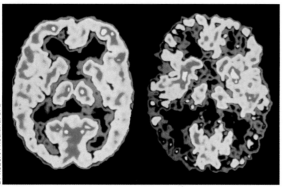

Dr Robert Friedland/SPL

A PET scan can be used to study blood flow in the brain. For example, if someone is talking during a PET scan, the areas of most blood flow in the brain will be the areas used during talking and the scan detects these areas. Cognitive activity and other types of brain activity can be tracked in this way and much information has been found about the functions of different parts of the brain. Language involves a number of brain areas because the individual has to find the word, prepare to speak it and then say it. By asking someone to think of words, read words, speak words and other such tasks, researchers can find which part of the brain works for a particular language function.

Reasons for using PET scans as a research method

PET scanning is mainly carried out for medical purposes, e.g. to check the damage made by a stroke or to check other nervous system problems. However, PET scans can also be used in research to map how the brain works. For example, PET scanning can be used in the study of schizophrenia to see which parts of the brain are working. The scans can then be compared with scans of the brain of a person without the illness so that more can be learnt about it. Epilepsy and other conditions can also be studied by looking at the blood flow in the brain.

> **Studies involving the methodology** Raine et al. (1997) (see page 254) used PET scanning to study the brains of murderers who pleaded not guilty by reason of insanity and compared them with a control group of non-murderers. They found numerous significant differences in the working of their brains.

Evaluation of PET scanning: strengths

- PET scanning, as all scanning techniques, is a reasonably non-invasive way of studying inside the brain (and body). The individual has to have the radioactive tracer injected, which is invasive, but the images are taken from outside the body, which is less dangerous and less distressing than surgery. Surgery for research purposes is carried out using animals, so scans using humans are more ethical for that reason. PET scanning is therefore a reasonably non-invasive and ethical way of researching the brain.
- As with all scanning techniques, there is validity — the scan seems to measure what it claims to measure. It is not easy to check validity when it comes to cognitive functions such as using language. However, when speech was studied using PET scanning, it was confirmed that what was previously thought to be the area for speech (found by examining the brains of people who had speech problems when they died) was indeed the area of activity (Broca's area). So scanning seems to be a valid measure.
- PET scanning is reliable because it can be repeated and the same results found. This can be tested — for example, whenever someone speaks the same area of the brain is used. The same areas of the brain are consistently found for different activities, which means the method is reliable.

Evaluation of PET scanning: weaknesses

- The use of the radioactive tracer is an invasive procedure and so there are ethical implications for the individual. The researcher must follow ethical guidelines carefully. Injecting someone with a substance is not something to be done lightly. There has to be informed consent and a good reason for carrying it out. The scan itself can make some people panic because having one's head inside a tube can be a claustrophobic experience and this must be fully explained to the participant.
- Although the activity shows up quite clearly on the image, it is difficult to isolate different brain functioning precisely. For example, people can read passages of text

Unit 2

while being scanned but they would almost certainly be using other parts of their brain as well. So although PET scanning is valid up to a point, it is hard to claim from a scan exactly which part of the brain is performing which function and this is often the aim of the research. Consequently, the validity of any claims can be criticised.

> **Study hint** To find out exactly what you need to know about any topic, read the AS specification carefully. You will see you don't have to be able to evaluate scanning techniques. They are evaluated here to help you in understanding such issues as reliability and validity. When you are revising, you need to know exactly what is required.

Table 4.6 *Strengths and weakness of PET scanning*

Strengths	Weaknesses
• PET scans are valid because their findings match other findings and they do measure what they claim to measure (e.g. the area pinpointed for speech is the same as that found by other methods) • PET scans are reliable; they are replicable and the same areas are highlighted (e.g. Broca's area for speech)	• They are ethical up to a point because they are relatively non-invasive compared with surgery; however, the injection is invasive. They can be distressing • It is hard to pinpoint exact areas of the brain so even if PET scans are clear, they are still fairly broad in their imaging

MRI scanning techniques

MRI scanning uses magnetic resonance imaging. A strong magnetic field is passed over the body. The whole body may be inside a tube, which can be claustrophobic. The process is noisy, but not painful. MRI scans are affected by movement, so the person has to keep very still. The effect of passing the magnetic field over the chosen area, which could be just the head, is measured and images are produced which are then interpreted.

An MRI scan gives cross-sectional views of the body, like a CT scan, and can produce images from different angles. MRI scans do not show activity to the same degree as PET scans, but they can measure blood flow. Before an MRI scan, a dye, called a contrast medium, is injected into the body to help show up body organs and relevant areas.

> **Studies involving the methodology** De Bellis et al. (2001) (see page 292) used MRI scanning to see if the volume of three areas of the brain (grey matter, white matter and corpus callosum) changed with age and sex of children aged between 6 and 18 years. They found that, with increasing age, grey matter decreased; white matter and the corpus callosum increased. They also found that these changes were greater in males than in females.

Evaluation of MRI scanning: strengths

- As with PET scanning, there is validity because what is found by the scan is then often found in reality. They are accurate in checking for abnormalities in the brain and rest of the body.
- Compared with surgery, MRI scans are non-invasive (apart from the injected dye). As a research method, surgery involving humans is unlikely. However, it is carried

out on animals. MRI scanning is, therefore, a more ethical way of studying the brain and the rest of the body, partly because it is non-invasive and partly because it means animals do not have to be used.

- MRI scanning is replicable. It can be repeated and the same results found. It is a scientific method because the resulting images can be checked by more than one person and the interpretation checked for objectivity. The images generated are evidence that the MRI scanner measures what was previously difficult to measure.

Evaluation of MRI scanning: weaknesses

- MRI scans are stressful because an injection has to be given, they are extremely noisy and can make people feel closed in. This sort of stress should not be imposed on a participant without careful consideration of ethical guidelines and issues.
- MRI scanning only measures particular things. There are, for example, clear images of soft tissue and body organs, but brain activity is not measured. This means that knowledge from such scans is limited.

Study hint Although for your course you are only asked to describe the two types of scans, your understanding of them would enable you to compare them. If what you are asked to do in your course would mean you can use the information in a certain way, then you might be asked to do just that. So it is useful to prepare for such questions and when more than one aspect of an area of knowledge is asked for, be ready to make comparisons.

Table 4.7 Strengths and weaknesses of MRI scanning

Strengths	Weaknesses
• They are valid in that what is found by the scans is real • They are scientific, replicable and reliable	• They are not completely ethical because an injection has to be given and having the scan is uncomfortable • Only certain information can be found from MRI scans, so in that sense they are limited

Comparing MRI and PET scanning techniques

Table 4.8 shows some comparison points between MRI and PET scans.

Table 4.8 A comparison of MRI and PET scans

Issue	MRI scan	PET scan
Non invasive	Yes — except for an injection of dye	Yes — except for an injection of radioactive tracer
Can study activity in the brain	No — studies tissues and looks for abnormalities, although can measure blood flow	Yes — the tracer picks up activity in the brain
Needs interpretation	Yes — from images generated by computer	Yes — from images generated by computer
Scientific method	Yes — objective technique that is the same for everyone	Yes — objective technique that is the same for everyone
Validity	Yes — measures what it is claimed that it measures; can be fairly unspecific	Yes — measures what it is claimed that it measures; unspecific because the brain is active in so many areas
Reliability	Yes — expensive and difficult to set up initially, but can be repeated easily	Yes — expensive and difficult to set up initially, but can be repeated easily

Issue	MRI scan	PET scan
Generalisability	Yes — same structures found for all people; specific problems relate to individuals	Yes — same brain functions found for all people; specific problems relate to individuals
Uses magnets	Yes — strong magnetic field used to scan parts of the body	No
Uses radioactive tracer	No	Yes
Focus on biological issues	Yes	Yes

The experimental research method

The biological approach uses experiments, and issues about carrying out experiments are important here. These issues have been dealt with in depth for the cognitive approach (Unit 1), but are covered briefly here because they are also required for Unit 2. Some of the issues in this methodology section relate to inferential statistics, which is a topic that you need to understand thoroughly.

How to carry out an experiment

- **Develop an experimental hypothesis.** The hypothesis is the statement of what is expected and is explained in Chapter 2.
- Choose participants using a sampling technique. You need to know about random, stratified, volunteer/self-selected and opportunity sampling. Check that you understand these different techniques. They are explained in Chapter 1 and briefly reviewed in Chapter 3.
- Identify the independent variable (IV) and the dependent variable (DV) (see Chapter 2 and page 298 in this chapter).
- Decide on the number of conditions and the design. The three types of experimental design (repeated measures, matched pairs and independent groups) are covered fully in Chapter 2.
- Decide on the experimental group and control group if appropriate. The control group shows what would happen if the independent variable were not manipulated and gives a baseline measure to test changes against (see Chapter 2 and page 298 in this chapter). Not all experiments have a control group, for example, studies of different groups of participants to compare.
- As far as possible, plan the study to avoid problems with reliability, validity and generalisability. This means having strict controls and standardised instructions, so that the study can be replicated and so tested for reliability. It means making the test as realistic as possible so that it represents real-life issues and is valid. This includes making the setting as close to real life as possible, so that there is an attempt at ecological validity. It means careful sampling to avoid bias, so that the findings can be generalised to the target population.

Using inferential statistical tests

In Chapter 3, you were introduced to the idea of using inferential statistical tests. A Spearman's rank correlation coefficient test was explained, together with a brief explanation of what the result of the test meant. However, no explanations of why that test was used or how to interpret the test result were given. This section covers how to choose a test and what the result of a test means. The Mann-Whitney U test is also explained because you have to carry out this test in the practical for this approach.

Descriptive statistics and inferential statistics

Descriptive statistics describe the data. You learnt about them for the cognitive approach. Descriptive statistics include:

- **measures of central tendency** — the mode, median, mean
- **measures of dispersion** — the range (and standard deviation, although you do not have to know this)

Descriptive statistics also include graphs and charts.

Inferential statistics draw inferences about the data, rather than merely describing them. Inferential statistics involve the use of statistical tests. The AS course includes three statistical tests:

- **Spearman rank correlation coefficent** (psychodynamic approach)
- **Mann-Whitney U** (biological approach)
- **Chi-squared** (learning approach)

Alternative and experimental hypotheses look for either *differences* between variables or for *relationships* between variables:

- The Spearman test is a test for relationships and correlations.
- The Mann-Whitney U and the Chi-squared tests are thought of as tests of difference.

Inferential statistics (the tests) examine whether the variables being studied are different or related enough to draw conclusions to that effect. This section explains why this is important and how to draw conclusions from statistical tests.

Practice 4.2

Decide whether each of the following studies is testing for a difference between variables or for a relationship. If testing for a relationship, a test of correlation is required; if testing for a difference, a test of difference is required.

Study 1 To see if the number of words generated on a topic while undergoing a scan is linked with length of time in education.

Study 2 To see if women have more activity in a certain brain region than men, when participants carry out a language task while undergoing a PET scan.

Study 3 To see whether men do better than women on a driving-test circuit where obstacles have to be avoided.

Answers are at the end of Chapter 4.

Choosing and using a statistical test

In order to use statistical tests you need to know about:

- levels of measurement
- levels of significance
- what 'N' is (or for the Chi-squared test what *df* is)
- participant (experimental) design
- whether a difference or a relationship is being tested for
- what 'critical value' means

Participant designs

Chapter 2 explains in detail about **participant designs**:

- **repeated measures** — the same participants for each part of a study
- **independent groups** — different participants for each part of a study
- **matched pairs** — different participants for each part of a study but matching those participants on important variables

These three participant designs are used when *differences* between variables are tested. Chapter 3 explains about correlation design, which looks at *relationships* between variables.

Alternative, experimental and null hypotheses

A hypothesis is the statement in a study of what is expected:

- The alternative hypothesis is the statement itself; it becomes an experimental hypothesis when the research method is an experiment.
- The alternative hypothesis is the 'alternative' to the null hypothesis; the null hypothesis is important where inferential tests are concerned.

Null hypothesis

The null hypothesis is the statement that what is predicted is *not* going to be true and any difference or relationship found is due to chance. A statistical test examines how far it is the case that the statement of what is expected will not happen. The question is, 'What is the probability of the results being due to chance?'

For example, for the alternative hypothesis 'women are better at language tasks then men', the null hypothesis would be 'any difference found between men and women with regard to language tasks is due to chance and not due to the independent variable (which in this case is gender)'. Remember that the independent variable (IV) is what is being manipulated in a study (in this case gender) in order to measure differences in the dependent variable (DV), which is what is measured as a result of the manipulation of the independent variable (in this case score on a language task).

Practice 4.3

For each of the following alternative hypotheses, write out a null hypothesis.

Alternative hypothesis 1 There is a positive relationship in that the number of words generated on a topic while undergoing a scan increases with length of time in education.

Alternative hypothesis 2 There is a difference between the sexes and women have more activity in a certain brain region than men when participants carry out a language task while undergoing a PET scan.

Alternative hypothesis 3 There is a difference between men and women when performing on a driving test circuit where obstacles have to be avoided.

Answers are at the end of Chapter 4.

Directional (one-tailed) and non-directional (two-tailed) hypotheses

Earlier chapters have discussed alternative and experimental hypotheses and how to make them directional (one-tailed) or non-directional (two-tailed). When using statistical tests, in order to judge whether or not the test result is significant, you have to know whether the hypothesis is one-tailed or two-tailed.

- **Directional (one-tailed) hypothesis** — the statement predicts not only a difference or a relationship but also the direction of the results, e.g. whether there will be a positive correlation or whether women will be better drivers.
- **Non-directional (two-tailed) hypothesis** — the statement predicts a difference or a relationship but does not give the direction of the difference or relationship, e.g. that gender affects driving or that there will be a relationship between gender and language ability.

Practice 4.4

For each of the following three hypotheses, decide whether it is directional (one-tailed) or non-directional (two-tailed).

Hypothesis 1 There is a positive relationship in that the number of words generated on a topic while undergoing a scan increases with length of time in education.

Hypothesis 2 There is a difference and women have more activity in a certain brain region than men, when participants carry out a language task while undergoing a PET scan.

Hypothesis 3 There is a difference between men and women when performing on a driving test circuit where obstacles have to be avoided.

Answers are at the end of Chapter 4.

Levels of measurement

There are three levels of measurement covered by the AS course.

- **Nominal data** are in the form of categories, simply putting data into sets. For example, categorising answers as 'yes' or 'no' is putting them into categories. There are no scores; the number of 'yes' answers and the number of 'no' answers are the data. The Chi-squared test (Chapter 5) is a test for nominal data. In terms of detail of data, nominal data are the lowest level of measurement.
- **Ordinal data** are ranked data, such as ratings. When data are put into a hierarchy (such as rating a day for whether it is cold or hot on a scale of 1 to 10), then they are ranked and are ordinal data. In terms of detail of data, ordinal data are the 'middle' level of measurement.

■ **Interval data** are data where real measurements are involved. For example, if temperature were recorded in degrees Celsius, that would be interval/ratio data, as would, for example, measurements of time, height, blood pressure and age. Interval/ratio data are scores that have equal intervals between them. For example, if you are 2 years older than one friend and 4 years older than another friend, then the numbers (number of years) have mathematical meaning. This is important because inferential tests for **interval/ratio data** involve calculations because the data are mathematical. In terms of amount of information provided, interval/ratio data are the highest level of measurement.

> **Interval data** and **ratio data** are not exactly the same, but are treated as such for the purposes of your course.

Practice 4.5

Here are some measures. Decide which level of measurement applies to each.

Measure 1 Whether a person is aggressive or not.

Measure 2 Reaction time to a stimulus shown on a screen.

Measure 3 How attractive we rate people to be.

Answers are at the end of the Chapter 4.

Choosing a statistical test

There are many different statistical tests, but for AS psychology you need to know only three. You need to know that:

■ if the study is a correlation, then the test to choose is the Spearman rank correlation coefficient test
■ if the study is an independent groups design and the data are nominal, then the test to choose is the Chi-squared test
■ if the study is an independent groups design and the data are ordinal or interval/ratio, then the test to choose is the Mann-Whitney U test.

Levels of significance

Your interest in psychology may be because you want to learn about people, how they think and, for example, how you make your own decisions. However, you need to know that the results of the studies from which such conclusions are drawn are sound results. Therefore, it is worth learning about levels of significance. The statistical test will see if the null hypothesis, which claims that any difference or relationship is due to chance, is true. So the test is to see if what was found was found by chance.

Calculating the odds of something being due to chance

There will be chance factors in any study. The idea is to decide what is down to chance and to be able to determine whether a difference or relationship is significant. Two examples of calculating odds are:

■ Imagine that a scientist found a vaccine for a life-threatening illness but also found that, although there was only a 1 in 100 000 chance of getting the illness there was a 1 in 100 chance that the vaccine would lead to a different life-threatening illness. It is a safe bet that nobody would have the vaccine.

■ Imagine that a personality test gave a 1 in 50 chance of finding the right employee for your company, but interviewing gave a 1 in 10 chance of finding the right person. You would choose the interview.

People work on such odds all the time but do not always know what they are. We cross the road regularly but may be more likely to be afraid of flying even though, according to figures, crossing the road is more dangerous. What statistical tests do is to calculate the odds of results being due to chance. When we know the odds of something being due to chance, we can decide whether to accept something as knowledge or not.

Accepted levels of significance in psychology

In psychology, anything that occurs due to chance in more than 1 in 20 cases is not accepted as knowledge. So, if you test 20 people to see if women gossip more than men, and more than one person goes against your hypothesis (perhaps there are several gossipy men in the sample), then this is not accepted as knowledge. Similarly, if you test 100 people and more than five people go against your hypothesis, then these are odds of more than 1 in 20, so this is also not accepted. The statistical test works out that likelihood for you. In psychology:

■ results are often accepted as statistically significant if there is a 1 in 20 likelihood or less of the results being due to chance
■ results are nearly always accepted if there is a 1 in 100 likelihood or less of the results being due to chance

The example above of a vaccine for a life-threatening illness is dramatic and possible in medical research. In psychology, however, most findings are not so dramatic and some chance factors have to be accepted. There are so many difficulties in measuring the variables in psychology studies that it is accepted that a level of 1 in 100 or even 1 in 20 may be due to chance.

'The probability that results are equal to or less than 1 in 20 due to chance' or 'the probability that results are equal to or less than 1 in 100 due to chance' are the phrases that you will be using. You will be accepting your results as statistically significant if you find one of those two probability levels. If you find that the results are significant at the probability that 1 in 1000 or less are due to chance, then that will be a highly significant result. If the results are more than 1 in 20 likely to be due to chance, you would not accept them because they are not statistically significant.

Instead of using '1 in 20' or '1 in 100' it is customary to use the mathematical (decimal) equivalent. Expressed as decimals:

■ 1 in 20 (5 in 100) is 0.05   ■ 1 in 1000 is 0.001
■ 1 in 100 is 0.01

The correct number of zeros goes in front of the probability. For example:

■ 1 in 1000 is expressed as 0.001   ■ 1 in 10000 is expressed as 0.0001
■ 2 in 1000 is expressed as 0.002   ■ 2 in 10000 is expressed as 0.0002

Suppose you have to convert a probability (e.g. 1 in 200) to a decimal:

- Find the lowest number needed to multiply the second figure (200) by to obtain a number such as 10; 100; 1000; 10000. (In this example, the number to choose is 1000.)
- The number needed to multiply 200 by is 5.
- Then, multiply both numbers by 5. This gives 5 in 1000, which expressed as a decimal is 0.005.

> ### Practice 4.6
>
> Convert the following probabilities into decimal form:
>
> **1** 1 in 200   **3** 1 in 10 000
>
> **2** 1 in 50   **4** 1 in 2000
>
> *Answers are at the end of Chapter 4.*

> **Study hint** It is worth making a note of what p ≤ 0.05 and p ≤ 0.01 mean because this question can be asked in the exams:
> - *p* means 'probability of the results being due to chance'
> - ≤ means less than or equal to
> - 0.05 means 1 in 20
> - 0.01 means 1 in 100

Similarly, 2 in 200 is 10 in 1000 (multiply both by 5) which expressed as a decimal is 0.01; 6 in 500 is 12 in 1000 (multiply both by 2) which expressed as a decimal is 0.012.

The way of expressing 'the probability that results are equal to or less than 1 in 20 due to chance' is:

$$p \leq 0.05$$

where p = the probability of the results being due to chance; ≤ means less than or equal to; 0.05 means 1 in 20.

'The probability that results are equal to or less than 1 in 100 due to chance' is expressed as $p \leq 0.01$.

When the likelihood of the results being due to chance is 1 in 1000, the probability is $p \leq 0.001$. The values p ≤ 0.05, p ≤ 0.01 and p ≤ 0.001 are examples of levels of significance. A **level of significance** is the probability that the results are due to chance. In psychology, $p \leq 0.05$ (1 in 20) is the probability at which the results are accepted as being statistically significant.

Choosing a level of significance

Whether the researcher chooses a lenient level of significance (e.g. 1 in 20 or $p \leq 0.05$) or a stricter one (e.g. 1 in 100 or $p \leq 0.01$) depends on what is being tested. If the test has been carried out previously and found to be true, it might be reasonable to ask for 1 in 100 ($p \leq 0.01$) of the results or fewer to be due to chance. If the study is new, and it is not known what is likely, then a result of 1 in 20 ($p \leq 0.05$) being due to chance might be a good result. It also depends on how 'serious' the consequences of the study might be. If a new education programme is launched on the basis of a study that has a high likelihood of its results being due to chance, then 1 in 20 might not be acceptable. (This is a rather high likelihood — it means that out of every 20 children, 19 do whatever is predicted.)

The meaning of *N* and *df*

Statistical tests differ, but they all need either N or *df*.

N is easy — it is the number of participants/number of scores. If there are 20 scores (from 20 people), N = 20. The Spearman test and the Mann-Whitney U test both use N. However, for the Mann-Whitney U test on an independent groups design there are two values for N. There will be one number of participants (N_A) in one condition and another number or participants (N_B) in the other condition. If there is the same number of participants in each condition, N_A and N_B are the same; if the number of participants in each condition is different, then N_A and N_B are different.

df stands for 'degrees of freedom'. The inferential test for the learning approach is the Chi-squared test, which uses *df*, not N. **Degrees of freedom (*df*)** refers to the number of values in the final calculation that are free to vary. Consider the data in Table 4.9:

- If you know that the total of a row is 20 (e.g. row 1 in Table 4.9) and there are two numbers in the row, one of which is 15, the other number must be 5 and has no freedom to vary. The first score (15) has the freedom to vary; the second score (5) does not.
- If you know that the total of a column is 20 (e.g. column 2 in Table 4.9) below) and there are two numbers in the column, one of which is 5, then other number must be 15 and has no freedom to vary. The first score (5) has the freedom to vary; the second score (15) does not.

A table that has two rows and two columns has a degree of freedom of 1. This is calculated as number of rows minus 1 multiplied by number of columns minus 1, which is 1 overall:

$$df = (r-1)(c-1)$$

where r = number of rows and c = number of columns.

For the data in Table 4.9:

$$df = (2-1) \times (2-1) = 1 \times 1 = 1$$

So for a two-by-two table, *df* is always 1.

Table 4.9 A two-by-two table

	Column 1	Column 2	Total
Row 1	15	5	20
Row 2	15	15	30
Total	**30**	**20**	**50**

> **Study hint** You might just want to learn that for a two-by-two table (two rows and two columns), *df* is always 1; for a three-by-two table (three rows and two columns or three columns and two rows), *df* is always 2. You don't have to know what degrees of freedom means, just that *df* means degrees of freedom.

Choosing a Mann-Whitney U test

For this approach you are asked to carry out a practical that uses an independent-groups design and generates at least ordinal data. This is so that you will have to carry out a Mann-Whitney U test to see if your results are statistically significant. A Mann-Whitney U test is used when a study looks for a difference and uses an independent groups design with at least ordinal-level data (the data can be interval/ratio).

Carrying out a Mann-Whitney U test

If you have studied the psychodynamic approach you already know how to carry out a Spearman test. A Mann-Whitney U test is similar. The formula may look complicated but, as with the Spearman test, a step-by-step approach can be taken.

$$U_A = N_A N_B + \frac{N_A(N_A + 1)}{2} - \Sigma R_A \qquad U_B = N_A N_B + \frac{N_B(N_B + 1)}{2} - \Sigma R_B$$

Suppose that a group of seven females and a group of eight males are set the task of completing an eight-piece jigsaw and the time (seconds) taken to complete the jigsaw is recorded. The hypothesis is that males will be better than females at jigsaws (males are supposed to be better than females at visuospatial tasks). When following the steps, refer to Table 4.10.

Step 1: If one group is smaller, this is group A. If there are the same number of participants in the group, call one group A. (Here, $N_A = 7$; $N_B = 8$)

Step 2: Rank all the scores together as if they are one set of scores from one group.

Step 3: Consider the groups separately and find the total (ΣR_A) of the ranks for group A. (Here, $\Sigma R_A = 79$.)

Step 4: Find the total (ΣR_B) of the ranks for group B. (Here, $\Sigma R_B = 41$.)

Table 4.10 *Scores (time in seconds that it took) for males and females doing an eight-piece jigsaw (made-up scores)*

Participants, $N_A = 7$ (Step 1)	Scores for females	Rank (from all 15 participants) (Step 2)	Participants, $N_B = 8$ (Step 1)	Scores for males	Rank (from all 15 participants) (Step 2)
1	123	13	1	95	8
2	89	5	2	78	2
3	140	14	3	102	10
4	97	9	4	79	3
5	110	12	5	84	4
6	150	15	6	93	7
7	104	11	7	62	1
			8	92	6
Total rank, R_A (Step 3): 79			Total rank, R_B (Step 4): 41		

Steps 5 to 9 provide a test result (U_A) for group A.

Step 5: Multiply N_A by N_B. (Here, $7 \times 8 = 56$)
Step 6: Add 1 to N_A and multiply the result by N_A. (Here, $(7 + 1) \times 7 = 56$.)
Step 7: Divide the answer to Step 6 by 2. (Here, $56 \div 2 = 28$.)
Step 8: Add together the answers to Step 5 and Step 7. (Here, $56 + 28 = 84$.)
Step 9: Subtract the answer to Step 3 from the answer to Step 8. (Here, $84 - 79 = 5$.)

This result is U_A. (Here, $U_A = 5$.)

Steps 10 to 15 provide a test result (U_B) for group B.

Step 10: Multiply N_A by N_B. (Here, $7 \times 8 = 56$.)
Step 11: Add 1 to N_B and multiply the result by N_B. (Here, $(8 + 1) \times 8 = 72$.)
Step 12: Divide the answer to Step 11 by 2. (Here, $72 \div 2 = 36$.)
Step 13: Add together the answers to Step 10 and Step 12. (Here, $56 + 36 = 92$.)
Step 14: Subtract the answer to Step 4 from the answer to Step 13. (Here, $92 - 41 = 51$.)

This result is U_B. (Here, $U_B = 51$.)

The smaller of U_A and U_B becomes U and is the number to look up in statistical tables to see whether or not the result is significant. For the example given, U_A is the smaller than U_B, so $U = 5$.

Sections of a critical values table for the Mann Whitney U test

To find out if the results of a statistical test are significant, you have to look it up in a critical values table (see Table 4.11).

If your number of participants is not included in this table you will need to find a full table in a statistics book or on the internet. To be significant, the value of U has to be equal to or less than the critical values shown in Table 4.11.

Note that the table given here assumes a one-tailed 'test' is appropriate, which means that the hypothesis being tested is directional. For a non-directional hypothesis, a two-tailed test is appropriate and a different table would be needed.

Table 4.11 *Critical values of U for a one-tailed test, level of significance $p \le 0.05$*

N_A	N_B				
	8	9	10	11	12
7	13	15	17	19	21
8	15	18	20	23	26
9	18	21	24	27	30
10	20	24	27	30	33
11	23	27	31	34	37
12	26	30	34	38	42

Tables of critical values can be found in statistics textbooks.

Assuming that you need a one-tailed test and have calculated the U value, all that you have to do is to compare the critical value for the number of participants in each group with your U result. If your own U is larger than the critical value, then the data from your study are not significant at $p \le 0.05$ (assuming the hypothesis is one-tailed).

In the example, the hypothesis was that males would be better at jigsaws. This is a directional hypothesis (it gives direction, because it says males will be better), so a one-tailed test is suitable. The test gave a value of $U = 5$. This is less than 13, which is the critical value when N_A is 7 and N_B is 8 (Table 4.11). Therefore, the result is statistically significant and supports the hypothesis.

Evaluating laboratory experiments: validity, reliability, and generalisability

For the biological approach, you are asked to consider the usefulness of laboratory experiments. These issues are considered with regard to both human participants and to the use of animals in laboratory experiments. Advantages and disadvantages are covered, in terms of practical issues, ethical issues and credibility. At the end of the section on using animals there is a table linking such issues to validity, reliability and generalisability.

The study by Raine et al. (1997) is useful as an example because it uses PET scanning and can be thought of as a laboratory study — the independent variable is manipulated and the dependent variable measured, with controls in place, including a control group. As the independent variable (the murderers) is naturally occurring the study is, in a way, a natural experiment although the control group is planned. The same issues regarding validity, reliability and generalisability apply here.

Validity

Validity is found when a study measures what it claims to measure. For example, did the PET scanning in the study of murderers who pleaded not guilty by reason of insanity (Raine et al. 1997) really measure their tendency to murder? Since laboratory experiments involve manipulation of the independent variable and operationalising the dependent variable to make it measurable, often what is being investigated and what is being measured are not valid (real life).

Reliability

Reliability is found when a study is repeated and the same results are found. For example, the study by Raine et al. (1997) built on previous work that had highlighted particular areas of the brain as being linked to aggression. When it was found that the same areas differed in the murderers' brains, this meant that the study had more reliability than if it had been a stand-alone study. In general, because laboratory experiments involve careful controls of both setting and participant variables, they are replicable and can be tested for reliability.

Generalisability

Generalisability is found when the sample used in a study represents the target population well enough for the results from the sample to be said to be true of the target population. For example, Raine et al. (1997) studied murderers who pleaded not guilty by reason of insanity, so the findings should perhaps be generalised only to that category of murderer. They studied mainly men, so perhaps they should generalise their findings only to men. The generalisability of the results of laboratory experiments is similar to that of other research methods because it is the sampling that determines it, rather than the research method.

Table 4.12 *Evaluation of laboratory experiments: validity, reliability and generalisability*

	Positive aspects	Negative aspects
Validity	If both the independent and dependent variables are naturally occurring, as with Raine et al. (1997) (the working of the brain is 'real' as was whether the participants were murderers or not) then they can be valid	If the independent variable is manipulated (e.g. participants having to read while being scanned), then this is not very valid. If the dependent variable can be interpreted differently (e.g. the murderers in the study by Raine et al. (1997) were anxious, which affected their brain functioning), then the experiment is not valid
Reliability	There are careful controls of all variables except the independent variable, so replicability and reliability are why the research method is chosen	Being replicable does not necessarily mean that a study is reliable — it has to be repeated in order to find that out. Study findings do contradict one another; the findings are then questionable with regard to reliability
Generalisabilty	If the sampling is random or chosen to be representative in some other way, and the sample is large enough, then experimental results are as generalisable as those of any other research method	If the sample is opportunity, volunteer or otherwise biased, then the findings are not generalisable to the target population

Using animals in laboratory experiments

Studies in psychology can use animals. You will learn about the use of animals in both the biological and learning approaches. According to the American Psychological Association about 8% of psychological research involves the use of animals; this is likely to be in the USA, but similar figures apply elsewhere. A number of species is used, around 90% of which are rodents and birds, mainly rats, mice and pigeons. Only around 5% of the animals are primates; cats and dogs are studied rarely.

There are both practical and ethical considerations, including issues about credibility, with regard to the use of animals in psychological research. In this section, some research using animals is described to give you an understanding of the sorts of studies that are carried out. The use of animals in experiments is then evaluated and the advantages and disadvantages of using animals summarised.

Research using animals in laboratory experiments

Animals are used in a number of areas of study, e.g. language use, memory and processes of learning. The biological approach covers the nervous system, how the brain works and the effects of genes. All these areas have been studied using animals; some examples are given here.

Studying genes

Mice have been used to find out how certain genes affect behaviour. Mice are useful for experiments because they breed quickly and the arrangement of genes along their chromosomes is similar enough to humans for the studies to be meaningful. Genes can cause abnormalities in humans; mice are tested to see if that particular gene causes the same abnormality in mice. For example, mice have been used in experiments on deafness.

Rats have been used to study Parkinson's disease and gene therapy. Researchers used drugs to replicate in rats the symptoms of Parkinson's disease. They then used gene therapy to try and reverse the symptoms — with some success.

Studying the nervous system

Rats have been used in investigations of the effects of antipsychotic drugs on the brain structure and on the nervous system within the brain. The changes caused by antipsychotic drugs appear to be:

- increased size of the striatum — it is thought that this increased size is due to increased blood flow and structural changes in the neurones
- increased density of glial cells in the prefrontal cortex
- increases in the number of synapses and changes in the synapses

Structures such as the prefrontal cortex are explained later in this chapter, as are glial cells and how synapses work.

Other studies include using mice to investigate changes in neurotransmitters when the mice were put under stress. Stress is an area that is often studied using animals.

A study using monkeys was carried out to see if control over a situation affected stress levels. It was found that in a trial the monkey with control developed more ulcers than the monkey that had no control over the situation, so it was concluded that having control over a situation can be stressful. However, other studies show that not having control is stressful, so conclusions are uncertain. Also in the study (Brady, 1958) monkeys who could learn were given the control. Those that could not learn were not, so the sampling was biased.

Studying the functions of the brain

Research has been carried out into the way that antipsychotic drugs affect the brain and its nervous system. Most of this research has been carried out on rats and the findings have been generalised to humans. The research needs to be replicated in humans because of the differences in brain structure and function between rats and humans. Some of the findings have come from MRI scans of humans, however, so animal studies are not the only way of researching the area.

Other research is into the effect of physical activity on the processes of ageing. Studies involve animals — usually rodents — exercising, for example, on a wheel. Exercise has been shown to protect animals from developing some age-related diseases. The researchers concluded that this was because there was an increase in the levels of certain neurochemicals that can prevent disease. It was also found that the plasticity of the brain was improved by exercise. Plasticity means being able to use different areas of the brain in place of other areas.

As far back as 1950, Lashley was investigating brain function in rats by using ablation (removing part of the brain). He systematically removed parts of rats' brains to see what effects this would have on memory.

Rats have been used to find the effect of sleep deprivation. They not only became distressed, but died, because of the deprivation.

Explore Using the internet or some other source, find some other studies that use laboratory experiments on animals to investigate the brain. Find out about the parts of the brain, e.g. the striatum. Look up the issue of antipsychotic drugs. If they alter the brain, should they be used?

Table 4.13 *Some of the areas where animals are used*

Animals used	Area studied
Mice	Genes associated with abnormalities in humans — to gain understanding of such issues
Rats	Symptoms of Parkinson's disease — and gene therapy to see if it could work
Rats	Antipsychotic drugs — to see how they change the brain itself (both its structure and the nervous system)
Mice	Stress — to find changes in neurotransmitters to gain understanding
Monkeys	Stress — to see what effect having control over the situation has
Rodents	Exercise — to see if it helps prevent the processes of ageing
Rats	Memory — to see what parts of the brain perform which function
Rats	Sleep deprivation — to see its effects

Evaluation of the use of animals in psychological research

There are practical advantages and disadvantages with using animals in research.

Practical advantages

It is usually, but not always, more practical to use animals than humans:

- Most animals used in research are small and can be handled.
- In studying genetics, it is useful to be able to study more than one generation in a short time. Therefore, animals that have a short gestation period and reproductive cycle are useful because successive generations can be obtained relatively quickly.

> Humans are animals, but for your course 'animals' refers to non-human animals.

- Some animals (e.g. mice) have similar sorts of brain areas and chromosomal function to humans which is useful for comparative purposes.
- Using animals in research can have practical benefits for the animals as well as for humans. For example, by knowing more about some animal species, zoos are able to care for them better.
- There are practical reasons why it is useful to use animals when studying the effects of drugs. The drug may need to be administered daily over days or weeks, which — ethical considerations aside — is more practical using animals. Some studies require examination of brain tissue after drug treatment, or need drugs to be administered to specific sites of the brain. These are procedures that can be carried out more practically on animals.
- Studying the process of ageing using humans is not practicable because the study might have to run over 80 years. On average, rats live for 2 years and monkeys live from 15 to 20 years. The shorter lifespans mean that results are found more quickly, which is again a practical reason for using animals.
- Laboratory experiments that need participants of a certain size, age, or genetic structure and which might need, for example, to restrict participants to a certain diet or to control their environment in some way are more practically carried out using animals.
- Evidence that findings from animal studies can be applied to humans comes from such studies as using cats and bulls and stimulating the limbic system, which affects their levels of aggression. It has been shown that in humans as well the limbic system relates to aggression. This supports the idea of using animals for practical reasons rather than humans.

If Darwin had not put forward the theory of evolution, which holds that human animals and other animals have evolved separately but from common beginnings, animals may not have been studied to find information about humans. However, because the theory of evolution is largely accepted, such studies are considered useful.

Box 4.1 **Practical reasons for using animals**

- Relatively small.
- Relatively easy to handle.
- Some have relatively short gestation periods.
- Some have relatively short reproductive cycles.
- Some (e.g. mice) have a similar brain structure to humans.
- Some (e.g. mice and rats) have a short lifespan (2 years).
- Some procedures have to be carried out daily.
- Some procedures require accessing specific parts of the brain that might then be damaged.
- Some procedures require strict control over the environment.

Practical disadvantages

- Animals are not the same as humans, so there can be problems in generalising results of studies on animals to humans. Even if an animal has a similar brain structure to humans it will not be identical.
- In animal studies, a variable is often isolated, e.g. exercise. Humans could follow a programme of increased exercise but there would be other areas of their lives that might also changed. Conclusions from animal studies often do not take into account the complexity of 'real' life situations.
- In order to study some diseases (e.g. Parkinson's) they have to be artificially reproduced in animals, which is not the same as a person developing the disease. Therefore, what is studied might not be valid.
- There is doubt about the credibility of animal studies. For example, what is being studied is often not the same as the situation for humans, e.g. drug-induced symptoms of Parkinson's disease or replication of control over a stressful situation for monkeys. Mice have similar chromosomal functioning to humans, which makes the findings from gene studies useful. However, when considering the whole organism, it does not seem credible to conclude that mice function in the same way as humans.

For all the reasons listed, we can say that the comparison between animals and humans is not credible. For example, simply because they have shorter reproductive cycles, live fewer years and have different brain structures, it is not credible to apply findings from such studies to humans. There is evidence that findings from animal studies cannot be applied to humans. The drug thalidomide was found to be safe when tested on rabbits but when pregnant women used it, many babies were affected by the drug.

Explore Using the internet or another source, investigate what the drug thalidomide was developed for and what its effects were.

Using animal studies assumes a **reductionist** approach to studying human behaviour because it reduces such behaviour to isolated variables (e.g. exercise or one set of symptoms in a disease). Such studies can give useful results, such as when determining drug therapy for a specific set of symptoms. An argument against reductionism is that studies should be **holistic**, e.g. humans should be studied as a whole, including not only their biological make-up but also their social situation and environment. Laboratory experiments using animals take a reductionist view, so their credibility can be questioned by giving a holistic argument. Use the internet or some other source to find out more about reductionism and holism.

Box 4.2 Practical reasons for not using animals in research

- The brains of animals are not exactly the same as those of humans. There are important differences, so results are not generalisable.
- Their genetic structures are also not the same. Therefore, findings about genes may not apply to humans, so the results are not generalisable.
- Human lives are complex and factors rarely occur in isolation.
- Some diseases (e.g. Parkinson's) have to be replicated in animals by using drugs and so might not be the same as the disease itself. Therefore, studies might lack validity.
- Using animals may not be credible.

Ethical advantages of using animals

The main ethical reason for using animals is that procedures can be carried out on animals that for ethical reasons cannot be carried out on humans. For example:

- **lesions**, which involve damaging brain structure
- **ablation**, which involves removing part of the brain

The American Psychological Association (APA) states that psychologists should only undertake research with animals for a clear scientific reason. The knowledge that comes from the research should increase understanding of behaviour, increase understanding of the species being studied or 'provide results that benefit the health or welfare of humans or other animals'. Otherwise the research should not be carried out. The British Psychological Society (BPS) takes a similar view.

Other reasons include:

- Drugs have been developed that would not have been developed without the use of animals, e.g. drugs to treat mental illnesses, such as antipsychotic drugs.
- It is argued by some that humans should improve their own quality of life by whatever means. This is called '**pro-speciesism**'.
- More is learned about the animal species in question and the knowledge is used to improve their care.

Look up what Green (1994) and Grey (1991) say about the ethics of using animals in research so that you can explore the arguments further.

Box 4.3   Ethical reasons for using animals in research

- In general, procedures can be carried out that cannot be carried out on humans and this benefits humans. For example:
  - ablation: removing parts of the brain to see what happens
  - lesioning: damaging parts of the brain to see what happens
- Pro-speciesism suggests that we ought to do all we can to protect our own species.
- Drugs have been developed that could not otherwise have been developed.
- The knowledge obtained can also improve the lives of the animal species in question.

Cost–benefit analysis: a decision cube (Bateson 1988)

It is said that a decision cube should be used to see whether a study should be carried out or not. There are three dimensions in the decision-making process:

- what benefit (either for animals or humans) the findings of the study are likely to have
- the cost of the study in terms of pain and suffering
- scientific quality going from poor to excellent

If the benefits are not very high, the cost (suffering) is high and the research is not well planned, then it should not be carried out. If the benefits are high, the cost (suffering) quite low and the research is well planned, then it should be carried out.

Guidelines for the use of animals in laboratory experiments and other research

The APA has published ethical guidelines for the treatment of research animals in its *Ethical Principles of Psychologists and Code of Conduct*. The APA also has other guidelines — *Guidelines for Ethical Conduct in the Care and Use of Animals* — that set standards for psychologists who use animals in research. The scientific community also sets standards. In the USA, the American Association for the Accreditation of Laboratory Animal Care (AAALAC) is the recognised body for accrediting institutions that use animals. Accredited institutions are inspected every 3 years. In the UK, the Society for Neuroscience also has guidelines. These are summarised in Box 4.4.

Box 4.4   Guidelines for using animals in research

- Researchers must have a Home Office licence and certificates.
- Anaesthetics must be used appropriately by someone who knows about them.
- Senior staff must supervise studies.
- Caging and social environment must suit the species.
- If the animal is to be deprived this must be monitored and suffering kept to a minimum.
- Animals must not be subjected to avoidable stress or discomfort.
- Anaesthetic must be given if possible when surgical procedures are involved.
- If no anaesthetic is given blood pressure and heart rate must be monitored to understand the pain involved and researchers must take action to alleviate the pain or end the experiment.

- No more animals must be used than necessary.
- Living animals should only be used when necessary.
- Alternatives should always be sought.
- Research animals must be acquired and cared for according to National Institute of Health (NIH) guidelines.
- Restraints that animals cannot easily adapt to should only be used if there is no alternative.
- There should be reasonable time between experiments so animals can recover and rest.

Source: Society for Neuroscience Guidelines for Animal Research

Ethical disadvantages when using animals in studies in psychology

It is fairly clear what the ethical disadvantages are when using animals in studies, particularly in laboratory experiments. The list of guidelines in Box 4.4 highlights the problems.

- In laboratory experiments, animals are likely to be confined more than is normal; they are either in an unfamiliar environment or bred for the purpose, neither of which is very ethical.
- Surgical procedures are used, which is likely to cause the animals pain (or at least discomfort), which again is not very ethical. In some studies, animals die because of the procedures. The guidelines help to make the studies ethical to an extent, e.g. specifying the use of the minimum number of animals. However, those that are used are still caused pain and discomfort.
- Animal species are not sufficiently different from humans for them to be treated as 'objects' and not as 'participants'. However, in general animals are not treated as conscious beings in the way that humans are.

Study hint In spite of the argument that animals deserve ethical treatment, do not use ethical guidelines for humans when discussing ethical issues regarding the use of animals in research. For example, although it is the case that animals do not have the right to withdraw and cannot give informed consent, it is not appropriate to use those arguments because they concern consciousness; it is accepted that humans are conscious beings but non-human animals are not.

A counter-argument about the use of animals

Some researchers have put forward arguments that using animals is not as unethical as might be thought. For example, Grey (1987) argued that:

- when rats were deprived of food it did not cause them distress. They were usually fed after the experiment, which was once a day, which was enough. Even if they were not fed then, their body weight was maintained at 85% of what it would be if they fed normally, and that this is a healthy weight
- when rats were given electric shocks, the size of the shock was what would cause a tickling sensation in humans

By looking at the detail in this way Grey helped to show that depriving rats of food and giving them electric shocks might not be as unethical as thought previously.

It is also suggested that some species (e.g. insects) do not feel pain, although this is still being researched.

Alternatives to using animals in laboratory experiments

Animal laboratories are expensive and labour intensive, so in practical terms it makes sense to look for alternatives. Ethical guidelines say that where possible alternatives must be used. However, there are problems with alternatives:

- Animals can be studied in their natural setting. However, such studies are usually for purposes other than investigating brain structure and function, so do not replace animal experiments.
- Other alternatives are using plants and tissue cultures or computer simulations. However, plants do not have a nervous system and tissue cultures cannot develop alcoholism, autism or learning disorders. Computer simulations are only useful if they draw on knowledge obtained from live organisms so are not a substitute for animal studies, although they may help to limit the numbers of animals used.

Even when studies are carried out in some other way, they are usually replicated on living organisms to test out the findings; those organisms tend to be animals.

> **Explore** Use the internet or some other source to investigate the claim that some animals do not feel pain. Research in this area is on-going and it is interesting to consider how such issues are investigated.

Box 4.5 Some ethical reasons for not using animals

- Many animals feel pain.
- Animals in experiments are not in their natural surroundings and are in unfamiliar, and, therefore, distressing conditions.
- Animals should be treated ethically; they are not sufficiently different from humans to be treated as objects.

Table 4.14 *Strengths and weaknesses of using animals in laboratory experiments in psychological research*

Strengths	Weaknesses
• **Ethical** — can be used when it would be unethical to use humans	• **Limited** — strong guidelines have to be followed
• **Practical** — can be more practical than using humans (e.g. animals used are easier to handle, have shorter life spans, and shorter reproductive cycles)	• **Hard to generalise** — differences that make animals useful (e.g. different life spans and different reproductive cycles) can make findings hard to generalise to humans
• **Fairly generalisable** — some animals have similar brain structures and chromosomal functioning to humans, so findings can be generalised quite successfully to humans	• **Human behaviour is likely to be more complex** — variables can be isolated and focused upon in a laboratory experiment, but human behaviour is likely to be more complex; this also means validity is questionable
• **Reliable** — careful controls mean that the experiments are replicable, so can be repeated and results are shown to be reliable	• **Lack of credibility** — findings from animal studies might be so hard to generalise, that there is a complete lack of credibility

Examination-style questions

1 How are twin studies used in psychology? In your answer, explain the research method and give at least one example of a twin study. *(6 marks)*

2 Evaluate the use of adoption studies as a research method. *(6 marks)*

3 Describe two scanning techniques used in psychological research. *(6 marks)*

4 Evaluate the use of animals in studies in psychology. In your answer, consider issues of ethics, practicality and credibility. *(8 marks)*

Extension questions

1 Compare the usefulness as research methods of twin studies, adoption studies and studies of twins reared apart. Discuss their relative strengths and weaknesses. *(12 marks)*

2 Give arguments for and against using animals in psychology. Include in your arguments at least three examples of studies using animals to gain information within the biological approach. *(12 marks)*

Content

The biological approach in psychology covers a large number of topics, e.g. stress, antipsychotic drugs, memory, sleep deprivation and gene therapy. For the AS course you study relatively few topics. You have to to be able to:

■ describe briefly the role of the nervous system and neurotransmitters in human behaviour

■ describe briefly the role of genes in behaviour (including the nature–nurture debate)

■ describe how genes, hormones and brain functioning affect the development of gender behaviour

■ evaluate the influence of biological factors on gender development and compare this with explanations of gender development from the psychodynamic and learning approaches

When comparing the three explanations of gender development you should include methodological issues of how they were arrived at, e.g. whether animals were used in studies.

The role of the central nervous system and neurotransmitters in human behaviour

The **nervous system** has two main parts, the central nervous system and the peripheral nervous system. The **central nervous system (CNS)** consists of the brain and spinal cord. The brain is within the skull and the spinal cord is within the vertebrae. In the embryo, a tube separates into the brain and the spinal cord and there are then

further subdivisions. The brain contains a number of areas. Those that are important for your course are shown in Table 4.15.

Table 4.15 Some important parts of the brain

Brain part	Function	Approach
Striatum	Important role in controlling movements and thinking	Biological approach (effects of antipsychotic drugs; use of animal laboratory experiments)
Hippocampus	Short-term memory occurs	Cognitive approach
Ventricles	Schizophrenia	A2
Corpus callosum, connects the two hemispheres	Brain lateralisation; sex differentiation	Biological approach
Amygdala	Emotions and aggression	Biological approach — Raine et al.
Hypothalamus	Regulating eating and drinking and motivated behaviours	Biological approach
Hemispheres	Brain lateralisation	Biological approach

Other parts of the brain include:

■ the thalamus — near the base; passes on information from the senses
■ the cerebellum — stores well-learnt practical skills
■ the cortex — the most recent development of the brain for humans, which stores information and is involved in problem solving and decision making

There are too many parts to explain them all, e.g. the suprachiasmatic nucleus is the body clock that keeps bodily rhythms going.

Figure 4.1 Parts of the brain and the spinal cord

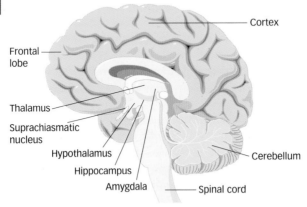

Explore Using the internet or some other source, look up split-brain studies. These are studies in which the corpus callosum has been split, often to help those with epilepsy; the resulting behaviour is studied. Sperry carried out such studies, so you could start by looking up his work.

Neurotransmitters

Neurotransmitters (e.g. dopamine and noradrenaline) are chemical messengers that act between the neurones in the brain. This allows the brain to process thoughts and memories.

The nervous system consists of neurones and glia. Glial cells carry out repairs, act as insulators and remove waste products from the brain; research is still going on into the role of glia. **Neurones** are cells that receive and transmit messages, passing them from cell to cell. At one end, a neurone has dendrites, which are finger-like structures surrounding a nucleus. From the nucleus there is long extension called an axon, which reaches to an axon terminal (see Figure 4.2).

Figure 4.2 *How synapses work*

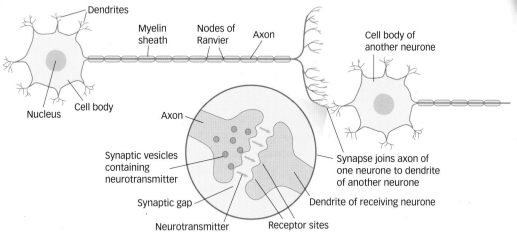

The axon terminal of one neurone reaches to the dendrites of another neurone. Between the terminal and the dendrites there is a gap called a **synapse**. The synaptic gap or synaptic cleft sits between two neurones. On one side, at the dendrites, there are receptors of a certain shape prepared to receive the neurotransmitter from the other neurone. If the neurotransmitter fits the receptor the message is passed on; if it does not, the message is blocked. **Receptors** can be thought of as locks — if a certain chemical (neurotransmitter) fits like a key then the message is received and continues along that neurone to another neurone and so on. Manufactured drugs work in this way. They mimic natural neurotransmitters, more or less fit certain receptors, are received like neurotransmitters and the message from them 'works'. Some drugs block the message. They 'fit' the receptor, so the natural neurotransmitter cannot pass the message on because the receptor is not available.

Explore Use the internet or some other source to find out more about how messages are passed by means of neurotransmitters. You could also find out more about neurotransmitters, such as the possible role of dopamine in schizophrenia and any links to Parkinson's disease. You could research how drugs work, either so-called recreational drugs (e.g. cocaine) or antipsychotic drugs (e.g. chlorpromazine).

The role of genes in human behaviour

You need to know about:
- the effect of genes on a person's make-up
- the genetic explanation for gender behaviour and development

Explaining the term 'gene'

A **gene** contains a set of instructions and is a carrier of information. Each individual human has a **genotype,** which is the genetic constitution. Each person also has a **phenotype,** which is what the individual becomes when their genes interact with each other and with the environment. Genes are inherited — 50% from each of our biological parents.

A gene consists of a long strand of **DNA** (deoxyribonucleic acid). A chromosome is a double chain of DNA. One of the functions of DNA is to control gene activity.

Genes contain bases (chemicals) called guanine (G), cytosine (C), adenine (A) and thymine (T) arranged along the gene. The coding sequence (three-letter combinations of G, C, A or T, each coding for an amino acid) contains the instructions as to what that gene will produce. The sequence is copied to produce an RNA (ribonucleic acid) molecule. RNA then organises the synthesis of proteins that act according to the genetic instructions. Transfer RNA (tRNA) transports amino acids to the ribosomes of the cell and messenger RNA (mRNA) acts as a model to form proteins. The proteins dictate how the organism develops.

A model of DNA

Phototake Inc./Alamy

The **genome** is the term for all the genes in a cell. It is thought that the human genome has just under 3 billion base pairs and around 20 000 to 25 000 genes. The genetic message contains millions of combinations of base pairs in DNA carried on chromosomes. Humans have 23 pairs of chromosomes in each cell (apart from egg and sperm cells). Genes can be physically linked so that if one gene is inherited the other gene is also inherited.

Some genes always lead to certain characteristics; these are called **dominant genes.** To produce a characteristic, dominant genes need to be on only one of a pair of chromosomes. Some genes need more than one copy to produce a characteristic; these are called **recessive genes.** Recessive genes have to be on both chromosomes of a pair for the characteristic to occur. If a recessive gene is present on only one of the pair of chromosomes, the characteristic will not appear in that particular organism. However, they can be passed on, so the characteristic might appear in a future generation. Characteristics can be aspects of appearance (e.g. eye colour), personality (e.g. shyness) or behaviour (e.g. aggression). Genes do not control all human characteristics because the environment also has a part to play.

Examples of the effects of genes on humans

- Human chromosome 4 has a marker known as G8. It is not yet known what G8 contributes, but the gene for Huntington's disease lies close to it. If a parent and child both have Huntington's disease, then in 98% of cases they both have the same form of G8 marker. This suggests that the gene for Huntington's disease travels with the G8 marker.

■ Some diseases and characteristics are sex-linked in that they are controlled by the sex genes. This is why some diseases/characteristics are more common in one particular sex, e.g. most colour-blind people are men.

■ If one parent contributes two copies of chromosome 21, then the child has three copies and the consequence is Down's syndrome.

Explore Use the internet or another source to look up the story of the decoding of the human genome, which was carried out in 2003. Then consider the claims of Dr Craig Venter who stated in September 2007 that he had decoded the 'real' human genome. Think about why understanding the human genome is important. For example, look up chromosome 19 to find out what diseases are associated with it. Look up Huntington's disease to see why understanding genetics is important — but be aware that you are a student of psychology and must stick to ethical guidelines, including taking care when spreading information about what you learn. These issues are about people and Huntington's is a serious disease.

Cancer involves damage to the DNA and the damage occurs as the cells divide. For example, in one form of leukaemia, almost every white blood cell carries an unusually small chromosome 22. The bone marrow produces damaged cells that reproduce more quickly than other cells and the disease spreads. It appears that chromosome 22 is smaller because part has broken off and transferred to chromosome 9. This transfer leads to a new abnormal protein being produced that speeds up cell division. However, there may be other factors involved when cancer develops, such as environmental triggers.

Environmental triggers on genes

Sometimes genes do not influence physical characteristics unless the 'right' environmental conditions occur. One example is phenylketonuria (PKU). You might be aware that all babies born in the UK have a blood sample taken from their heels immediately after birth. This is to test for PKU, a disease that leads to brain damage. It is known that if a child's diet is carefully controlled the damage from PKU can be averted, i.e. the effect of the gene can be avoided.

Explore Some viruses contain RNA and can be templates for protein synthesis. A retrovirus uses an enzyme (a protein) to make DNA from its RNA. If this DNA is then incorporated into a chromosome, the retrovirus will continue to be produced and may even be inherited. It is difficult to 'treat' an illness caused by a retrovirus. The HIV virus that can lead to AIDS is a retrovirus; retroviruses might be linked with schizophrenia. Use the internet or another source to investigate this fairly new area of research further.

Understanding the Individual

The nature–nurture debate

The genotype is the genetic constitution of an individual; the phenotype is the result of interaction between inherited characteristics and the environment. Psychologists are interested in separating nature (inherited characteristics) from nurture (experiences) because they want to find causes for behaviour.

The effects of nature on behaviour

The phrase 'effects of nature on behaviour' means the influence of genes and other biological structures. To discuss someone's nature, it would be necessary to consider the effects of neurotransmitter functioning, brain structure, genetic make-up and other related issues. The biological approach provides much information about the way 'nature' influences behaviour.

The effects of nurture on behaviour

The phrase 'effects of nurture on behaviour' means the effects of everything other than biological aspects — style of upbringing, experience of schooling, peer-group influences, position in the family (e.g. middle child), social and cultural influences, and other similar issues. For example, children who watch a lot of violent television may be more likely to behave aggressively; children who have not made secure attachments with their main caregivers may find it less easy to form secure relationships when they are older.

Interaction of nature and nurture

Some areas in psychology (e.g. personality, depression and alcoholism) are often studied by looking at 'nature'. Some areas (e.g. criminal behaviour and phobias) are studied by looking at 'nurture'. In fact, most areas in psychology, including depression, alcoholism, criminal behaviour and phobias, are studied by looking at how nature and nurture interact to produce such behaviour.

For example, stress arises when people think that they do not have the resources to cope. Stress involves a biological reaction that gets the body ready for 'flight or fight' and then something in the environment triggers that biological reaction. Aspects of both nature and nurture are needed to explain stress.

Study hint As well as an understanding of the meaning of 'nature' and 'nurture', you need to have some examples so that you can discuss the nature–nurture debate.

Biological explanations for gender development

As well as having a general understanding of how neurotransmitters work, how genes work and what the nature–nurture debate is, you also need a more in-depth understanding of the biological explanation for gender behaviour and gender development.

- **Gender** is the term usually used when referring to the development and behaviour of the different sexes in relation to environmental and social aspects.
- **Sex** is the term usually used when referring to biological aspects of males and females.

Genes and sex determination

Apart from sperm and egg cells, every cell in the human body contains 46 chromosomes (23 pairs). Individual sperm and egg cells have unpaired 23 chromosomes.

To form a new organism, 23 chromosomes come from the mother's egg cell and 23 chromosomes come from the father's sperm cell. The two unpaired sets combine to make 23 unique pairs. A male baby (XY) receives an X chromosome from his mother and a Y chromosome from his father; female babies (XX) get an X chromosome from each parent.

> **Explore** Look at the Science Museum website (**www.science-museum.org.uk**) or visit the Science Museum in London where there is a quick guide to genes and how they work.

Genes and gender development

In the very early stages of development, an embryo starts to generate hormones and genes start organising the brain along gender lines. Studies (e.g. Vilain, 1964) of mice have identified 54 genes where activity levels vary according to gender.

In mammals, the X and the Y chromosomes (the sex chromosomes) determine whether the fertilised egg develops into a male or female organism. In humans, females have twice the number of X chromosomes as males; males have only one X chromosome and the Y chromosome is important. Humans with only the X chromosomes are female.

Research as to how genes affect gender development has been carried out on animals, where the processes of distinguishing between the sexes can be different from in humans. For example, in roundworms, fertilised eggs with one X chromosome become males; those with two X chromosomes become hermaphrodites. **Hermaphrodites** have characteristics of both males and females. Fruit flies, like humans, have two X chromosomes for females and one X and one Y chromosome for males.

> **Study hint** Note that the use of animals in gene studies is common. Use examples like this when discussing methodology and the use of animals in laboratory experiments and when evaluating research methods and research findings.

These examples show that genes start influencing the embryo immediately after conception. An important feature is which sex

organs start to develop. This is governed by DNA in the genes and is processed through RNA and proteins.

Normal sex differentiation in humans

There are four main steps in normal sex differentiation in humans:

- **Step 1:** fertilisation determines the genetic sex, according to the chromosomes contributed from the sperm and egg cells. The 23 chromosomes in an egg cell include an X chromosome; the 23 chromosomes in a sperm cell include either an X chromosome or a Y chromosome.
- **Step 2:** the fertilised egg divides to form a large number of identical cells. During the development of the embryo the cells differentiate to form the various body organs, including the sex organs. Both males and females at this stage have a gonadal ridge and, after 6 or 7 weeks' gestation, two sets of internal ducts, the Mullerian (female) ducts and the Wolffian (male) ducts. At this stage, the external genitalia appear female.
- **Step 3:** the gonadal ridge becomes either an ovary or a testis. In males, it develops into testes because of a product from a gene on the Y chromosome. In females, there is no Y chromosome; other genes trigger the gonadal ridge to develop into ovaries.
- **Step 4:** hormones then act to enable the different sexes to develop. Mullerian (female) inhibiting substance (MIS) and androgens are the two important hormones. MIS prevents the growth of the female Mullerian ducts (the uterus and fallopian tubes) which are present in all foetuses up to this point. Androgens are also secreted and affect the growth of the Wolffian ducts. Ovaries do not produce androgens, but testes do. The Wolffian ducts do not grow when ovaries develop; MIS is not produced either, so the Mullerian (female) ducts can develop. For male development, MIS is needed to stop female duct growth and androgens are needed to stimulate male duct growth. External genitalia remain feminine in the absence of androgens; in the male, androgens allow the masculine external genitalia to develop.

Box 4.6 Normal sex differentiation

- Genetic sex is determined through XX (female) and XY (male) chromosomes.
- Testes develop in an XY foetus; ovaries develop in an XX foetus.
- An XY foetus develops Wolffian ducts; an XX foetus develops Mullerian ducts.
- An XY foetus masculinises the female genitalia to make them male; an XX foetus retains the female genitalia.

Abnormal sex differentiation

- Problems with sex differentiation can occur at any of the stages explained above. For example, problems can arise at fertilisation — boys with XXY chromosomes develop Klinefelter's syndrome and girls with XO chromosomes have Turner's syndrome (page 271).

- There can also be abnormality when there is a gonad that cannot develop into a testis or an ovary, e.g. if the gene (SRY) is absent or deficient. Under these circumstances, despite the presence of the Y chromosome, the XY foetus does not receive the SRY signal to develop testes.
- Incorrect Mullerian or Wolffian duct development also causes problems. For example, MIS secretion might not be accompanied by androgens, or the foetus might not respond to androgens, in which case the foetus will have neither male or female internal duct structures. Lack of MIS but with androgen secretion can led to a foetus having both male and female duct structures.

Explore Use the internet or some other source to investigate abnormal sex differentiation, looking in particular at issues other than Klinefelter's syndrome and Turner's syndrome, because these are explained here. Consider issues for the individuals and investigate what treatment (if any) is offered. Find out what intersex means.

Abnormal development: Klinefelter's syndrome

Klinefelter's syndrome (named after the person who first described it) occurs in about one male in every 500 to 1000 males. Men with Klinefelter's syndrome have an extra X chromosome, so are XXY. Their testes are small and their fertility is much reduced; they may be sterile. Small, low-functioning testes means they have low testosterone (a hormone) levels. There can also be other differences — they may find language learning difficult and they can have slightly increased breast tissue. It seems that the extra X chromosome is kept because of a problem when the sex cell divides. XXY males can be treated by testosterone treatment and therapies, although the genetic variation cannot be reversed.

Explore Use the internet or some other source to investigate Klinefelter's syndrome further. It is a relatively new discovery, made in the mid-1900s. Those with the syndrome tend to have specific body types, although this is not a reliable way of diagnosing XXY males. Consider possible treatments of XXY males, including both practical and ethical considerations. For example, should this syndrome be regarded as a disease?

Abnormal development: Turner's syndrome

Turner's syndrome is a disorder that affects girls. The condition occurs in about 1 in 2500 births of girls worldwide and is more common in pregnancies that do not go to term. It is caused by a missing X chromosome and is, therefore, a genetic disorder. Girls with Turner's syndrome are short and their ovaries do not work properly, so most are infertile. They are at risk of particular health problems. There is no cure, but there are treatments (e.g. growth hormone) available.

The gene (SHOX) is important for growth and development and occurs on the X chromosome. Missing one copy of this gene is probably what causes girls with Turner's syndrome to be shorter than average. Most girls with Turner's syndrome do not produce the sex hormones oestrogen and progesterone at puberty. Without

hormone treatment, such girls will not develop breasts or have periods. Girls with Turner's syndrome are of normal intelligence. They have good verbal and reading skills but can have problems with maths, memory skills and fine movements. Turner's syndrome does not appear to be inherited and the cause of the problem with one of the X chromosomes is not known. It seems to be a random error.

Hormones and gender development

Like neurotransmitters, **hormones** carry messages. However, the messages are passed much more slowly because hormones travel in the bloodstream. They affect numerous processes such as growth, development, mood and metabolism. They are produced by endocrine glands, which are groups of cells and include the pituitary, pineal, thyroid and adrenal glands. They are also produced by males in the testes and by females in the ovaries. A very small amount of hormone can cause large changes in cells and too much or too little can cause problems.

The 'female' hormones are oestrogen and progesterone; the 'male' hormones are androgens, such as testosterone. Collectively, these are called **reproductive hormones**. These reproductive hormones dictate gender differences and cause the male and female brains to develop differently. The fourth step in developing sex differentiation (page 270) after fertilisation involves the release of hormones, e.g. androgens are needed to form male genitalia.

Such hormone differences can affect health and lifestyle throughout a person's life and there is some evidence that in adulthood the brain is still changing because of hormones. For example, more females develop pain syndromes like fibromyalgia and they also tend to suffer more from mood disorders, such as depression and anxiety. On the other hand, more men than women are likely to develop alcoholism and to abuse drugs.

Hormones also affect sex differences in the brain, possibly changing it throughout the life span. Hormones can affect working and reference memory. **Working memory** is used in everyday tasks and decision making; **reference memory** is used to refer back to information that has been stored.

> **Working memory** is short-term memory; **reference memory** is long-term memory.

In one study, the ovaries were removed from adult female rats so that oestrogens would not be produced. The rats were then given estradiol (a form of oestrogen). Low levels of estradiol improved working memory, but high levels impaired both the working and reference memories. Estradiol also influenced cell growth in the brain.

It has been shown that the effects on cell growth are different in males and females. For example, in females, high levels of estradiol first increased, and then stopped, the production of new cells in part of the **hippocampus.** However, the same processes did not seem to be at work in the male brain.

> The **hippocampus** is involved in short-term memory and produces new cells throughout the organism's life.

The reproductive hormones may also have influence in the experience of pain and may be why some diseases associated with chronic pain (e.g. fibromyalgia) occur more frequently in females. PET scanning can be used to see how the brain responds to pain. In one study, men had an increase in the amount of endorphins released compared with women and women reported more feelings of pain. At first, all the women in the study had low levels of oestrogen, because they were in the early phase of their menstrual cycles. The women were then given oestrogen and tested at a time when their natural levels of oestrogen were high (a different point in the menstrual cycle). More endorphins were released and the women rated the pain as less severe. It was concluded that hormones affect brain responses differently in males and females. This is, therefore, evidence that hormones affect gender behaviour.

Genes dictate differences in the production of hormones, including that of reproductive hormones. Therefore, when looking at sex differences, it is difficult to separate the effects of genes and hormones — the two are related in affecting differences in gender behaviour and development

Abnormal development: androgenital syndrome

Androgenital syndrome is a genetic disorder that is caused by a deficiency in the hormones aldosterone and cortisol and by overproduction of androgens. Males may have an enlarged penis and small testes; females may have ambiguous genitals, failure to menstruate, a deep voice and excessive hair. Androgenital syndrome can be caused by congenital adrenal hyperplasia. Part of the adrenal gland, (the adrenal cortex) makes three steroid hormones that are secreted into the blood stream and are necessary for normal health. Congenital adrenal hyperplasia is linked with the adrenal cortex and these three hormones:

- **cortisol** — controls stress responses and helps to control blood sugar levels
- **aldosterone** — regulates salt levels and sends messages to the kidneys about such levels, thus controlling sweating or the release of salt in urine
- **androgens** — male hormones, including testosterone. Testosterone controls the growth of pubic hair and the onset of puberty. It is also produced by the testes (a small amount is also produced by the ovaries)

If, during development, the adrenal gland does not produce enough cortisol, then the pituitary gland is stimulated to release the hormone ACTH. This travels in the bloodstream to the adrenal glands and can cause the adrenal cortex to increase in thickness, which is called being 'hyperplastic'. The increased size of the cortex is accompanied by increased testosterone production, which can cause early sexual development. In females, this excess testosterone causes abnormal genital development in the embryo; in adult females it causes unwanted hair growth and

Unit 2

irregular periods, i.e. androgenital syndrome. Substitute therapy to correct the cortisol levels can stop the production of excess testosterone, bringing levels back to normal. These issues show that hormones affect sex differentiation and gender development.

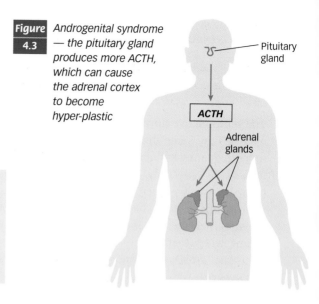

Figure 4.3 *Androgenital syndrome — the pituitary gland produces more ACTH, which can cause the adrenal cortex to become hyper-plastic*

Pituitary gland

ACTH

Adrenal glands

Explore Use the internet or some other source to look up congenital adrenal hyperplasia. Find some case studies to see how it affects people and find out what treatments are offered.

Brain structure and gender development: brain lateralisation

The brain is divided into two hemispheres (halves). It is claimed that the left hemisphere controls language and the right hemisphere is concerned with visuospatial ability and perception. Studies have suggested that the brains of males and females differ with regard to the use of the two hemispheres, with, in general, males using the right hemisphere more and females using both hemispheres. The corpus callosum is the bundle of fibres that connects the two hemispheres of the brain; it is said to be larger in women. This ties in with the idea of women using both halves of the brain more equally than men do.

There are also supposed to be gender differences in visuospatial ability. The idea is that male brains are more **lateralised** — males have more of a preference for one hemisphere; females use both hemispheres, so are less lateralised. The right side of the brain is for visuospatial functions and as males appear to use that side more, they are said to be better at visuospatial tasks. It is assumed, therefore, that males are better at mathematics and at tasks such as map-reading.

However, a **meta-analysis** of many studies did not find such differences. For example, the corpus callosum does differ between individuals, but it is hard to show that there are consistent gender differences. These theories were put forward in the 1980s and there is now some doubt about them, although there is still broad agreement. A problem is that there have been many studies and some findings are contradictory. However, there a tendency to agree that there are gender differences in brain lateralisation because evidence from studies still points in that direction.

It is thought that the larger corpus callosum in women (if indeed there is this difference) would lead to better fluency in speech and thought. Therefore, there would be better communication between the two hemispheres in females, which could explain female intuition and their superior ability in understanding body language.

Further evidence that there are gender differences in brain structure comes from the finding that another brain structure — the anterior commissure, which communicates sensory information — is larger in women, and appears to be larger in male homosexuals.

Evidence for brain lateralisaton includes:

- It was thought that damage to the left hemisphere would lead to problems with verbal tasks and damage to the right hemisphere would lead to difficulties in visuospatial tasks. However, some studies working with people who had damage to only one side of the brain show that this is true for men, but not for women.
- Women with Turner's syndrome (XO genotype) use both sides of the brain even more than usual and display very 'feminine' behaviour.
- Men who do not have normal exposure to androgens in the womb tend to use both sides of the brain more.
- From work with rats, it is thought that high levels of testosterone slow neurone growth in the left hemisphere, which again points to differences.
- The general suggestion from tests that females do better in language tasks, tasks of verbal fluency, speed of speaking and in mathematical calculation tasks. For example, they can match items better. Males are better at spatial tasks such as maze performance and mental rotation tasks.
- In patients with damage to the left hemisphere, speech difficulties occur more often in males.

One problem is that although blood flow in the brain can be measured to show where activity is, the activity may not occur because of different brain structure, but because of different strategies used. Another problem is that the development of the brain is not just about the biology; it is also affected by the environment of the embryo. There is interaction between nature and nurture and differences in male and female brains are likely to be a product of their biology and their environment.

> **Study hint** Use these sorts of examples when discussing the nature–nurture debate.

A study of male-to-female transsexuals found that, compared with a control group of men, the transsexuals were better at verbal memory tasks but worse at mental rotation tasks. This could be evidence for there being biological reasons for feeling like a female in a male body. On the other hand, environment affects brain development. Groups of both male and female transsexuals did not show brain lateralisation; they used both sides of the brain more equally.

Tasks tend to focus on verbal and spatial abilities, so perhaps those differences are found because those tasks are used. Some researchers suggest that the right hemisphere deals with well-established tasks and the left hemisphere deals with new tasks. Perhaps the left analytical side can deal better with tasks where there is no script? You can see where the idea of women being able to multitask comes from.

Table 4.16 *Gender differences in the use of the two halves of the brain*

Research method	Result(s)	Conclusion
Male-to-female trans-sexuals did tests and were compared with a control group of males	Male-to-female transsexuals were better at verbal tasks and worse at spatial tasks	There are differences in hemisphere use between males and females. Male-to-female transsexuals may have biological reasons for wanting to change sex.
A group of both male and female transsexuals was used	Both used both hemispheres fairly equally	Either there are not sex differences in how the two halves of the brain are used or both types of transsexual have 'female'-type brains
Testing of males to find hormone levels	Males who do not have the usual amount of androgens during development in the womb tend to use both sides of the brain	There are sex differences in how the two hemispheres are used and this links with levels of reproductive hormones during development in the womb
Rats were given varying levels of testosterone	High levels of testosterone may tend to slow neurone growth in the left hemisphere	Males have high levels of testosterone, which might explain their tendency to use the right hemisphere more
People with damage to the left hemisphere are studied	Speech difficulties occur mainly in males	Males are more reliant on using one half of the brain and cannot use the other half to back-up when there are problems
Both males and females doing tests	Females tend to be better at language tasks, speed of speaking and arithmetical calculations. They also match items better. Males do better in spatial tasks, such as maze performance and mental rotation tasks.	Males do well in tasks controlled by the right hemisphere and less well in tasks controlled by the left hemisphere, whereas females are better at using both halves. This is evidence for sex differences in the use of the two hemispheres.
Brain scanning is used to examine brain structure	The corpus callosum appears to be larger in females than in males, although the evidence is contradictory	If the corpus callosum is larger this might mean transfer of information is easier, which might be why females use both halves of the brain more equally
Brain scanning is used to examine brain structure	The anterior commissure, which communicates sensory information, is larger in females and in homosexual men	There are sex differences in brain structure
Working with patients with brain damage to one hemisphere	Damage to the left hemisphere leads to problems with verbal tasks and damage to the right hemisphere leads to difficulties with visuospatial tasks — in males but not in females	This is more evidence that males prefer the right side of the brain whereas females can use both sides more easily
Studying women with Turner's syndrome	They are more 'feminine' in many ways and use both sides of the brain efficiently and more equally than usual	There are sex differences in brain lateralisation

Abnormal brain development: the effects of child abuse and neglect

Child abuse and neglect appear to lead to brain abnormalities. A baby is born with all the neurones the individual will have but the brain carries on developing through childhood and adolescence and can be damaged by environmental influences.

Some effects of abuse and neglect are problems with the limbic system, which is a network of brain cells where emotions are controlled. Abuse can cause disturbances in the limbic-system cells that can lead to seizures and other abnormalities that show up on an electroencephalogram (EEG). An EEG measures electrical activity in the brain. In cases of child abuse or neglect, all the abnormality was shown to be in the left hemisphere. It is thought that in people who have been abused, the left hemisphere abnormalities are linked to depression and memory deficits.

The corpus callosum, which links the two hemispheres, is smaller in those who have been abused as children. In studies, there was a 24% to 42% reduction in the size of parts of the corpus callosum in boys who had suffered neglect; sexual abuse seemed to have no such effect. In girls, there was a reduction of 18% to 30% in the corpus callosum in cases of sexual abuse, but neglect had no effect. It is concluded that the reduction in size of the corpus callosum means less activity between the two hemispheres, which might lead to noticeable changes in mood.

The other conclusion is that there are sex differences in how the two halves of the brain are used and are affected. The findings of these sorts of studies come from MRI scanning, in which blood flow to the brain is measured.

Animal studies are also carried out. When investigating how changes to brain structures such as the corpus callosum might occur, the researchers found that neglect and trauma led to increased production of cortisol and decreased production of the thyroid hormone. These changes affected (among other areas) the development of neurotransmitter receptors in the amygdala and hippocampus — areas that relate to fear and anxiety. The conclusion is that stress caused by child abuse and neglect may cause changes in levels of certain hormones and neurotransmitters that in turn affect the brain structures, and that males and females might be affected differently. In rats too gender differences in response to stress have been found.

Study hint These findings show that it is difficult to study the structure of the brain, the role of neurotransmitters and the role of hormones separately because they are connected. You are likely to be asked to comment about these as *different* aspects of biological functioning in humans, but it is worth noting that, in fact, they interact with and affect each other.

Evaluation of the biological explanations for gender development

Biological explanations for behaviour are difficult to evaluate because it is hard to find weaknesses in biological research methods. For example, it is difficult to criticise the findings of a PET scan because the picture tells the story. However, it is important to evaluate all findings in psychology. Some evaluation points were mentioned earlier; they are summarised in this section. Comparisons of the biological explanations for gender development with explanations from the psychodynamic approach and learning approaches can be used in evaluation of biological explanations.

Strengths

- The results of biological explanations are based on tests that can be repeated, e.g. injecting rats with additional testosterone or using MRI scanning in humans to detect blood flow. The results are replicable and can be shown to be reliable.

■ Different research methods are used and tend to come up with similar findings. For example, tests using male and female participants tend to suggest that males are better at mental rotation tasks. Studies using scanning show that the right side of the brain is where such tasks are carried out and that language tasks are more left-brain oriented. Other studies show that male-to-female transsexuals do not carry out such tasks as well as they perform language tasks. All these findings add up to the same conclusions, which suggests that they are valid.

Weaknesses

■ Studies of genes and hormones are usually carried out on animals, so the findings may not be applicable to humans. There is a difficulty in generalising from animals to humans because of the differences between them.

■ The focus is on biological aspects. For example, it is found that there are sex differences in the use of the two hemispheres. MRI scanning shows blood flow in different areas when similar tasks are carried out and the conclusion is that different brain functioning is taking place, i.e. that the two sexes have different biological brain functions. However, it might be that the two sexes use different strategies and that their brain structure and function is the same. Strategies can come from upbringing. For example, girls learn to play more quietly and are encouraged more with language and writing whereas boys learn to play more roughly and more physically. These influences might affect their strategies in tasks, which are often tests of language ability, at which males do not perform as well as females.

Table 4.17 *Strengths and weaknesses of biological explanations for gender development*

Strengths	Weaknesses
• There is reliability because the studies are replicable and are replicated; measures (e.g. injecting rats with testosterone or using MRI scanning in humans to measure blood flow) are objective	• There is a problem with generalisability because many findings come from animal studies; there are important differences in the human brain, so such findings may not be relevant to humans and may not be credible
• There is validity because different studies using different research methods have similar findings (e.g. such sex differences in brain lateralisation)	• Biological aspects are difficult to study without reference to the environment; for example, male and female children are reinforced for different behaviour; this may mean that they use different strategies to do tasks, rather than that they have different brain structures

Examination-style questions

1 Describe how neurotransmitters work. Include an explanation of synaptic transmission in your answer and give one example to illustrate. *(6 marks)*

2 Describe the role of genes in sex assignment. *(4 marks)*

3 Explain how hormones work in sex assignment. Include one example of abnormal sex assignment that is due to hormones. *(6 marks)*

4 Evaluate the biological explanation of gender behaviour/development. *(6 marks)*

Studies in detail

For the biological approach, you have to know, in detail, a study of identical male twins in which one was brought up as a girl (Money 1975) and one other from a choice of three:

■ a study of schizophrenia (Gottesman and Shields 1966)
■ a study of brain differences in murderers (Raine et al. 1997)
■ a study of sex differences in how the brain matures (De Bellis et al. 2001) — *this is covered in more detail on the CD-ROM.*

Money (1975)

This study is about a boy infant who was brought up as a girl. It is summarised here as a case study because it is about one individual and is an in-depth investigation. However, other cases were also considered in the study.

Aims

The aim of the study was to gain information about situations in which babies were brought up as the opposite sex from that which had been assigned to them. One case in particular is detailed.

Procedure

The study considers 45 cases of genetic males reassigned and brought up as females. Of these, 43 had defective penises and two were cases of infantile ablatio penis (the penis is removed for some reason). All the cases were treated at Johns Hopkins hospital. The age range of the 45 cases studied was from infancy to adulthood; some were married women. There was continuous long-term follow-up and each could be matched with someone similar at birth and brought up as male. Most of the study focuses on one child who was brought up as a girl after a circumcision procedure went wrong. This child had an identical twin brother so there was a natural control.

Case description

At 7 months, one of a pair of identical twins suffered a 'surgical mishap'. During circumcision, the electric current used was too strong and his penis was ablated

flush to the abdominal wall. There followed much discussion about what to do about this baby. A plastic surgeon suggested reassignment as a girl. The parents were not sure what to do and then they saw John Money on a television programme talking about an adult sex reassignment male-to-female transsexual. When the baby was 17 months old, the parents chose sex reassignment and changed the child's name, clothing and hairstyle. Later, hormone replacement and surgery were used. When Money first met the parents he gave them confidence, based on other cases, that the child would 'be' a girl and would conform to the sex of her rearing. The parents were guided about what to say to family, friends and their other child. There was follow-up for almost 9 years after surgery with the parents making annual visits to Money. He collected data from the parents, asked the child questions and made his own observations.

The mother first changed the child's hairstyle and clothes, putting the baby into slacks and blouses and later into dresses. The child had feminine things such as bracelets and hair ribbons and the mother said that the child preferred to wear dresses and was proud of her long hair. By the age of four and a half years, the little girl was said to be much neater than her brother. The mother treated them differently, including explaining what their function would be as adults, emphasising 'mummy' and 'daddy' role behaviour. As they grew older, the two children copied the role behaviour of their same-sex parent. The family talked openly about their sex differences, such as saying that girls have babies. The daughter tried to help the mother tidy up and clean; the boy could not have cared less about it. The girl wanted dolls for Christmas and the boy wanted a garage with cars. The mother said she would like them both to go to college but seemed to feel that this was more important for the boy 'since he will be earning a living for the rest of his life'. The mother was both very observant and a good reporter. 'I found that my son, he chose masculine things like a fireman or a policeman…I asked her and she said she wanted to be a doctor or a teacher.'

The girl had many tomboy traits such as abundant physical energy, a high level of activity, stubbornness and being dominant in a girl's group. The mother tried to teach her to be 'more quiet and ladylike'. The girl seemed to be the more dominant twin. At the end of the study, the twins were 9 years old. The girl talked about a visit to the zoo and liking the monkeys. She was asked what animal she would like to be and she said 'a monkey because a monkey can climb and swing on its arms'. Money asked her if she would like to be a girl or a boy monkey and she said 'a girl one — I am already a girl'. Money pointed out that eventually she would have to be told the truth because too many of her family knew the truth for it to be kept a permanent secret.

Case analysis

Money concluded that the girl's behaviour was 'so normally that of a little girl'. He listened to the mother's information and noted the liking of wearing dresses, the intention to become a doctor or teacher when she grew up and the comment about being a girl monkey. He compared this with the twin boy's desire to be a fireman or policeman. However, there were other issues that were not commented upon, such as the girl's liking for physical activity and climbing. Money commented that the mother was a good observer and thought that her own female behaviour and her comparisons between girls and boys when talking to the twins had helped the girl to adapt.

Conclusions

It was concluded from the study of the twins and of the other cases, that 'gender identity is sufficiently incompletely differentiated at birth as to permit successful assignment of a genetic male as a girl. Gender identity differentiates in keeping with the experiences of rearing'. From all the cases, it was concluded that 'with surgery and hormonal therapy it is possible to habilitate a baby with a grossly defective penis more effectively as a girl than as a boy'. It is more effective to surgically create female organs than to create male organs, which is why the genetic males were brought up as females, rather than brought up as males with corrective surgery. Parents need education and counselling when a baby needs corrective surgery of the sex organs. With help, the study concluded that it is possible to rear the child avoiding ambiguity and uncertainty of gender.

An update on the case analysis and conclusions

Case studies are about individual people and they usually end with conclusions from the researchers. However, sometimes, those individuals identify themselves later and an update to the conclusions can be added. This is the case in Money's study. This is a sensitive story, all the more so because the male-born twin who was brought up as a girl committed suicide.

David Reimer was brought up as a girl called Brenda. When he decided to tell his story more information came to light. Money had said that Brenda was happy as a girl, but David Reimer explained that this was not so. It appears that Brenda did not like wearing dresses and refused to play with dolls. She would beat up her brother – and indeed Money did report that Brenda was the dominant twin.

It is possible that Money knew that Brenda was not happy as a girl and also that David had reassumed the identity of a boy. However, Money only followed the case until the children were around 11 years old, so it is not clear that Money deliberately lied.

Brenda's mother attempted suicide and the father turned to alcohol. Brian, who was Brenda's brother, turned to crime and became clinically depressed. When Brenda was 14 years old, she was told the truth. David said that suddenly everything made sense and he felt that he was not crazy after all. He underwent surgery and turned back into a male. In his twenties, he was depressed and twice tried to commit suicide. However, he married and his wife was a support for him.

At around the age of 30, David met a psychologist called Diamond, who published a paper about him, showing that Money's conclusions were wrong and should not be

used to justify bringing up babies whose sex was indeterminate as one sex or the other.

In 2000, David Reimer published a book about his life. In 2002, his brother died of an overdose of antidepressants. David had marital difficulties, was unemployed, and his brother had committed suicide. He was an angry person who suffered from depression, so any of these reasons may have led to his suicide. His mother and brother suffered from depression, which indicates a genetic tendency in the family. However, it is likely that his upbringing contributed to his problems.

The nature–nurture debate

Money's case study indicated that nurture is the strongest influence on upbringing because a genetically male baby was brought up apparently successfully to be a girl. However, David Reimer's story shows the opposite — that nature is the strongest influence on upbringing. Despite being brought up as a girl, his 'maleness' came through. Another aspect of the nature–nurture debate that helps to explain this case is the genetic implication that clinical depression was in the family.

Evaluation of the study by Money (1975)

There are clearly strengths and weaknesses of Money's study because the participant in the case study reported that he was not happy as a girl.

Strengths

- There is a lot of detail about Brenda, her likes and dislikes and her role in the family. This is an in-depth and detailed look at an individual and his/her family. The data are qualitative and rich, so can be analysed in depth. Qualitative data are more valid than quantitative data because of this richness and detail.
- More than one person contributed to the data. The mother carried out most of the observations, but the father attended the annual visits and could either agree or disagree with her accounts. Money also asked Brenda questions and could observe what she was like. This means that there is some reliability, as the data were gathered from more than one source.

Weaknesses

- Money's conclusions were denied by the participant in the study. This means that the findings were not valid because they did not represent the situation at the time. If the person the case study is about says the results are not correct, then this means that the data are not valid.
- It is difficult to generalise the findings to other situations in which there are problems with sex assignment. This is a unique case. That is highlighted, for example, by considering the genetic explanations for David Reimer's mental state and depression. His mother and brother also suffered from clinical depression and both he and his brother committed suicide at a young age. This could have been because of the study, but might not have been. It is difficult to generalise the findings from such a unique and complex situation.

| Table 4.18 | Strengths and weaknesses of the study by Money (1975) |

Strengths	Weaknesses
● The case study is detailed and longitudinal, so there is validity — the data are qualitative and gathered from more than one source	● The study lasted 9 years, but later the participant revealed that he was not happy as a girl, and he chose to live as a man — so, in fact, there was no validity
● The case study has data from more than one source — observation, information from both parents, Brenda's own contributions — so there is reliability	● It is hard to generalise from a unique case like this; not everyone brought up as a girl, although genetically male, will have the same experiences

Raine et al. (1997)

Raine et al. (1997) used PET scanning to look for differences in brain functioning between murderers who pleaded not guilty by reason of insanity and a control group.

Aims

The study aimed to show that the brains of murderers who pleaded not guilty by reason of insanity were different from the brains of non-murderers. Raine et al. investigated whether brain dysfunction predisposed people to violent behaviour.

Background literature: previous research

Previous studies linked certain parts of the brain to violent behaviour:

■ EEGs, neurological and cognitive testing suggest that there is a link between brain dysfunction and violent behaviour. The prefrontal cortex and different functioning of the two hemispheres (which implicates the corpus callosum) are thought to be important.

■ Recent mapping techniques have found reduced electrical activity in the left angular gyrus in violent offenders.

■ Some experimental animal research suggests that the limbic structures (e.g. the amygdala and hippocampus) and the thalamus are involved in aggression.

Study hint You do not need to know detail about the parts of the brain mentioned here. However, it is important to note the reasons for the study as they will help you to understand the results and conclusions.

Raine et al. (1997) listed these regions and studied them both in murderers pleading not guilty by reason of insanity and in a control group. A preliminary study of 22 such murderers and 22 'normal' participants gave some support for prefrontal dysfunction in the murderers.

Procedure

In the study there were 41 murderers pleading not guilty by reason of insanity and 41 controls. The main participants (average age 34.3 years) were 39 men and two women who had been charged with either murder or manslaughter (labelled murderers in this study). All had been referred to the University of California Irvine

Imaging Center to obtain evidence relating to a 'not guilty by reason of insanity' defence or to gather evidence for some other part of their trials to do with incompetence. The group consisted of 23 people with a history of brain damage, six schizophrenics, three people with a history of substance abuse, two had an affective disorder, two had epilepsy, three were diagnosed as hyperactive or with a learning disability and two had paranoid personality disorder. None was on medication. The control group was formed by matching each murderer with a normal participant of the same sex and age, and who was similar in other ways, e.g. there were six schizophrenics. None of the control group was on medication. The group (average age 31.7 years) consisted of 39 males and two females.

This study is a matched pairs design — there is a clear attempt at matching individuals. The independent variable is whether or not the participant is a murderer; the dependent variable is the measures of brain activity as found by PET scanning.

PET scanning procedure

The procedure of the study was as follows:

- Each participant carried out a practice test.
- 10 minutes later, a fluorodeoxyglucose (FDG) trace was injected.
- The participant then completed a continuous performance task and target recognition was recorded.
- After a 32-minute period of FDG uptake, the participant was taken for a PET scan of the head and images of slices of the brain were produced.

Brain regions were identified by:

- the cortical peel technique — slices were examined and glucose values for each region of interest were compared with those of other areas in a slice
- a box technique — 2 cm^2 boxes of brain area were examined and linked scan results to the suggested areas for violence

> **Study hint** The above information is useful when describing the use of PET scans, so it is worth learning it as an example.

Results

In the tasks that were carried out before the PET scans there were no differences in performance between the two groups.

Raine et al. presented the results for the cortical and sub-cortical regions of the brain separately. The cortical regions are the lobes of the cerebral cortex; the sub-cortical regions are the other regions of interest.

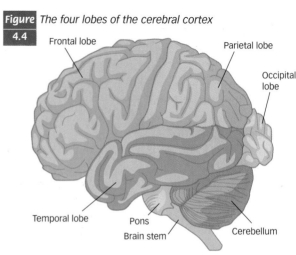

Figure 4.4 The four lobes of the cerebral cortex

Frontal lobe
Parietal lobe
Occipital lobe
Temporal lobe
Pons
Brain stem
Cerebellum

Results for the cortical regions were as follows:

- Prefrontal lobe — the murderers had lower glucose metabolism relative to the controls in some of the prefrontal areas.
- Parietal lobe — the murderers had lower glucose metabolism than the controls, particularly in the left angular gyrus and bilateral superior parietal regions.
- Temporal lobe — there were no significant differences between the murderers and control group.
- Occipital lobe — the murderers had higher glucose metabolism than the controls.

Results for the sub-cortical regions were as follows:

- Corpus callosum — the murderers had lower glucose metabolism in the corpus callosum than the control group.
- Amygdala — the murderers had reduced activity in the left amygdala and greater activity in the right amygdala than the controls.
- Medial temporal lobe, including the hippocampus — the murderers had reduced left activity and greater right activity than the controls.
- Thalamus — the murderers had greater right thalamic activity than the controls.

The effects of handedness, injury and ethnicity

Raine et el. also looked at other variables where the groups differed and that could have affected the results. They had not managed to match the groups in terms of handedness (left-handed or right-handed), injury (relevant head injuries) and ethnicity. On checking these variables, they found:

- Six murderers were left-handed. They were compared with the right-handed murderers and only some slight differences were found. It was concluded that handedness would not have affected the results.
- Fourteen of the murderers were non-white. They were compared with white murderers and no significant differences were found.
- Twenty-three murderers had a history of head injury. They differed from the other murderers on only one measure — lower activity in the corpus callosum.

Conclusions

It was concluded that murderers pleading not guilty by reason of insanity have:

- reduced glucose metabolism in the bilateral prefrontal cortex, the posterior parietal cortex and the corpus callosum
- abnormal activity in the amygdala, thalamus and medial temporal gyrus, including the hippocampus

These findings support the idea that violence has biological causes.

The researchers looked at how the biological deficits that they found translate into violence, with the following conclusions:

- Prefrontal deficits can result in impulsivity and loss of self-control, as well as emotionality and an inability to modify behaviour.
- Limbic deficits show the amygdala is associated with aggressive behaviour, both in animals and humans. The amygdala (part of the limbic system), hippocampus

and prefrontal cortex govern the expression of emotion and the thalamus relays information. The hippocampus is thought to modulate aggression (in cats) and there is other evidence linking the limbic system to aggression, emotion and control.

- The posterior parietal cortex seems to be linked to cognitive functioning. For example, reductions in glucose metabolism in the left angular gyrus have been correlated with reduced verbal ability. Cognitive dysfunction could mean educational and occupational failure, which may lead to crime and violence.
- A dysfunction in the corpus callosum may explain hemisphere differences because the corpus callosum links the two hemispheres. The right hemisphere has been said to generate negative effects in humans and may be in the murderers less regulated by the left hemisphere. Studies of rats reinforce this idea.

Findings show that neural processes underlying violence are complex and that there is no single mechanism in the brain that causes violence. 'Violent behaviour probably involves disruption of a network of multiple interacting brain mechanisms that predispose to violence in the presence of other social, environmental and psychological predispositions' (Raine et al. p. 503).

Overall, murderers pleading not guilty by reason of insanity seem to have different brain functioning from controls.

Evaluation by Raine et al. (1997): factors that might have affected the conclusions

The researchers looked at some extraneous factors that may have affected their results and concluded that they were controlled for sufficiently:
- Forty-one is a reasonably good sample size for PET scanning.
- The strengths of the effects were large enough to draw fairly firm conclusions.
- All but one of the areas that they thought would be important gave significant results, so the findings of earlier studies are supported.
- Areas that they thought would not be important (because of earlier research) were not important.
- The groups were well matched; areas that were not matched (e.g. handedness) were tested, so comparisons between the two groups could be drawn fairly. However, head injury may have affected the brain activity of the murderers.
- All the participants could do the tasks, so there did not seem to be differences in attention, although IQ was not measured. However, low IQ should have given higher cerebral glucose metabolism. The murderers had lower glucose metabolism, so reduced IQ does not seem to account for the differences.

Consideration by Raine et al. of the strengths and limitations of their conclusions

Raine et al. (1997) commented on the strengths and weaknesses of their conclusions:
- This is the largest sample ever imaged.
- The control group includes some good matching.
- The images produced by PET scanning are not particularly clear.

- There was no psychiatric control group.
- Findings only apply to one group of murderers pleading not guilty by reason of insanity, not to all violent offenders.
- The findings do not say that violence is biological.
- The findings do not say that murderers who plead not guilty by reason of insanity are not responsible for their behaviour.
- The study does not give the causes of the brain dysfunctions.
- The findings cannot be generalised to all murderers.
- The control group did not include non-violent criminals.

Evaluation of the study by Raine et al. (1997)

Strengths

- PET scanning was used and such scans can be interpreted objectively by more than one researcher. Therefore, the results tend to be reliable. PET scanning is a scientific method because there is objectivity and replicability and the procedures are controlled.
- A large group was involved. The researchers pointed out that this was the largest sample that had been used in a PET scan study (up to 1997). There were sufficient people in each group for conclusions to have been fairly firm and generalisation might have been possible to other murderers pleading not guilty by reason of insanity.

Weaknesses

- The results can only be generalised to murderers pleading not guilty by reason of insanity because that was the specific group studied. The findings (results and conclusions) cannot be said to be true of all violent offenders, even though it was violence that was being studied.
- The brain dysfunctions cannot be found by the study. The findings describe the differences but do not *explain* them. It could be that such differences were present from birth and are biologically given. However, it could also be that such differences came about from environmental influences and that, although they are biological differences, they are not caused biologically. This is an example of the nature–nurture debate and how it is difficult to separate the two when looking for causes of behaviour.

Table 4.19 *Strengths and weaknesses of the study by Raine et al. (1997)*

Strengths	Weaknesses
● PET scanning is an objective technique and the results can be interpreted by more than one researcher; it is a scientific method and is likely to give reliable findings	● Hard to generalise beyond murderers pleading not guilty by reason of insanity as there were no violent criminals in the control group
● Largest sample size (up to 1997) for PET scanning and large enough for useful comparison with the control group and for generalisation to murderers pleading not guilty by reason of insanity	● Does not show biological causes for violence because environment can cause brain differences

Unit 2

Gottesman and Shields (1966)

Gottesman and Shields (1966) carried out a study into whether schizophrenia might be caused genetically. They compared **MZ twins** with **DZ twins** to see how often when one twin had been diagnosed with schizophrenia (or some similar psychosis) the other twin had a similar diagnosis. If MZ twins showed a higher **concordance** rate than DZ twins then it could be suggested that schizophrenia has, at least in part, a genetic basis.

> **MZ (monozygotic) twins** are identical; **DZ (dizygotic) twins** are non-identical.
>
> **Concordance** means agreement. If one twin has a characteristic and the other twin also has it, then there is concordance; if one twin has a characteristic and the other twin does not have it, there is discordance.

Background

Previous twin studies had shown a difference in concordance for schizophrenia between MZ and DZ twins and had concluded that there is a genetic basis for schizophrenia. However, the methodology (in particular, sampling) of these studies had been criticised. Gottesman and Shields (1966) set about their study with such criticisms in mind and were careful to detail their sampling to address such criticisms. The research method is a twin study; both **primary** and **secondary data** are gathered.

> **Study hint** Gottesman and Shields (1966) is an example of a twin study. Use it when describing twin studies as a research method.

> **Primary data** are gathered first hand by the researchers. **Secondary data** are data that have been gathered previously.

Aims

Gottesman and Shields (1966) aimed to study twins, at least one of whom had been diagnosed with schizophrenia, to see whether schizophrenia has a genetic basis. They also aimed to replicate other studies to see how far their findings agreed with each other and with their own findings. They felt that, despite the criticisms, previous studies had shown a genetic basis for schizophrenia and they aimed to carry out their own analysis to see how far their findings fitted with those of other twin studies.

Procedure

Sampling

The researchers accessed records from 1948 from the Maudsley and Bethlem Royal Joint Hospital, which was a short-stay psychiatric hospital with a large outpatients department. There were 16 consecutive years in which information about twins had been recorded. By March 1964, there had been 392 patients of the same sex who said that they were twins; 47 of the patients had been diagnosed as having schizophrenia. Other twins were diagnosed in such a way as to suggest that they might develop schizophrenia, e.g. having obsessions. More twins were followed up who were known to have been diagnosed with schizophrenia after they had left the hospital. Twenty-one more pairs were found. Altogether, 68 patients were one of pairs of twins and had a diagnosis of schizophrenia or a related psychosis. Three patients were discounted because they were from Ghana, Jamaica and Barbados. Three patients were discounted because it was not easy to tell if they were MZ or DZ twins. So 62 patients remained. These were from 52 pairs of twins where only one was represented in the sample and five pairs of twins where both were represented in the sample.

Assessing zygocity

Zygocity is whether a twin is an identical (MZ) twin or a non identical (DZ) twin. The researchers used three measures to test zygocity:

- blood tests
- fingerprint analysis
- assessment of resemblance between the twins

Table 4.20 *Zygocity of the pairs in the sample*

	MZ pairs	DZ pairs	Total pairs
Female	11	16	27
Male	13	17	30
Total	**24**	**33**	**57**

There were 31 males and 31 females in the group, born between 1893 and 1945 aged between 19 and 64, with an average age of 37. After the testing, the researchers felt that their decisions regarding zygocity were accurate.

Data collection

Data were collected by:

- using hospital notes
- case histories for the twins
- tape recordings of 30-minute samples of verbal behaviour gathered by semi-structured interviews
- personality testing
- a test to examine thought disorders

So there were multiple ways of collecting data.

Results

The results were reported in terms of concordance using the following criteria:

- Category 1: pairs in which both twins were diagnosed as having schizophrenia.
- Category 2: pairs in which one twin has schizophrenia and the other has a psychiatric diagnosis that is not schizophrenia.
- Category 3: pairs in which there appears to be psychiatric abnormality from some of the researchers' own measures.
- Category 4: pairs within normal limits.

Table 4.21 *Numbers and percentages of pairs of twins in the four categories*

Category of twins	Number of MZ pairs	% of MZ pairs	Number of DZ pairs	% of DZ pairs
1 — both diagnosed with schizophrenia	10	42	3	9
1 + 2 — both diagnosed schizophrenia or similar	13	54	6	18
1 + 2 + 3 — where one has schizophrenia and the other is 'abnormal'	19	79	15	45
4 — where one has schizophrenia and the other is 'normal'	5	21	18	55
Total	**24**	**100**	**33**	**100**

In MZ twins, 79% fall into the overall category that when one twin is schizophrenic, the other has some abnormality. This compares with 45% of DZ twins. The researchers also examined gender effects and found that the concordance rate for females was slightly higher. However, of the 13 male MZ pairs there were five pairs who both had schizophrenia; of 11 female MZ pairs there were also five pairs who had schizophrenia. This suggests no real gender effect. When they examined the severity of the schizophrenia, they found that for MZ twins the concordance rate for severe schizophrenia was 75% and for mild schizophrenia it was 17%; for DZ twins the figures were 22% for severe schizophrenia and 0% for mild schizophrenia.

Conclusions

The researchers thought that the diathesis-stress model best explained the results. This suggests that behaviour comes partly from genetic predisposition and partly from environmental triggers. Gottesman and Shields (1966) thought that particular genes predispose someone to schizophrenia by lowering the threshold for coping with stress. Even if it is thought that there is a single gene for schizophrenia (Gottesman and Shields believe there is a set of genes) the explanation still stands — that there is a genetic tendency that is triggered by the environment.

However, the researchers also considered that there might be different forms of schizophrenia, some of which might not be genetically caused. As there were 14 pairs of identical twins in which only one twin had been diagnosed with schizophrenia, this means that it cannot be completely caused by genes.

The researchers suggest further investigation into these discordant twins. They raised some questions:

- Had the twin with schizophrenia been misdiagnosed?
- Should the non-schizophrenic twin be considered to have schizophrenia, even if not diagnosed?
- Might the non-diagnosed twin still develop schizophrenia?
- What in their lives might have led to one twin being diagnosed with schizophrenia and the other twin not?

Case history data suggested that some diagnoses needed more information. For example, one patient had been a prisoner of war and had brain damage, which might explain the symptoms, rather than it being 'in the genes'. In other cases, there were upbringing and life-history differences that may have led to one twin being diagnosed and not the other.

Gottesman and Shields (1966) concluded that the different twin studies agree and that their study supported previous findings. Therefore, they felt that the finding that there is a genetic element in schizophrenia is reliable. They compared 11 studies and, although there were methodological criticisms such as the sampling, they felt the results of the studies to be compatible. Studies from other cultures suggest a low concordance rate (e.g. Finland and Norway), and more studies need to be done in different cultures. For example, a Norwegian study found low concordance rates, and a Finnish study finding no concordance at all. They suggested that there might be different gene patterns that could explain these different findings and that more studies from different cultures are needed.

Overall, they concluded that the identical twin of someone with schizophrenia is at least 42 times as likely to have schizophrenia as someone from the general population; a fraternal twin of the same sex is at least nine times as likely. Therefore, genetic factors appear to be responsible for the specific nature of most schizophrenias. Genes are necessary for it to occur but environmental triggers may also be necessary.

Evaluation of Gottesman and Shields (1966)

Strengths

- The study replicates other studies and the results are supported by those studies, which means that they are likely to be reliable. For example, with regard to the difference between concordance rates when schizophrenia was severe or mild, Inouye (1961) in Japan found a 74% concordance rate for those with progressive chronic schizophrenia and 39% when twins had mild transient schizophrenia. These figures are similar to those of Gottesman and Shields.

- The study addresses criticisms of previous studies by detailing the sampling carefully, so that it was understood which twins were included and why. There is much detail about the different diagnoses, e.g. whether it was schizophrenia, some other psychosis or a different abnormality.

Weaknesses

- The researchers point out that a concordance rate simply notes whether, if one twin has an abnormality, the other has it too. It would be useful to have information about the degree of the abnormality – for example, a scale from 'having schizophrenia' through 'other psychiatric diagnoses' to 'some abnormality' to 'normal'.

- Although figures are given to link schizophrenia to genes, there is no evidence to explain the illness, apart from there being some genetic link. The researchers suggest that there might be different forms of schizophrenia. They also suggest that some of the diagnoses might have come from life experiences (such as being a prisoner of war), rather than being genetic. The study did not readily distinguish between reasons for schizophrenia. Both qualitative and quantitative data were gathered and there was rich detail but this detail was not explored thoroughly, so the reasons for developing schizophrenia were not clear.

 Table 4.22 *Strengths and weaknesses of Gottesman and Shields (1966)*

Strengths	Weaknesses
• The findings agree with findings of previous studies so there is reliability because the studies replicate each other in so far as they examine schizophrenia in MZ and DZ twins • Issues such as sampling are dealt with carefully; these issues were criticised in previous studies, so the study addresses problems with previous studies	• Concordance rates measure only whether or not schizophrenia occurs, rather than a continuum from severe schizophrenia to some other abnormality • The study suggests some genetic link; it fails to give any more detail about explanations for schizophrenia or whether there are different types of schizophrenia; it is descriptive rather than explanatory

De Bellis et al. (2001)

De Bellis et al. (2001) carried out a study using MRI scanning to find out if there are sex and age differences in brain development during childhood and adolescence. The study aimed to investigate three areas of the brain to find out if the volume of those areas changed over time from childhood to adolescence and whether there were differences between the sexes. De Bellis et al. (2001) used MRI scanning, measured the relevant areas and then tested the results for age and sex differences, both separately and together. Previous studies had shown a reduction in grey matter and increases in white matter and in the corpus callosum over time.

Overall, the volume of grey matter showed the expected decrease and the volume of white matter and the corpus callosum size showed the expected increases with age. There were also sex differences, in that although the increases and decrease concerned the same areas, the degree of change was less in females than in males.

This study is covered in more detail on the CD-ROM.

> **Study hint** De Bellis et al. (2001) used volunteer sampling and a cross-sectional design. They used MRI scanning as their main method and they paid special attention to the ethics and practicalities of the study. They also used more than one rater of the scans and mention using a blind technique. In their study there is a possible confounding variable. The study is, therefore, a useful example of the methodological issues.

Examination-style questions

1 Describe Money's (1975) study of sex reassignment. Then, add subsequent information from the participant, so that the whole case study is described. *(6 marks)*

2 Evaluate Money's (1975) study of sex reassignment, including comment on ethical and methodological issues. *(6 marks)*

3 You will have studied one study from Raine et al. (1997), Gottesmann and Shields (1966) or De Bellis et al. (2001).

a For one of these studies describe the procedure. *(4 marks)*

b For one of these studies describe the findings (results and/or conclusions) *(4 marks)*

Extension question

Choose two studies from Money (1975), Raine et al. (1997), Gottesmann and Shields (1966) or De Bellis et al. (2001) and compare the procedures and the findings (results and/or conclusions). *(12 marks)*

Key issues

You have to study one key issue of relevance to today's society and apply concepts and ideas from the approach to that issue. Concepts and ideas include research, studies and theories. Two of the three key issues suggested for your course are covered here. The other is summarised below and covered in more detail on the CD-ROM. However, you do not have to choose one of these — you can choose any issue.

Is autism an extreme male brain condition?

Explore Look up the work of Simon Baron-Cohen, who is a professor at Cambridge and has worked on autism and related issues such as the theory of mind. Find out about him as a person so that you have some background to his work because this will help you to remember, and make your studies interesting.

There has been recent interest in the idea that autistic people have extreme male brain tendencies, i.e. that autism could result from an exaggeration of the normal male brain. The main researcher in this area is Professor Simon Baron-Cohen.

Describing the issue

Autism is a condition that children develop, rather than being a disease. In general, it is characterised by the child not being able to empathise with others and not being able to show love or emotions. According to Baron-Cohen, children with autism seem to have systemising ability; they find it hard to understand people, but they are good at making sense of the world. Some children with autism have a low IQ, so sometimes this systemising takes the form of an obsession, such as staring at a leaf or memorising train timetables. There is an **autistic spectrum**, which means that other conditions connected with autism and which share certain features are included on a **continuum** of autism.

A **continuum** is a graded scale from one point to another.

The continuum is from mild Asperger's syndrome, through Asperger's syndrome to autism. The higher up the scale, the more severe are the effects of the condition on the individual (and family and friends). People with Asperger's syndrome function normally but find it hard to read the emotions of others; those with autism are low-emphathising and high-systematising. Males are supposed to be less able to empathise and to have more ability in systems and visuospatial tasks, so a possible explanation for autism is an 'extreme male brain'. There are females who are autistic, but there are many more males with the condition. For Asperger's syndrome, the ratio of males to females is 10:1. The suggestion is that all males have some autistic traits, but that there is a difference in degree. Autism tends to run in families, which suggests a genetic link.

The suggestion that males are better at systems and less good at emotions has evidence from studies of children. In general:
- girls like to play with dolls; boys like lorries and building toys
- girls are quieter; boys like to play roughly
- girls are more verbal and like gossip more; boys are more spatial
- girls show more verbal aggression, which means they have to know how their victims feel; boys are more aggressive physically

Even though such studies can be criticised, these generalisations show why it is thought that autism links to the male brain.

Application of concepts and ideas

You have to be able to explain this issue using concepts and ideas from the approach. Here is a list of suggestions that you might like to include in answers about this issue:

- The explanation rests on the idea that males seem to use the right hemisphere more and to be less able than females to use both hemispheres effectively.
- Boys' brains grow more quickly than girls' brains and those with autism show such growth to an extreme degree.
- The amygdala is the area of the brain in which emotions are centred and young children with autism have an abnormally large amygdala area with what seems to be an increased density of smaller neurones.
- Male foetuses produce androgens in their testes and female foetuses produce testosterone in their adrenal glands, so girls could be exposed to abnormally high levels of testosterone, which might explain why autism also occurs in girls.
- One study carried out by Baron-Cohen's team showed that girls are more empathising and boys are more oriented to systems. One-day-old babies were set so they could look either at the researcher's face or at a ball of the same size at a distance of 8 inches. The researcher's face moved naturally; the ball moved mechanically because it was mounted on a stick. Of 44 boys tested, 19 looked at the ball for at least 10 seconds longer than at the face, 11 preferred the face and 14 had no preference. Of 58 girls tested, 21 preferred the face, ten preferred the ball and 27 had no preference.
- Studies show that women make more eye contact and are better at decoding body language than men. It is concluded that women are better at social contact, and it is thought that this might be linked to testosterone levels in the developing foetus. Girls, who have less testosterone, are better at social contact; boys, who have more testosterone, are worse.
- Baron-Cohen has used questionnaires to test for systematising and emotional abilities between genders and has found such differences. However, more research is needed to draw firm conclusions.

Are transgender operations ethical?

When an individual wants to change sex, a transgender operation may be carried out. Various treatments are offered to make this change successful for the individual.

Describing the issue

It is difficult to discuss the ethics of procedures such as transgender operations because it is not clear what makes people want to change sex. In some people, their biological make-up means that their sex allocation has been incorrect, so it can be understood that such people are 'trapped' in the wrong gender and wish to change. However, it is not always accepted that sex allocation is biological or, importantly, that sex allocation can be ambiguous or even wrong. So examining biological evidence as to how sex allocation takes place can help when discussing the ethical issues related to transgender operations.

- If the cause is biological, then transsexuality is likely to be 'treated' as other conditions are treated and it would seem unethical not to offer treatment.
- If the cause is social — if it is considered that individuals can change themselves — then perhaps it would seem unethical to offer 'treatment'.

So whether transgender operations are ethical depends on what is thought to be the cause of transsexuality and where the 'blame' lies. Transsexual individuals suggest that it is unethical not to offer them surgery and accept their new gender. People who are not transsexual find it harder to understand. Transsexuals put the issue forward so urgently because they want to gain self-determination as well as legal and medical recognition.

Some other points include:

- There is evidence of transsexuality from the ancient world and castration and penectomies were common in, for example China. The Christian world did not accept this, however.
- Male-to-female surgery began in 1951 in the UK (e.g. Roberta Cowell) and in the 1930s in Germany.
- Hormone therapy dates back to the early 1920s, although in China a version of hormone therapy was being used hundreds of years ago.
- A transsexual in 1970 was told he/she could not marry as a female as he/she was still legally a man in spite of an operation.
- There are legal aspects that are important and leave transsexuals in limbo.

Application of concepts and ideas

The psychodynamic, biological and learning approaches all offer explanations for transsexuality. Here you need to focus on the biological approach but brief explanations from the other approaches will help in comparing the approaches and also in explaining ethical issues:

- According to the psychodynamic approach, boys identify with their fathers through castration fear and girls identify with their mothers because of penis envy. There is no room for any other gender feelings. It could be that an overly protective mother and an absent father lead a boy to identify with his mother. However, some boys with absent fathers are very close to their fathers and develop 'normally'. So the psychodynamic approach does not explain transgender behaviour well. According to the learning approach, gender behaviour comes from reinforcement of appropriate behaviour from those around us. Money (1975) describes a case study in which a boy was reared as a girl and 'became' a girl. However, subsequently it was found that the boy was not happy as a girl and he acted as male as an adult, so the learning approach also does not explain transgender behaviour well.

- The biological approach can explain sex differentiation, including abnormalities and differences. For example, an X chromosome comes from the mother and the father provides either an X chromosome (which will lead to a girl, XX) or a Y chromosome (which will lead to a boy, XY). This indicates that there are two sexes in humans, which suggests that transsexuality occurs because of the environment.
- However, abnormalities are found, e.g. XXY (Klinefelter's syndrome) and XO (Turner's syndrome). Here these are called 'abnormalities', but this is a value judgement and they can be called 'differences'. It is interesting from an ethical point of view because 'abnormalities' suggests that individuals have a right to 'treatment' and so transgender operations are ethical.
- Many of the differences between people — that can be called abnormalities — are to do with how the body reacts to hormones. Excess testosterone and the way the organism reacts to androgens can cause differences. Transsexual individuals may have had different levels of such hormones.
- Levels of hormones can affect brain structures, e.g. use of the two halves of the brain and the size of the corpus callosum, which passes information between the two hemispheres.
- There is some evidence from transsexuals that their abilities reflect their gender with regard to brain lateralisation. This is evidence for transsexuality being a genuine biological difference. If it is a biological difference, relevant operations would be ethical perhaps.
- A laboratory model of transsexuality has been developed in rats by changing their hormone patterns. This is evidence that transsexuality has a biological basis.
- Autopsies have shown brain differences between gay and straight men, which is evidence for biological factors in sex differentiation.
- Early experiences also shape the brain, so it is possible that transsexuality is caused by these early experiences. However, this still suggests that such individuals are entitled to 'treatment', including surgery and it would be unethical not to offer such surgery. This is because their brains have been shaped by circumstances that they have not chosen, although choosing an operation does not make it ethical.

Does taking drugs during pregnancy have a harmful effect?

The question of whether taking drugs during pregnancy has a harmful effect covers both recreational drugs (e.g. alcohol and nicotine) and other drugs (e.g. heroine).

The issue also covers medication. Not only might drugs affect the pregnant woman, but there is also the effect on the baby to consider. The effects of drugs are usually concerned with neurotransmitters and synaptic transmission, but hormonal transmission can also be affected.

This issue is covered in more detail on the CD-ROM.

Examination-style question

1a Describe one key issue that can be explained using concepts and ideas from the biological approach. Remember to describe the issue, *not* the ideas from the approach. *(4 marks)*

b Use evidence from the biological approach to explain the issue you described in answer to part (a). *(6 marks)*

Extension question

Discuss the biological approach. Include some key ideas from the approach and illustrate your points by using one suitable key issue. *(12 marks)*

Practical: a test of difference

As with the other approaches, you have to carry out a practical to put some of the methodology into practice. The practical for the biological approach is a test of difference using an independent groups design and gathering ordinal or interval/ratio data. A practical is given in detail here to help you to understand what is required and the issues you need to cover. This practical looks at gender differences because that is a main theme for this approach. However, your course plan will probably choose a practical for you. For example, you could use a task such as map reading (males would be expected to be better) or verbal ability, such as solving a list of anagrams (females would be expected to be better).

Aim

The aim is to see if there are gender differences in the time it takes to do an eight-piece jigsaw of the sort used in playgroups. Such jigsaws are not too difficult but they take long enough to make the scores meaningfully different. The aim is to see if males are better at such visuospatial tasks.

Research method

Hypotheses

■ The experimental hypothesis is that male participants will complete an eight-piece jigsaw in fewer seconds than female participants.

- The null hypothesis is that any difference in the time taken to complete the jigsaw is due to chance.

Variables

- The independent variable is gender, because that is the variable of interest.
- The dependent variable is what is measured, which is the time in seconds taken to complete the jigsaw.

Method

The study uses an experimental method because there have to be controls to make sure that the independent variable (IV) is all that is different and is the only factor that could cause the change in the dependent variable (DV). Gender cannot be manipulated and is naturally occurring, so the study is a natural or quasi experiment. This is a test of difference — one variable is considered to see its effect on another variable.

> **Study hint** Keep notes about your practicals in preparation for revision because you are likely to be asked questions about them in the exam.

Design

This is an independent groups design. No participant can be both male and female, so there must be different participants in each group.

Controls

Controls make the study scientific. They ensure that only the independent variable is different and so can be the only factor causing the change in the dependent variable. Controls for this study are:

- Participants are chosen carefully so that they are not different in terms of such factors as age, e.g. you would not want all the males to be a lot older than the females. However, it is not a matched pairs design.
- The instructions are the same for all participants (standardised instructions).
- The study is carried out in the same setting each time, so that there is control over **situational variables**.
- The participants all use the same jigsaw.
- There is careful observation of when to start and stop the stop-watch.
- The participants only see the jigsaw when they are ready to carry out the task, so that there can be no forward planning.

Preparing for the study

- Find a suitable jigsaw and a suitable room for the study.
- Write out standardised instructions. This is a simple study, but you still need to attend to ethical issues and be clear about what the participants have to do.

- Plan how you will find the participants, including choosing your sampling method, which will probably be opportunity sampling. Try to find at least ten male and ten female participants.
- Choose your time of day and get permission, as required.

Carry out the study

- You can work on your own, but it would be a good idea to have someone helping you who can do the timing and can concentrate on getting it right for each participant.
- Read out the instructions, check that you are giving the right to withdraw, that you have informed consent and that your study is ethically sound.
- You could have another jigsaw for a practice run.
- Let the participant see the jigsaw. Start the timer. Stop the timer when the last piece is correctly inserted.
- Record the times carefully, alongside the gender of the participant.
- Tell the participant the time taken and explain the purpose of the study and a little about the background, such as about brain lateralisation.

Present the results and carry out the analysis

Table 4.10 in the methodology section gave some suggested times, a suggested table and a worked example of a Mann-Whitney U test. Using your own results, draw up a similar table and carry out a Mann-Whitney U test. Use critical value tables to find out whether or not U is significant. You will need a one-tailed 'test' and you can choose $p \leq 0.05$ as a significance level. The level of measurement is interval because it is time in seconds. Calculate the mode, median, mean and range for the two sets of scores and tabulate them. These are descriptive statistics. Draw up a graph of the results, perhaps a bar chart of the two means.

Conclusions

You need to draw conclusions about whether the males in your sample were quicker at finishing the jigsaw than the females. Consider individual scores and whether one particular participant had such a different score from the others in the group that this affected the overall results.

Evaluating your study

Consider your findings in the light of validity, reliability, credibility, and generalisability:
- **Validity** refers to how far the findings (results and conclusions) represent real life.
- **Reliability** refers to whether, if the study were to be done again, the same results would be found.

- **Credibility** refers to whether the findings are believable and accepted, including whether they fit a common-sense interpretation.
- **Generalisability** refers to whether from the sample used the results can be said to be true of the whole target population.

Validity of the findings

The study used the time taken to complete an eight-piece jigsaw as a test of visuo-spatial ability. This may not be a valid measure, although it does seem a reasonable interpretation because the shapes have to be visualised mentally to see where they fit. However, one jigsaw may not be sufficient; other measures of such abilities might have made the findings more secure with regard to visuospatial skills. Completing a simple jigsaw may only measure one element of such abilities. There is some doubt about the overall validity of the task — people do jigsaws, but they do other visuospatial tasks more often. Adults are unlikely to do eight-piece jigsaws in their everyday lives.

The setting is not natural, so there is a lack of ecological validity. A more valid study might be one in which the participants have to find their way around an area, or do some other natural task in a natural setting.

Reliability

The study used good controls so could be repeated to see if the findings are reliable. Other studies have found that males are better at visuospatial tasks, which reinforces the idea that the findings are reliable.

Credibility

The findings are credible because they are reliable. If the study were to be repeated, it is likely similar results would be found. This means that the findings are credible. Credibility links to validity, in that if the findings relate to real life, they are more credible.

It would be interesting to carry out a brief survey to see if, in general, people think that males are better at visuospatial tasks. This would see if there is credibility in terms of common sense and everyday thinking. There is a general feeling that females are bad at map reading and giving directions, so to that extent the finding that males are better at visuospatial tasks is credible.

Generalisability

Generalisability depends on the sampling technique used and how far the sample represents the target population. The target population is everyone as it was hypothesised that males are better at visuospatial tasks than females. The number of participants will be small to generalise with confidence, and the sample might be biased because opportunity sampling (if that is what you used) can be biased. The sample needs to be examined, e.g. the age of the participants and any differences, other than gender, that there might be between them. If there are participant variables (e.g. age) that may have contributed to the findings, then the findings are not easily generalisable.

Examination-style questions

1 When studying the biological approach you will have carried out a test of difference using an independent groups design and gathering at least ordinal level data. Use your study to answer the following questions:

a Briefly outline the aim(s) of your study. *(2 marks)*

b Explain the procedure of your study. *(4 marks)*

c Explain why you carried out an inferential statistical test on your results. *(3 marks)*

d Outline two weaknesses of your study. *(4 marks)*

Extension question

When studying the biological approach you will have carried out a test of difference using an independent groups design and gathering at least ordinal level data. Design such a study and give justifications for your decision-making choices. Include in your answer the aim(s), hypothesis, independent and dependent variables, ethical considerations and procedure. *(15 marks)*

Answers to the practice boxes

Practice 4.1 on p. 238

Study 1 Find mothers diagnosed as suffering from depression and whose children have been adopted. Find the children. Check the children for signs of depression (perhaps when they are older). Check the adoptive mothers for depression. If the adopted children with depressed biological mothers have depression, this is evidence for some genetic factor causing depression. This is true if the adoptive mothers do not suffer from depression.

Study 2 Find twins that were reared apart throughout their childhood. Check how similar they are, particularly if they have not met one another. Alternatively, check how similar they were when they first met as adults. If they are similar as adults, that similarity is likely to be genetic.

Study 3 Find MZ and DZ twins. Give both the IQ test. See how different the scores are between the two twins. If the scores for the MZ twins are more similar than the scores for the DZ twins, then this indicates at least some genetic cause for IQ.

Practice 4.2 on p. 245

Study 1 This is looking for a relationship between the number of words generated and the length of time in education. Whenever there are two scores (number of words and time in education) for each participant a correlation test is carried out. This study is not investigating whether the number of words is caused by the length of time in education, only to see if the two are related.

Study 2 This is looking for a difference between men and women. Gender is the independent variable and the amount of brain activity is the dependent variable. This cannot be a correlation because gender does not give a score or a rating, there are only male and female. This would be an independent groups design as the two groups are naturally defined as either male or female.

Study 3 This is looking for a difference between men and women. Gender is the independent variable; the number of obstacles hit on the driving course is the dependent variable. This is an independent groups design, not a correlation.

Practice 4.3 on pp. 246–47

Alternative hypothesis 1 The null hypothesis is 'any relationship found between the number of words generated and length of time in education is due to chance'.

Alternative hypothesis 2 The null hypothesis is 'any difference found between men and women in brain activity when doing a language task is due to chance'.

Alternative hypothesis 3 The null hypothesis is 'any difference found between men and women and their driving ability is due to chance'.

Practice 4.4 on p. 247

Hypothesis 1 This is directional (one-tailed) because a positive relationship is predicted — the number of words is expected to increase with length of time in education.

Hypothesis 2 This is directional (one-tailed) because women are predicted to have more brain activity when doing a language task than men.

Hypothesis 3 This is non-directional (two-tailed) because the hypothesis does not say whether men or women will perform better.

Practice 4.5 on p. 248

Measure 1 Nominal — people would be allocated as 'aggressive' or 'not aggressive'.

Measure 2 Interval/ratio — reaction time is a real measure. Reaction time is likely to be measured in seconds and seconds are equal intervals.

Measure 3 Ordinal — people would have to be ranked in order of attractiveness. You could argue this is nominal because people could be allocated as 'attractive' or 'not attractive', although having to say *how* attractive they are does suggest ratings.

Practice 4.6 on p. 250

(1) 1 in 200 is 5 in 1000; decimal form is 0.005
(2) 1 in 50 is 2 in 100; decimal form is 0.02
(3) Decimal form of 1 in 10 000 is 0.0001
(4) 1 in 2000 is 5 in 10 000; decimal form is 0.0005

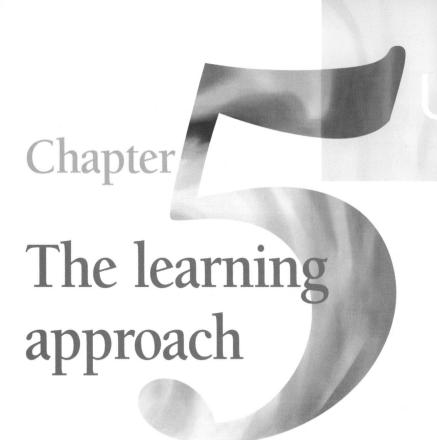

Chapter 5

The learning approach

Psychology is the study of the brain and behaviour and the learning approach focuses on behaviour. In the early 1900s, there was focus on consciousness — for example, Wundt investigated how people think and remember. He studied such issues by asking people to introspect, which means thinking about their own cognitive (thinking) processes. At the same time, there was focus on the unconscious, as seen by Freud's psychodynamic approach. However, other researchers realised that neither the conscious nor the unconscious is easily measurable scientifically. Emphasis on the 'mental' became emphasis on the 'physical', which for psychology meant behaviour. These researchers focused on observable actions. In behaviourism the focus is on measurable behaviour — for example, Pavlov showed that at least some of a dog's behaviour was the result of learned associations.

Study of interest Shedletsky and Voineskos (1976) carried out a study in Canada to investigate the success of a token economy programme (giving tokens as rewards to encourage desired behaviour) in psychiatric patients. Most studies show that such a programme can work in the hospital itself but few studies examine what happens once the patients are discharged. This study followed up patients and also followed up other patients who had experienced a different programme. Effectiveness was measured by discharge rates, how the patient got on in the community and readmission rates. It was found that neither programme was particularly effective in helping rehabilitation outside the hospital. The conclusion was that, as well as behavioural programmes, patients require other measures of support.

5

Everyday example Learning theories can be applied to the training of animals. For example, to train a dog to bark for a biscuit, you would hold the biscuit towards the dog so that the dog is aware of it and then you would withhold the biscuit. As soon as the dog barks, you would give it the biscuit. After repeating this several times, the dog would learn that the reward follows the bark. This is an example of positive reinforcement.

Summary of learning objectives

Definitions
You have to be able to define the terms:
■ classical conditioning, extinction and spontaneous recovery
■ operant conditioning, positive and negative reinforcement, punishment, primary and secondary reinforcement
■ social learning, imitation, modelling, observation, vicarious reinforcement
■ stimulus and response

Methodology
The methodology you have to cover includes:
■ observation as a research method, including participant, non-participant, overt, covert and naturalistic observations
■ inferential statistics, including:
  – levels of measurement
  – reasons for the choice of a Chi-squared, Spearman or Mann-Whitney U test
  – comparing observed and critical values to judge significance
■ the laboratory experimental research method as it is used with human and animal participants and ethical guidelines when using human participants

Content
The content covers:
■ classical conditioning
■ operant conditioning
■ one treatment or therapy based on the principles of either classical or operant conditioning
■ social learning theory
■ gender development as explained using learning theories
■ comparison of the explanation of gender development according to the learning approach with those of the psychodynamic and biological approaches

Studies in detail
You have to be able to describe and evaluate in detail:
■ the Bandura, Ross and Ross (1961) study of how aggressive models might be copied by children
■ one other study from Watson and Rayner (1920), Skinner (1948), and Pickens and Thompson (1968)

Three of the four studies are described and evaluated in this chapter. *The other study is summarised below and covered in detail on the CD-ROM.*

Key issues

You have to be able to describe one key issue that can be explained using concepts and research from the learning approach. Three key issues are suggested in the specification and two are explained here to help you choose. The other is summarised below and covered in detail on the CD-ROM. However, you could choose a completely different key issue relevant to today's society.

Practical

You have to:

- carry out an observation that focuses on some aspect of learning theory and carry out a Chi-squared test on your data
- evaluate your results in terms of validity, reliability, generalisability and credibility

One suggested practical is given in this chapter. You (or your teacher) could choose a different practical.

Study hint Make the summary of learning objectives into a checklist. Table 5.1 gives a suggested list. However, you could add detail, which would help you learn.

Table 5.1 *A checklist of what you need to know for the learning approach and for your progress*

I need to know about	Done	More work	I need to know about	Done	More work
Define classical conditioning, extinction and spontaneous recovery			Operant conditioning, including positive and negative reinforcement and punishment		
Define operant conditioning, positive reinforcement, negative reinforcement, punishment, primary reinforcement, secondary reinforcement			Primary and secondary reinforcement		
Define social learning, imitation, observation, vicarious reinforcement			Social learning theory, modelling, imitation, observation, vicarious reinforcement		
Define stimulus and response			Stimulus and response		
Participant and non-participant observations			Gender development according to learning theories		
Covert, overt and naturalistic observations			Comparing the explanantions of gender development given by the three approaches		
Qualitative and quantitative data			Bandura, Ross and Ross (1961)		
Ethics of using human participants in studies			One study from Skinner (1948), Pickens and Thompson (1968), and Watson and Rayner (1920)		
Define inferential statistics, levels of measurement, levels of significance, critical and observed value			One key issue		
Reasons for choosing Chi-squared, Spearman and Mann-Whitney U tests			One observation practical		
Laboratory experiments using both animals and humans			Evaluation of the practical in terms of reliability, validity, credibility and generalisability		
Classical conditioning, including extinction and spontaneous recovery					

5

Definitions

The following terms are defined in the content section of this chapter:

- classical conditioning
- extinction
- spontaneous recovery
- operant conditioning
- positive reinforcement
- negative reinforcement
- punishment
- primary reinforcement

- secondary reinforcement
- social learning
- imitation
- observation
- modelling
- vicarious reinforcement
- stimulus
- response

An introduction to the learning approach

This chapter is about how human behaviour is learned. The learning approach focuses on how nurture shapes individuals in terms of their environment, e.g. family, peer group, social and cultural situations. For the learning approach it is as if the individual is born 'blank', ready to be shaped into the person that they become. The research methods used are scientific, e.g. laboratory experiments using both animals and human participants.

Study hint It is useful to study the approach as a whole rather than the methodology, content, studies in detail, key issues and practical as separate sections. Read the chapter as a whole, taking in some of the information but without taking notes or learning the terms. After reading the whole chapter, you can then start learning in earnest.

Key assumptions

The learning approach is the approach that focuses most on environmental influences. It includes behaviourism, which, at the start of the twentieth century, developed from other aspects of psychology. By the end of the nineteenth century, when Freud was developing his psychodynamic approach, other people were moving from philosophical thinking to more psychological questions. Wundt, for example, used introspection to answer such questions as how we remember. **Introspection** involves participants thinking about their thinking or how they process information and then explaining those processes to the researcher. Wundt is credited with setting up the first laboratory for the subject. However, as introspection was the method used to collect data, they were not measured carefully and it was difficult to draw scientific conclusions. Ebbinghaus and other researchers were working at that time. These researchers were scientific in their approach, setting up controlled studies.

In response to the problems in drawing conclusions from the research being carried out, the behaviourists, for example Watson, chose to study measurable and observable behaviour. Others — such as Pavlov, who was carrying out laboratory experiments with animals to investigate physiological (biological) responses — were publishing findings about behaviour that were scientifically gathered. The theory of operant conditioning developed from Watson's work; that of classical conditioning developed from Pavlov's studies. Behaviourism comprises classical and operant conditioning. Later, Bandura developed social learning theory. Classical conditioning, operant conditioning and social learning theory are the three theories that you will study.

Explore   Using the internet or some other source, look up Wundt and Ebbinghaus to see how these early researchers studied psychological aspects of behaviour. Then look up Watson and Pavlov to find out about the beginnings of behaviourism, which forms the basis of the learning approach.

Focus on the environment

The learning approach holds that the environment experienced shapes people, by means of reinforcements, to develop in specific ways. For example, young children learn to speak a particular language by copying their parents and family. A baby babbles sounds such as 'mmm' and, in return, the parents say 'mum'; the baby, to get attention, repeats the sound. Such reinforcement leads to talking. Punishment can also shape behaviour. When people are punished for an action, they are less likely to repeat it — unless that punishment is the only attention they receive, in which case they may repeat the behaviour because attention itself becomes rewarding.

Focus on scientific methods

Behaviour is difficult to study and it is yet more difficult to draw scientific conclusions. Therefore, specific actions are isolated and studied to find out what leads to those actions or what would stop them. A single piece of behaviour — for example, a rat pressing a lever to receive a food pellet — is studied to see when the rat presses the lever and how quickly it learns to press the lever for the reward. Such a study would involve an independent variable (e.g. a red light when the rat gains the food or a green light, when it does not). All other variables are controlled. A dependent variable (e.g. how often the rat presses the lever when the red, but not the green, light is on) is then measured. Scientific principles such as these are a feature of the learning approach. Behaviourists saw that it would be difficult to build knowledge if data were not reliable, so they turned to measurable aspects of behaviour and to scientific methodology.

Types of learning to illustrate the learning approach

General principles of classical conditioning

Classical conditioning is about how a stimulus is associated with a response. It applies *only* to the conditioning of reflexes. Human reflexes include, for example, a fear response, eye blinking in response to certain stimuli, knee-jerk reactions and breathing. However, most behaviour goes beyond reflex actions, so classical conditioning is limited in its application.

Study hint When asked to give ideas that underpin the learning approach, avoid giving the particular theories. Instead, consider the underlying principles — for example, the focus on experience within an environment and the desire to build a body of knowledge using scientific methods. You could, however, use the three types of learning explained below to illustrate points about environmental influences or the scientific approach. Alternatively, you could choose a different underpinning idea, such as that using animals in laboratory experiments means that the findings can be applied to humans.

Fear can be conditioned. For example, a fear response to something in an individual's life (such as stress) could occur in a lift. From then on, that person might be afraid of being in a lift because the response was associated with the lift (see page 333 for more detail).

Pavlov

Explore Use the internet or some other source to look up Pavlov's work with dogs. In the early 1900s, he started off the idea of learning by association and classical conditioning. You could consider ethical issues involved with using animals in laboratory experiments and draw on material that you have learned within the biological approach.

General principles of operant conditioning

Most behaviour is voluntary, not reflex. Operant conditioning examines voluntary behaviour and considers how rewards and punishments shape it. For example, schoolchildren may work hard for the reward of gold stars, so their behaviour (hard work) is repeated for the reward (a gold star). Other children might not work hard and be punished by being given homework. These are the sorts of principles involved in operant conditioning.

Explore Use the internet or some other source to look up the work of B. F. Skinner, who, in the mid-1900s, explained the idea of operant conditioning. He used many laboratory experiments involving animals. Consider the problems of generalising from animal studies to humans — is it fair to say that what is found in animals is necessarily true of humans?

Skinner

General principles of social learning

Social learning theory, explained by Bandura from about 1960, shows how people learn by observing other people, particularly those they look up to, i.e. their role models. Not all learning is reinforced or involves reflexes. The social learning theory suggests that much of what is learnt comes from watching others and copying them.

Explore Use the internet or some other source to look up the work of Bandura, focusing on social learning theory. You could also find out what he investigated later, e.g. self-efficacy.

Examination-style questions

1 Define the terms 'extinction' and 'spontaneous recovery'. *(6 marks)*

2 Explain two ways in which the learning approach differs from the biological approach. *(4 marks)*

3 Explain two ways in which the learning approach differs from the psychodynamic approach. *(4 marks)*

Extension question

Compare the biological, psychodynamic and learning approaches in terms of their underpinning beliefs about the study of the brain and behaviour. *(12 marks)*

Methodology

This textbook has worked through the approaches in the order of the specification, so this methodology section has a smaller amount of new material than the methodology sections for the other approaches. This section focuses on observation, which is an important technique in psychology. The learning approach also features aspects of inferential statistics; the Chi-squared test is new and is detailed here. The learning approach methodology also includes information about laboratory experiments and ethics, covered earlier (see pages 103 and 150). All aspects of the methodology section of this approach are at least mentioned here. If you need to know more, refer back to where the issue is covered in detail within another approach.

Study hint This is the last of the five chapters, so you have nearly covered all the key terms you need to know about with regards to methodology. Using the checklists near the start of each chapter, make a list of all the terms and check that you know what they mean. This can be a daunting exercise — so work with one or two friends, taking it in turns to define the terms. Working together is a good way to learn. You could even turn the exercise into a quiz.

The observational research method

You might think that all research methods in psychology involve observing people's behaviour, which of course is right — up to a point. Scanning may involve some observing of behaviour and it is essential to look at the images produced, but this is not an observational research method. Case studies may involve observation because in-depth data are gathered. However, although they may use observations, the research method is case study. In laboratory experiments, scores may come from the observation of behaviour. For example, you will study Bandura's work — he set up laboratory experiments to observe whether or not children copy aggressive behaviour. However, this is not an observational research method and it is important not to call this an observation. It is an experiment — even though there is an element of observation. It is an experiment because there were careful controls of sampling, allocation to groups, control over the behaviour watched by the participants and over what was carried out at each stage of the study. The independent variable was carefully manipulated.

The observational research method features observation as the main way that data are gathered, without setting up an experiment or using scanning techniques or any other research method. In an observation, behaviour is observed and recorded without controlling all aspects of the study and an independent variable is not manipulated, as it is in an experiment. There might be an independent variable such as gender, but it is likely to be naturally occurring. There are a few structured observations, but most are naturalistic.

Structured observations (rarely used)

Occasionally observations are structured so that the same situation is repeated with different participants and researchers observe what happens. There is no manipulation of an independent variable (that would make the study an experiment). However, there is manipulation of the setting and situation, which

> Structured observations are used in child psychology, which you might study at A2.

makes the observation structured. It is not often that observing behaviour in a structured (artificial) situation is useful because a main point of observations is to obtain valid results. Sometimes a **structured observation** can be set up to organise, but not destroy, natural interactions. Structured observations have the advantage of being replicable. Therefore, they can be tested for reliability. However, this is not a common research method. Usually, even if observations are made, structured situations are experiments.

Studies involving the methodology Mary Ainsworth used structured observations. She set up a situation that she called the 'strange situation' and then observed interactions between mothers and their infants to examine attachment patterns. The interactions were watched through a one-way mirror and all the data were gathered by observation. Apart from the situation, everything else was natural. The 'strange' situation involved the mother and child together 'normally' in a strange place and then a stranger entering the room. The observations were to see what the child did when the mother was both in and out of the room, with or without the stranger being present.

Naturalistic observations

Most observations, in which data are collected by observation only and there is no manipulation by the researcher, are naturalistic observations. Naturalistic observations take place in the participant's natural setting. The different ways of designing a naturalistic observation are outlined here. When observations are referred to in this methodology section, they are naturalistic observations.

Participant or non-participant observations

- **Participant observations** — observers are part of what they are observing; they are involved in the activity, group or situation. An example of participant observation is infiltration of a group by a researcher in order to find out more about how the group works or when a researcher is already part of the group. So someone could be a member of the team and could observe, for example, team cohesion.

- **Non-participant observations** — observers are not part of what is happening. They sit away from the activity and are not involved in it. Examples of non-participant observation are when researchers are studying a childcare programme but are not part of that programme or when they are studying team cohesion in sports psychology but are not members of the team.

> **Studies involving the methodology** Donna Weston reports on a naturalistic observation of parents and their children from birth to around 18 months, recording patterns of communication. Five non-participant observers observed day-to-day interactions in the home weekly. They wrote up the story and scored the behaviour on a scale. (If a parent had carried out the observation and scored the behaviour, that would have been participant observation.)

Evaluation of non-participant observations: strengths

- The observer has no other role to play and so can concentrate on observation and be impartial and objective.
- Recording the data is easier in non-participant observations and the observer can record more data, more efficiently. A non-participant observer might be able to make notes during the study whereas a participant observer might not be able to do that until afterwards.
- A non-participant observer should be able to carry out time sampling and tallying more systematically than a participant observer.

Evaluation of non-participant observations: weaknesses

- The observer in non-participant observations has to be nearby and is likely to be noticeable, which would affect the situation. The observations would lack validity because what is recorded is not 'normal'.

- Compared with participant observation, the observer may have insufficient understanding of what he/she is observing to record valid data. A participant observer would have useful background knowledge that would help in understanding the data.

Table 5.2 *Strengths and weaknesses of non-participant observations*

Strengths	Weaknesses
• Non-participant observers are objective. They can stand back from the situation better than participant observers • Non-participant observers can record data more easily than participant observers because they have the time to concentrate • They can use time-sampling when tallying, which might be difficult when participating and observing at the same time	• Non-participant observers are likely to affect the situation just by their presence • Non-participant observers might miss the relevance of some interactions or might misunderstand something, whereas participant observers have the advantage of shared understanding with the participants

Evaluation of participant observations: strengths

- The observers in participant observations do not disrupt what is happening — they are are not additional people who would affect the situation. Therefore, ecological validity is greater because the observers do not affect the situation and make it unnatural.
- The observers in participant observations are likely to have additional information that they can offer as data. They are likely to obtain more data from the observations because they would have better access to such data. They are likely to observe things that non-participant observers would miss.
- It is not normally easy to get access when carrying out a study. Therefore, another strength is obtaining **access** because participant observers are present already.

> **Access** is the term for entering a situation in order to gather data.

Evaluation of participant observations: weaknesses

- The observers may be so involved in the situation that they cannot step back sufficiently to make the observations. Non-participant observers can observe all the time; participant observers also have other roles.
- Because the observer is part of the group, participant observations are hard to replicate. Therefore, it is difficult to check for reliability.

Table 5.3 *Strengths and weaknesses of participant observations*

Strengths	Weaknesses
• There is ecological validity because the observation is in the natural setting, including not having a stranger present • A participant observer is likely to gather valid data because the setting is natural and what occurs is also natural	• The observer may be too involved to record all the data, partly because they cannot step back from the situation and partly because they have another role • They are difficult to replicate because it is not easy to find an observer who is also a member of the group

Covert and overt observations

- In a **covert** observation the participants do not know that the observation is taking place — it is being done secretly.
- In an **overt** observation the participants know that the observation is taking place and they are aware of all aspects of the study.

Evaluation of covert observations: strengths

- Because the participants in covert observations are unaware of the study, the behaviour being observed is likely to be natural. Therefore, the data are valid.
- In covert observations the observer can maintain a distance (literally if a non-participant observer; figuratively if a participant observer) from the participants and can, for example, make notes without being concerned about the effect this is having on the participants. The participants are not aware of the study and so will not be looking at what the observer is doing.

Evaluation of covert observations: weaknesses

- Covert observations are usually unethical. Ethical guidelines:
  - ask for informed consent, which could not be obtained
  - do not allow for participants to be distressed, which they may be on discovering that they have been observed secretly
  - do not allow secret observations if the situation is not public (observations in a public place are permitted)
- Non-participant observers may find observation difficult because they cannot be helped by the participants to find a suitable place to watch from. It is not easy to observe behaviour secretly because, in practice:
  - the observers have to be in a suitable position to gather the necessary data
  - in a participant observation the observer may need to do something different from the norm, thus making secrecy difficult

Table 5.4 *Strengths and weaknesses of covert observations*

Strengths	Weaknesses
• Behaviour of the participants is likely to be natural because they are unaware that they are being observed; therefore, there is validity	• They are often not ethical because there is no informed consent; if they are not carried out in a public place, they go against ethical guidelines
• The observation is easier because the observer can carry out the study without the participants watching what the observer is doing	• The observer cannot be helped by the participants (e.g. to find a suitable place for observation) because the participants are unaware that the study is taking place

Evaluation of overt observations: strengths

Strengths of overt observation include:

- It is much more ethical than covert observation — for example the participants can give informed consent and can be offered the right to withdraw.
- The observer can ask for help in setting up a suitable place for observation.

■ Participant observers can ask for help in getting data to which they might not usually have access.

Evaluation of overt observations: weaknesses

■ The participants may not act normally because they know that they are being observed. Therefore, the data might not be valid.

■ Participant observers may find it difficult to carry out their duties as the people being observed would be aware that the observers are taking on different roles. If the observation were a non-participant observation then this is less of a problem.

Table 5.5 *Strengths and weaknesses of overt observations*

Strengths	Weaknesses
● They are ethical because informed consent can be gained and the right to withdraw can be given	● The participants know that they are being watched so might not act in a natural way. Therefore, there is doubt about validity of the data
● Observers can ask for help to set up the study (e.g. where to observe from)	● It might be difficult to carry out because the observers themselves would be watched to see what they are doing

Study hint Be ready to describe each aspect of observation (covert, overt, non-participant, participant and naturalistic). Prepare descriptions worth about 4 marks each. You also need to be able to identify these aspects and to be able to use them, for example, in a study scenario. If you cannot describe a term fully, then use an example to show understanding and perhaps contrast one aspect with another. For example, to describe overt observations you could briefly contrast them with covert observations. However, don't spend long doing this because you must say what the aspect is, not what it is not.

Inter-observer reliability

It could be said that observations are one-off situations that are hard to replicate because they take place at one moment in time and involve naturally occurring events. However, if there is more than one observer, their observations can be compared. The separate sets of data are recorded and then tested to see if there is a correlation between them. If there is a correlation then it is said that the observation has **inter-observer reliability**, which is a strength.

Recording data from naturalistic observations

When observations are carried out, the data have to be recorded and how they are recorded is important. A single observer, for example, can only observe when not writing things down and can, in any case, only observe certain aspects of the situation. Two observers can do better and inter-observer reliability can be tested. However, a system for recording observations must be agreed. Much depends on whether the study needs qualitative or quantitative data or both.

■ **Qualitative data** involve attitudes or emotions; detail, rather than numbers, is important.

■ **Quantitative data** are numerical; they are useful when analysing results. If quantitative data are required, tallying can be used as a way of recording.

Tallying

Tallying involves making a mark each time a behaviour (or whatever is being observed) occurs.

There needs to be an initial observation session, preferably with more than one observer, in which categories of behaviour are recorded so that all the researchers know what behaviour should be tallied. For example, if observing boys and girls in a nursery to look for gender-specific behaviour, it would first be necessary to record some gender-specific behaviour in order to list what is relevant and what is likely to be seen in that nursery. In the nursery, there might, for example, be bikes, a climbing frame, a painting corner and books; there might be a play mat with cars, a play-dough session, a large wooden train set and a soft play area. The toys and play equipment available will guide the play behaviour and researchers need to decide on their categories before gathering the data. When they have the categories, they can then draw up a table for tallying. An example is given in Table 5.6.

Time sampling

If you carry out tallying for your practical, there will be one important problem that needs addressing. You need to know when to make a tally mark. If a child plays with play dough, you make a mark. Do you then wait until the child does something else? Playing with play dough may continue for ages. One way round this is to use **time-sampling**, which means making a tally mark every minute or other chosen interval. This provides a better picture of what the child has been doing during the observation.

Table 5.6 shows data (artificial) from two observers who watched two children each, one boy and one girl (i.e. two boys and two girls were observed). Since the observers watched different children, inter-observer reliability could not be tested. However, the observers were trained in the use of the categories by watching a video before-hand, to ensure that they would note the same behaviour.

Table 5.6 An example of the use of tallying to examine gender-specific behaviour in a nursery. A mark was made every minute for each child, over a session of about 2 hours

Play behaviour	Boys	Girls
Playing on the climbing frame	丅卌 ////	///
Playing in the book corner	///	丅卌 //
Painting	丅卌	////
Playing in the Wendy houses	丅卌 ///	丅卌 //
Riding on bikes	丅卌 丅卌 //	丅卌
Playing quietly alone	////	丅卌 丅卌 ///
Playing with other adults	丅卌 丅卌 /	丅卌 ///
Watching, not playing	///	丅卌 ///
Playing with play dough	丅卌	丅卌 丅卌 //

Evaluation of naturalistic observation: strengths

■ The setting is natural, so there is ecological validity. **Ecological validity** means that:
  – the setting is real life and the data are, therefore, real
  – the study, with regard to the setting, gathers the data that it claims to gather

If an observation is not carried out in a natural setting, you cannot be sure that natural behaviour is being observed.

- Detail that can be gathered in naturalistic obervation. Observation can potentially capture all the behaviour exhibited at that time, (provided that there is more than one observer). Observers can record speech, actions, interactions, body language, information about the setting and emotions. Other research methods tend not to be able to gather so much detail (except case studies with observation used as a research method within the study).

> **'Validity'** means that the study measures what it claims to measure, which means that it gathers real-life data; **'ecological'** refers to the setting of the study.

Evaluation of naturalistic observations: weaknesses

- The observer makes decisions about what to record and, in some cases, what categories to use and into which categories particular behaviour should be placed. So there is an element of interpretation, which means that the study could involve subjectivity, which is not a scientific way of carrying out research.
- Data gathered by an observational research method tend to lack generalisability because an observation at that moment in time is specific. It is difficult to generalise from that specific situation to other situations, even if they are similar. Tallying gives quantitative data, but there is some interpretation involved; observations often gather qualitative data and a specific situation is involved. For these reasons, generalisation is difficult.

Table 5.7 *Strengths and weaknesses of naturalistic observations*

Strengths	Weaknesses
• Observations take place in the natural environment of the participant, so there is ecological validity	• There might be subjectivity because the observer has to choose what to observe and what to record
• They gather much in-depth data and detail, which is difficult using any other research method; data are often qualitative and rich; even when quantitative, the data can be detailed	• An observation is of one group or individual at one moment in time, so the data are not generalisable to other people at different times

Practice 5.1

Using the terms covert, overt, participant, non-participant, inter-observer reliability and naturalistic, explain the research method used in the following study. Make sure that you use each term in such a way that makes it clear that you understand it:

'A study was carried out to see if girls chose different toys from boys. The study took place in a local nursery; children aged between 2 and 4 years were observed. There were two observers both sitting to one side of the nursery, on opposite sides of the room. The nursery staff, parents and children were aware that a study was taking place and had agreed to take part.'

Answers are at the end of Chapter 5.

Inferential tests

Some points about inferential testing:

- The detail of what you need to understand about inferential tests is covered in Chapter 4.
- The Mann-Whitney U test is explained in Chapter 4 (page 251); the Spearman test is explained in Chapter 3.
- For the learning approach, you need to know how to carry out a Chi-squared test.
- A summary of issues involved in inferential testing is given here.

Choosing and using an inferential test involves some careful steps/calculations but, taken one at a time, none of them is difficult. You need to know a lot about your study first, including the level of measurement of the data, your design, whether your hypothesis is one- or two-tailed and whether your study involves looking for a difference or a relationship between the variables. Then you can choose and run your test.

Choosing a test

The chapter on the biological approach gives detail about choosing a test. The information is summarised here:

- Determine the **level of measurement** — nominal (categories), ordinal (ranked data) and interval/ratio (real mathematical scores).
- Review the alternative (experimental) hypothesis to see if it is directional (one-tailed test needed) or non-directional (two-tailed test needed). Directional means that the hypothesis states the predicted direction of results (e.g. boys play more noisily and girls are more involved in quiet play).
- Review the hypothesis to see whether a difference or a relationship is predicted. If a relationship is predicted, then a test for **correlation** is needed (Spearman's rank correlation coefficient). The tests of difference in your course are the Mann-Whitney U test for ordinal or interval/ratio data and the Chi-squared test for nominal data.
- Review the study to find the participant design. If the hypothesis is testing for a relationship, then the design is a correlation. If the hypothesis is testing for a difference the design is either:
  - matched pairs or repeated measures (taken as one design for the purpose of inferential testing) *or*
  - an independent groups design (Mann-Whitney U test for ordinal or interval/ratio data; Chi-squared for nominal data)
- Choose a level of significance. For your purposes, $p \leq 0.05$ or $p \leq 0.01$ level of significance is suitable. A probability of 0.05 means a 1 in 20 likelihood that the results are due to chance; 0.01 means a 1 in 100 likelihood. With these probability levels, the results are accepted as statistically significant.
- Write out the null hypothesis, which says that any difference or relationship predicted by the alternative (experimental) hypothesis is due to chance and not due to the manipulation of the independent variable.

- Choose the Spearman test if the hypothesis predicts a correlation and the level of measurement of data is at least ordinal. Both scores must be on a scale that can be ranked.
- Choose the Mann-Whitney U test if the level of measurement of the data is ordinal or interval/ratio, if the hypothesis predicts a difference and it is an independent groups design.
- Choose a Chi-squared test if the level of measurement of the data is nominal, the hypothesis predicts a difference and it is an independent groups design.
- Carry out the relevant test using the step-by-step instructions in the relevant chapter. (Spearman test is in Chapter 3; Mann-Whitney U test is in Chapter 4; Chi-squared test is in this chapter).
- Find the relevant statistical table. There is more than one table for the Mann-Whitney U test so check that it is the correct one for your chosen level of significance. Determine whether the test must be one-tailed or two-tailed. Tables can be found in statistics textbooks and on the internet.
- For the Spearman test and the Mann-Whitney U test, find N, which is the number of participants. For the Mann-Whitney U test, where the participant design is independent groups, there are two N scores (because there are two groups).
- For the Chi-squared test, find the degrees of freedom (df). For a two-by-two table, $df = 1$. The degrees of freedom, df, is the number of rows minus 1 multiplied by the number of columns minus 1. Step-by-step instructions for calculating this are given in Chapter 4 (page 251).
- Use the tables to find the critical value for the test. This depends on df and/or N, the level of significance and whether the test is one- or two-tailed.
- Check the result of your test against the critical value. For the result to be significant and the null hypothesis (that the resulting data are due to chance) to be rejected, the Mann-Whitney U test requires the result (U) to be equal to or *less* than the critical value; the Chi-squared and Spearman tests requires the result (χ^2 and rho respectively) to be equal to or *greater* than the critical value.
- Note whether your null hypothesis is rejected (or whether the test is significant).

The Chi-squared test

Preparing data for a Chi-squared test

To show how to carry out a Chi-squared test, some tally data from Table 5.6 are used. A Chi-squared test can test for more factors than those given here. However, the most straightforward Chi-squared test is when there is a **two-by-two table**, as used here.

> A **two-by-two table** consists of two rows and two columns.

The columns in this example are the two sexes, boys and girls. The rows could be any of the categories but the sensible thing is to choose two categories in which boys and girls have shown different behaviour. For this example, the two rows are 'playing on the climbing frame' and 'playing in the book corner'. There were differences in other categories (e.g. playing alone), but the chosen categories involve toy use because the purpose of the study was to investigate children playing with toys.

Table
5.8 *A two-by-two table for a Chi-squared test*

Play behaviour	Boys	Girls	Total
Playing on the climbing frame	9	3	**12**
Playing in the book corner	3	7	**10**
Total	**12**	**10**	**22**

For this example, 22 behaviours were recorded — 12 for boys and ten for girls; 12 on the climbing frame and ten playing in the book corner.

Carrying out the Chi-squared test

A Chi-squared test is carried out when:
- the data are nominal
- the study is testing for a difference
- the participant design is independent groups

Here, the independent variable is gender, so there are bound to be different people in the two conditions, so this is an independent groups design.

First label the cells in the two-by-two table, as in Table 5.9.

In a Chi-squared test using a two-by-two table, the expected values for the four cells (A, B, C and D) are calculated and then compared with the observed values (Table 5.9).

Table
5.9 *Observed values (artificial) for a Chi-squared test*

Play behaviour	Boys	Girls	Total
Playing on the climbing frame	9 (Cell A)	3 (Cell B)	**12**
Playing in the book corner	3 (Cell C)	7 (Cell D)	**10**
Total	**12**	**10**	**22**

The formula for the expected value is:

$$\frac{\text{total of the row of cells} \times \text{total of the column of cells}}{\text{total of all cells}},$$

where

total of the row of cells = total of the row of cells containing the required cell

total of the column of cells = total of the column of cells containing the required cell

Data found from Table 5.9 are:
- observed frequency for cell A = 9
- observed frequency for cell B = 3
- observed frequency for cell C = 3
- observed frequency for cell D = 7
- row total for A and B = 12
- row total for C and D = 10
- column total for A and C = 12
- column total for B and D = 10
- total observations = 22

Using cell A as an example:
Step 1: Find the total of the row containing the cell. (Here, row total = **12**.)
Step 2: Find the total of the column containing the cell. (Here, column total = **12**.)
Step 3: Multiply the answer to Step 1 by the answer to Step 2. (Here, 12 × 12 = **144**.)
Step 4: Find the overall total of observations. (Here, overall total = **22**.)
Step 5: Divide the answer to Step 3 by the answer to Step 4. (Here, 144/22 = **6.55**.)

This is the expected value for the cell. (Here, the cell is A.)

Repeat Steps 1 to 5 for each cell. The results are shown in Table 5.10.

Table 5.10 Expected values for cells A, B, C and D

Step	Cell A	Cell B	Cell C	Cell D
Step 1: Find the total of the row containing the cell	12	12	10	10
Step 2: Find the total of the column containing the cell	12	10	12	10
Step 3: Multiply the answer to Step 1 by the answer to Step 2	12 × 12 = 144	12 × 10 = 120	10 × 12 = 120	10 × 10 = 100
Step 4: Find the overall total of observations	22	22	22	22
Step 5: Divide the answer to Step 3 by the answer to Step 4	144/22 = 6.55	120/22 = 5.45	120/22 = 5.45	100/22 = 4.55
Expected value for cell	6.55	5.45	5.45	4.55

Redraw the two-by-two table, giving both the observed (*O*) and the expected (*E*) frequencies (Table 5.11).

Table 5.11 Observed (O) and expected (E) frequencies

Play behaviour	Boys	Girls	Total
Playing on the climbing frame	9 (*O*); 6.55 (*E*)	3 (*O*); 5.45 (*E*)	**12**
Playing in the book corner	3 (*O*); 5.45 (*E*)	7 (*O*); 4.55 (*E*)	**10**
Total	**12**	**10**	**22**

The formula to find the Chi-squared result is:

$$\chi^2 = \Sigma \frac{(O - E)^2}{E}$$

where Σ = the sum of
O = the observed results
E = the expected result

Referring to Table 5.11 and using cell A (boys) as an example:
Step 1: Subtract E from O. (Here, 9 − 6.55 = **2.45**.)
Step 2: Square the answer from Step 1 (multiply the answer to Step 1 by itself). (Here, 2.45 × 2.45 = **6.00**.)
Step 3: Divide the answer to Step 2 by E. (Here, 6.00/6.55 = **0.92**.)

The results for all four cells are shown in Table 5.12.

| Table 5.12 | Calculating χ^2 for the study of gender and development |

Step2	Cell A	Cell B	Cell C	Cell D
Step 1: Subtract *E* from *O*	9 − 6.55 = 2.45	3 − 5.45 = −2.45	3 − 5.45 = −2.45	7 − 4.55 = 2.45
Step 2: Square the answer from Step 1	2.45 × 2.45 = 6.00	−2.45 × −2.45 = 6.00	−2.45 × −2.45 = 6.00	2.45 × 2.45 = 6.00
Step 3: Divide the answer to Step 2 by *E*.	6.00/6.55 = 0.92	6.00/5.45 = 1.10	6.00/5.45 = 1.10	6.00/4.55 = 1.32
Squaring numbers removes the minus sign				

The final step is the calculation of the value of Chi-squared (χ^2). This is obtained by adding together all answers (in this case, four) for Step 3. In this example:

$$\chi^2 = 0.92 + 1.10 + 1.10 + 1.32 = \mathbf{4.44}$$

This is the value of Chi-squared.

Is the Chi-squared test result statistically significant?

For a two-by-two study, the degree of freedom, *df*, is always 1. As you will probably choose to do a two-by-two study, the critical table value for *df* = 1 is displayed here (Table 5.13). If you carry out a study with, for example, a three-by-two table, *df* is 2, so that part of the critical values table is also shown in Table 5.13.

To find the degree of freedom, *df*:

Step 1: Subtract 1 from the number of rows. (For a two-by-two table, 2 − 1 = 1.)
Step 2: Subtract 1 from the number of columns. (For a two-by-two table, 2 − 1 = 1.)
Step 3: Multiply the answer to Step 1 by the answer to Step 2. (For a two-by-two table, 1 × 1 = 1.)

The answer to Step 3 is the degree of freedom. For a two-by-two table, *df* = 1.

| Table 5.13 | Critical values for Chi-squared when df = 1 or 2 |

	Level of significance, *p*, for a one-tailed test			
	0.05	0.025	0.01	0.005
	Level of significance, *p*, for a two-tailed test			
df	0.10	0.05	0.02	0.01
1	2.71	3.84	5.41	6.64
2	4.60	5.99	7.82	9.21

The example given here tested the hypothesis that toy use is different depending on gender. This is a non-directional hypothesis because it does not predict which toys which gender will play with more. The test required is a two-tailed test. If the $p \leq 0.05$ level of significance is chosen, this means that it is accepted that the probability of the results being due to chance is 1 in 20 or 5% and the null hypothesis will be rejected. At this level of significance, when *df* is 1, the critical value to be equalled or exceeded is 3.84. In the example given, the Chi-squared value is 4.44. This is greater than 3.84, so the null hypothesis is rejected and the alternative

5

hypothesis is accepted — there is a difference in toy use depending on gender and that boys play more on the climbing frame with girls staying in the book corner. Note that before the test was carried out it was possible to see the difference by reading the two-by-two table. However, the test is carried out to find whether or not the result is statistically significant.

> **study hint** You do not need to memorise how to carry out the inferential tests. However, you need to know how to choose a test, when to use each of the three tests given in the specification and how to interpret the result of the test using critical value tables. You also need to know how to use a level of significance and what is meant by the result of a test being significant (or not).

Describe and evaluate the laboratory experiment as a research method

You need to be certain that you can describe and evaluate the laboratory experiment as a research method. A description and some evaluation issues are given briefly here. Each aspect is more fully detailed elsewhere in the course, so review any aspects that you are not sure about by referring to the relevant methodology sections in the other chapters.

Description

- A laboratory experiment takes place in controlled and, therefore, artificial conditions.
- An independent variable is manipulated.
- A dependent variable is measured to see the result of manipulating the independent variable.
- The aim is a cause-and-effect relationship, rather than a correlation.
- The procedures are scientific, e.g. control of extraneous variables to avoid **confounding variables** being responsible for the results.
- Standardised instructions and standardised procedures are put into place as controls, and the experimenter maintains objectivity.
- In a repeated measures design, either the order of conditions is randomised or counterbalancing is used to control for order effects.
- Careful sampling produces a sample that represents the target population.
- Some experiments in psychology involve the use of animals.

Evaluation

When evaluating a research method, both strengths and weaknesses should be considered.

Strengths

- A laboratory experiment is replicable because of the controls. Therefore, it can be tested for reliability. Reliability is a requirement of science. If a study is repeated and the same results are found, then it is reliable. For a body of knowledge to be built up, data must be reliable.

- Careful sampling techniques and careful controls such as using standardised instructions mean that results tend to be generalisable to the target population. This means that the data can be used to predict outcomes, which is another requirement of science.
- Careful controls allow a cause-and-effect relationship between the variables to be claimed, i.e. that manipulation of the independent variable causes the changes in the dependent variable.
- Careful controls (e.g. counterbalancing in a repeated measures design, making sure that there are no extraneous variables and controlling for experimenter effects) mean that objectivity is maintained, which is yet another requirement for science.

Weaknesses

- The controlled artificial setting means that there is no ecological validity and the situation is unlikely to be representative of real life, so the results are not as generalisable as might be thought. Validity exists when what is measured is about real-life issues and is also what is claimed to be measured.
- The controlled conditions mean that what is measured is not likely to relate to real life because artificial conditions produce artificial behaviour. Therefore, laboratory experiments may not be valid.
- There may be a lack of credibility. The results of a laboratory experiment might not be valid to the extent that the findings are not useful. For example, some experiments use animals; it might not be credible to claim that the same result would apply to humans.
- Careful operationalisation of the independent and dependent variables so that they are measurable means that they may be artificial, so nothing meaningful is measured.
- It is possible that the participants could guess the purpose of the study just by taking part. In this case there could be demand characteristics, in which the participants give the responses that they think the experimenter wants. This causes bias.

Describe and assess ethical guidelines for the use of human participants

The issue of ethical guidelines for human participants was covered in the social approach and extended in the psychodynamic approach. To make sure that your work is ethical, you will have reviewed the guidelines when carrying out practicals. Some guidelines for the use of human participants are listed briefly here:

- British Psychological Society (BPS) guidelines are to be followed for all research in psychology. In March 2006, a new *Code of Ethics and Moral Conduct* was produced by the BPS.

Study hint The learning approach uses animals in experiments, so also review the guidelines for the use of animals (see Chapter 4).

- All participants have the right to withdraw their data both throughout the study and at the end.
- Informed consent should be obtained before the study starts. If consent cannot be fully informed, because that would affect the study, then this must be made clear to participants who should be debriefed to make sure that everything is fully understood.
- A debrief at the end of the study must be given to check that participants do not want to withdraw their data, to make sure that they leave in the same state as when they started and to make sure that they have no questions or anxieties. The debrief is also to make sure that they have understood what the study is about and how the data will be used.
- The researcher must be competent to carry out the study and must check with other competent individuals to make sure that ethical guidelines are being followed.
- There should preferably be no deceit involved in the study. However, where there has to be some deceit because of the nature of the study, then a debrief must fully explain the issues and participants must be happy about having been deceived.

Examination-style questions

1 Outline an example of an overt participant observation, a covert participant observation, an overt non-participant observation and a covert non-participant observation (you can make up the examples). *(8 marks)*

2 Outline an actual study that is a laboratory experiment using animals. Give two ways in which ethical considerations are important for that study. *(8 marks)*

3 Outline two strengths and two weaknesses of observation as a research method in psychology. *(8 marks)*

Extension question

Choose one research method other than observation and compare it with observation in terms of strengths and weaknesses. Include issues of validity, reliability, generalisability and credibility in your answer. *(12 marks)*

Content

The learning approach comprises classical conditioning, operant conditioning and social learning theories. You need to know:
- some of the main features of the three theories
- one therapy from either classical or operant conditioning, so that you can apply the ideas and see how they can be used to help people
- how operant conditioning and social learning theory explain gender development and behaviour

You have to able to evaluate explanations for gender development and behaviour and compare the explanations given by the learning, biological and psychodynamic approaches.

Main features of classical conditioning

Classical conditioning is a theory of learning that examines how a response is associated with a stimulus to cause conditioning. It is illustrated by Pavlov's work with dogs.

Stimulus–response learning

A stimulus is something that produces a response. In classical conditioning, the response is either a reflex or an automatic behaviour. The stimulus is what is done to the person or animal; the response is how the person or animal responds to the stimulus. Neither classical nor operant conditioning examine what happens between the stimulus and the response — they do not consider cognitive (thinking) processes. Classical conditioning is a stimulus–response (S–R) theory.

Explore When considering stimulus–response learning, it is sometimes said that between the stimulus and the response there is a 'black box'. This is because learning theories do not look at what happens between the stimulus and the response, which could be cognitive processing. Use the internet or some other source to look up this idea of a 'black box'. A similar idea associated with the learning approach is that people are born a 'blank slate' ('tabula rasa' in Latin) and develop only through their learning experiences. Research the idea of a 'blank slate'. The ideas of a 'black box' and a 'blank slate' are useful when discussing learning theories.

In classical conditioning, the responses to stimuli are reflex actions, i.e. they are *involuntary* responses. Examples include blinking to a puff of air, knee jerking to a tap on the correct part of the knee, sneezing because of certain stimuli, showing a startle response (fear) to, maybe, a noise, and a fight-or-flight response when there is a threat.

Classical conditioning explains how someone can be conditioned into a response from a stimulus that is not the one that would naturally produce that response. For example, if you sneeze when flowers are in the room, and your aunt's house always has flowers, you may 'learn' to sneeze whenever you see your aunt because you associate her with the flowers and the flowers lead to the response of sneezing. A diagram is a good way to explain the process of classical conditioning and the example of Pavlov's dogs will show you how the idea came about.

Figure 5.1 illustrates classical conditioning processes:
■ The process starts with an **unconditioned stimulus** (UCS) that automatically provokes an **unconditioned response** (UCR). The stimulus and the response are called unconditioned because the response is bound to happen, e.g. a dog salivating (dribbling) in response to food.

- The **unconditioned stimulus** (UCS) is then paired (+) with a **conditioned stimulus** (CS). This will be the conditioned stimulus (CS) although at first, before conditioning is complete, it is a neutral stimulus (NS) so is sometimes called that. In one of Pavlov's studies, the CS/NS was a bell. The unconditioned stimulus (UCS) still gives the **unconditioned response** (UCR) as before, which is salivation.
- After a few pairings, the conditioned stimulus (CS) on its own produces the response of salivation. The response is now a **conditioned response** (CR) — it is conditioned to occur in response to the stimulus of the bell alone.

Figure 5.1 *Classical conditioning*

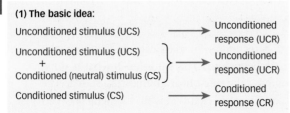 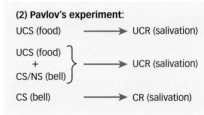

Figure 5.2 *The Little Albert conditioning experiment*

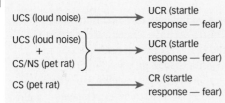

Some other examples of classical conditioning are explained later when therapies are considered (page 325). Another example is explained in the study of Little Albert by Watson and Rayner (1920) (page 355). Figure 5.2 shows Little Albert's conditioning experiences. Little Albert was a baby who learned to fear a pet white rat as part of an experiment.

> **Explore** Conditioning can be found in a number of situations, some of which lead to problems for the individual. For example, prisoners of war can be conditioned into fearing whatever was associated with fear in the prison camp. It has been suggested that soldiers in the war in Iraq learned to fear the smells round about them. On returning home, similar smells brought back the horrors of the experiences and the fear, i.e. Gulf War syndrome. Use the internet or some other source to look up such incidents and see how classical conditioning might have been the way responses were learned. Of course, Gulf War syndrome could have a physical cause unconnected with conditioning. Consider the different explanations, including classical conditioning, and the effects on the individuals concerned.

Extinction and spontaneous recovery

As well as the main principles there are other aspects of classical conditioning, for example:

- **Extinction** — how does the conditioning disappear?
- **Spontaneous recovery** — if the conditioning has disappeared can it reappear?

Extinction

Extinction occurs when the association between the unconditioned stimulus (UCS) and the conditioned stimulus (CS) no longer occurs; after a few trials of separating the two stimuli, the learned response is extinguished. In one of Pavlov's examples, the bell was no longer rung when the food was presented. After a little while, the dog did not salivate to the sound of the bell alone — the association was extinguished.

Spontaneous recovery

After extinction, the association sometimes recurs for no apparent reason. The conditioned stimulus (e.g. the bell) suddenly produces the response (e.g. salivation) that was conditioned previously. The reappearance of a conditioned response is called spontaneous recovery. For example, if you have a startle response (fear) to loud noises and were shopping when there was an incident nearby involving shouting and some disturbance, you might learn a fear of shopping. If you then went shopping (you might need help to achieve this) and there was no noise or disturbance, then you could unlearn the association (this is not easy to achieve if a person has a phobia). This would mean that your fear response to shopping has been extinguished. However, it might suddenly reappear at a later date without the noise, which would be spontaneous recovery.

Unit 2

Practice 5.2

Think of other occasions when a response might be learned in this way. Consider how advertising (page 362) aims to make an association between a conditioned stimulus (the product) and a response (e.g. salivation to a certain brand of chocolate or a 'sexual' response to a product). Maybe you can think of an association that you or someone else has made, such as a fear. When you have thought of one or two examples of learning by classical conditioning, draw a diagram to represent the processes.

An example answer is given at the end of Chapter 5.

Main features of operant conditioning

Operant conditioning differs from classical conditioning because it considers the learning of *voluntary*, rather than involuntary, behaviour. The idea is that when people behave in a particular way and are rewarded for that behaviour, then they will repeat it; if they are punished for it, they will stop the behaviour. Operant conditioning also differs from classical conditioning because the consequences come after the response whereas in classical conditioning the stimulus comes before the response.

Reinforcement and punishment

Reinforcement is the central feature of operant conditioning. The theory identifies two types of reinforcement, both of which encourage repetition of the desired behaviour:

■ **Positive reinforcement** is when something desired (a reward) is given in response to a behaviour, e.g. if children tidy their rooms as asked and are given additional pocket money as a reward. They have been reinforced to tidy their rooms because they want to receive the additional pocket money.

Understanding the Individual

327

■ **Negative reinforcement** is when something undesired is taken away in response to a behaviour, e.g. if people do not like the loud music in one restaurant, they will go to a quieter restaurant instead. They have been reinforced to go to the other restaurant because they want to avoid the loud music.

Punishment is different from reinforcement because it is discouraging behaviour, not encouraging it. Negative reinforcement encourages behaviour to avoid something unpleasant. **Punishment** means doing something unpleasant to stop the behaviour, e.g. a child who is behaving badly in a shop (perhaps shouting at a parent) might be punished by not being allowed to play with his or her friend as arranged previously. This is to stop the child behaving badly. An issue here is that punishment does not help to achieve the desired behaviour, it only stops undesired behaviour. Therefore, it is not usually recommended. If it is the only attention someone gets, then punishment can be rewarding, which is another reason for it not usually being used in therapy or when wanting to change someone's behaviour.

Table 5.14 *Positive reinforcement, negative reinforcement and punishment*

Feature of operant conditioning	How behaviour is elicited
Positive reinforcement	A reward of something good is given because of the behaviour. The behaviour is repeated
Negative reinforcement	The reward of the removal of something unpleasant is given because of the behaviour. The behaviour is repeated
Punishment	Something unpleasant happens because of the behaviour. The behaviour is not repeated

Practice 5.3

For each of following three examples of behaviour decide whether it is an example of positive reinforcement, negative reinforcement or punishment.

Behaviour 1 John continues with his driving lessons because the instructor says he is doing very well and will soon pass his test.

Behaviour 2 Jenny stops going to her driving lessons because she does not like how the instructor criticises her.

Behaviour 3 Jean's driving instructor shouts at her for going through a red light so she does not do it again.

Answers are at the end of Chapter 5.

Punishment versus negative reinforcement

It was suggested above that a child could be punished for shouting at a parent by not being allowed to play with a friend. Perhaps on another occasion, the child behaves well in order to avoid being prevented from playing with his or her friend, so he or she is allowed to play with the friend. In this example, the child's behaviour was negatively reinforced — the child behaved well in order to avoid something that he or she did not like. So, if the child behaves well, that is through negative reinforcement; if the child stops behaving badly, that is through punishment. The difference is whether or not the punishment is given. If it is given, that is punishment. If it is avoided by behaving differently, that is negative reinforcement.

How operant conditioning is studied

Skinner (e.g. 1935) is a key researcher linked with developing the theory of operant conditioning. He used animals so that he could isolate measurable behaviour and reinforce it in various ways to investigate the effect(s). For example, he developed various ways of reinforcing rats using food pellets, which, because the rats were hungry, rewarded them. His apparatus included levers and coloured lights. He could vary the conditions so that, for example, food was only released if the rat pulled the lever when a red light was on and not when a green light was on. The rats quickly learnt to press the lever when the red light was on.

Thorndike (e.g. 1911) also carried out experiments to examine operant conditioning principles. He used a puzzle box with a single exit that could only be opened by a system of levers. A cat was placed in the box and food was placed just outside the box. The cat moved around in the box, trying to get out because of the food. When moving about, the cat accidentally pressed levers and gradually learned by trial and error how to open the box. Then the cat could get the food, which was the reward. This sort of learning, in which the solution is hit upon by trial and error, and a reward is given so that the behaviour is repeated, is called '**trial-and-error**' learning. Thorndike stated that this was the **law of effect** — if the effect of the learning (to get out of the box) is good (obtains food) then the behaviour is learned and repeated. Learning takes place because of what happens after the action.

Figure 5.3 A drawing of a Skinner box showing a typical experiment using a rat, a light and a lever with food as a reward

Figure 5.4 A drawing of the type of box used by Thorndike

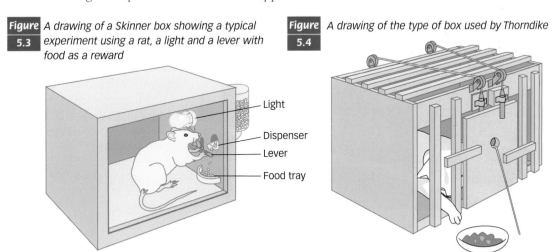

- Light
- Dispenser
- Lever
- Food tray

Skinner's studies using rats and other animals, and Thorndike's work with cats are both examples of positive reinforcement because the animals are carrying out the behaviour to obtain a reward. Another study about rewards and reinforcement (Skinner 1948) is covered in the Studies in detail section of this chapter. *Another example (Pickens and Thompson 1968) is summarised later in this chapter and covered in more detail on the CD-ROM.*

Shaping behaviour

One important aspect of operant conditioning is that the complete desired behaviour may not be exhibited immediately so that it can be reinforced. The outcome (the desired behaviour) might have to be shaped by reinforcing steps towards that behaviour. **Shaping** is when behaviour is arrived at by:

- rewarding moves towards the desired behaviour
- then, waiting for an action that is nearer to the desired behaviour
- finally, waiting for the actual behaviour before offering the reinforcement

For example, for an advertisement, a squirrel was taught to conquer an assault course. The whole course could not be achieved in one attempt. It was necessary to reward each part of the course until the squirrel had learnt the whole course, i.e. shaping was used. Similarly, teaching a pigeon to roll a ball towards small pins (as in tenpin bowling) can be achieved by shaping. At first the pigeon is rewarded for pecking near to the ground; the reinforcement is then withheld until the pecking is near the ball. Subsequently, the reward (food) is not given until the ball is hit. Then the ball has to be hit in the right direction before food is given, and so on, until the ball hits the pins.

Explore Thorndike explained the law of effect and also put forward other laws. Use the internet or some other source to investigate Thorndike's research into operant conditioning.

A pigeon in an operant conditioning study in which the pigeon learns to peck an object to obtain food

Training orcas at Sea World

Explore Use the internet to find out how the principles of operant conditioning are used by some zoos and similar institutions to teach behaviour. Training at Sea World, for example, uses such principles.

Primary and secondary reinforcement

- **Primary reinforcement** — the reward is a basic need (food, drink, warmth and shelter). For example, when a pigeon pecks at a disk to obtain a food pellet, the food is a primary reinforcement.
- **Secondary reinforcement** — the reward is something that can satisfy a basic need but is not in itself a basic need. For example, when a child is given additional pocket money that in itself is not a basic need but it could be used buy a basic need, such as food.

Evaluating the use of animals in laboratory experiments

Both operant and classical conditioning use animals in laboratory experiments. Some practical issues are given here which you could use when evaluating theories that use animals in studies.

Reasons for behaviourists to use animals in experiments include:

- Animals are fairly easy to handle.
- In ethical terms, experiments can be carried out on animals that cannot be carried out on humans.
- Animals can learn something new, which it is fairly certain that they have not experienced before, so learning is testable.
- Laboratory studies mean strict controls.
- Objectivity can be achieved.
- Measurable stimuli and responses can be isolated from other experiences.
- Experiments are fairly easy to repeat and quite cheap (e.g. more animals can be obtained).
- Darwin's ideas about evolution suggested that animals could be studied and the findings applied to humans.

Problems with using animals in experiments include:

- There are brain differences between humans and animals, so generalisation is difficult.
- Ethically, the rights of animals must be acknowledged.
- It is not certain that animal learning is the same as human learning.
- There could be factors involved other than the stimulus–response situation set up by the experimenter.
- Animals do not have the same emotional responses as humans, which might affect generalisation of the findings to humans.
- Animals are different from each other and respond differently to different stimuli.
- Laboratory experimenters are not natural, so the findings are not valid.

Evaluation of operant and classical conditioning theories as explanations of human behaviour

Strengths

- In both operant and classical conditioning objective measures and careful controls are used when researching the concepts. Both theories are studied scientifically. Some behaviour is isolated and a way of measuring it is devised. The behaviour is then tested and, because of the controls, scientific conclusions can be drawn. For example, Skinner (operant conditioning):
  - isolated animals in a cage, to control all variables other than the independent variable
  - varied the independent variable in such a way that the differences being introduced were clear
  - measured the dependent variable carefully

In this way, cause-and-effect conclusions could be drawn.

> **Study hint** You need to be able to evaluate operant conditioning as an explanation of gender behaviour. Evaluation of both operant and classical conditioning is covered here to help your understanding.

Unit 2

■ Both types of conditioning can be used in therapy (see pages 325 and 327) and so have real-life applications to society. Therefore, they are useful theories.

Weaknesses

■ Both operant and classical conditioning mainly involved animals. The differences between humans and animals make it difficult to draw conclusions from animal studies and generalise the results to humans. For example, cats may learn to get out of a puzzle box by trial and error and, once rewarded, they may repeat the behaviour to get more rewards. However, humans would be likely to use problem-solving techniques together with previous experience to work out how to open the box, which is not trial-and-error learning. Therefore, generalising findings from animal studies to say they apply to humans may not be useful.

■ Both operant and classical conditioning theories — partly because the studies use animals and partly because the studies are experiments — lack validity. Studies isolate behaviour to investigate it scientifically, which means reducing such behaviour to a small part of 'normal' activities, so the results are not true to life. The situation is not valid because laboratories are used; the concepts might not be valid if they apply just to small parts of overall behaviour.

| Table 5.15 | Strengths and weaknesses of operant and classical conditioning theories as explanations of human behaviour |

Strengths	Weaknesses
● Studies use experimental method and controls so they are scientific and cause-and-effect conclusions can be drawn ● Both can be applied in therapies and so they have practical applications	● Studies use animals, so generalisability and credibility are in doubt ● Studies are laboratory experiments and use animals, so validity is in doubt

Treatments/therapies and operant and classical conditioning

You need to know one treatment or therapy that uses the principles of either operant or classical conditioning. Three therapies are suggested in the specification; all three are explained here to help you choose. Study all three therapies, because this will help you to understand how the two types of conditioning work and you will be able to use them as examples. If you wish, you could choose a different therapy.

Systematic desensitisation

Systematic desensitisation is based on the principles of classical conditioning. Classical conditioning theory indicates how a stimulus and an involuntary response are associated. One such response is a **phobia**, which is a fear response thought to be acquired through classical conditioning processes. A phobia is not just any fear:

■ It is a fear that prevents normal functioning in life.
■ It is irrational, and the phobic person needs treatment to help overcome the fear.

One way of overcoming a phobia is to use systematic desensitisation (SD), which was developed by Wolpe, a South African psychiatrist. It is sometimes called **graduated exposure therapy**.

Systematic desensitisation involves a step-by-step approach (systematic) to get the person used to the phobic object or situation (desensitised). The idea is that the phobia has been learned through classical conditioning, so it can be unlearned in the same way. Instead of the fear response to the phobic object or situation, a relaxed response is required. People are taught to relax their muscles (not easy to learn) and they are then introduced gradually to the object or situation. People might also be taught to imagine happy scenarios, meditate, and maybe to try and change their thinking about the phobic object; these ideas focus on reducing the anxiety and replacing it with a relaxed response.

The gradual introduction involves a hierarchy — from a slight introduction (e.g. a photograph), through to a little more exposure (e.g. a film) and so on, through to the real object or situation. Individuals undergoing therapy set up the hierarchy for themselves, so that it is meaningful for them. If people relax at each stage, then they should be relaxed with the object present. Systematic desensitisation is also used to treat anxiety disorders other than phobias. Figure 5.5 shows how a phobia of going out shopping can be explained using classical conditioning principles; Figure 5.6 shows the result of a systematic desensitisation process to overcome the phobia.

| **Figure 5.5** | *How a phobia of going out shopping is explained using classical conditioning principles* |

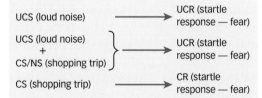

| **Figure 5.6** | *The final stage of systematic desensitisation to overcome a 'shopping' phobia* |

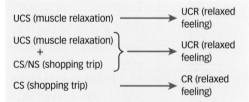

A fear of going out (e.g. to go shopping) can be limiting and can be diagnosed as a phobia. Having agreed to systematic desensitisation, sufferers learn to relax. While relaxing, the idea of going out a short distance is introduced, then going a little further, going with someone on a bus, and so on, until they manage eventually to go shopping alone, which is the goal.

Explore The specific example of fear of going out shopping is given here as a phobia. However, if someone has agoraphobia, which means fear going out at all, then systematic desensitisation has been found to be less effective, perhaps because the phobia is so general. It is not easy to test the effectiveness of systematic desensitisation. Research this area using the internet or some other source.

Some issues with systematic desensitisation

- Although the therapy can be shown to work using classical conditioning principles, there are also operant conditioning principles at work. People with phobias avoid the phobic object or situation. The phobic object or situation is unpleasant; the individual avoids it through negative reinforcement. Systematic desensitisation

could work because the object or situation is no longer unpleasant, and so no longer needs to be avoided. This is an alternative explanation of why systematic desensitisation works. However, it does not explain the phobia as thoroughly as classical conditioning because it does not explain why the phobic object or situation became unpleasant in the first place.

■ Although systematic desensitisation is usually thought to be a therapy based on the learning approach and learning theory, an element of the cognitive approach is involved when the relaxation is being taught. For example, to relax, the individual is taught to think differently about the phobic object. Systematic desensitisation has sometimes been referred to as a cognitive behavioural therapy because of this element. However, as the concept is based firmly on classical conditioning principles, it is considered in AS psychology as a therapy based on behaviourism and learning theory.

Evaluation of systematic desensitisation as a therapy: strengths

■ Compared with other therapies that deal with phobias (e.g. flooding), systematic desensitisation is a fairly ethical procedure. Flooding involves 'immersing' a person with a phobia in his/her fear until he/she becomes more calm. The principle is that maintaining fear uses energy, and the energy will run out with time.

> **Explore** Use the internet or some other source to research into the use of flooding as a therapy for phobias.

■ Systematic desensitisation has a clear rationale based on classical conditioning principles. Therefore it can be explained to people, which can give them confidence that the therapy will work. This does not *make* the therapy more successful, but if it is more likely to be accepted, then that is more successful. If the explanation for the phobia follows the same principles as the therapy, then this makes sense.

■ The therapy has been shown to work. For example, a study in Spain (Capafons et al. 1998) showed that systematic desensitisation was successful in overcoming a fear of flying. The programme had three phases and the focus was on relaxation by stopping negative thoughts about flying:
 – The first phase was training in relaxation and imagination.
 – The second phase focused on setting up the hierarchy for travelling by plane.
 – The third phase was the presentation of the hierarchy along with the focus on stopping negative thoughts.
There were 20 patients with 21 other people in a control group. Success was measured by self-report, interview and recording biological factors when the patients were in a simulated situation. The results showed that the programme worked.

Evaluation of systematic desensitisation as a therapy: weaknesses

■ There are other factors besides classical conditioning involved, e.g. operant conditioning principles and cognitive processing. This does not make the therapy less successful, but does question the reasoning behind it.

- Although systematic desensitisation is useful for phobias and anxiety disorders it is not useful for other mental health issues, such as psychoses. The individual needs to be able to learn to relax and has to be involved in the whole process; not everyone can do this.

Table 5.16 *Strengths and weaknesses of systematic desensitisation*

Strengths	Weaknesses
• It is more ethical than other therapies for phobias (e.g. flooding) because it involves a gradual exposure to phobic objects or situations and individuals are involved fully in their therapy	• Not everyone can learn to relax and take such a central part in therapy; it is only useful for some mental health issues, and not, for example, for psychoses
• The therapy has a clear rationale based on classical conditioning that can both explain the phobia or anxiety and also remove it	• There are issues such as operant conditioning principles and cognitive processes being involved, so the explanation — resting on classical conditioning — is not the whole story
• Studies show that the therapy is successful (e.g. Capafons et al. 1998 showed that it helped to overcome a fear of flying)	

Aversion therapy

Aversion therapy is based on classical conditioning principles. It is used for addictions, e.g. addiction to alcohol. Other areas in which aversion therapy is used include using nasty-tasting substances on the fingernails to discourage nail biting and using electric shocks to discourage certain types of behaviour.

Aversion therapy uses the principles of classical conditioning. The therapy replaces the pleasure response with an aversion response (e.g. pain or something unpleasant).

Using the example of alcoholism, in order to be free from the addiction, the pleasure response given by alcohol has to be replaced by an aversion response. In treating alcoholism, a pre-scribed emetic drug (that makes people feel, or be, sick) is paired with the alcohol. After a few trials, alcohol will make the person feel sick even in the absence of the drug.

Figure 5.7 *Aversion therapy used to treat alcoholism*

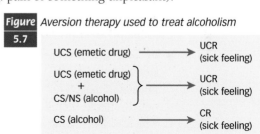

It is important that during the therapy people drink soft drinks, so that they are not conditioned to feel sick in response to all drinks.

Study hint Sometimes, to treat alcoholism, a drug is prescribed that people are told will make them ill, so they don't drink because they fear being ill. However, this treatment does not use classical conditioning principles because the alcohol is not paired with an involuntary action (feeling sick), rather with a cognitive thought. It is important to note that classical conditioning involves only involuntary actions. Always check that the behaviour being conditioned is involuntary.

Explore Aversion therapy was discussed on the website of the American Society of Addiction Medicine in 2003 (www.asam.org). Use this website or some other source to find out more about the therapy.

Aversion therapy and homosexuality

Aversion therapy has been used (and still is, in some situations) to try to convert homosexuals to heterosexuality. In 1994, the American Psychological Assocation (APA) said that aversion therapy is dangerous and does not work. From 2006, the use of aversion therapy to treat homosexuality has been said to violate the APA codes of practice. Its use for that purpose is illegal in some countries.

When used to 'help' homosexual men become heterosexual, electric shocks were given when the men looked at images of naked men; no shocks were given when they looked at images of naked women. The idea was to change their conditioning, so pain was paired with looking at images of naked men but not with images of naked women.

One gay man, Billy Clegg-Hill, was reported to have died from coma and convulsions caused by injections of apomorphine that were given to make him sick during aversion therapy. The aim was to get him to pair sickness with images of naked men in order to 'cure' him. This case was reported in 1996, although it occurred in the 1960s. He did not volunteer for therapy; he was arrested for homosexuality and sentenced by a judge to compulsory treatment. Aversion therapy features in some films, including *One Flew Over the Cuckoo's Nest* and *Clockwork Orange*.

> **Explore** An important aspect of psychology is how studies and knowledge change over time and how social issues are addressed at different times in history. For example, homosexuality used to be considered a mental illness and at one time it was also illegal. Use the internet or some other source to investigate this issue, partly to help in understanding aversion therapy and partly to see how things have changed.

Evaluation of aversion therapy: strengths

- In some situations aversion therapy has been shown to be successful. Follow-up studies have shown that it achieved better abstinence rates (people stopped the undesired behaviour) than other treatments. Those receiving aversion therapy did not discharge themselves more frequently than patients on other programmes, which indicates that ethical problems with this therapy are no greater than with other therapies. In spite of criticisms on ethical grounds, aversion therapy has been claimed to work well. Seligman (1966) said that 50% of gay men who received the therapy did not continue homosexual practices.
- It rests on a clear theoretical explanation of how the behaviour being treated came about. A therapy that has a clear rationale is likely to be more acceptable to people — bearing in mind that today such therapy is neither part of a punishment nor a legal requirement.

Evaluation of aversion therapy: weaknesses

- As Seligman later reported, most of the men studied when he reported that the therapy was successful were bisexual. When true homosexual males were studied, the treatment was much less successful. Other studies have suggested a 99.5% failure rate and at least one gay man has died.

- There are ethical issues involved in using aversion therapy because those administering the therapy have power over the patient. Patients may be asked to give permission for the therapy to take place but they may not feel that they have the power to decline. As was seen when the therapy was used for homosexuality, society decides which behaviours are acceptable and which ought to be changed.

Table 5.17 *Strengths and weaknesses of aversion therapy*

Strengths	Weaknesses
• Studies have shown greater success than with other therapies; in 1966, Seligman reported a 50% success rate (later questioned because the sample may have been biased)	• According to some studies, the success rate is almost negligible; one gay man died from a drug administered as part of the therapy
• The therapy rests on the clear rationale of classical conditioning; therefore, it can be explained to patients, which might help them when choosing the therapy	• Ethics are important, particularly given that the patient is unlikely to be the one with control over the situation

Token economy programmes

Token economy programmes are based on operant conditioning principles. Operant conditioning theory has led to the development of ways to help people change their learning by using rewards as reinforcements. You may have watched television programmes in which families with disruptive children are helped to enable the family to function better. The advice is usually to reward good behaviour and to ignore unwanted behaviour — perhaps, if a young child is involved, by using a 'naughty step', where the child has to stay while being ignored for a set amount of time, rather than being punished. One method of shaping behaviour, based on operant conditioning, is the token economy programme (TEP).

Token economy programmes can be used in prisons, mental health units and schools. The aim is to obtain the desired behaviour through a system of rewards:
- The tokens act as rewards and can be used to purchase something that is desired — this is the 'token' part of the therapy.
- People are 'paid' in tokens as a reward for acting in a desired way — this is the 'economy' part of the therapy.
- It is a 'programme' because there has to be a plan — the people involved have to be clear about what is to be rewarded and by how much each time.

Rewards have to be given consistently by all the staff involved. People involved in the programme have to understand what they have to do to gain the rewards and how they can exchange them. Token economy programmes are used in schools when other reinforcements (classroom rewards and teacher attention) have not worked. For example, they can be used for children with attention deficit disorder. The tokens can be chips or stars, for example, or points.

These are the steps in using a token economy programme:

Step 1: Identify the behaviour that has to be changed
A few behaviours are selected to be changed. The behaviours must be outlined clearly

and everyone involved in the programme must understand them. If possible, they should be positive — asking people to 'remain quiet at meal times' is better than asking them 'not to shout at meal times'. It is the positive behaviour that is desired, rather than just the absence of the negative behaviour. The behaviour must also be observable, so that everyone is clear when it occurs and what is to be rewarded.

Step 2: Select the tokens and decide what they can be exchanged for
Actual plastic tokens can be useful, but points can be used. Decide how to give them out if they are tokens, and where they should be kept. If they are points, decide how to record them clearly.

Step 3: Make sure that the tokens or points 'buy' significant rewards
It is important that the rewards have meaning for the individual concerned and that they are worthwhile. Individuals could maybe help to make a list of what they would like. If what the tokens or points buy is not rewarding enough, there will be no motivation to perform the behaviour.

Step 4: Set goals that are achievable
The individuals involved need to know what they have to do to earn the tokens or points. The goals should be achievable, but not necessarily easy. They can be adjusted as the behaviour improves. Knowing what is to be rewarded is not difficult if it is a particular behaviour, but if it is a percentage improvement in something, then this must be clear to everyone.

Step 5: Explain the whole programme to the individuals concerned
The programme must be clear to the individuals so that they know what the tokens are for and can repeat the behaviour to gain more tokens. If they are not clear what the desired behaviour or goal is, then the programme is not likely to work.

Step 6: Feedback on progress
Individuals need feedback on their progress and, if they are not doing the correct thing to earn the token, they need guidance. There can be some element of punishment, such as **response cost** — tokens are either withheld or taken away for undesirable behaviour. It is recommended that this only happens after a few weeks of the programme. Response cost can also be used if part of a goal has not been met, rather than just if undesirable behaviour is shown.

Step 7: Provide the reward
At some stage, there must be a time for the tokens or points to be exchanged for rewards. If no tokens have been earned, there should be no fuss about the individual not getting a token; the person should just be informed that a token has not been achieved. No critical comments should be made.

Step 8: Reviewing the programme
As people make progress, goals can be reviewed. People might also be given more tokens or the tokens could be exchanged more often. There should be praise to go with the programme. If there is no further progress, an earlier goal can be returned to.

Explore Barkley (1990) has discussed the use of token economy programmes in schools. Investigate the work of Barkley to find out more about such programmes. Azrin has also been involved in the development of such programmes, so investigate her work.

Evaluation of the use of the token economy programme: strengths

- The token economy programme has been seen to work — and quickly. O'Leary and O'Leary (1976) point out that such programmes work in schools. The powerful incentives produce the desired behaviour, possibly because the recognition is immediate and tokens may be given at the time of the desired behaviour.
- The programme can be adjusted to suit each individual. The rewards the tokens buy can be personal and the goals can be set individually. This is a therapy that can be focused clearly; it is not a group therapy. If necessary, each individual can be rewarded differently. Therefore, the programme is likely to be more successful because it can address specific difficulties.

Evaluation of the use of the token economy programme: weaknesses

- The system is time consuming. In schools, formal token programmes are used by only about 30% of teachers. The system requires an investment of time, which is difficult when staff are busy. If staff do not all focus on the programme, then it is likely to fail.
- The programme is targeted at a certain situation. Once outside that situation, the individual may not exhibit the shaped behaviour. Therefore, the programme might have limited application. For example, in a prison setting, the person may behave as desired but that behaviour may not be exhibited in the outside world.

Table 5.18 *Strengths and weaknesses of the token economy programme*

Strengths	Weaknesses
• It has been found to work in schools (O'Leary and O'Leary 1976); this is possibly because the rewards are immediate and powerful • The programme can be aimed at individuals; therefore, it is likely to be successful because it will focus on their goals and the rewards can be tailored around individual needs and preferences	• There are practical difficulties; for example, the programme is time-consuming and all staff have to work together cohesively, which is not easy to achieve • The behaviour may not generalise to a situation outside where the programme is run, which limits the application of the therapy

Main features of social learning theory

The third main type of learning, apart from classical and operant conditioning, is social learning. Social learning theory (SLT) explains that learning can occur by observation, imitation and modelling.

Observation, imitation and modelling

Social learning theory was developed by Bandura, one of whose studies is explained in the next section. It seemed clear that not all behaviour was conditioned because some behaviour appeared without conditioning. So, alongside (not replacing) operant conditioning, social learning theory suggests that people learn by observing others. This is

Explore Use the internet or some other source to look up Mineka's work with monkeys, where observational learning can be found. This will help to illustrate the principles of social learning theory.

observational learning — people watch what others do and copy their actions, thus learning new behaviours. Some animals, e.g. monkeys, have been found to use observational learning as well.

There are steps in observational learning:

- First, the behaviour is **modelled** by a role model. A **role model** may be a parent, a friend, someone in a peer group, a media personality or any person who is significant in some way. A role model tends to have some importance for the observer.
- The observer **identifies** with the role model.
- The behaviour is **observed** and noted.
- The behaviour is **imitated** and so it is learned. Whether it is repeated again depends on reinforcements and rewards.

Not all behaviour is imitated; it depends on the model and also on the consequences of the observed behaviour. If the model's behaviour is seen to be punished then it might not be imitated; if it is seen to be rewarded, it is more likely to be imitated. Reinforcement is motivational and people are more likely to imitate behaviour if they are motivated to do so, possibly because of the likelihood of rewards. Social learning theory, therefore, accepts an element of thinking in the processes of learning, which was not considered in either classical or operant conditioning theories. 'Modelling' entails the role model being identified with and involved as well as meaning the role model 'demonstrating' the behaviour.

Cognitive processes in observational learning

There are cognitive elements involved in observational learning. When observing, the learner has to pay attention to the important, not the incidental, parts of the action, and has to record the information in memory, which younger children may find more difficult than older children. Motivation is also important as the consequences of the action for the role model are involved in deciding whether or not to carry out the behaviour. The child must also have the physical ability to carry out the action. Therefore, the issues that govern whether a modelled behaviour is imitated are that:

- it is observed
- it is attended to
- it is stored in memory
- it is rewarded in such a way that there is motivation to reproduce the action

Behaviour that is learned through observation may not be exhibited until some time after the learning has taken place.

Results of studies showing the most likely occasions when behaviour is imitated

Bandura carried out studies to investigate when children are likely to imitate behaviour. He found that:

- Aggressive male models are imitated more than aggressive females. This may show relevance — aggression is seen as more appropriate in males in the US society in which Bandura worked.

- Boys are more likely than girls to imitate an aggressive male model. This shows relevance — male models are more relevant to boys.
- Role models that show consistency are more likely to be imitated. If a person says one thing and does another (inconsistency), this is confusing. Actions are imitated more than words.
- Boys tend to show physical aggression when they imitate aggression and girls tend to be more aggressive verbally.

Vicarious learning

Vicarious reinforcement is a term used to explain that reinforcement can occur through others being reinforced. Vicarious reinforcement is connected with observational learning — social learning theory explains that learning takes place through direct reinforcement *and* indirect (vicarious) reinforcement. It examines how imitation is affected by perceived reinforcements and punishments. Examples include:
- vicarious reinforcement — a person works hard because a colleague has been rewarded for hard work
- vicarious punishment — someone does not park in a particular place because he or she has seen someone get a parking ticket there
- vicarious extinction — people stop doing something because they have seen that people are not rewarded for doing it

There are four aspects to vicarious reinforcement:
- the **modelling effect** — people copy directly a behaviour that they would not have carried out before seeing it modelled
- the **eliciting effect** — the observer copies the behaviour, but slightly differently
- the **disinhibiting effect** — someone who would not normally carry out a particular action does so after seeing someone else do it with no negative consequences
- the **inhibitory effect** — people stop doing something because they see a role model being punished for the behaviour

Important factors in vicarious learning

Models are more likely to be imitated:
- if they are similar to the observers. However, similarity is in the mind of the observer, e.g. a girl might imitate a celebrity who she thinks she is similar to, even though others would not recognise the similarity
- if they are perceived by the observers as important or prestigious
- if the behaviour is observable — the more observable the behaviour, the more likely it is to be imitated

Evaluation of social learning theory as an explanation of human behaviour

Evaluating a theory helps in understanding and is useful when applying the theory to a situation. For example, social learning theory is used to explain why violence on television seems to be imitated. In order to evaluate this, it is necessary to be able to evaluate the theory itself as an explanation of human behaviour.

Strengths

■ There is a great deal of experimental evidence to support social learning. Much of this is the work of Bandura, but others have also found that behaviour is observed and then imitated. It is not difficult to set up a situation in which a distinctive behaviour is modelled and then to watch to see if it is imitated, as it often is. This has been found in studies with children and with some animal species.

■ The theory is useful in explaining human behaviour and can be applied as a therapy. For example, obsessive compulsive disorder is sometimes treated by using operant conditioning principles and shaping. One piece of obsessive behaviour is chosen and the patient is rewarded for not carrying out that behaviour. Observational learning can be used alongside the system of rewards. Someone the patient trusts can carry out the desired behaviour and the patient can see that the consequences are not unpleasant. For example, people with obsessive compulsive disorder may not be able to touch things without afterwards washing their hands many times. Someone trusted can keep touching an object without hand washing so that it can be seen that there are no bad consequences.

Weaknesses

■ Behaviour might not be exhibited immediately. Therefore, it is difficult to test for observational learning. Experiments show only specific behaviours at a specific time, so the results are limited and there might be a lack of validity in the findings.

■ Some experiments are carried out on animals. Therefore, there are the usual issues involved in claiming that behaviour shown by animals is also true of humans, given the differences between them.

> The animals used are often monkeys and chimpanzees, which are close to humans in evolutionary terms. So the evidence from animals could be quite strong.

Table 5.19 *Strengths and weaknesses of social learning theory as an explanation of human behaviour*

Strengths	Weaknesses
● There is a great deal of experimental evidence to support the theory and the behaviour that is learned is visible, so the evidence is strong	● There might be a lack of validity as the behaviour might not be exhibited immediately, so it might be thought that no learning had taken place, when, in fact, it had
● The theory gives rise to practical applications such as in therapy and in explaining, for example, why violence on television or in media games might be copied	● Studies are often carried out on animals and it can be difficult to generalise to humans from animal studies

The learning approach and gender development

The learning approach draws on operant conditioning and social learning theory to explain gender behaviour and how it is learned. A main issue for the learning approach is that all behaviour is learned through experiences and interaction with the environment. The approach does not consider genetic influences or sex differences between males and females. The view of the learning approach is that any differences would be down to their learning experiences.

Reinforcement, behaviour shaping and gender development/behaviour

Operant-conditioning principles suggest that gender behaviour is shaped through patterns of reinforcement and punishment just like other behaviour. Even when first born, male and female babies are treated and reinforced differently. Little boys are seen as tough, strong and 'big'; little girls are seen as pretty, delicate and 'sweet'. Studies have been carried out in which babies have been dressed as the opposite sex to see how they are treated. In one study in a doctor's surgery, a mother was asked to look after a baby for a short time while the baby's mother went to see the doctor. The baby was 'wrongly' dressed. The babysitting mother was, for example, more likely to offer a hammer rattle to a 'boy' baby than to a 'girl' baby (Smith and Lloyd 1978). However, a review of 23 studies in which babies were dressed up as 'boys' or 'girls' (Stern and Karraker 1989) showed that adults did not always respond to the labelling, whereas young children did.

In general, learning theory suggests that according to the law of effect, people repeat an action if it is rewarded and do not repeat it if it is punished. Boys are more likely to be rewarded, possibly by attention rather than direct rewards, for 'male' behaviour in society; girls are more likely to be rewarded for 'female' behaviour. Children may be punished for inappropriate gender-specific behaviour. So, gender behaviour is learned though reinforcement and punishment. It can be shaped gradually by reinforcing certain behaviours, leading to an overall type of gender behaviour, just as language use is shaped by reinforcing sounds and gradually reinforcing only the correct words.

Modelling and gender development

Social learning theory also offers an explanation for gender development. Gender behaviour can develop through vicarious learning, although for this to happen a child would have to identify with one particular gender, which is not likely to be the case when very young. Adopting gender behaviour through observational learning can happen when a child is older. Bandura showed that boys are more likely to imitate male models and that girls copy female models. Social learning theory suggests that people imitate behaviour that they observe in people similar to themselves, which again emphasises gender. Behaviour that is rewarded is also likely to be repeated. Therefore, if children copy gender-appropriate behaviour (for which they are more likely to be rewarded — as shown by operant conditioning) then they are more likely to keep repeating that behaviour. Two issues that are important in observational learning are **relevance** and **identification**:

- Behaviour that is seen as **relevant** is likely to be imitated. Gender behaviour is likely to be seen as relevant, although this involves cognitive factors that are not explored in great detail by social learning theory.

- Observational learning occurs when the individual **identifies** with the model and copies the behaviour. Identification is more likely to occur with a relevant role model, who is likely to be someone of the same gender.

Evaluation of learning theories and how they explain gender development/behaviour

Gender behaviour can be explained by both operant-conditioning principles and social learning theory. Criticisms of both theories can be used as criticisms of their explanations for gender development; strengths of the theories can be used as strengths of their explanations for gender development.

Strengths

- Such learning can be observed. Observations have been carried out that show girls copying their mothers and boys copying their fathers, and the evidence for this sort of imitation is strong. Observations also show that girls and boys play with different toys and that the toys are gender specific for a culture. (However, this is not to say that the behaviour comes from observational learning or reinforcement. There is an issue here with whether a behaviour comes from nature or nurture. For example, girls might inherently prefer 'girl' activities). Overall, however, the strength of the explanations given by learning theory is that they investigate observable behaviour that can be tested using scientific and objective research methods and methodology. This is what behaviourism set out to do in the first place, and so is a strength of its explanations.
- Learning theories have been tested using animals and similar behaviour patterns have been found. If a behaviour can be replicated in a laboratory situation using animals then this is strong evidence for it taking place. Observational learning has been found in animals as well as in humans, which is additional evidence supporting the theory. Operant conditioning principles also work in some animal species. Although using animal studies to draw conclusions about humans has been criticised, they can be replicated and provide reliable evidence.

Weaknesses

- Learning theory explanations for gender behaviour cannot easily account for similarities across different societies with different norms and customs. If all gender behaviour is learned through imitation and reinforcement, then it would be expected that there would be different gender behaviour in societies with different customs — however, there are similarities. For example, there are developmental sequences that are similar between different cultures, such as when children first learn their gender identity.
- There are differences between male and female babies at birth. For example, girls seem to be more sensitive to noise than boys and this is unlikely to be learned. New-born baby girls maintain eye-contact with a speaking adult for longer than new-born boys. Girls maintain eye-contact with a silent adult differently than with a talking adult; boys do not show this difference. These are examples that do not seem to be learned because, for one thing, they occur too early in life

for learning to have taken place. Taken together, they tend to suggest different abilities or interests with regard to communication.

Table 5.20 *Strengths and weaknesses of learning explanations for gender behaviour*

Strengths	Weaknesses
• Learning explanations test observable behaviour in experimental conditions and so are developed using objective scientific method • Animal studies show that learning explanations can also explain animal behaviour and that such explanations are reliable	• Learning theory explanations should mean that different cultures exhibit different gender behaviour, but there are developmental sequences that are similar between cultures • In new-born babies, there are gender differences that cannot have been learned, so not all differences in gender behaviour can be explained by learning theories

An overview of explanations for gender development

Gender behaviour: the psychodynamic approach

Freud had a unique view of how children develop gender behaviour. He explained that boys, in order to resolve the Oedipus complex, identify with their fathers and take on their fathers' behaviour and moral code. This is because their feelings for their mothers produce guilt; it is only by 'becoming' their fathers that they can resolve this guilt. Girls identify with their mothers to avoid feelings of guilt, although in a slightly different way. So, from around the age of 4 or 5 years, children identify with their same-sex parents and take on their behaviour and code of behaviour.

Gender behaviour: the biological approach

The biological approach explains how gender behaviour comes from genes and hormones. Briefly, a male has an X and a Y chromosome; a female has two X chromosomes. These chromosomal differences lead to different development of the foetus. One resulting difference is in the amounts of hormones, e.g. males have more testosterone. These hormonal differences cause differences in development. They are the reasons for the development of physical differences, e.g. different genitalia and levels of body hair. There are also differences in the brains of males and females.

Study hint Gender development, sex differences and gender behaviour are not treated differently by your course because all three approaches discuss development in some form — they all consider gender behaviour across time as the child grows. The biological approach focuses on sex differences rather than gender behaviour only because 'sex' is the biological term and 'gender' is the 'social' term. There is, however, no need to differentiate between the two terms (development and behaviour).

Biological sex differences are present at birth (and before). They affect people throughout their lives and also interact with the environment. So, there is a strong focus on nature but also a focus on nurture. It seems that female babies are hardier, sleep and eat in more regular patterns, are more sensitive to pain, mature faster and are more socially responsive. Female babies are in general more cooperative. Male babies are more assertive, more ready for rough-and-tumble play and more restless. They tend to sleep less, be more active and cry more and be more difficult to pacify. There are also differences in temperament. Of course, male babies differ a great deal

from each other, as do female babies. There are innate factors other than sex differences that lead different children to develop in different ways.

Gender behaviour: the learning approach

One type of learning is operant conditioning, which claims that when a behaviour
is rewarded, it is repeated. Learning theories suggest that children learn gender
behaviour by imitating relevant role models, who tend to be the same gender as
themselves. They are also positively reinforced for appropriate gender behaviour
because it meets with approval; inappropriate gender behaviour meets with disap-
proval. They learn vicariously, which means that if the role model is reinforced for a
certain behaviour, the children are more likely to repeat it. As appropriate gender
behaviour in adults tends to be reinforced, children are more likely to imitate it.

Comparing the psychodynamic and biological approaches

Similarities between the psychodynamic and biological approaches are that they
both examine:

- biological features, e.g. inherited processes of personality development (id, ego
  and superego) in the psychodynamic approach and genes and hormones in the
  biological approach
- environmental influences, e.g. parents and society with regard to development
  of the superego for the psychodynamic approach and the influence on brain
  development of issues such as abuse in the biological approach
- nature and nurture with regard to development
- case studies such as Little Hans in the psychodynamic approach and the Money
  study in the biological approach

Differences between the psychodynamic and biological approaches include:

- The psychodynamic approach is about mental aspects (e.g. id, ego and superego);
  the biological approach is physiological (e.g. genes and hormones).
- The psychodynamic approach looks at gender development (e.g. norms and
  behaviour); the biological approach examines sex assignment.
- The psychodynamic approach cannot use scientific measures because the
  concepts (e.g. superego) are not measurable; the biological approach uses scientific measures of measurable aspects (e.g. chromosomes).
- The psychodynamic approach does not use animal studies; the biological approach
  uses animals to investigate, for example, the effects of hormones on brain
  development.

> **Study hint** If an exam question asks you to make comparisons, give points from both sides.
> For example, you could say that both the biological and psychodynamic approaches focus
> on biological differences. Or you could say that they both focus on biological aspects, with
> the biological approach looking at genes and hormones. Or you could say that they both
> focus on biological differences, with the biological approach looking at genes and
> hormones and the psychodynamic approach considering the id and the unconscious. This
> last point adds detail to the general comparison point about biological aspects and is
> more thorough.

Comparing the psychodynamic and learning approaches

Similarities between the psychodynamic and learning approaches include:

- They both look at development of behaviour according to norms. The psychodynamic approach looks at gender being related to same-sex parent behaviour; the learning approach looks at repeating behaviour that has been rewarded. Both these types of behaviour are desired by society.
- They both use the concept of identification. The psychodynamic approach says that at about 5 years children identify with the same-sex parent; the learning approach says children imitate their same-sex parent as a model.
- Neither approach considers brain or hormonal differences.

Differences between the psychodynamic and learning approaches include:

- The psychodynamic approach allows for biology in the form of inborn characteristics (e.g. the role of the unconscious and the development of the id, ego and superego); the learning approach holds that development after birth comes from the environment.
- The psychodynamic approach is more 'nature'; the learning approach is all 'nurture'. The psychodynamic approach does have aspects of nurture (e.g. conscience and superego are provided by parents and society).
- The psychodynamic approach collects qualitative data from case studies; the learning approach uses experiments and objective scientific method.
- The psychodynamic approach studies concepts, such as the id and the unconscious, that are not measurable; the learning approach studies measurable behaviour only.
- The psychodynamic approach does not use animal studies; the learning approach uses animals and maintains that conclusions drawn from animals can be applied to humans.

Comparing the learning and biological approaches

Similarities between the learning and biological approaches include:

- Both use scientific method, favouring experiments and quantitative measures. They both look for cause-and-effect relationships. The biological approach, for example, examines the relationship between hormones and characteristics; the learning approach, for example, looks at the relationship between rewards and behaviour being repeated.
- Both use animal studies to find cause-and-effect relationships. The biological approach uses mice, for example, to see how gender behaviour is influenced by hormones; the learning approach uses rats to see what effect rewards have on pressing levers for food.

Differences between the learning and biological approaches include:

- The biological approach focuses on nature and how inborn characteristics (e.g. genes and hormones) lead to certain gender behaviours; the learning approach concentrates on nurture and how upbringing leads to certain gender behaviours (e.g. girls use language better, boys are noisier).
- The biological approach focuses on sex assignment (biological make-up); the

learning approach looks at gender behaviour and development which is connected with upbringing.

■ The biological approach uses case studies (e.g. Money 1975); the learning approach (apart from some case studies of imitation of behaviour, such as violence on television) uses fewer case studies.

The explanations for gender development given by the three approaches are summarised in Table 5.21.

Table 5.21 *Comparison of the three approaches and explanations for gender bahaviour/development*

Feature	Psychodynamic approach	Biological approach	Learning approach
Influence of genes	Inherited tendency to Oedipus complex	XX for females and XY for males	Not considered
Influence of environment	Need parents to identify with in phallic stage	External environment (e.g. abuse or neglect) can affect development	Completely responsible for gender behaviour and development — pattern of reinforcements and also role of models such as parents and peers
Influence of neuro-transmitters and hormones	Not considered	Influential; if hormones are not produced or reacted to normally, gender development can be affected strongly	Not considered
Sex assignment	Gender development is focused on more than sex assignment	Sex assignment is the main focus	Gender behaviour is focused on more than sex assignment
Scientific study	No — evidence difficult to find and tends to be qualitative	Yes — laboratory studies, reductionist, scanning and animal studies	Yes — laboratory studies when considering reinforcement; what is measurable is not as clear as in the biological approach
Focus on social norms	Yes — a boy identifies with his father and takes on his norms and values (similarly for girl and mother)	Not considered	Yes — social norms are required and reinforced; modelling (e.g. copying parental behaviour) also leads to following social norms
Concept of identification	Yes — with same-sex parent, but with unique explanation	Not considered	Yes — with role models
Use of case studies	Yes — focuses clearly on case-study evidence	Yes — particularly case studies of abnormal development	Possible — such as of a person who appears to have committed a crime because of modelling — but less likely than in the other two approaches
Use of animal studies	No	Yes — findings from animal studies used to draw conclusions about humans	Yes — when considering reinforcements; less so when looking at social learning

An interactional approach: nature and nurture

Psychology has no single paradigm (conceptual framework). This is shown in your course as you look at five of the approaches to psychology. For example, one approach considers biological aspects and another focuses on cognition. You have also looked at how social factors, environment and experiences affect people. In some approaches, the focus is on nature and inherited characteristics, in others it is on nurture and experiences. However, it is more likely that what people become is due to a combination of nature and nurture, not working separately, but interacting even from before birth.

Biologists have shown that baby girls like to gurgle at humans whereas boys are happy watching geometric designs. Learning theorists suggest that parents reinforce what is seen in their society to be appropriate behaviour. For example, it could be that girls are better communicators because they are born with a focus on communication or they might be better at language because their parents expect that and reward them for linguistic skills and focus on language more in the toys that they buy. It seems likely that there is a continuum from having good language skills to having poor language skills, with more girls at the 'good' end and more boys at the 'poor' end. (Of course, there are boys who have good language skills and girls who have poor language skills.) It is probably not even useful to ask whether biological preferences and tendencies guide how babies are responded to, or whether learning guides their biological development. The conclusion is usually that it is neither possible nor desirable to separate biology from learning.

Examination-style questions

1 Using an example in your answer, describe the principles of classical conditioning. *(4 marks)*

2 Imagine that you are helping someone to train a dog to sit beside the person on command. Using operant conditioning principles, outline the advice you would give and explain why you would give this advice. *(6 marks)*

3 Using social learning theory, explain why girls might play 'house' and boys might prefer to play with cars. *(6 marks)*

Extension question

Evaluate how successfully the learning approach explains how gender behaviour develops. You could consider issues such as how strong the evidence is, how the different theories within the approach explain such behaviour and whether or not other approaches are better at explaining such behaviour. *(12 marks)*

Studies in detail

For the learning approach you have to know, in detail, a study of how children might copy aggressive behaviour that they have seen in adults (Bandura, Ross and Ross 1961) and one other from a choice of three:

- a study of Little Albert who was conditioned to fear objects that he did not fear previously (Watson and Rayner 1920)
- a study of how a pigeon learns behaviour that seems to link with a reward (Skinner 1948)
- a study of how rats exhibit behaviour because of being reinforced by cocaine (Pickens and Thompson 1968) — *this is covered in more detail on the CD-ROM.*

Bandura, Ross and Ross (1961)

One reason for this study being prescribed for your course is that it is an experiment with clear controls and procedures, so it is useful as an example for methodological issues. It provides evidence for observational learning and social learning theory and is straightforward to learn and remember.

Aims

The study has several aims, reflected by the number of hypotheses. The general aim is to see whether children will imitate behaviour, not at the time they see it, but later, even if it was not rewarded. The hypotheses were:

- Participants exposed to an aggressive model would later reproduce aggressive acts similar to those modelled.
- Those exposed to non-aggressive models and those who had no modelled behaviour (a control group) would not produce aggressive acts.
- Observation of non-aggressive behaviour would inhibit subsequent behaviour. Therefore, control group participants (who saw no modelled behaviour) would show more aggression than the group that saw non-aggressive behaviour.
- Participants are more likely to copy same-sex models than opposite-sex models. This is based on the idea that parents tend to reinforce sex-appropriate behaviour.
- Aggression is more a masculine behaviour, so boys will be more aggressive than girls, particularly when the model is aggressive.

Procedure

The participants were 36 boys and 36 girls, aged from 37 to 69 months, who were enrolled in the Stanford University Nursery School. There was also a male role model, a female role model and a female experimenter. There were eight experimental groups, each with six participants and a control group of 24 participants. Half the participants in the experimental group had an aggressive model, half had a non-aggressive model. The groups were subdivided into an equal number of boys and girls in each group and further subdivided so that half had a model of the same sex and half had a model of the opposite sex.

Before the study, participants in the experimental and control groups were matched for their original levels of aggression. They were rated on five-part scales covering:

- physical aggression
- verbal aggression
- aggression towards objects
- aggressive inhibition

They were rated by an experimenter and a nursery-school teacher, both of whom knew the children well. The two judges achieved a high level of inter-rater reliability. Participants were then grouped into threes according to the aggression ratings, and were allocated randomly to either the control group, a group that watched an aggressive model or a group that watched the non-aggressive model.

Study hint So far in this study you have read about the use of a control group, the use of hypotheses and the use of inter-rater reliability. Check that you fully understand these terms. This study is suitable to use when describing what the terms mean.

Figure 5.8 *The design of the study by Bandura, Ross and Ross (1961)*

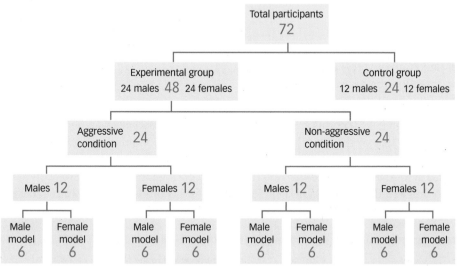

Participants were taken individually into one corner of a room and were seated at a table with materials to occupy them. A model then went to another corner of the room where there was a mallet, a toy set and a Bobo doll. A Bobo doll is a plastic doll (over 1.5 metres tall) that is on a wide base and can be punched but returns to its original position. The children did not have access to a mallet, a Bobo doll or a toy set — they had different play materials. In the non-aggressive condition, the model played with the toy set and was subdued. In the aggressive condition, after a minute of playing quietly the model acted aggressively towards the Bobo doll. The aggressive acts were carefully modelled so that if they were repeated later, this could be observed clearly. For example, the doll was laid on its side and the model sat on it and punched it. In another aggressive act, the model struck the doll on the head with the mallet. There was also verbal aggression, such as the model saying 'sock him on the nose…' and verbal comments that were not aggressive. The control group underwent the same procedures with regard to play, but there was no model present.

The participants were then taken to a different area and were shown some attractive toys that they started to play with. They were then told that the toys were not for them, they were special, and they were not allowed to play with them anymore. This made the children frustrated. This was to make sure that their emotional levels were similar before the next phase.

Each child was then taken to another room where there were many sorts of play materials. The toys included a Bobo doll similar, but not identical, to the one they had seen, a mallet and the toy set, together with other toys. Some of these were toys

with which the child could be aggressive, such as a toy gun and a ball with a face on it hanging from the ceiling; some were 'non-aggressive' toys.

There were two judges who watched through a one-way mirror and recorded each child's play behaviour. One of the judges did not know the child or to which condition they had been allocated. By having more than one judge inter-observer reliability could be tested.

Results

Three types of imitation were measured:

- imitation of verbal aggression
- imitation of physical aggression
- imitation of non-aggressive verbal responses

In the 'aggressive' condition, there was much verbal and physical aggression that resembled that of the model. In the 'non-aggressive' condition and in the control group very little aggressive behaviour was found; around 70% of these participants had a zero score for aggression. About one-third of those in the 'aggressive' condition also imitated the model's non-aggressive responses; no one in the other two conditions made such remarks.

Table 5.22 *Mean aggression score for experimental and control group participants*

| | | Experimental group | | | | |
| | | Aggressive condition | | Non-aggressive condition | | |
		Female model	Male model	Female model	Male model	Control group
Physical aggression	Girls	5.5	7.2	2.5	0.0	1.2
	Boys	12.4	25.8	0.2	1.5	2.0
Verbal aggression	Girls	13.7	2.0	0.3	0.0	0.7
	Boys	4.3	12.7	1.1	0.0	1.7
Mallet aggression	Girls	17.2	18.7	0.5	0.5	13.1
	Boys	15.5	28.8	18.7	6.7	13.5
Non-imitative aggression	Girls	21.3	8.4	7.2	1.4	6.1
	Boys	16.2	36.7	26.1	22.3	24.6
Gun play	Girls	1.8	4.5	2.6	2.3	3.7
	Boys	7.3	15.9	8.9	16.7	14.3

The mallet was used aggressively on objects other than the Bobo doll to a greater extent by those in the 'aggressive' and control conditions than by those in the 'non-aggressive' group. Perhaps modelling subdued non-aggressive behaviour leads to less aggression. This was particularly true for girls. Girls who observed a non-aggressive model, performed a mean number of 0.5 mallet aggressive responses compared with 18.0 for girls in the 'aggressive' condition and 13.1 for girls in the control condition.

In the non-aggressive group, boys produced more imitative physical aggression than girls but they did not differ with regard to verbal aggression. Male participants showed more physical and verbal aggression, more non-imitative aggression and more aggressive gun play when exposed to the aggressive model than girls did.

Girls exposed to the female aggressive model performed more verbal imitative aggression and more non-imitative aggression than boys, although there were only small numbers in the groups from which to draw conclusions.

In general, it seemed that a male model had more influence on behaviour than a female model. Apart from mallet aggression, there were no significant differences between the 'non-aggressive' group and the control group. However, this was because exposure to the female model in both the 'aggressive' and the 'non-aggressive' conditions did not differ from the controls. This masked the finding that, regarding the male model, there were large differences between the 'non-aggressive' group and the control group. Comparing controls and the 'non-aggressive' group regarding the male model, participants were less aggressive in all measures than the control group.

An interesting finding regarding social learning theory in general was that girls spent more time than boys playing with a tea set and colouring books and boys spent more time in exploratory play with guns. No sex differences were found with regard to farm animals, cars or other toys. It was also interesting that those who were in the 'non-aggressive' condition spent more time sitting quietly and not playing.

> **Study hint** When carrying out your practical, use this information about the different play behaviour of boys and girls.

Conclusions

The study shows that not all behaviour is shaped by reward or punishment. Some behaviour is learned through observation and observed behaviour can later be reproduced. Observing aggressive behaviour may weaken social inhibitions, particularly if the behaviour is performed by adults and observed by children.

This study is important because it did not involve reinforcement of the modelled behaviour and yet it was later imitated. The male model appeared to be more imitated than the female model. This might have been due to sex typing because boys imitated physical aggression more than girls but did not differ with regard to verbal aggression. Maybe what is imitated depends on social norms and values.

Evaluation of the study by Bandura, Ross and Ross (1961)
Strengths

- The study was a carefully set up and controlled laboratory experiment. For example, care was taken to get the children into a similar emotional state before the observation and to set up measurable acts that could be recorded. This means that cause-and-effect conclusions could be drawn because the variables were isolated and operationalised, with controls.
- The reliability of the measurement of the dependent variable. Two judges were used and their observations were checked for reliability. One judge did not know to which condition the child had been allocated, i.e. a 'blind' procedure was used to avoid bias when recording the play behaviour. Therefore, the results were reliable.

Weaknesses

- The study lacked validity. It could be claimed that the setting was realistic as the rooms were set up to be like the nursery rooms with which the children were familiar. However, the situation was not valid because the adult either deliberately punched and kicked the Bobo doll or was deliberately subdued. In either case, this was not a natural situation — all the more so because the doll and other materials were placed in the room where the children were observed. They may have thought that they were supposed to act towards the doll in the same way that the model had acted.

- The study can be criticised on ethical grounds. The researchers do not explain in any detail how permission was obtained for the study, though it might be assumed that the university had an ethical committee who oversaw the study. However, even if this were the case, the children observed an adult being aggressive and then copied that behaviour. For some children, there was modelling of both verbal and physical aggression. Parents were not mentioned in the study, so they may not have given permission.

Table 5.23	Strengths and weaknesses of the study by Bandura, Ross and Ross (1961)	
Strengths		**Weaknesses**
• The study has controls with operationalisation of variables, so cause-and-effect conclusions can be drawn; for example, the aggressive acts were set up so that they could be observed later • There is reliability because two judges observed the behaviour and their scores could be compared; one judge did not know to which condition a child had been allocated, so was not biased		• The situation was not natural; the children might have thought that they were supposed to hit the Bobo doll, given that they had seen adults doing it • The study might not be ethical because children observed verbal and physical aggressive acts and repeated them; how ethical issues were dealt with was not clearly explained

Watson and Rayner (1920)

Watson and Rayner (1920) carried out a study using classical conditioning principles to see if they could cause a human baby to develop a fear that he did not have previously. This was to test whether classical conditioning worked with humans. This study is important because not many studies of classical conditioning using humans have been carried out.

Aims and background

Watson and Rayner (1920) set out to gather experimental evidence for classical conditioning in humans. They needed a reflex action that occurred in response to a stimulus and some other behaviour to condition to cause that reaction. In infancy, there are some instinctive emotional reactions such as fear, rage and love. The researchers felt that there must be some way in which the range of emotional reactions becomes increased because humans have emotional reactions to many stimuli. They thought that these early reactions were increased through associations developed by classical conditioning. They also thought that a child's early experiences in the home were like being in a laboratory where such conditioning takes place. This led them to find a baby whom they could condition to have an emotional response to something new.

The researchers aimed to find out:

- whether they could condition fear of an animal by simultaneously presenting the animal and striking a steel bar to make a loud noise to frighten the child
- whether the fear would be transferred to other animals and objects
- the effect of time on the conditioned response

Procedure and results

Watson and Rayner (1920) chose Albert B as the participant for their study. He had been reared from birth in a hospital environment because his mother was a **wet-nurse** in a home for invalid children.

A **wet-nurse** breastfeeds babies.

Albert was healthy from birth and was well-developed, stolid and unemotional, so they thought they could do him 'relatively little harm' by carrying out their experiments. This background is important because it may affect what you think about the ethics of the study. It also affects the conclusions, because it is important that he was relatively fearless. This was an experiment, not a case study, because they did not gather in-depth information about Albert. It was a single-case experiment because there was only one participant. It was well controlled, there was careful manipulation of the independent variable (IV) (though it changed through the study) and careful measurement and recording of the dependent variable (DV).

Watson and Rayner (1920) tested Albert for fear reactions when he was about 9 months old. They introduced a white rat, a rabbit, cotton wool and other stimuli and filmed his reactions. He showed no fear whatsoever. The mother and hospital attendants witnessed some of these events. The researchers also banged a hammer against a suspended steel bar to make a loud noise. They found a fear response — the baby's lips puckered and trembled and he had a sudden crying fit. This was the first time he had cried in the laboratory where the tests took place.

Establishing a conditioned emotional response

The researchers did consider whether what they wanted to do was ethical but they decided that Albert would in any case have worrying situations once he went to nursery. They waited until he was 11 months old and checked again that he had no fear. The procedure and results at 11 months 3 days are shown in Table 5.24.

Table 5.24 *Little Albert: procedure and results at 11 months 3 days*

Procedure	Resulting response
A white rat (real) was presented to Albert	He reached for it with his left hand
As his left hand touched the rat, the bar was struck behind his head	He jumped and fell forward but did not cry
Just as his right hand touched the rat, the bar was struck again	Albert jumped violently, fell forward and started to whimper

The researchers waited for 1 week before continuing the experiment. The rat was then presented suddenly to Albert, without a sound. He reached out tentatively, but did not touch the rat. He was then given blocks which he played with without a problem. They concluded that there had been some effect from the conditioning.

The experiment continued as summarised in Table 5.25. The conclusion was that the conditioning had been successful.

Transfer of fear to other objects

The researchers then continued with the study to see if there was a transfer to other objects. The results at 11 months 15 days are shown in Table 5.26.

They concluded that the conditioning of rat with fear had lasted for 5 days. The experiment was continued, using different stimuli (Table 5.27).

Table 5.25 *Little Albert: procedure and results at 11 months 10 days*

Stimulus	Response
Rat + sound	Albert started to fall over immediately; he did not cry
Rat + sound	Fell to the right; he did not cry
Rat + sound	Fell to the right; he did not cry
Rat presented alone	Puckered face, whimpered, and withdrew his body to the left
Rat + sound	Fell to the right and began to whimper
Rat + sound	Stared and cried; did not fall
Rat alone	Albert started to cry immediately, turned and started to crawl away

Table 5.26 *Little Albert: procedure and results at 11 months 15 days*

Stimulus	Response
Blocks alone	Played well
Rat alone	Whimpered, turned away
Blocks	Played and smiled
Rat alone	Leaned to the left, fell and crawled away
Blocks	Smiling and happy

Table 5.27 *Little Albert: use of different stimuli at 11 months 15 days*

Stimulus	Response
Rabbit alone	Immediate negative responses; leaned away, whimpered, burst into tears
Blocks	Played well and energetically
Dog alone	Not as violent a reaction as to the rabbit; tried to crawl away but only cried when dog approached his head
Blocks	Played well
Fur coat	Withdrew to left side and began to fret; began to cry when coat brought nearer
Cotton wool was presented wrapped in paper with some cotton wool showing	Not the same negativity, but played with the paper; withdrew his hand from the wool itself
Hair	Negative response but okay with hair of two observers
Santa mask	Negative behaviour

At 11 months 20 days, when the researchers introduced the rat alone, Little Albert's response was less marked than previously. The researchers decided that the association had weakened so they renewed it.

Table 5.28 *Little Albert: renewal of association at 11 months 20 days*

Stimulus	Response
Rat + sound	Violent reaction
Rat alone	Fell to left side and strong reaction
Rat alone	Fell over to left and crawled away; no crying and gurgled happily
Rabbit alone	Leaned to left and whimpered a little
Blocks	Played well

The researchers then tried to condition the fear to the dog and the rabbit (Table 5.29).

Fear could, therefore, be transferred to other objects.

The experiment was then moved from the dark room where the previous studies had taken place to a lecture room in the presence of four people. This was to study the effect of different surroundings (Table 5.30).

It was concluded that there were transfers to different stimuli and to a different situation.

The effect of time on conditioning

The final part of the experiment took place when Little Albert was aged 1 year 21 days.

The researchers concluded that conditioned emotional reactions lasted longer than 1 month, though became a little weaker. On that day, when he was 1 year 21 days old, Albert was taken from the hospital, as had been going to happen in any case. The researchers could not, therefore, remove the conditioned emotional responses. They felt that the responses would last for a life time.

Table 5.29 *Little Albert at 11 months and 20 days: rabbit and dog were the stimuli*

Stimulus	Response
Rabbit alone	Whimpered and leaned over
Rabbit + sound	Violent fear reaction
Rabbit alone	Whimpered and leaned over
Rabbit alone	Whimpered, but wanted to reach out to the rabbit as well
Dog alone	Whimpered and held hands away from dog
Dog + sound	Violent negative reaction
Blocks	Played well

Table 5.30 *Little Albert at 11 months and 20 days: the effects of a different setting*

Procedure	Resulting response
Rat alone	No fear reaction but hands held away
Rabbit alone	Slight fear reaction; turned away a little
Dog alone	Turned away and cried
Rat alone	Slight negative reaction
Rat + sound	Jumped but did not cry
Rat alone, moved near	Began whimpering as rat brought near
Blocks	Played well
Rat alone	Withdrawal and whimpering
Blocks	Played well
Rabbit alone	Pronounced reaction
Dog alone	Did not cry until the dog barked

Table 5.31 *Little Albert at 1 year 21 days: the effect of passage of time on conditioning*

Stimulus	Response
Santa Claus mask	Negative
Fur coat	Negative
Blocks	Played
Rat	Negative
Blocks	Played
Rabbit	Somewhat negative
Dog	Cried

The results of Watson and Rayner's (1920) study on Little Albert are detailed in Tables 5.24 to 5.31. To summarise briefly, each time the blocks were given to Albert

Unit 2

he played with them happily and each time the rat was presented, after it had been paired with the noise, there was a negative response. Little Albert's fear of a white rat and other similar animals and objects can be explained using classical conditioning principles (Figure 5.9).

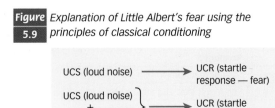

Figure 5.9 *Explanation of Little Albert's fear using the principles of classical conditioning*

When objects similar to the white rat, such as cotton wool, a rabbit and a Santa Claus mask were presented, Albert responded negatively. Therefore, there was a conditioned emotional response, as the researchers had thought there would be. It was generalised to other similar objects and animals and, albeit somewhat reduced, it lasted over time. Note that during the experiment the researchers had to reintroduce the pairing of the unconditioned and conditioned stimulus.

Conclusions

A conditioned emotional response can occur in humans after only a few pairings of stimuli, but the pairings might have to be repeated. The conditioned response can be transferred to other similar objects. Albert was removed from the study, so there was no means of seeing if the responses could be extinguished.

Evaluation of the study by Watson and Rayner (1920)

Strengths

- The Little Albert study was carefully documented; witnesses helped to record the data and there were strict controls. Albert's reactions were recorded carefully, the setting(s) were controlled and only one variable was changed at a time. If it could have been repeated ethically, it would have been replicable and could, therefore, have been tested for reliability.
- The study is evidence that classical conditioning occurs in humans. Pavlov had shown that it exists in dogs, but it might have been difficult to generalise the results to humans had Watson and Rayner (1920) not carried out this study.

Weaknesses

- The study is not ethical. The researchers made sure that Albert was not easily frightened and they thought that the experiment was acceptable because he would have frightening experiences at nursery. However, there is little doubt that he was distressed. They allowed him to rest between experiments, but continued even when they saw how distressed he was. They did not extinguish the fears, so it is possible that they remained with him. However, 1 month later his fear responses had started to weaken, so it is possible that they disappeared when the unconditioned and conditioned stimuli were no longer paired.

Edexcel AS Psychology

- The study may not be valid. The setting and tasks were artificial. It could be argued that a noise from a hammer and steel bar could represent a real-life noise and that playing with white fur and animals is natural. However, the setting was not natural and Albert was in a laboratory situation, which may have made him initially fearful.

Table 5.32	Strengths and weaknesses of the Little Albert study by Watson and Rayner (1920)	
Strengths	**Weaknesses**
• The experiment was well-designed and controlled; for example, the independent variable each time was clear and the dependent variable (the behaviour) was measured and recorded carefully • The study showed that Pavlov's ideas about classical conditioning (from his work with dogs) could be said to be true of humans	• It was not ethical because Albert was distressed throughout and even though he was distressed the study continued for weeks • The setting was a laboratory and, therefore, artificial; the study lacked ecological validity and perhaps validity with regard to the task

Skinner (1948)

Skinner carried out many studies of the processes involved in operant conditioning and used laboratory experiments with animals for this purpose.

Aims and background

Skinner (1948) was interested in how reinforcement led to behaviour in animals. For this study, he wanted to see if *any* reinforcing situation would yield a response, even if that situation was not reinforced *deliberately*. He knew that a particular behaviour could be chosen and reinforced deliberately by giving a reward when the behaviour happened, so that it would be repeated. However, he wondered if any behaviour that occurred and was reinforced (though not deliberately by a researcher) would be repeated. At the end of this study, he called such behaviour 'superstitious' because the connection had not been planned.

Procedure

The experiment was run with eight pigeons. Two observers noted the pigeons' behaviour, which was also recorded photographically (100 photos in 10 seconds).

Each pigeon was starved to 75% of its usual 'well-fed' weight. For a few minutes each day, it was put into a cage into which a food hopper could be swung so that the pigeon could eat from it. The hopper was held in place for 5 seconds and was then swung out, so that the pigeon could no longer eat. This happened at regular intervals during the day. The food was the reinforcement. The hopper was swung in with no attention being paid to what the pigeon was doing. This was to ensure that the pigeon was not rewarded for a specific behaviour such as pecking in a certain spot or hopping from side-to-side. The idea was to offer the food but without any particular behaviour being rewarded deliberately.

Results

In six of the eight trials, the observers agreed about which behaviour had been re-inforced:

- One bird turned anticlockwise, making two or three turns between reinforcements.
- One pushed its head into the upper corners of the cage.
- One showed a head-tossing response.
- Two showed a pendulum motion with their bodies.
- One made incomplete pecking movements towards the floor.

In the other two birds conditioning processes were not clearly marked.

It seemed that the bird executed a response when the hopper appeared to give a reward of food. The bird then carried out that response as if it were causing the reward (hopper) to appear. If the hopper reappeared within a period that was too short for extinction (behaviour stopped) to have taken place, then the behaviour was conditioned and strengthened further. The birds rapidly repeated the response while awaiting the return of the hopper. Photographs showed that the shorter the interval between reinforcements, the more marked the conditioning; longer intervals resulted in the birds carrying out other responses in different parts of the cage. The sooner a second reinforcement appeared, the more likely it was that the second response would be the same as the first and the stronger was the association. Fifteen seconds was an effective interval for this study, but Skinner concluded that this would depend on the strength of the drive and the species being studied.

The study was then extended. A 1-minute interval produced different responses. At first there was a lot of energy, but the bird settled gradually on a particular well-defined part of the response, e.g. a sharp movement of the head was exaggerated until the bird started turning. This involved taking steps until the stepping response became another main feature. The stepping response made an electrical contact that produced a sound that could be recorded. When the hopper no longer appeared, the bird continued to do the side hopping. Extinction was only found after a 10–15 minute interval. When the hopper reappeared after this interval, there was gradual reconditioning. However, the previous response was replaced with a new response, suggesting that retention of learning is brief.

Conclusions

The bird behaved as if there was a connection between the behaviour and the response but there was no such causal link. This resembles superstitious behaviour, such as good luck rituals in humans.

Evaluation of the study of superstition in pigeons by Skinner (1948)

Strengths

- There is inter-observer reliability because there were two observers who agreed about the observed behaviour. For example, both agreed that one bird turned anticlockwise for two or three turns and that another bird made pecking movements towards the floor. Reliability is important in a scientific study because the findings are then more secure and if the study is repeated the same results are likely to be found.

■ There were controls, such as the timing of the introduction of the hopper into the cage using a clock, so that there was no likelihood that a particular behaviour was reinforced deliberately. Other controls were that the cage was the same size in each experiment and the birds were starved systematically. Experiments need good controls so that cause-and-effect conclusions can be drawn.

Weaknesses

■ The study used animals and it might not be credible to draw conclusions about humans by relying on data from pigeons. Humans have motivation and think about their behaviour; it is assumed that pigeons do not think in the same way.

■ It studies one particular aspect of behaviour separated from normal behaviour. It is possible that there is some validity in the conclusion that pigeons learn to link a certain action with a reward. However, this is short-lived learning — the behaviour was changed or lost quickly. Real behaviour, outside laboratory conditions, is likely to be more complex and last longer, so the study lacks validity.

Table 5.33 *Strengths and weaknesses of the study by Skinner (1948)*

Strengths	Weaknesses
● There was inter-observer reliability because when the results of two observers were compared they agreed ● The study was well-controlled — for example, the accurate timing of swinging the hopper to avoid inadvertently re-inforcing a particular behaviour, using the same cage and starving the birds in the same way	● There was lack of generalisability because the study involved pigeons and there are important differences between pigeon and human behaviour, so relating the processes to humans is difficult ● There was lack of validity because the situation was limited and unnatural

Pickens and Thompson (1968)

Pickens and Thompson (1968) is an example of an animal study that can be used when discussing ethical guidelines with regard to animals. Pickens and Thompson worked with rats in laboratory conditions to investigate the use of cocaine as a re-inforcement for behaviour using the principles of operant conditioning.

They found that cocaine acted as a reinforcer for behaviour such as lever pressing, and the rats only responded if the rewards followed the response, otherwise there was extinction. There were other findings too, such as that the dosage and when the drug was given are important. If the dosage of cocaine was too high or too low, the cocaine did not act as a reinforcer.

This study is covered in more detail on the CD-ROM.

Key issues

You have to study one key issue that can be explained using concepts and ideas from the learning approach. The specification suggests three issues, two of which are covered here. *The other is summarised below and covered in detail on the CD-ROM.* However, you do not need to choose one of these — you can choose any issue.

The influence of advertising on people's behaviour

The issue of the influence of advertising can be related to classical conditioning and social learning theory.

Describing the issue

Advertising is used to persuade people to buy a product. There are television and cinema adverts, newspaper adverts and posters. All are targeted towards particular groups. It is likely that most people think that they are not affected by advertising, yet companies know that sales go up when adverts are shown. For example, an advert with a phone number — perhaps for mortgages, savings or insurance — immediately generates a large increase in the number of calls, which seems proof that advertising works. Adverts can be targeted towards a particular age group, gender, or socioeconomic group; they tend to focus on a combination of these factors. They use celebrities and powerful images. The questions are: 'why do advertisements work?' and 'how does making advertisements draw on knowledge of learning theory?'

Explaining the issue

- Each advertisement focuses on a particular group of people, according to age, gender, social class or some other feature. The advertisement then models the group's behaviour because research evidence from social learning theory says that people imitate those who are similar to themselves.
- Advertisements also use prestigious models, such as football 'heroes' and other celebrities because research has shown that people imitate those seen as having prestige.
- Vicarious learning suggests that people imitate behaviour that is clearly observable, so advertisements use close-ups, e.g. a close-up of unwrinkled skin when advertising an anti-ageing product.
- Based on the ideas of classical conditioning, advertisements pair involuntary behaviour with a product. For example, beautiful women and handsome men are used in advertising because they elicit an involuntary arousal response. When the beautiful woman or man is paired with the product, after a few trials, the product

alone elicits the response. For example, in advertisements, a certain make of car will be driven by an attractive woman so that the car will elicit an arousal response in men. Alternatively, the well-dressed attractive woman might result in the car being bought by more females because they aspire to be that attractive woman.

- Operant conditioning can also be involved in the success of advertising because it is linked to vicarious reinforcement. If an attractive female is seen to be rewarded for certain behaviour, such as wearing a certain perfume, then this behaviour is likely to be imitated.

Formula One driver Lewis Hamilton — a vehicle for advertising

Explore Study some advertisements and make notes about how they use classical conditioning. Find the involuntary response first, then you will be able to find the pairing of the unconditioned and conditioned stimuli. Then look for advertisements that demonstrate the principles of social learning theory, such as using a powerful role model. For example, in 2007, Lewis Hamilton did exceptionally well in Formula One motor racing and his sponsors featured him immediately in advertisements for their products.

The increase in female violence to changing role models

There has been an increase in female violence, one cause of which could be cultural images that are being copied. If fun and liberation are perceived to be the rewards for female violence then it is more likely to be imitated. Violent female role models such as in *Kill Bill* may be portrayed as 'sex goddesses'. This pressurises girls to conform to the behaviour because it is likely that they will get positive reinforcement for doing so in the form of admiration from their peers.

This issue is covered in more detail on the CD-ROM.

The influence of role models on anorexia

It has been claimed that anorexia could be caused by cultural images such as 'size-zero' models.

Describing the issue

Anorexia is an eating disorder characterised by being extremely underweight (about 15% lower than it should be) and refusing to eat properly, if at all. Sufferers tend to see themselves as fat even when they are painfully thin. Anorexia usually starts in the teenage years. Girls stop menstruating because their bodies 'shut down'. Boys also suffer from anorexia, but less so than girls, although the rate of anorexia in boys is rising.

Anorexia is less common outside the Western world. In Britain, it is thought that up to 1% of girls in school and university are anorexic but exact figures are hard to obtain. It is common in some professions, such as models and ballet dancers. Anorexia is self-induced either by not eating or by doing too much exercise or by a combination of these behaviours. There are side effects such as losing interest in socialising, tiredness, feeling cold and stomach pains. Anorexia can last for years. Without treatment, sufferers become ill and may die.

Explaining the issue

- Social learning theory suggests that people imitate role models; celebrities and people with prestige are likely to be imitated.
- People who are perceived as similar are also imitated. Therefore, girls are likely to imitate female role models, rather than male role models.
- As the trend in the 2000s is for 'size-zero' catwalk models it is not surprising, given the principles of social learning theory, that wanting to be thin is commonplace in young people; anorexia can follow that desire.
- Anorexia can also be explained by operant conditioning, because of the rewards for being thin and the negative reinforcement against being fat. If peers tease fat children, then to avoid being teased, they will stop eating in order to be thin. If peers are envious of thin children, they will do what they can to become thin, including not eating.

Victoria and David Beckham — if thin models and celebrities act as role models, it is likely to lead to girls under-eating

- It could be said that the current focus on an 'obesity crisis' will lead to an increased desire to be thin in order to avoid the criticism of being obese. This would be an example of negative reinforcement.
- There are, however, alternative explanations for anorexia. For example, the psychodynamic explanation is that it prevents a girl, who may want to remain a child because of fixation at an early developmental stage, from growing up.
- Cross-cultural differences in levels of anorexia tend to support the explanation for anorexia given by the learning approach because different types of behaviour and social norms are likely to be modelled in different countries. Therefore, if in another culture, there is less emphasis on being thin, then fewer people will try to be thin.

Practical: an observation

For the learning approach you have to carry out an observation. The one suggested here is an observation of young children playing, so will be non-participant. You are free to choose a different observation.

Ethical issues with observation

The suggested practical is an observation of children playing, so there are ethical issues to consider. The best approach is to use a video or DVD of children playing because then you are not interrupting their play or affecting the situation and the children will not be affected. Of course, while the video or DVD was being made, they could have been affected. Ethical guidelines should be followed:
- Individual children must not be identified or discussed.
- Informed consent is needed.
- Those obtaining the data have to be competent to do so.
- The right to withdraw has to be given to the children, parents and staff involved.
- Afterwards, the participants should watch the video/DVD to be sure that they were debriefed properly and had agreed that their data could be used.

There are various videos and DVDs available, so you do not have to use a local nursery or playgroup. Alternatively, you might be able to use a television programme with a short extract of children playing. Child development or childcare courses use such material and educational television programmes produce them. Data that other people have gathered are **secondary data** although, as you will be gathering the actual data by talking or some other means of recording, you will be collecting **primary data**.

If you have access to a nursery or playgroup where you are known, then you could obtain the relevant permission to carry out an observation to collect primary data, but be guided by your teacher. There are particular ethical issues with regard to children, so you will need to obtain special permission. If you have access to children within your family, then you could collect your own data. However, you still need to obtain permission.

Background

The aim of the observation is to examine some aspect of the theories within the learning approach. It is difficult to observe classical conditioning because reflexes — involuntary behaviour — are involved. It is easier to observe voluntary behaviour, so the focus is on operant conditioning or social learning theory. Operant conditioning suggests that people act in response to rewards, reinforcement and punishment. Children repeat behaviour for which they are reinforced, so an observation could look for reinforcements and see if children respond to them. Social learning theory suggests that people imitate others and have models whom they copy. So an observation could look for behaviour that imitates the behaviour of others.

This practical looks at society's focus on gender behaviour with regard to children's play behaviour. According to learning theories:

- children play differently according to their gender because they are reinforced for doing so by their parents, family and other carers *or*
- they play differently because they accept their gender and copy the behaviour of others of the same gender

Gender is the focus of the observation. It is assumed that you are using a recording of play behaviour.

Aim

The aim is to test the idea that children are reinforced to act in a way that suits their gender. Previous studies have suggested that girls play more quietly than boys and that boys are more physical in their play.

If you are using a secondary source, this is a non-participant naturalistic observation. Assume that it is an overt observation because the children would probably have been aware that their behaviour was being recorded. In some ways you will simply be counting behaviour categories rather than doing an observation yourself, but this is for ethical reasons so is counted as an observation. You are simply using a recorded situation instead of being there. You must explain this when discussing your study. You are not examining the content of the video or DVD itself so this is not a content analysis.

Hypotheses and variables

- The null hypothesis is that any differences between boys' and girls' behaviour in the book corner and on the climbing frame are due to chance.
- The alternative hypothesis is that there is a difference in play behaviour in these two areas which is due to gender. This is a non-directional hypothesis because it is not predicted which gender will play more in which task.
- The independent variable is gender; the dependent variable is the number of tally marks made, using time sampling, for each activity.

Design

Here it is assumed that you are using a video or DVD that includes a short section of children playing in an area that has, among other things, a climbing frame and a book corner. The study is simplified here — you could observe other aspects of play, depending on the material available. Time sampling with tallying is used to measure the amount of activity on both tasks. This is an independent groups design because the children are in different gender groups. Prepare tables in which to record the results.

Watch the material through once to familiarise yourself with how to record the activity. You will only be able to record what has been filmed, which will affect the findings, but as long as there is sufficient time for each activity, that is acceptable for this practice study. Using secondary data means that you will watch each activity and record whether those using it are boys or girls. This is different from recording primary data for play activity, when you would have chosen one particular boy and one particular girl to study. Watch the material again to make sure that you are recording accurately. Alternatively, if you are working in a group, compare your tally with another member of the group. This is a check of inter-observer reliability.

Carrying out the study

Use the tables that you have prepared and give yourself room for the tallying. Gather the data by watching and recording. You will probably find that you can record more than one tally mark per minute; make sure that you record at regular intervals. Repeat the observation and compare your tallies.

Analysing the results

From the raw tally data, draw up a two-by-two table so that you can carry out a Chi-squared test. This is the correct test because you have nominal data, as you made tally marks according to the two categories of play and whether the children playing in the categories were girls or boys. It is an independent groups design because the children are in different gender groups. It is a test of difference because the alternative hypothesis states that there is a difference in play behaviour depending on gender. For the practical outlined here, data are given in Table 5.34. Refer to the methodology section of this chapter (page 318) for details of the Chi-squared test.

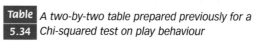

Table 5.34 A two-by-two table prepared previously for a Chi-squared test on play behaviour

Play behaviour	Boys	Girls	Total
Playing on the climbing frame	9	3	**12**
Playing in the book corner	3	7	**10**
Total	**12**	**10**	**22**

The example given here tested the hypothesis that activity use is different depending on gender. This is a non-directional hypothesis, so the test required is a two-tailed test. If the level of significance chosen is $p \leq 0.05$, it will be accepted that

5

the probability of the results being due to chance is 1 in 20 (5%) and the null hypothesis will be rejected. At this level of significance when df is 1, the critical value that has to be equalled or exceeded is 3.84. In this example, the value of Chi-squared is 4.44 (page 321). This is greater than 3.84 so the null hypothesis is rejected and the alternative hypothesis, that there is a difference in activity use depending on gender, is accepted; boys are seen to play more on the climbing frame and girls spend more time in the book corner. Note that before the Chi-squared test was carried out it was possible to see the perceived difference by looking at the two-by-two table.

Applying issues of validity, reliability, generalisability and credibility

Validity

Validity refers to the degree to which findings are 'real life'. This study used a video or DVD of real play behaviour, so the results are likely to be valid. It is a naturalistic observation, so there is ecological validity and the task itself is valid because it is natural play behaviour.

There is the problem of the play being recorded. However, you will not know whether there was someone operating the camera or whether it was left rolling discreetly. Therefore, you cannot comment about how the recording would affect validity. Assume that the play behaviour you focused on was some way through the recording and that by then the children would have forgotten about the presence of the camera, which is likely to be the case. Unless, of course, you noticed some aspect of their play that seemed unnatural, perhaps because of the recording.

Reliability

Naturalistic observations may not be reliable because behaviour is often observed at one moment in time. If that is the case, the study cannot be repeated to test for reliability. However, here, if you watched the material twice and your tallies were similar, or if you compared your results with those of someone else in your group, then there is reliability. If your results were similar to those of another person in your group, then there is inter-observer reliability.

Generalisability

Whether the results are generalisable to other situations depends on the sampling. You may not have been able to observe many children, you will not have chosen the sample and you probably do not know the background of the children or the setting, all of which affect generalisability. You can only say that your results are true of that situation; you cannot say that the situation is typical of all similar settings. Therefore, there is a lack of generalisability.

Credibility

The lack of generalisability affects the credibility of the study. You might have found the only short period when more boys climbed and more girls were reading books. You would need to use more than one setting and more than one period of behaviour before you could claim that boys and girls showed different play behaviour. To claim credibility, you would need to show that your results were valid, reliable and generalisable.

Study hint Make notes about the issues of validity, reliability, generalisability and credibility of your observation in preparation for an exam question about these areas.

Answers to the practice boxes

Practice 5.1 on p. 316

The study was a naturalistic observation because it took place in the children's nursery, which was their natural setting. It was an overt observation because the children and staff knew that it was taking place. There was nothing covert about it; the study did not take place in secret, which would have been difficult because the presence of the observers would have had to be explained. The observation was non-participant because the researchers were not nursery staff. They could not be participants, because the participants were children and the observers were adults. There were two observers so there was the potential for inter-observer reliability.

Practice 5.2 on p. 327

beautiful woman (UCS) ⟶ arousal/desire (UCR)

beautiful woman (UCS)
+
car being advertised (CS/NS) ⟶ arousal/desire (UCR)

car being advertised (CS) ⟶ arousal/desire (CR)

Practice 5.3 on p. 328

Behaviour 1 Positive reinforcement,
Behaviour 2 Negative reinforcement
Behaviour 3 Punishment

Index

Note Numbers in **bold** type refer to definitions of terms

Edexcel AS Psychology

N

N (number of scores) **250**

Native American folk story, *War of the Ghosts* 116–17

natural experiments **102**, 103–07

nature–nurture debate **232**, 238, 268, 282, 346–48

negative correlation **178**

negative reinforcement **328**

nervous system, effects of drugs on rats 255

neurological decay 122–23

neurones **265**

neuroses 164, **186**, 187,194, 213

neurotransmitters 228, 231, **263**, 264–65

Niesser and Harsch, on *Challenger* crash 145

nominal data **155, 247**

nomothetic theory **164**

non-directional (two-tailed) hypothesis 95, **96, 247**

nonsense syllables 131
Peterson and Peterson 151

norm 63

'normal' achievement 46

normal sex differentiation in humans 270

nurses and obedience to doctor 59–61

O

obedience 2, 3, 11, **35**
to authority 77
drop in level 47
interview on 83, 84
in male and female soldiers 31
in society 69
theory of 41–44
in war situations 78

obedience levels studies 27, 35
in Dutch experiment 44–51

objectivity 169, 170
in interviewing **20**, 21

observation 64, 309, 310, **316**, 339

observational learning approach, **340**, 365–69

observational research method 309

observed, steps in observational learning **340**

observers in nurses experiment, Hofling 59

Oedipus complex 161, **177**, 192, **193**, 214–15
and gender 345

oestrogen ('female') 231

old age in memory 144

open-ended questions 10–16

operant conditioning theory 307, 327–32, 344
in anorexia 364–65
rewarding behaviour 345
strengths and weaknesses 339
treatment 332–39

operationalising **96, 149**

opportunity sampling **34**, 35,**150, 185**
advantages and disadvantages 34, 35

oral stage **191**

order effects **100, 151**

ordinal data **155, 247**

out-group prejudice 54, 55, 56

overt **313**
strengths and weaknesses 313–14

P

pain administration in Australia 51

paired associated tasks **131**

pairs of related words 124, 131

parenting styles 216, 221

Parkinson's disease, experiment with rats 255

participant design 100, **246**

participant observations 311, 312

participants 27–28, 37
distress 52
in questionnaires **8**
Reicher and Haslam study 71

participant variables **97**

passage of time effect 136

Pavlov, Ivan 303, 307, 308
work with dogs 325

Penfield, W. G. 122, 123

penis damage at birth 279–80

penis envy **193**

perception 109

perceptual analysis 112

permeability **72**

personal data **9**

personality parts 188

personal 'selves' 54